Microsoft

Windows Azure™ Step by Step

Microsoft®

Windows Azure™ Step by Step

Roberto Brunetti

Published with the authorization of Microsoft Corporation by:
O'Reilly Media, Inc.
1005 Gravenstein Highway North
Sebastopol, California 95472

ISBN: 978-0-7356-4972-9

1 2 3 4 5 6 7 8 9 M 6 5 4 3 2 1

Printed and bound in the United States of America.

Microsoft Press books are available through booksellers and distributors worldwide. If you need support related to this book, email Microsoft Press Book Support at *mspinput@microsoft.com*. Please tell us what you think of this book at *http://www.microsoft.com/learning/booksurvey*.

Acquisitions and Development Editor: Russell Jones
Production Editor: Teresa Elsey
Editorial Production: Online Training Solutions, Inc.
Technical Reviewer: Brian Keller
Indexer: Ginny Munroe
Cover Design: Twist Creative • Seattle
Cover Composition: Karen Montgomery

This book is dedicated to Barbara for her support in every important step of my life.

—Roberto

Contents at a Glance

Table of Contents

Acknowledgments

A book is the result of the work of many people, but usually only the author name appears on the cover.

First, I want to thank Vanni Boncinelli for his effort in reviewing all the chapters for both technical aspects and linguistic troubles. This is my first English-written book. Without him, the editor would have rejected all the chapters.

I also want to thank Russell Jones for his patience in responding quickly and precisely to all of my rookie questions and for supporting me from the beginning of this writing.

Many thanks go to Brian Keller: he has reviewed not only the text but every line of code two times, because during the writing process Microsoft released the SDK 1.3, which was significantly different from the previous version around configuration and the Visual Studio IDE add-in. Brian also had to re-review all the portal screenshots, because the Windows Azure user interface was completely redesigned in Silverlight as of January 2011.

One of the most important people to thank is Victoria Thulman, who guided me in the process of copyediting all the chapters. Her patience with my mistakes and incorrect assumptions was immeasurable.

Gabriele Castellani and Giuseppe Guerrasio wrote the foreword and have supported me since 2008, when Microsoft first announced Windows Azure at PDC 08.

Fabio Santini and Mario Fontana have given me the opportunity to work with many Italian Microsoft partners and with a wide range of application scenarios: you can find those experiences reflected in many of this book's pages.

Last, but not least, thanks to Paolo Pialorsi, who introduced me to Russell Jones one year ago.

Now, the book is complete: thanks again to all of you.

Foreword

When Roberto asked us to write a foreword for this book, he made us happy for several reasons. First, it's a pleasure introducing you to the work of one of the members of DevLeap, a group of professionals who have always been distinguished by the quality and the clarity of their teaching materials and courses. Second, the topic discussed in this book touches one of the most important issues for the future of our profession: cloud computing, and in particular, the Windows Azure Platform, which is the first application infrastructure specifically conceived and built for the cloud.

The evolution of networks and the growing diffuseness of the Internet, after having transformed the way people consume content, are on the verge of changing the way we think about concepts such as computational power and storage capabilities. We are used to thinking of those as related to local physical machines, but the advent of cloud computing is leading toward a revolution in how we access computational and storage resources. Thanks to the Windows Azure Platform, huge data centers easily provide the computational power, storage, services, and applications developers need to develop their own solutions, transforming them into services accessible on demand.

Providing technologies and infrastructures that we are already familiar with, within an on-demand infrastructure, helps to reduce management and hardware and software maintenance and licensing costs and to constantly increase available computational power and storage capacity.

In this book, Roberto accompanies us through the world of the Windows Azure platform and services, providing us with detailed but still basic explanations about the objectives and features of the major components of this new platform and telling us how we can leverage this platform to host our own services and applications. Ranging from the core of the Windows Azure Platform to its deployment and monitoring services, from SQL Azure to full integration with the development tools, this book guides us in discovering the main aspects of this new technology, from a concrete, development-oriented perspective and with plenty of practical examples, in line with the philosophy that has always inspired any DevLeap activity. Case studies and practical tips regarding the use of the services and the most efficient implementation strategies show the best way to approach the Windows Azure Platform, allowing us to ride this new technological wave, which is expected to significantly improve our chances to leverage computational power, storage, and basic services, from the beginning.

Here begins a new and interesting journey toward a new technological frontier. The only thing you need to do to jump aboard and start exploring this application platform under Roberto's guidance is to press F5!

Giuseppe Guerrasio
Architect Evangelist
Developers & Platform Evangelism
Microsoft Italy

Gabriele Castellani
Developer & ITPro Evangelist Manager
Microsoft Italy

Introduction

Windows Azure is the Microsoft cloud computing platform that lets developers leverage its powerful, scalable, and fault-tolerant infrastructure to build successful applications.

Windows Azure Step by Step provides an organized walkthrough of the Windows Azure platform and its related technologies. The text is decidedly introductory; it discusses every released component, discussing theory interspersed with simple but effective procedures you can follow, and offering downloadable code examples you can use to jump-start your learning about the Azure platform and as a basis for your own explorations.

The book provides coverage of every Windows Azure platform component that has been released to production by Microsoft as of the time of this writing, as well as some related technologies, such as WCF Data Services, OData, and the ADO.NET Entity Framework.

Who Should Read This Book

This book's goal is to aid .NET developers who want to start working with the components of the Windows Azure platform—from the operating system to SQL Azure and Windows Azure AppFabric. A solid knowledge of the .NET Framework is helpful in fully understanding the code examples and following the exercises using Visual Studio. The content of this book should also prove useful to software architects who need an overview of the components they plan to include in the overall architecture of a cloud-based solution.

Who Should Not Read This Book

If you have already been working with the Windows Azure platform, this book is probably not for you. This book is an introductory guide to developing applications that leverage the platform.

Assumptions

This book expects that you have at least a minimal understanding of .NET development and object-oriented programming concepts. Although Windows Azure can run all .NET language platforms and many third-party (and open source) runtimes, this book includes examples in C# only. If you are not yet familiar with C#, you should consider reading John Sharp's *Microsoft Visual C# 2010 Step by Step* (Microsoft Press, 2010) first.

The Web Role examples assume a basic understanding of ASP.NET Web Forms technology, although the code examples don't use any advanced ASP.NET features.

Organization of This Book

This book is divided into eleven chapters, each of which focuses on a different aspect or technology within the Windows Azure platform.

- Chapter 1 provides a technical overview of cloud computing scenarios and a flavor of Windows Azure.
- Chapter 2 analyzes the various components of the platform and guides the reader through the Windows Azure Management Portal to start using it.
- Chapter 3 introduces Hosted Services, instances, virtual machines, and roles.
- Chapter 4 is dedicated to the construction of a simple application that leverages the Storage Account feature to store and retrieve blobs.
- Chapter 5 maintains the focus on the Storage Account, explaining the main concepts around tables and queues, and introduces the Worker Role feature.
- Chapter 6 dives deep into important aspects such as billing, security, management certificates, and affinity groups.
- Chapter 7 is dedicated to Windows Azure AppFabric, one of the platform components built on the Windows Azure Operating System.
- Chapter 8 focuses on WCF Data Services and guides you through the creation of an Entity Data Model and the use of the "Astoria" project to expose this model with REST and OData protocols.
- Chapter 9 is dedicated to SQL Azure, the SQL Server cloud brother.
- Chapter 10 leverages the Windows Azure services from an on-premises application and different programming environments.
- Chapter 11 is dedicated to the application architecture.

Conventions and Features in This Book

This book presents information using conventions designed to make the information readable and easy to follow.

- In most cases, the book includes exercises for Visual C# programmers. The presented code and procedure are purposely kept as simple as possible, so you can probably gain insight by studying the C# examples even if you are a Visual Basic programmer.
- Each exercise consists of a series of tasks, presented as numbered steps (1, 2, and so on) listing each action you must take to complete the exercise.

- Boxed elements with labels such as "Note" provide additional information or alternative methods for successfully completing a step.
- Text that you are supposed to type (apart from code blocks) appears in bold.
- A plus sign (+) between two key names means that you must press those keys at the same time. For example, "Press Alt+Tab" means that you hold down the Alt key while you press the Tab key.
- A vertical bar between two or more menu items (for example, File | Close), means that you should select the first menu or menu item, then the next, and so on.

System Requirements

You will need the following hardware and software to complete the practice exercises in this book:

- One of the Windows 7 editions, Windows Server 2008 with Service Pack 2, or Windows Server 2008 R2.
- Visual Studio 2010, any edition (multiple downloads may be required if you use the free Express Edition products)
- SQL Server 2005 Express Edition or higher (2008 or R2 release), with SQL Server Management Studio 2005 Express or higher (included with Visual Studio; Express Editions require separate download). To work with SQL Azure, you need SQL Server Management Studio 2008 R2.
- A computer capable of running Visual Studio 2010.
- An Internet connection to work with Windows Azure. You can also try all the samples using the local emulator.

Depending on your Windows configuration, you might require Local Administrator rights to install or configure Visual Studio 2010 and SQL Server 2008 products.

Code Samples

Most of the chapters in this book include exercises that let you interactively try out new material learned in the main text. All the example projects, in both their pre-exercise and post-exercise formats, are available for download from the web:

http://go.microsoft.com/FWLink/?Linkid=217915

Follow the instructions to download the AzureSbs.zip file.

Note In addition to the code samples, your system should have Visual Studio 2010 and SQL Server 2008 installed. The instructions below use SQL Server Management Studio 2008 to set up the sample database used with the practice examples. If available, install the latest service packs for each product.

Installing the Code Samples

Follow these steps to install the code samples on your computer so that you can use them with the exercises in this book.

1. Unzip the AzureSbs.zip file that you downloaded from the book's website (specify or create a specific directory where you want to unzip the files).
2. If prompted, review the displayed end user license agreement. If you accept the terms, select the accept option, and then click Next.

Note If the license agreement doesn't appear, you can access it from the same web page from which you downloaded the AzureSbs.zip file.

Using the Code Samples

The zip file contains

- A directory for each chapter with sample code.
- Every chapter directory contains a Visual Studio solution you can open and work with.
- Chapter 7 contains four subdirectories, each of which contains a Visual Studio solution.

Every chapter contains the step-by-step procedure to recreate the sample so *you do not need any of the code samples* to complete the exercises. To complete an exercise, follow the list of procedure steps in sequence. Each chapter contains all the necessary steps for its exercises; in other words, you do not have to have completed the exercises in previous chapters.

How to Access Your Online Edition Hosted by Safari

The voucher bound in to the back of this book gives you access to an online edition of the book. (You can also download the online edition of the book to your own computer; see the next section.)

To access your online edition, do the following:

1. Locate your voucher inside the back cover, and scratch off the metallic foil to reveal your access code.
2. Go to *http://microsoftpress.oreilly.com/safarienabled*.
3. Enter your 24-character access code in the Coupon Code field under Step 1.

   (Please note that the access code in this image is for illustration purposes only.)

4. Click the CONFIRM COUPON button.

   A message will appear to let you know that the code was entered correctly. If the code was not entered correctly, you will be prompted to re-enter the code.

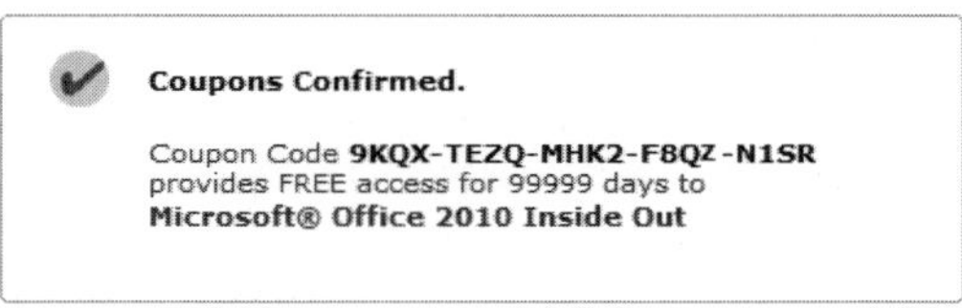

5. In this step, you'll be asked whether you're a new or existing user of Safari Books Online. Proceed either with Step 5A or Step 5B.

   5A. If you already have a Safari account, click the EXISTING USER – SIGN IN button under Step 2.

   5B. If you are a new user, click the NEW USER – FREE ACCOUNT button under Step 2.

   - You'll be taken to the "Register a New Account" page.
   - This will require filling out a registration form and accepting an End User Agreement.

- When complete, click the CONTINUE button.

6. On the Coupon Confirmation page, click the My Safari button.
7. On the My Safari page, look at the Bookshelf area and click the title of the book you want to access.

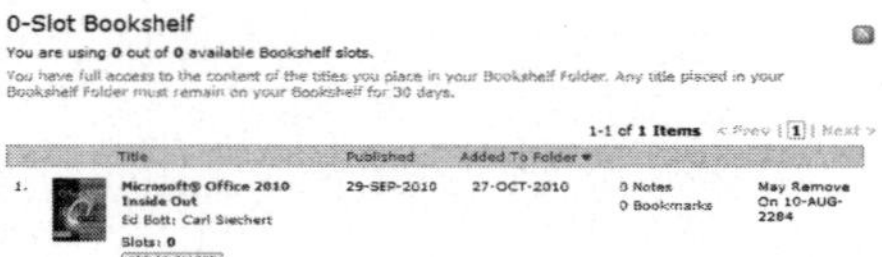

How to Download the Online Edition to Your Computer

In addition to reading the online edition of this book, you can also download it to your computer. First, follow the steps in the preceding section. After Step 7, do the following:

1. On the page that appears after Step 7 in the previous section, click the Extras tab.
2. Find "Download the complete PDF of this book," and click the book title.

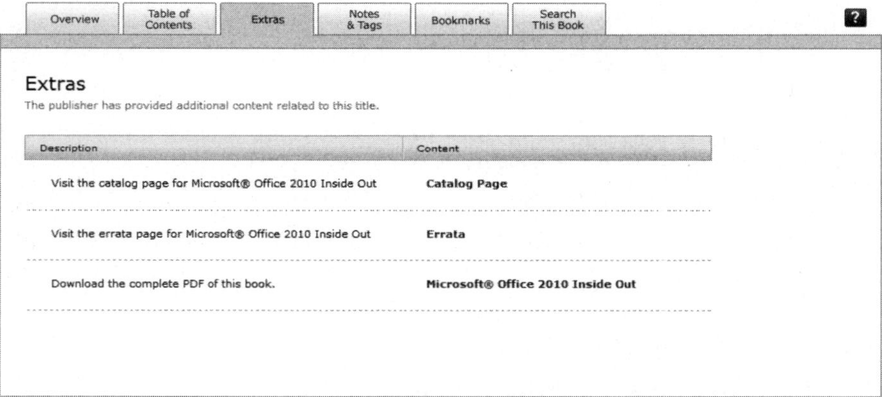

A new browser window or tab will open, followed by the File Download dialog box.

3. Click Save.
4. Choose Desktop and click Save.
5. Locate the .zip file on your desktop. Right-click the file, click Extract All, and then follow the instructions.

Note If you have a problem with your voucher or access code, please contact *mspbooksupport@oreilly.com*, or call 800-889-8969, where you'll reach O'Reilly Media, the distributor of Microsoft Press books.

Errata & Book Support

We've made every effort to ensure the accuracy of this book and its companion content. If you do find an error, please report it on our Microsoft Press site at oreilly.com:

1. Go to *http://microsoftpress.oreilly.com*.
2. In the Search box, enter the book's ISBN or title.
3. Select your book from the search results.
4. On your book's catalog page, under the cover image, you'll see a list of links.
5. Click View/Submit Errata**.**

You'll find additional information and services for your book on its catalog page. If you need additional support, please e-mail Microsoft Press Book Support at mspinput@microsoft.com.

Please note that product support for Microsoft software is not offered through the addresses above.

We Want to Hear from You

At Microsoft Press, your satisfaction is our top priority, and your feedback our most valuable asset. Please tell us what you think of this book at:

http://www.microsoft.com/learning/booksurvey

The survey is short, and we read every one of your comments and ideas. Thanks in advance for your input!

Stay in Touch

Let's keep the conversation going! We're on Twitter: *http://twitter.com/MicrosoftPress*

Chapter 1
Introduction to Cloud Computing

After completing this chapter, you will be able to

- Differentiate between IaaS, SaaS, and PaaS.
- Understand the approach Microsoft has chosen for its cloud strategy.
- Understand the basics of the Windows Azure platform.

This book is based on my personal experience in learning about, teaching, and developing cloud-based solutions that take advantage of the various components of the Windows Azure platform, which consists of Windows Azure Compute, Windows Azure Storage, Windows Azure AppFabric, and Microsoft SQL Azure. This chapter introduces the cloud computing philosophy that is the basis for any cloud-based project.

The home page for Windows Azure (Microsoft Corporation, Windows Azure website, 2011, *http://www.microsoft.com/windowsazure/*) states:

> *Microsoft Windows Azure provides a scalable and fault-tolerant environment that lets developers create powerful applications without the need to purchase and configure hardware and operating systems. Instead, you can simply rent what you need following the PaaS (Platform as a Service) model.*

Note Because URLs, UI names, and procedures may vary over time, some of them may be out of date by the time you read this. In that case, my best advice is to start looking for the information about the Windows Azure product on the Windows Azure home page (*http://www.azure.com*). Information included in this book was accurate at the time of writing.

Approaches to Cloud Computing

The idea behind any cloud computing proposal is for you to pay only for what you use, scaling up or down according to business needs. Vendors supporting cloud computing can interpret this statement differently, providing varying levels of services to achieve this result. The three approaches to cloud computing are Infrastructure as a Service (IaaS), Software as a Service (SaaS), and Platform as a Service (PaaS).

Infrastructure as a Service

Some vendors provide the infrastructure to build solutions, and you rent the hardware such as servers, load balancers, a firewall, and cables. You then configure these remotely and install your solutions on them. You can scale up by requesting more servers and reconfiguring the load balancer without purchasing more hardware. You can scale down at any time by reconfiguring the infrastructure you rented from the cloud service provider. This vendor approach is called *Infrastructure as a Service (IaaS)* because a customer can rent the infrastructure without having to forecast and provision for the highest possible demand in advance. In this approach, you are responsible for correctly configuring the rented infrastructure.

These are the most important points to remember about IaaS:

- The lower levels of the stack are managed by the vendor.
- Very few vendors actually provide an operating system. You are still responsible for managing everything, from the operating system to the applications.
- The obvious benefit of IaaS is that it frees you from the concerns of provisioning many physical or virtual machines.

Software as a Service

In another approach, you can rent a service offered by the vendor and then configure the service by using the interface provided by the vendor, without having to know what infrastructure the vendor uses to provide that service. This approach is called *Software as a Service (SaaS)* because you pay to use defined services. For example, Microsoft Exchange Online carries a per-mailbox charge. To configure it, you use a web application supplied by the vendor to request mailboxes, and name and dimension them. You receive a password for that user and nothing else is necessary—users can access their mailboxes immediately.

This proposed interface has little in common with the on-premises version of Microsoft Exchange. In an SaaS model, you do not have control over nor are you responsible for the hardware on which the service is installed. Similarly, you have no control over the operating system that runs the service, nor any control over the software apart from what the web user interface exposes to you. In other words, a vendor provides everything required to run the application, shielding you from all the underlying components.

Platform as a Service

The third approach is *Platform as a Service, or PaaS*. In this approach, you rent a platform on which you deploy your applications without configuring the infrastructure and without the limitations of the SaaS approach.

The Wikipedia definition for PaaS is as follows (Wikipedia, Platform as a Service, 2011, *http://en.wikipedia.org/wiki/Platform_as_a_service*):

> *...the delivery of a computing platform and solution stack as a service. PaaS offerings facilitate deployment of applications without the cost and complexity of buying and managing the underlying hardware and software and provisioning hosting capabilities, providing all of the facilities required to support the complete life cycle of building and delivering web applications and services entirely available from the Internet.*
>
> *PaaS offerings may include facilities for application design, application development, testing, deployment and hosting as well as application services such as team collaboration, web service integration and marshaling, database integration, security, scalability, storage, persistence, state management, application versioning, application instrumentation and developer community facilitation. These services may be provisioned as an integrated solution over the web.*

The Windows Azure platform fits best in the PaaS category, because it doesn't provide access to the underlying virtualization environment or operating system details such as the network interface, IP configuration, and disk management.

The key concepts to remember when dealing with PaaS are:

- The platform vendor provides and manages everything, from the network connectivity to the runtime.
- PaaS offerings reduce the developer burden by supporting the platform runtime and related application services.
- Developers can begin creating the business logic for applications almost immediately.
- PaaS, compared to traditional hosting solutions, offers the potential for significant productivity increases, because the cloud provider manages all the hardware and operational aspects of the cloud platform.

Cloud Services Defined

The responsibility of you and the vendor is summarized in the following figure.

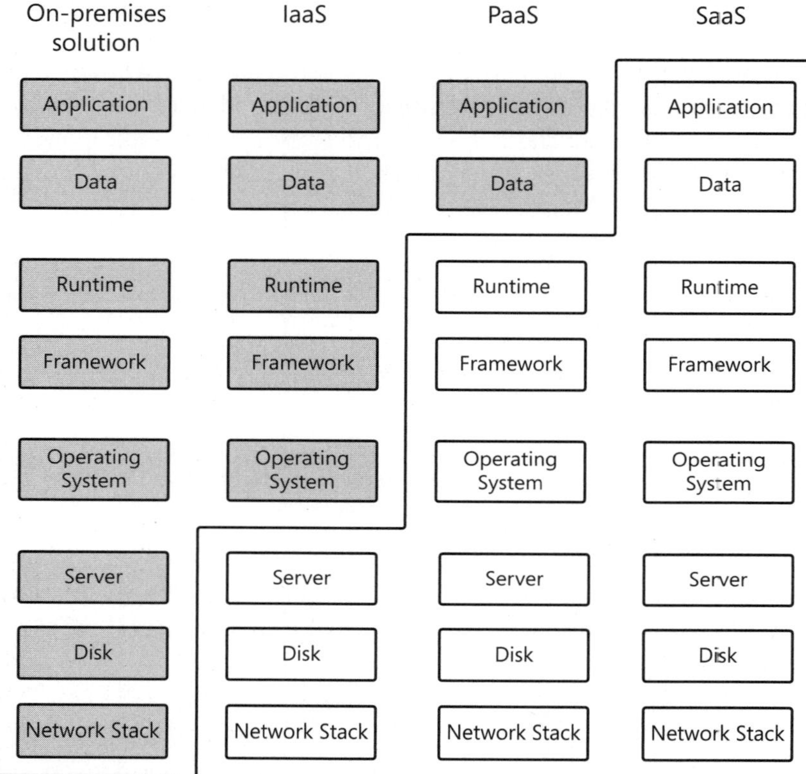

As you can see in the figure, despite significant differences among the various offerings in the cloud computing industry, vendors provide a set of services that you can rent so that you do not have to manage layers (presented as white, below the line).

The definition of cloud computing from Wikipedia is as follows (Wikipedia, Cloud Computing, 2011, *http://en.wikipedia.org/wiki/Cloud_computing*):

> *Cloud computing is Internet-based computing, whereby shared servers provide resources, software, and data to computers and other devices on demand, as with the electricity grid. Cloud computing is a natural evolution of the widespread adoption of virtualization, service-oriented architecture and utility computing. Details are abstracted from consumers, who no longer have need for expertise in, or control over, the technology infrastructure "in the cloud" that supports them. Cloud computing describes a new supplement, consumption, and delivery model for IT services based on the Internet, and it typically involves over-the-Internet provision of dynamically*

> *scalable and often virtualized resources. It is a byproduct and consequence of the ease-of-access to remote computing sites provided by the Internet. This frequently takes the form of web-based tools or applications that users can access and use through a web browser as if it were a program installed locally on their own computer.*

This definition points out two important aspects of these offerings: the usage of distributed resources (IaaS, SaaS, and PaaS), and the abstraction of the underlying technology from the developers. You already learned about the first aspect. The second aspect is important because you can manage abstracted resources such as distributed storage without having to know much technical detail about how to configure it, secure it, and distribute it.

Long-Term Vision

I can imagine a future in which all the physical aspects of data and programs are completely superfluous from a user point of view—but there is still a long way to go to reach that future.

Today, a commonly used acronym is *SOA (Service Oriented Architecture),* a term that defines an ecosystem of interconnected services that can exchange data and share processes, using common patterns and standards. A SOA service can be consumed by applications deployed on heterogeneous platforms that use different operating systems and have different programming environments. SOA defines interoperability concepts that work across systems and platforms. Each service may be implemented using different approaches and technologies—SOA simply defines the way these services communicate with each other and with client applications, giving the service developers the freedom to implement the internal logic however they desire. For example, a service implemented in the Microsoft .NET Framework uses other .NET Framework components and Windows APIs; it is completely different from a similar service written in Java or Ruby. Although each service might use different communication patterns internally, they all must adhere to the common communication contract to talk with other SOA services or clients.

The evolution of languages, operating systems, and frameworks has already provided a layer of abstraction for local platform concerns; for example, in most modern programming languages, you do not have to manage RAM directly. Instead, in today's garbage collected environments, you just have to release your instances correctly, and the framework takes care of allocating and releasing memory from the operating system. That abstraction means that the same code can work in a .NET Framework solution on a powerful notebook with 8 GB of RAM and in a Microsoft .NET Compact Framework environment running on a Windows CE device with 256 MB of RAM—even though the garbage collector works very differently between the two devices. I'm not saying that the same code can work everywhere; I'm saying that there are many differences between Windows and Windows CE, and some of those are made transparent to the developer by the .NET Framework.

Today's compilers do a great job abstracting the machine code. Operating systems abstract the details of memory, disks, and graphics devices, and runtimes such as the common language runtime (CLR) or the Java Virtual Machine (JVM) handle the physical details for you.

That's a strong start, but the next step is to remove the dependencies between the physical location of a resource and a piece of code that uses it to create a distributed system where you can deploy applications and services and provide an abstracted way to manage resources. From a consumer's point of view, location isn't important; instead, obtaining responses to his or her requests quickly and painlessly is important. From a developer's point of view, the main goal is to concentrate on application logic and avoid dealing with the distractions of the underlying environment.

Windows Azure as a PaaS Solution

With a PaaS, you don't need to know the technical details of every component or the difference between a RAID 0 and RAID 1 hard drive. You don't have to worry about or choose hard drive speed or capacity, and you don't need to know or have to care whether a drive is configured as C or D. You just ask the platform for a location to store some information and leave all the technical details up to the platform itself.

The Windows Azure platform hides these technical details completely, and instead provides APIs for managing resources in a logical way. You need only to create storage, choose a name, and then use an endpoint provided by the system to manage resources.

The idea behind Windows Azure is to provide a distributed operating system where you can deploy and run applications without dealing with the classic Windows interface. For example, you don't have to copy files to the Windows Azure file system, and you don't have to use the Internet Information Services (IIS) management console to configure sites, virtual directories, or application pools. In fact, you don't even have to know whether IIS exists behind the scenes.

If you want some disk space, you can just create a storage account and use the provided endpoint to manage resources on it. With PaaS, you can forget disks, storage area networks, and load balancer configurations when storing data in the cloud. You can use standards such as REST and HTTP to interact with this kind of storage. Where are the files stored? You just don't need to know. Are these the quickest disks available? You don't have to care; disk management (from the ordering phase to switching out a broken one) in a PaaS solution is implicit in the platform itself.

Using the Windows Azure platform, you cannot see the exact location of the disk space you rent, you cannot choose the UPS or the hardware manufacturer for disks or servers, you cannot choose your IPs, and you don't have to worry about computer names.

In a system like this, resource access must be done using the related service. Every API must be exposed as a remote web service. Although today's systems do not expose *every* API, you probably get the point.

In practice, PaaS is a kind of SOA for everything:

- You ask the storage service to save a new file.
- You ask the storage service to search for a file.
- You ask the platform management service to scale up or down according to your immediate needs.
- You ask the storage service to create a new folder.
- The service replies with a response you have to analyze.

You learn more details about how this works in the following chapters, but the basic idea is to write a program, deploy it somewhere, and execute it without ever knowing the physical location of the binaries and data. After the deployment phase, you can forget your software (apart from bugs) because the platform takes care of managing it by doing the following:

- Applying patches as soon as they become available.
- Replicating your data and runtime to provide fault-tolerance and load balancing.
- Managing disks and other hardware. For example, if a disk fails, the system immediately uses a replica without any intervention from you. You won't even notice the failure.
- Allocating more disks automatically when your data grows and reconfiguring the load balancer without any downtime.
- Restarting the system automatically if your application crashes.
- Providing more computational power when you request it, which you can do at any time. (You can also automate this task in Windows Azure, as you will learn in this book.)
- Moving your service to a new machine automatically, without your intervention, if the machine assigned to your application stops responding.

Great Opportunity for Small Businesses

In my opinion, cloud computing—particularly the Windows Azure platform—is a great opportunity for every organization and an incredible opportunity for small software houses. Without a cloud computing platform or infrastructure, a small company cannot compete with bigger organizations when creating applications that potentially have thousands of simultaneous users. It cannot afford to invest in expensive hardware.

A small company must take many aspects into account when creating a new solution, such as an e-commerce site, an advertising application, or a finance web application. The major considerations include not only the initial costs, but also the costs for skilled people to configure and maintain the following:

- Production and staging web servers
- A database cluster
- Routers and load balancers
- Firewalls and security software

In addition, there are fixed costs for the bandwidth required by an application as well as licensing costs for all the software. And that investment isn't limited to the company's initial needs. The company must buy enough web servers to create a fault-tolerant solution from the beginning, because the application requires that, starting with its initial deployment. The collateral damage incurred from failure can be even more expensive than the initial cost of preventing such a failure.

Apart from the often prohibitive initial costs of developing an application, a small company needs to find highly skilled people to configure the servers in the most appropriate and highest performing way. Often, this skill level must be found outside the company, which means additional costs in the early stages of the system. Using individuals outside of the company can also lead to many problems if something goes wrong after going to production, because the company employees have little or no internal knowledge about the system. In addition, hiring people with the necessary skillset (or training internal employees) can postpone the release date and raise the costs even further.

Finally, even after all this initial effort, assume the company deploys (or sells) the application, and that users start using it. If the number of users goes up, the company has to buy new hardware and reconfigure the entire system using its newly hired talent or an external consulting service. This can be a big problem when the application is successful, and the numbers go up too quickly. Even if the revenue coming from the application is higher than expected (which could then be used to improve the system), hardware failures and other troubles might be imminent. (As Murphy's Law says, "If something can go wrong, it will.").

A big company might have the necessary knowledge and fault-tolerant hardware to manage such events and, in this case, the problem would be fixed by internal personnel in a reasonable timeframe. But if the company has chosen an external consulting service, it has to spend some more money to fix the problem. Moreover, it must wait for service availability. Normally, small companies try to spend less money for external services by buying just what they think they will need—but sometimes they tend to underestimate Murphy's Law. On the other hand, if the number of users is lower than expected, the company has probably already wasted money on an oversized hardware setup.

If the company has a strong marketing department, it can try to advertise the application or service. Typically, such campaigns offer a trial period to new customers. In theory, this is good practice from a marketing point of view, but it can lead to a dramatic traffic spike during or immediately after the advertising campaign. This leads to two different problems:

- Trouble for existing users who want their money because of reduced service quality
- Trouble for trial users, who will not buy a service perceived as slow

If the application is an e-commerce site, you can imagine the problems that occur when a marketing campaign advertises the website. Existing customers start experiencing latency while browsing the site, and new customers will see a site that performs poorly. In a case like this, the simplest solution from a technical point of view is to increase the hardware level, but in reality, costs often make that approach impractical.

There is yet another factor to take into account. A higher-than-expected number of applications have what are called "peak times." For example, use of e-commerce applications can peak during holiday seasons, when a new product is launched on the market, or when a new fashion season opens. Similarly, a finance application typically has more traffic at the end of the month or fiscal year, and a travel application may have many peak times during the year preceding common holidays. Even an internal application has peak times that typically correspond to month-end tasks such as salary processing, or to the beginning and end of workdays.

If a company's application or website experiences different levels of load throughout the month or year, but the company has opted for a fixed model for the cost, there is an intrinsic incongruity—most of the time, the company has to pay more than needed for the ordinary activity just so it will be able to handle peak activity levels. Even worse, consider a case such as our hypothetical company, which, if it is not successful, will have completely lost the initial cost for hardware and licenses.

However, using cloud solutions, a small company can launch with minimal effort and expense. The following list describes the benefits of using a cloud-based infrastructure:

- There is no initial cost for the production web servers.
- There is no fixed cost for the bandwidth.
- No particular skills are required for the installation of the servers.
- There is no initial cost for database clusters.
- The skills required for configuring a database cluster are unnecessary.
- There are no routers or load balancers to buy or configure.
- There is no firewall and security software to purchase or configure.
- There are no skills required to secure the underlying system.

- There is no cost for the staging environment.
- There are no licenses to buy.

As the preceding list reveals, all the initial effort usually required by any on-premises solution is bypassed completely. You start paying only when you deploy your solution, and then you can adjust the computational power and the storage space to your actual needs—almost in real time. More importantly, you can reduce the computing power (and the costs) according to those needs as well. Finally, if the business turns out to be unprofitable, you can simply stop paying at any time.

Great Opportunity for Big Businesses

The same advantages and opportunities of cloud computing apply to big companies, although with some differences, for example:

- Big companies usually hire dedicated IT teams that probably already have the necessary skills to install, configure, and maintain an enterprise-class system.
- Big teams can handle the various aspects of a modern solution, from security tasks to networking performance to installation criteria.
- The same team can be used in different projects, reducing the per-solution costs.
- Big teams typically have fault-tolerant procedures and people dedicated to respond to alerts.
- Big companies may launch new businesses by using machines that are already in place and can meet the initial load.

Remember that on-premises solutions do incur variable costs over time: electrical power, IT people to install and configure new servers, and bandwidth.

Another set of concerns applies to both big and small companies:

- Configuring the same server so that it meets the needs of completely different projects can be problematic. For instance, one project might require some settings that are incompatible with the settings required by a different project.
- Scalability problems can occur when several applications share the same components.

From a technical point of view, using different servers and infrastructure for each application is ideal—but doing that has an impact on the total cost of solution ownership. In a cloud computing infrastructure, IT managers can separate applications and services from both a logical and physical perspective without buying the hardware in advance.

In my consulting experience, one of the biggest problems cloud computing faces in large organizations is the variable nature of the bill. Many organizations prefer to have a fixed amount of money allocated for a project rather than assume the risks of having variable costs.

Companies must shift their approaches to cloud computing. That shouldn't be too difficult, because it's the same sort of shift companies and people have been making for the last 20 years in many aspects of business and personal life. These changes include the following:

- **Phone carriers have changed their billing system.** I remember my childhood when there was only one way of paying—a monthly fee and a fixed cost fee for every call. Today you can choose among hundreds of difficult-to-understand rate plans. The same applies to any business contract. Cloud billing plans are very similar. They can range from a fixed rate for a fixed feature to a completely variable rate.
- **A growing number of people live in rented houses in many countries.** Buying a house can be a good investment, but hardware components don't acquire value over time. Many companies don't own the buildings where their offices reside. When they have a problem, they can request assistance from the owner. Ownership in the cloud is very similar: problems and patches fall within the owner's liability.
- **Many companies rent cars for their employee instead of buying them.** Renting typically has a fixed cost and some reasonable usage limit (such as mileage). You pay a higher fee only when you exceed that limit. Cloud computing is essentially the same as renting. You pay a fixed fee and accept some limits (such as those for bandwidth and storage), and pay a higher fee only when you exceed those limits.
- **Many companies already rent hardware such as personal computers, notebooks, and servers.** Again, the cloud platform is similar, but also includes the bandwidth, routers, firewalls, and so on.

Remember that, in the cloud, hardware is replaced not only when problems occur (such as when the plumbing in your house bursts), but also when new models become available. The electric power service you receive at home or in your office is another good example of the cloud approach. When new devices become available, such as a new type of electric meter, you do not have to install it yourself. I live in a small village in Tuscany, and a new meter with remote configuration and an LED display was installed in my house in 2004. I didn't pay anything for this new device; the costs were absorbed by the fees I was already paying to the electric company. In the same way, you don't have to pay anything when Microsoft installs new firewalls or routers in Windows Azure data centers.

Cloud computing also has an impact on open source systems, because cloud customers do not pay for licenses. The cost of licenses is included in the cloud rental fee. In on-premises solutions, open source fans state that one of the major advantages of open source operating systems over Windows-based operating systems is that they are free. In the cloud, this statement isn't applicable: customers pay a fee for the system, which includes servers and other hardware, and bandwidth. A customer can choose the cloud platform and compare these costs without worrying about licensing fees.

Windows Azure and Cloud Computing

Windows Azure is an operating system for the cloud (and hosted in the cloud) that completely abstracts the physical components of the system: the developer, as the customer, chooses the features, the components, and the level of Service Level Agreement (SLA) without the configuring of hardware or software on the assigned machines. To guarantee scalability and fault-tolerance, data stored in Windows Azure is replicated to three nodes, and the load balancer works in a completely transparent way. At the time of this writing, for computational power, a customer can choose among a range of five virtual machine types that can be described using only these components:

- **CPUs** You can range from a single processor at 1 GHz and greater to 8 cores if you want to leverage vertical parallelism.
- **RAM** Choose the size you need. The available range starts at 768 MB and goes up to 8 GB. You do not have to choose the vendor, the speed, or other characteristics.
- **Instance storage** Disk space starts at 20 GB and can expand to 2 terabytes per instance. You do not need to choose the speed, the controller, or the type of redundancy.
- **I/O performance** The choice is straightforward: low, moderate, or high.

The subscription fee can include some or all of these features. When a customer exceeds its limits, the billing system starts charging the surplus. Moreover, these features include everything you need. In five minutes, you can be up and running with a service or an application on the Windows Azure platform.

If you want to scale up, you can choose from a simple configuration file to increase the number of machines you are using, and within about five minutes, you obtain more machines. If you want to reduce your computing power, you can reduce the number of instances at any time. The billing system will stop charging for dismissed instances immediately.

You can also change the machine size at any time; however, it takes a slightly longer period of time to restart the service, because the platform needs you to redeploy the application. Such a redeployment operation usually takes about five minutes, after which you are up and running with new instances on new machines.

Costs are proportional to the chosen configuration, but—and this is significant—you can change the configuration as needed.

Every technical aspect of the deployment is Microsoft's responsibility. Fortunately, no one knows Microsoft Windows Server 2008 SP2 (the operating system on which Windows Azure is currently based at the time of this writing) better than Microsoft, and no one knows the .NET Framework internals, the operating system kernel, the IIS components, Microsoft SQL Server, and so on, better than Microsoft.

Similarly, for maintenance and security, no one can apply patches faster than Microsoft. Even if your administrators check newsletters or read feeds 24 hours a day, they will always be second to the Microsoft team, which applies patches to the Windows Azure platform automatically as soon as they become available.

Your application is deployed using a model that describes the application's needs. Developers can request a certain amount of disk space, and Windows Azure provides it automatically. However, you cannot request a specific SCSI (small computer system interface) controller or a RAID5 configuration—but you don't typically need to do that. The only thing you need to do is ensure that the application has sufficient disk space. If you achieve the required performance for your applications, because redundancy and scalability are assured, you don't need to know all the internal details. There is no added application value in knowing disk types. Moreover, you can avoid the inherent risks of choosing the wrong disks.

Windows Azure hides most of the details of an on-premises solution. Every resource is exposed as a service (such as the storage account service for managing files) using standard protocols. All the storage details are completely transparent to developers on every platform. Physical resources are exposed by the infrastructure as services so that developers don't need to write resource-specific code to handle details like these:

- Physical location of resources
- Installed hard disks
- Name of the servers
- Network path
- IIS virtual directory
- IPs of the requested machines

Likewise, the .NET Framework developers usually don't need to understand the way the garbage collector (GC) works internally; all they need to know is how to release objects properly to let the garbage collector do its work most efficiently. They don't need to ask the garbage collector to run to clean up memory—and in most cases it would be counterproductive to do so. Similarly, in the cloud, knowing internal details of the local storage service is unimportant, but opening and closing files correctly is fundamental.

To reach a remote resource, the application must call the service that exposes the resource itself. Technically, developers use the service URI to insert, update, or delete a resource, and use the OData REST pattern to query the service for existing resources.

This usually leads to a common question: does typical developer code work well in Windows Azure? The answer is that it depends. If you developed the application properly, decoupling it from dependencies and separating functionality into appropriate layers, the application will probably perform as well (or even better) in Windows Azure with few or no changes. (If you need to store files in shared storage, you will need to adapt some code.)

If the code is monolithic or you did not take full advantage of object-oriented programming (OOP) techniques, or the application consists of "spaghetti code" that mixes UI with business logic or data access logic, the application will probably need some adjustments to work with a different type of storage. However, generally, when the application works with SQL Server, you can probably port it to Windows Azure and SQL Azure with minimal modifications.

If you decide to use the Windows Azure storage service instead of SQL Azure as the storage service for your application, and you wrote a correctly layered solution, you can simply substitute your existing data access layer with the new one (or adapt your existing layer). The storage service exposes resources as an OData service using the same pattern used by Windows Communication Foundation (WCF) Data Services in .NET Framework (previously referred to as Microsoft ADO.NET Data Services in .NET 3.5). If you chose this type of data access technique for your on-premises client solution, you need only adapt the code to use the security model exposed by Windows Azure—and that's it.

The upcoming chapters walk you through the various services and features exposed by the entire Windows Azure platform. You start with a complete description of both the released and announced features in the next chapter, then begin writing code in the local simulated environment, and finally deploy the code to an instance in the cloud. You see how to use the storage service efficiently, and how to work with OData and WCF Data Services. The later chapters are dedicated to SQL Azure and the Windows Azure AppFabric, which represent two of the major components built on top of Windows Azure so far.

The last chapter is dedicated to a simple example application that uses OOP techniques and patterns to decouple the user interface and business layer from the data access components.

Summary

This chapter provided an introduction to cloud computing, starting with the basic idea and moving on to a brief introduction to Microsoft's cloud strategy. You saw some of the common patterns and theories behind this new wave in the computer industry.

Chapter 2

Introduction to the Windows Azure Platform

After completing this chapter, you will be able to

- Understand the basic workings of the Windows Azure platform.
- Create a service.
- Understand Worker Roles.
- Understand Virtual Machine Roles.
- Describe the purpose and architecture of Windows Azure AppFabric.
- Know how SQL Azure fits into the overall picture.

Chapter 1, "Introduction to Cloud Computing," discussed the general concepts and ideas that underlie Microsoft's cloud computing platform and infrastructure. The following excerpt from the Windows Azure website (Microsoft Corporation, Windows Azure website, 2011, *http://www.azure.com*) describes how the Windows Azure platform meets the needs of developers. The first two sentences recall what Chapter 1 explained: you pay only for what you use, scale up when necessary, and scale down according to business needs. This is true for every component of the platform:

> *Building out an infrastructure that supports your web service or application can be expensive, complicated and time consuming. Forecasting the highest possible demand. Building out the network to support your peak times. Getting the right servers in place at the right time, managing and maintaining the systems.*
>
> *Or you could look to the Microsoft cloud. The Windows Azure Platform is a flexible cloud–computing platform that lets you focus on solving business problems and addressing customer needs. No need to invest upfront on expensive infrastructure. Pay only for what you use, scale up when you need capacity and pull it back when you don't. We handle all the patches and maintenance — all in a secure environment with over 99.9% uptime.*

The chapter you are reading now focuses on the Windows Azure platform, starting with the operating system, and describes the way Microsoft is choosing to respond to the rise of cloud computing. It provides an overview of the major Windows Azure platform components. You see what these components are and how each functions to help you deliver and manage cloud applications.

In the next chapter, you create a simple application that takes advantage of the Windows Azure platform's scalability feature. You also publish that simple application to the cloud using the project portal.

Note Because URLs, UI names, and procedures may vary over time, some of them may be out of date by the time you read this. In that case, my best advice is to start looking for the information about the Windows Azure product on the Windows Azure home page (*http://www.azure.com*). Information included in this book was accurate at the time of writing.

The Operating System

The most important component of the platform is Windows Azure, the operating system created for the cloud. Like all operating systems, its purpose is to provide an abstraction from the physical hardware components and a set of services that every application can use. In other words, Windows Azure has the same role as a traditional operating system on any hardware platform.

It also has many similarities to—as well as many differences from—a traditional file system. Unlike a traditional operating system such as Windows 7, which abstracts a single box with its CPU, hard disks, keyboard, mouse, and graphics cards, Windows Azure abstracts a set of servers, providing a common platform for building services and applications in a completely virtual environment. In this environment, you work with servers, but you do not install the application on server A or server B; you deploy an application, but not on a specific disk C or D; and you do not have to configure the network card or the virtual directory to expose your services.

Like traditional operating systems, Windows Azure exposes a way to store data, called *local storage*. However, this storage doesn't consist of physical hard disks nor is it a traditional network share such as \\servername\sharename. Instead, Windows Azure provides shared storage. It provides CPU power—but not just the processors you can see when you open the case of a physical server. In fact, no one can see the actual disks or machines that host a Windows Azure solution; you just upload the application to the environment and let Windows Azure choose the best servers, disks, and load balancing strategies for a particular solution. You can describe your application's needs in a logical way. For example, you can request 1 GB of local disk space to cache remote resources, but you cannot force Windows Azure to deploy your solution on a specific disk or server. You can specify that your application needs to listen for HTTPS requests on port 443, but you cannot configure the IP address of the virtual node.

You can't install the current version of Windows Azure locally, but you can use a local development environment that *simulates* the cloud version of Windows Azure so that you can test your solutions before deploying them. Window Azure is not a product you can find in a shrink-wrapped software box on the shelf in some store, and there's no demo version you can download and try out on your local server. Everything is in the cloud. At the time of this writing, Microsoft is slated to release the Windows Azure appliance, and describes it like this: "The Windows Azure platform appliance consists of Windows Azure, SQL Azure and a Microsoft-specified configuration of network, storage and server hardware. This hardware will be delivered by a variety of partners" (Microsoft Corporation, Windows Azure website, 2011, *http://www.microsoft.com/windowsazure/appliance/default.aspx*).

As you learned in the previous chapter, the main advantages of this cloud-only approach are:

- You do not have to configure hardware, drivers, system components, or the operating system.
- You do not need an inbound Internet connection.
- You do not have to install and configure your own router, firewall, or obtain public IPs; consequently, you do not need network configuration expertise.
- You do not need to apply patches or monitor the system for hardware or software failures.
- Microsoft monitors and maintains the system 24 hours a day so that you don't have to do it on your own.
- The load balancer configuration is logical, not physical.
- You pay for services you need for a defined period of time. During high-use peaks, you can increment the number of "servers" simply by changing a number.
- You do not need to precisely dimension your hardware and buy it in advance.

Window Azure takes care of all these aspects for you. It can manage services automatically, basing its decisions on a completely logical configuration. You provide a set of rules that the Windows Azure "brain" (called *fabric*) follows to deploy your solution. This set of rules is called the *model*; it is a logical description of an application's configuration in the cloud.

Windows Azure uses the term *service* to identify every piece of code that can be exposed and used. For example, an ASP.NET application, a *while*-block that dequeues some messages, and a Windows Communication Foundation (WCF) service are all services. Each service can be hosted in the platform on different servers. Each server, or more precisely, each *node*, is based on Windows Server 2008 R2, so virtually any code that can run on-premises can run in the cloud as well.

The hosting environment is distributed on different nodes that are hosted by servers. Each server is part of a *server collection* that resides in a container. The *container* is like a big shipping container that you can see on the tops of barges and freight trains, and it is placed in a data center by plugging in a giant cable that provides network connectivity and electrical power. From this point on, Windows Azure takes care of everything. When you deploy a solution, you do not have to use a remote desktop to connect to one of these servers—in fact, you don't even have to know the name of the machine. Instead, you use the simple web interface shown in the following figure.

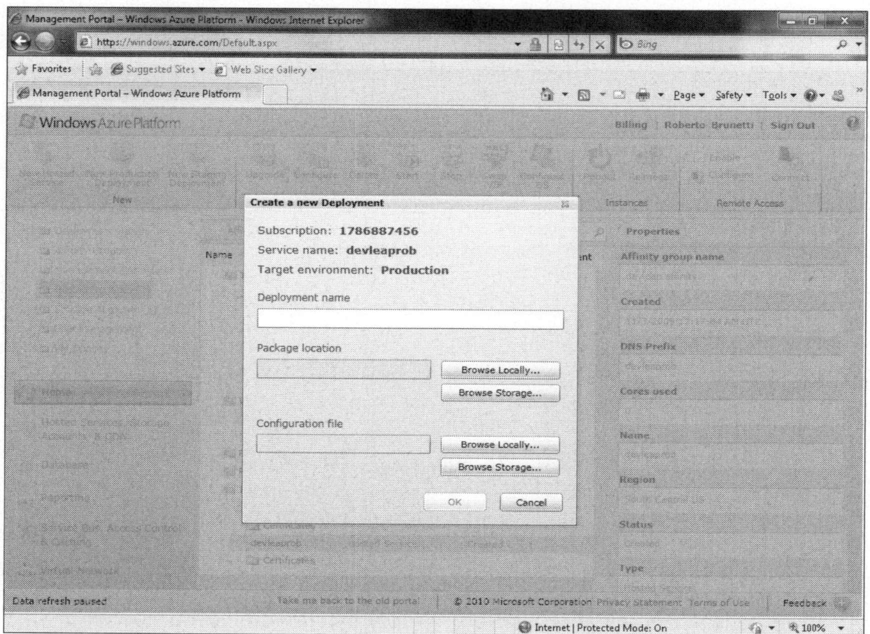

Completing this dialog box is the only task you have to do to deploy a solution and, as you can see, there is no physical component to configure. Microsoft Visual Studio builds the two files that the dialog box requests (Application Package and Configuration File) to deploy a service in the cloud automatically every time you create a cloud project. You will learn how to create a cloud project in Chapter 3, "Creating a Web Role Project."

The Application Package file is the result of compiling your cloud project. It contains the code that Windows Azure will deploy to every node. The Configuration Settings file equates to what I called a model earlier in this chapter. The simplest form of a model is shown in Listing 2-1.

LISTING 2-1 ServiceConfiguration.cscfg.

```
<?xml version="1.0"?>
<ServiceConfiguration serviceName="DevLeapCloudService" xmlns="">
  <Role name="WebRole1">
    <Instances count="1" />
...
  </Role>
</ServiceConfiguration>
```

This basic service model contains the configuration for a service, called DevLeapCloudService, that will be deployed to one node of the cloud (one of the virtual servers) as specified by the *Instances* element value.

As you can see, there is little in this configuration except for names and an instance count: you do not have to configure the IP address, create a virtual directory, copy the application files to the relative path on some remote disk, configure read access to that directory, and so on. You just create a service using the portal, and upload the binaries and the configuration file. You see how to do that in the next procedure.

Service Creation

To create a service that hosts some code, you have to create a new hosted service. You create that service from the main page of the portal (after logging in with a valid Windows Live ID).

Create a Service

1. Open the browser of your choice and go to *http://www.azure.com*.

   From this page, you can access useful information about the platform as well as the major links to the SDKs, as shown in the following figure.

2. You need to buy a subscription before you can work with Windows Azure. Click the Sign Up Now link or the Try link and choose the plan that best suits your needs.

If you just want to test the product, the portal provides some discounted offers at the time of this writing. These subscriptions might be a perfect opportunity to test your solutions in the cloud. Note that most MSDN subscriptions can also include Windows Azure platform subscriptions. I suggest reviewing all the offers available.

Note You can find detailed information about subscriptions and projects in Chapter 6, "Windows Azure Operating System Details."

3. After you activate your subscription, return to the home page, shown in the following figure.

Three links on the right side of the page take you to the various portals. The Windows Azure Developer Portal is the one you need to create your first Windows Azure Service. You learn more about the SQL Azure and AppFabric Portals and components later in this chapter.

4. Click on the Sign In To The Management Portal link to open the Management Portal. After logging on using your Windows Live credentials, you find the Getting Started page shown in the following figure.

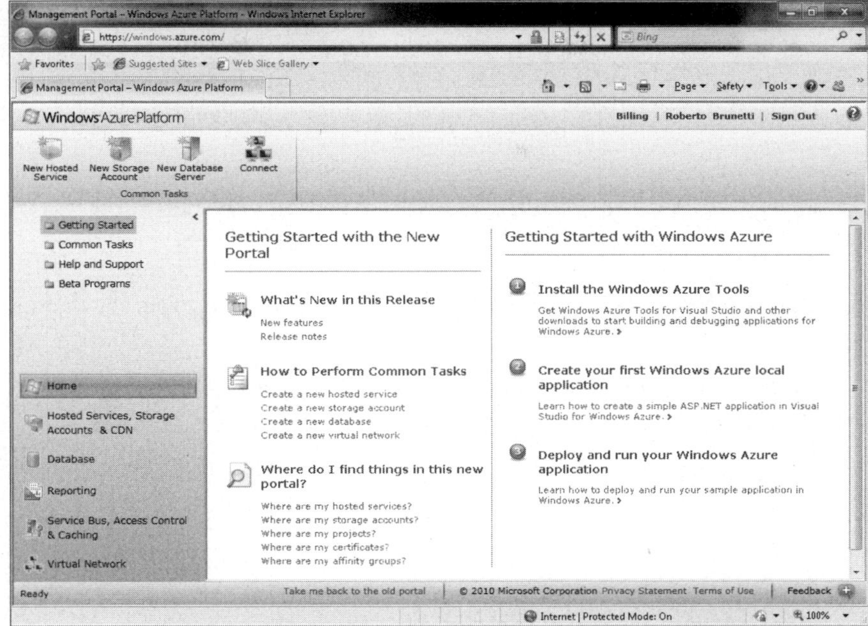

5. On the Getting Started page, click Hosted Services, Storage Accounts & CDN to manage your services. The home page for managing services is shown in the following figure.

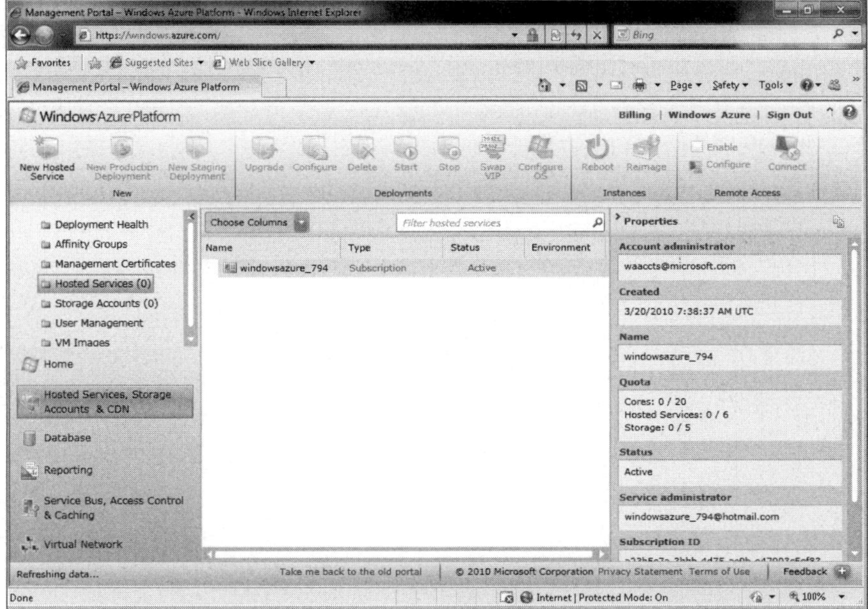

6. Click the New Hosted Service icon on the toolbar to create your new service. Assign the name **Demo** to the project and type a URL prefix for your service, as shown in the next figure. The URL prefix represents the Public Service Name for your service. The name you supply must be globally unique. The portal checks the availability of the name as you write.

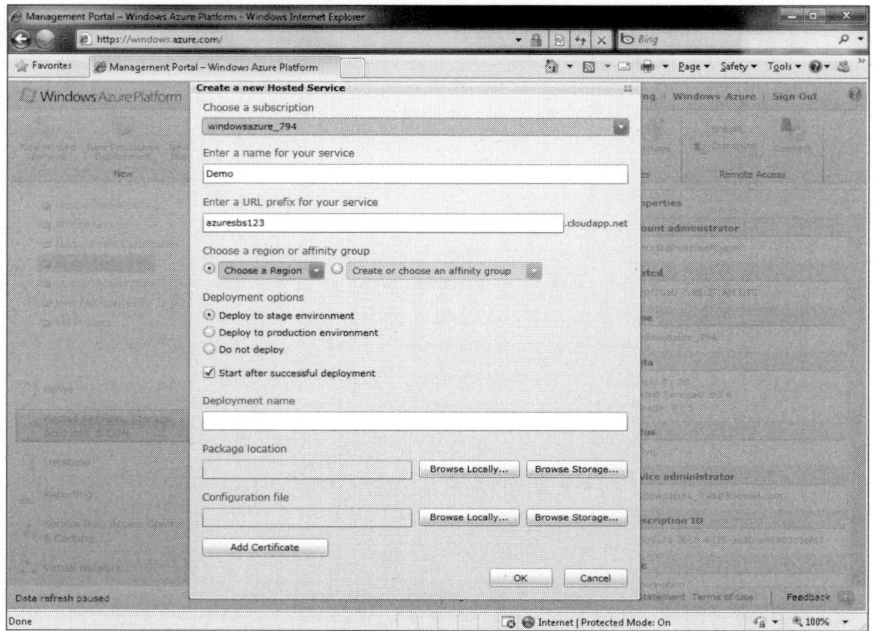

The service name is just a logical name and has no relevance during deployment. In practice, the label is useful for finding a service in the service list shown in the previous image and in the relative treeview menu.

7. Choose a region to host your service. You can select any region where Microsoft has a data center for Windows Azure. This option lets you host your code in a data center in your local region or in the region closest to your users.

Note The Choose A Region Or Affinity Group section is very important because you can define a group of related services that are guaranteed to be hosted in a single data center. See Chapter 6 for a detailed discussion.

8. In the Deployment Options section, select the Do Not Deploy option and click the OK button. (Don't worry about completing the other text boxes for now.) You now have a new hosted service. The next figure shows the user interface for managing a deployed service.

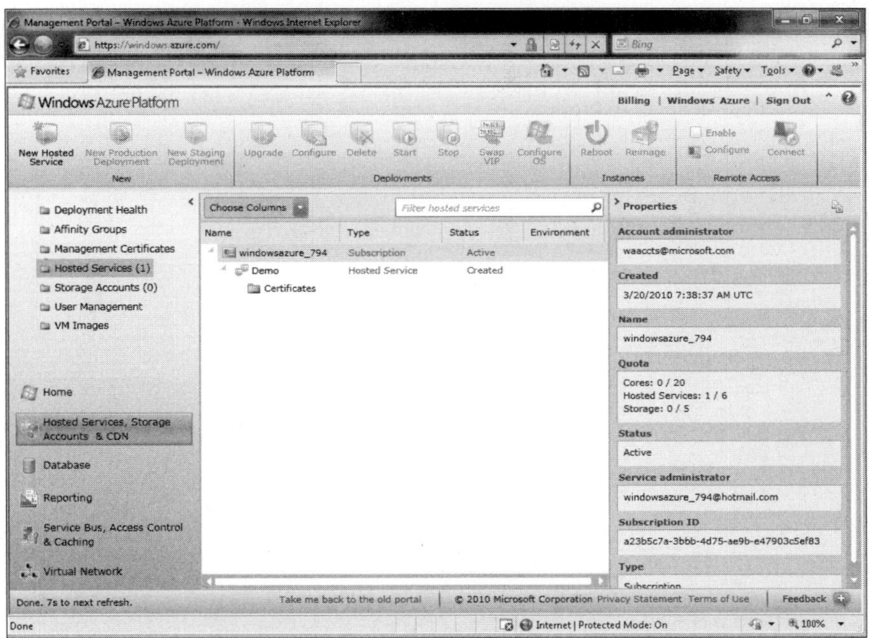

Congratulations! You created a hosted service in which you can deploy your solution using the easy procedure described at the beginning of this chapter. You also uploaded the binaries and the configuration file—that is, the model that describes the application's requirements. Chapter 3 is dedicated to explaining how to create the binaries and model using Visual Studio.

To review, to create a new solution, you have to:

1. Create a hosted service providing the name of the Service, the public URL, and the region.
2. Upload the cloud service package (the binaries) and the configuration file.

You learned that Windows Azure is an operating system and that it completely hides the physical details of the data center, servers, disks, and virtual directories. Because you don't need to worry about any of those aspects, you can deploy a solution with just two clicks.

Figure 2-1 shows you my Windows Azure subscriptions and projects.

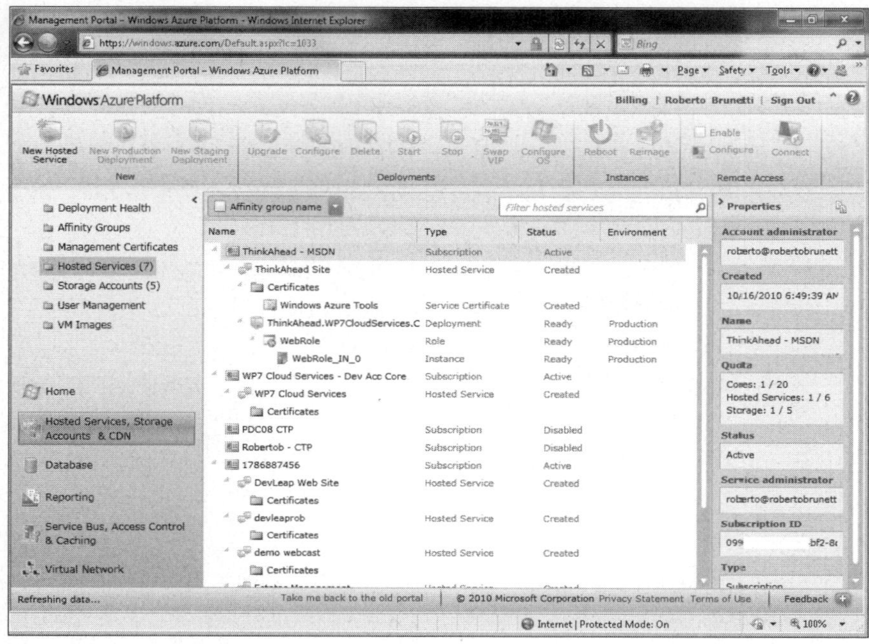

FIGURE 2-1 Home page for managing projects.

The two projects labeled as Disabled in the preceding screen are based on the first community technical preview (CTP) of Windows Azure. (The one called PDC08 –CTP is the first public release of Windows Azure in October 2008 that I used during the beta period.) The other three projects are, in the order they appear in the screen: a demo subscription that I used during training classes; my company's website *http://thinkahead.cloudapp.net*; and a set of hosted applications that expose services to Windows Phone 7 applications, which you can see at *http://wp7.thinkahead.it* (a DNS alias to my company's hosted services).

Save the Planet is a simple application composed of a hosted service and a Windows Phone client application. Users enter the actions they've taken to help the planet, incrementing a global counter visible to any application owner. The company developed a service in WCF to receive this kind of input and a database structure to store the data. Because users can receive notifications when the global counter reaches important goals, the company had to store the push channel URI someplace and create a service that sends notifications to the users. But many questions remain, such as how many users will buy the application. What will the frequency of their actions be—that is, how many requests will the company receive per hour? How many notifications will need to be sent? How many records will need to be processed? The answer to all these questions is that the company simply doesn't know!

Suppose the company bought some hardware to run the site on, and the number of environmentally conscious people using the application grew rapidly, thanks to advertising and word of mouth. In that case, the company might buy new hardware, but installing, configuring, securing, deploying, and testing the application on the hardware (in addition to other activities) would take time. Instead, the company decided to host the service on Windows Azure, so when the application became popular (it was the top-selling app in its category) in October and November, the company just incremented the number of instances. That took only a few seconds, and we did nothing but change a number in the model. You can click the Configure button of the deployed solution to increase the server capacity at any time. This increased capacity is shown in the next figure. In the figure are five configured instances of the Web Role for this application. (The Web Role is the front end hosting the WCF Services.)

It's useful to know that you can perform any of the operations described so far in this chapter programmatically, by calling the Windows Azure APIs. You can create a remote configurator that reads some data—let's say, the number of concurrent requests—and automatically increases or decreases the number of instances accordingly.

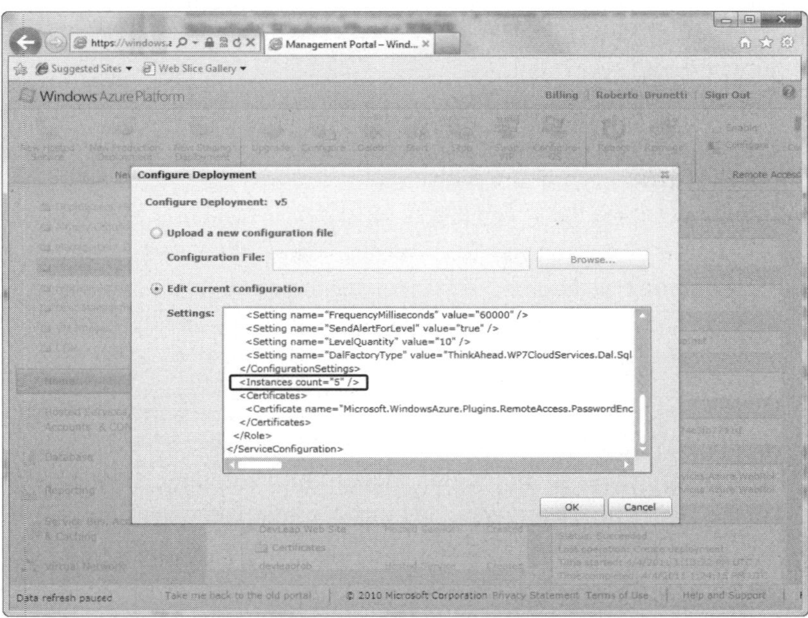

The convenience of the virtual configuration works in the opposite direction as well. If use of the Save the Planet application were to decrease dramatically after its initial momentum, the company could simply scale down its solution without idling or removing any hardware, reconfiguring load balancers, endpoints, machine, disks, and so on.

Every service hosted in Windows Azure can manage the resources exposed by the operating system using the appropriate APIs. For example, in the service model, you can request

40 GB of disk space for local storage, and then use the *RoleEnvironment* class to request a file path that you can use to manage that space. Windows Azure can allocate the 40 GBs on a local disk, so you cannot refer to directories and files using the classic path; instead, you have to ask Windows Azure for that location and then use the classic *System.IO* API, basing the root path on it. The local storage request, as well as the other settings in the model, let the Windows Azure fabric choose the best server to host the service. Local storage is nothing more than a space on a disk of the machine that Windows Azure has chosen to host the service: it is inaccessible from the outside, it cannot be shared among instances, and it is not guaranteed to survive a machine recycle or a crash. You can use this space to cache resources or store temporary files, but do not use it to store application data, session state, or any other data that you cannot recalculate quickly from the application code.

Windows Azure exposes two different environments for each hosted service: the Production environment shown in Figure 2-1, and a staging environment that you can create by clicking the New Staging Deployment button. Staging and production can use different models and different configurations, as well as different numbers of instances. You can configure the staging environment with a smaller instance number sufficient for testing the application, as well as a different connection string and path that use staging rather than production resources.

When you deploy a hosted service to the staging environment, you receive a temporary URL that is composed of a GUID followed by your service name. The staging environment is identical to the production environment in terms of the types of servers, network capabilities, processor types, and so on. You have to pay to host a service even in a staging environment, so the Windows Azure billing system starts to calculate usage time when you deploy a service, whether you do so in a staging or production environment. If you chose a pay-as-you-go subscription, your account is charged immediately; if you chose an offer with some hours included, your account will be charged only if you exceed your limit.

You can swap production and staging environments whenever you want—it takes just a moment. Typically, you deploy a new version to the staging environment, test it, and then press the VIP Swap button to move the staging version to the production environment and the old production code to the staging environment. If something goes wrong, you can immediately swap the two environments again to return to the previous situation and investigate the problem. The swap operation occurs in near real-time because Windows Azure fabric just adjusts the internal DNS, exchanging the pointers.

Chapter 3 is dedicated to creating and deploying a simple application using the Windows Azure Tools for Visual Studio.

In the following figure, the production environment is hosting the first version (labeled V1 in the screen) of the service. It is exposed on *http://azuresbs123.cloudapp.net*, which represents its public URL. In contrast, the staging environment is hosting the next version of the service (labeled V2) for testing purposes.

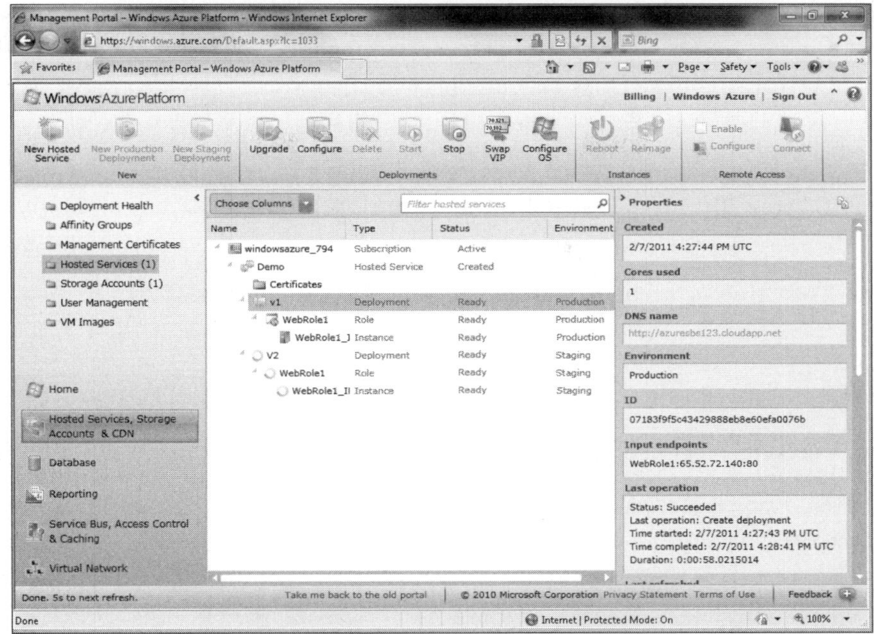

> **Note** The hosted service presented in the previous sentence (*http://azuresbs123.cloudapp.net*) was removed at the end of this writing, so don't try to use it!

During the test phase, the company used the temporary URL *http://<guid>.cloudapp.net* to reach the application's pages and services. When all tests are complete, the Swap VIP (Virtual IP) button switches the DNS pointers so that the real URL *http://azuresbs123.cloudapp.net* points to the machine hosting the second version of the service, and vice versa.

Windows Azure Storage

The Windows Azure operating system, as illustrated in the previous section, exposes a virtualized environment where you can host your services in a very simple fashion: you create a new hosted service and then deploy your solution without having to worry about any of the classic (and often painful) deployment issues.

The operating system lets you store three different kinds of resources: blobs, tables, and queues. You use *blob* storage to store files. *Tables* are a type of unstructured entity container, and you can use *queues* to decouple two applications. All storage resources are covered in the next chapters. To use these types of storage, you have to create a storage account project from the portal. Storage accounts are publicly exposed via HTTP, so you can reach a particular storage account (subject to security policy permissions) from virtually everywhere. Hosted services can use the storage account to store application data permanently (remember that local storage is local to the machine and is only temporary). Because the storage location is exposed via HTTP, an on-premises server application can use the same Windows Azure storage account as a hosted or mobile application as long as a connection is available.

Windows Azure exposes the storage account data using Internet standards such as HTTP, REST, and OData (Open Data Protocol), so it's accessible by just about any platform in our galaxy.

To create a new storage account, you complete a simple wizard available from the project portal.

Create a Storage Account

A storage account is the second project type you can create using the Windows Azure Portal.

1. On the main project page, click the Storage Accounts link in the upper-left menu, shown in the following figure.

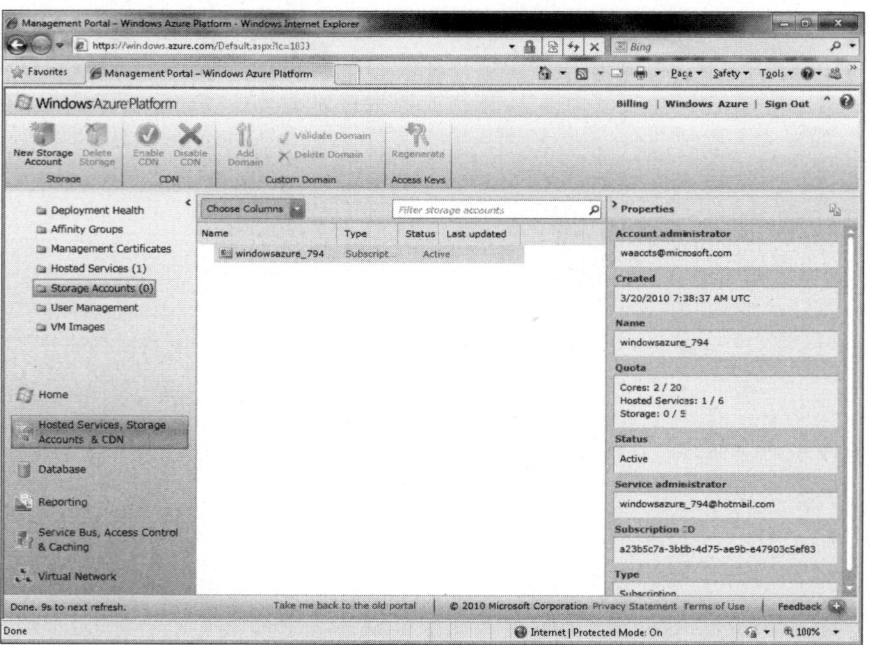

2. Click the New Storage Account button on the toolbar to open the Create A New Storage Account wizard, shown in the following figure.

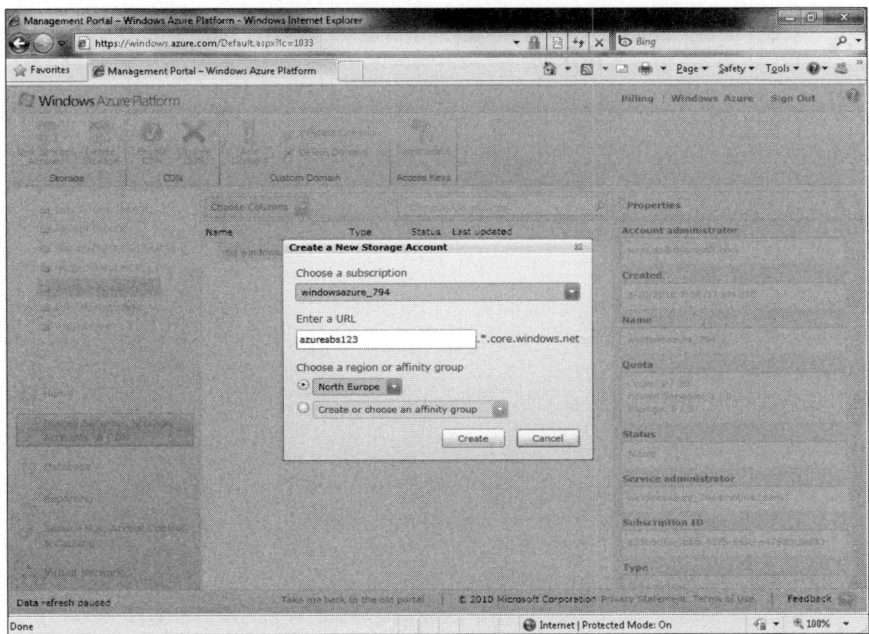

3. Type a unique URL for your service in the Enter A URL text box and select a region in the Choose A Region Or Affinity Group section. The service name you choose will form the suffix for the URI that Windows Azure exposes so that you can access the service.

   The Create Or Choose An Affinity Group option list box allows you to define a named group of servers to host your services and data. Windows Azure guarantees that the servers in an affinity group will be hosted in the same data center. Placing your services in the same affinity group will hold latency to a minimum.

4. Click the Create button to create your storage account. You see the screen shown in Figure 2-2.

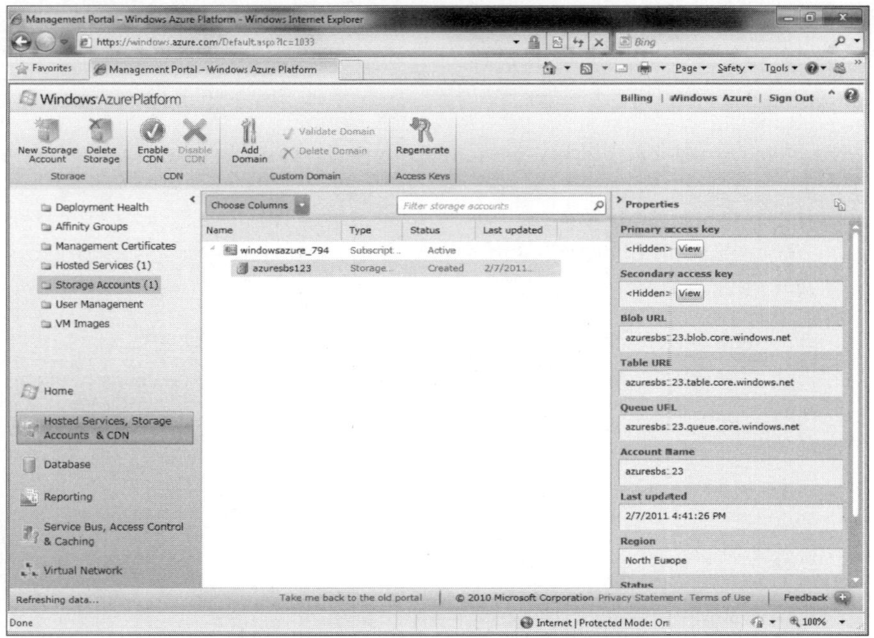

FIGURE 2-2 Storage account details.

If you followed all the steps in this procedure, you should end up, in theory, with an infinite space in which to store your data. This space is distributed across servers by an automatic load balancer, and by default it is replicated to three nodes, which guarantee a high level of fault tolerance. Note that you created this robust storage with just three mouse clicks—you didn't have to buy new hardware, configure it, or expose it to the outside world.

As you can see in Figure 2-2, you get three different endpoints for your storage, each one dedicated to a different kind of resource (I introduced these to you earlier, too):

- **Blob** This service is the persistent file system for every Windows Azure application. You use this endpoint to store images, documents, and other files. The blob can be organized in different containers.
- **Table** A table is a container of heterogeneous entities that you can store and retrieve using a key. A table has no predefined structure, and you can organize it in partitions, spreading different partitions across different servers to achieve an optimum level of scalability.
- **Queues** A queue can be used as a method to decouple applications, enabling asynchronous communication. Windows Azure exposes a simple service that any application on any platform can use to send messages to other applications.

Everything is exposed using standard protocols, so it's possible, for example, to make a REST query using the *PUT* method from a PHP (Hypertext Preprocessor) on-premises application to insert a blob in the storage, and then use code in a Windows Phone 7 Microsoft Silverlight application to perform a *GET* operation to retrieve the list of blobs in the storage. As you can see in Figure 2-2, you receive two access keys that you can use to secure access to your storage account. In the next chapters, you learn that these keys are equivalent. You learn more about using an Azure storage account and related code in Chapter 4, "Windows Azure Storage," and Chapter 5, "Tables, Queues, and Worker Roles," which are dedicated to describing this feature.

The billing method for the Windows Azure storage account is different from the billing method for Windows Azure Compute: you don't pay when you create a project as you do with a hosted service. The Windows Azure storage account charges transactions to the storage and the space occupied. I discuss this more in Chapter 6.

The Worker Role

The cloud storage account exposes a smart service so that you can build a queue solution to decouple one application from another. A perfect example is decoupling the front end of a web application (the Web Role) from the back end (the Worker Role). A *Worker Role* is a type of service that, by default, is not exposed with an endpoint but is instead dedicated to performing process operations in the back end.

An example of a Worker Role project might be an order-processing process that receives an order as a message in a queue from the front end. The front end is freed up immediately after it inserts the message in the queue.

You can adjust Web Role and Worker Role instances independently. If you want to accept more orders, you can increase the instances for the front-end. The queue will accept more orders without any problems, and the front-end thread that serves the user request can be placed in the pool to serve another incoming request. Similarly, if the queue length starts to increase, you can adjust the number of Worker Role instances accordingly.

Figure 2-1 showed the real-world deployment of the Save the Planet Windows Phone 7 application. The 11 instances of the Web Role process the WCF service call to increment the application's action counter. The Worker Role is a scheduled process that sends notifications to the client. The code scans a User Table to check the last date the current user performed an action to determine whether a user needs any notifications and if so, it sends the notification. The application scans the table once each minute, so it does not need more than one instance.

A Worker Role can open an external endpoint; in this way, it becomes reachable synchronously by a remote client or a Web Role in the cloud.

Worker Roles are hosted in different nodes from Web Roles. This is important because it means that you get charged for Worker Role instances separately from Web Role instances. For example, if you deploy both a Worker Role instance and a Web Role instance, you have to pay for a total of two instances.

The Virtual Machine Role

During the Professional Developers Conference (PDC) 2010, Microsoft announced the Virtual Machine Role functionality by which developers or IT Managers can transfer an on-premises virtual machine to the cloud. (This feature was first announced at PDC 2008 with the code-name RAW Mode.)

A Virtual Machine Role runs a virtual hard disk (VHD) image of a Windows Server 2008 R2 virtual machine (VM). The VHD must be created from an on-premises Windows Server machine, at which point the image can be uploaded to Windows Azure. After it is stored in the cloud, the VHD can be loaded on demand into a VM Role and executed. Customers can configure and maintain the operating system and use Windows Services, schedule tasks, and so on for the VM Role.

It is important to remark on the differences between the Web and Worker Role models and the VM Role model. At the time of this writing, Microsoft introduced the VM Role with this statement (Microsoft Corporation, Windows Azure website, 2011, *http://www.microsoft.com/windowsazure/compute/default.aspx*):

> *A Virtual Machine (VM) role runs an image (a VHD) of a Windows Server 2008 R2 virtual machine. This VHD is created using an on-premises Windows Server machine, then uploaded to Windows Azure. Customers can configure and maintain the OS and use Windows Services, scheduled tasks etc. in the VM role. Once it's stored in the cloud, the VHD can be loaded on demand into a VM role and executed. The VHD can be used as the base image for all instances of a VM Role.*

The statement clarifies that developers have to manage the virtual machine—configuring it, patching it, and updating it. A Web or Worker Role is a more flexible and automated environment.

Windows Azure AppFabric

Windows Azure exposes the base services for the entire platform. Microsoft has also released a set of products and technologies built on Windows Azure called the Microsoft Push Notification Service for Windows Phone 7. This is a Microsoft service hosted on the

Windows Azure operating system. Some of the Windows Live Services are already hosted on Windows Azure.

Windows Azure AppFabric is another set of services hosted on top of the operating system that provides a comprehensive middleware platform. Developers use Windows Azure AppFabric to connect application pieces together, manage identity and access control, cache remote resources, and create composite applications.

At the time of this writing, the official documentation (Microsoft Corporation, Windows Azure website, 2011, *http://www.microsoft.com/windowsazure/appfabric/overview/default.aspx*) describes Windows Azure AppFabric in this way:

> *Windows Azure AppFabric provides a comprehensive cloud middleware platform for developing, deploying and managing applications on the Windows Azure Platform. It delivers additional developer productivity adding in higher-level Platform-as-a-Service (PaaS) capabilities on top of the familiar Windows Azure application model. It also enables bridging your existing applications to the cloud through secure connectivity across network and geographic boundaries, and by providing a consistent development model for both Windows Azure and Windows Server.*
>
> *Finally, it makes development more productive by providing higher abstraction for building end-to-end applications, and simplifies management and maintenance of the application as it takes advantage of advances in the underlying hardware and software infrastructure.*

The middleware services run with the same paradigms described in this chapter and the preceding one: payment only for what you use, deployment, logical management, and autoconfiguration of lower-level services such as load balancers and a fault-tolerance strategy.

Windows Azure AppFabric was released in April 2010 with two important initial services: Service Bus and Access Control. Other services will be released in the CTP during 2011.

The Service Bus

The Service Bus service provides secure connectivity and messaging capabilities through which distributed and disconnected applications can talk together via the Service Bus pattern. The Service Bus is of course hosted in the cloud, so any application that has an Internet connection can access it. To start exchanging messages via the Service Bus from any application and platform, you create a new service namespace using the portal. The service uses Internet standards such as HTTP and REST to create services and exchange messages. As you will learn in Chapter 7, "Building an AppFabric Solution," if your service-oriented architecture (SOA) solution is based on WCF, adapting the solution to use the Service Bus involves only a few lines of code and some configuration settings.

At the time of this writing, Microsoft presents the Service Bus with this statement (Microsoft Corporation, Windows Azure website, 2011, *http://www.microsoft.com/windowsazure/appfabric/overview/default.aspx*):

> *The Service Bus provides secure messaging and connectivity capabilities that enable building distributed and disconnected applications in the cloud, as well as hybrid application across both on-premise and the cloud. It enables using various communication and messaging protocols and patterns, and saves the need for the developer to worry about delivery assurance, reliable messaging and scale.*

The following figure illustrates a typical Service Bus message flow. In this image, an on-premises application behind a firewall or a NAT registers itself on the service bus using a simple *POST* request to the service namespace URL (created in the portal). When authorized applications send messages to this public URL, the Service Bus acts as a relay; it forwards the messages to the on-premises applications. This technique eliminates the need to expose the on-premises application to the outside world. It also enables new applications to become part of the message flow. Any new application that needs to receive the same messages can register itself in the service namespace.

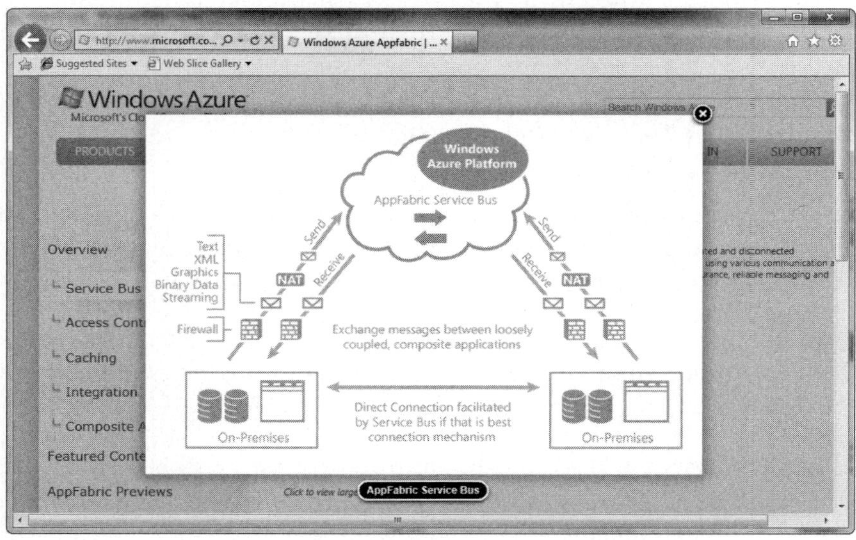

The Service Bus can relay messages that contain text, XML, graphics, binary data, and streaming data. It exposes classes to various programming environments using a set of SDKs. If an SDK is not available for a particular platform, developers can still use REST and HTTP to interact with the Service Bus nodes.

The Access Control Service

The second released piece of the Windows Azure AppFabric is the Access Control Service. At the time of this writing, the official documentation states (Microsoft Corporation, Windows Azure website, 2011, *http://www.microsoft.com/windowsazure/appfabric/overview/default.aspx*):

> *Access Control provides an easy way to provide identity and access control to web applications and services, while integrating with standards-based identity providers, including enterprise directories such as Active Directory®, and web identities such as Windows Live ID, Google, Yahoo! and Facebook.*
>
> *The service enables authorization decisions to be pulled out of the application and into a set of declarative rules that can transform incoming security claims into claims that applications understand. These rules are defined using a simple and familiar programming model, resulting in cleaner code. It can also be used to manage users' permissions, saving the effort and complexity of developing these capabilities.*

Authorization rules can be pulled out from an application and put onto the Windows Azure AppFabric Access Control. A developer can manage permissions and claims using both the developer portal and the provided command-line tool. Some third-party tools and free tools can facilitate the construction of these rules. (You can find these at *http://www.codeplex.com.* Use the term "Azure" in the search engine.)

Here's a possible scenario. A client application (represented on the right side of the following figure) sends the required claims to the public Access Control URL to access a remote application. The Access Control service checks the input claims against the defined rules, produces the output claims, and sends these claims in a secure token that the client application then sends to the remote application (on the left side of the figure). The server application can request permission to the AppFabric Access Control.

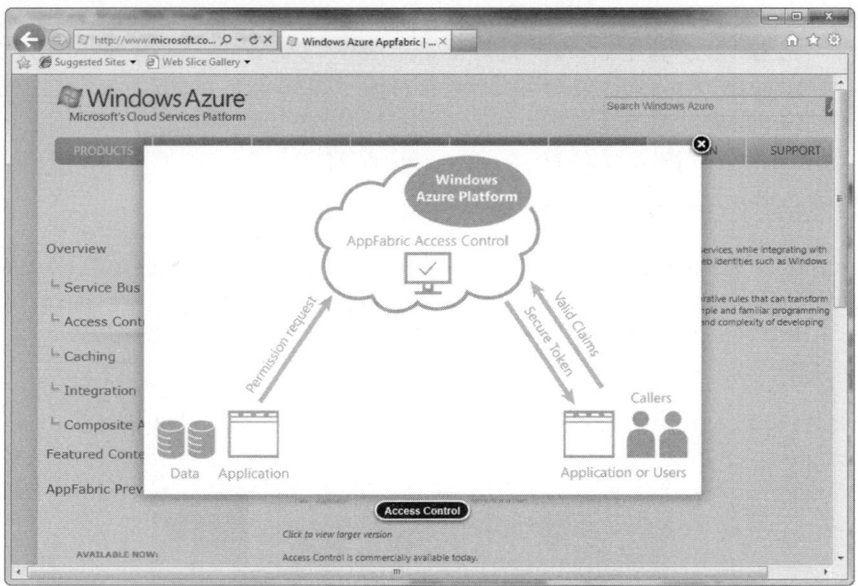

The Access Control service uses REST and the Web Resources Access Protocol (WRAP) to funnel claims back and forth to the applications. Because those are publicly exposed in the cloud, they can be used anywhere and on any platform. For example, at the time of this writing, no SDK exists for Windows Phone 7, but you can still use REST and HTTP to ask the Access Control Service for security claims and use those to send messages to the Service Bus.

Microsoft plans to release three additional useful components in the second half of 2011: the caching service, the integration service, and the composite application service, which I describe in the following sections.

The Caching Service

Caching supplies a distributed, in-memory, highly available application cache service for Windows Azure applications. This capability is provided using the same approach as other Windows Azure services use: no installation, no instance management required, and the ability to dynamically increase or decrease the cache size as needed.

You can use the developer preview—part of the CTP/Labs environment—to get an early look at these features. Just request access to the CTP using the link you can find in the portal in the Caching section.

Caching architecture is shown in the following figure.

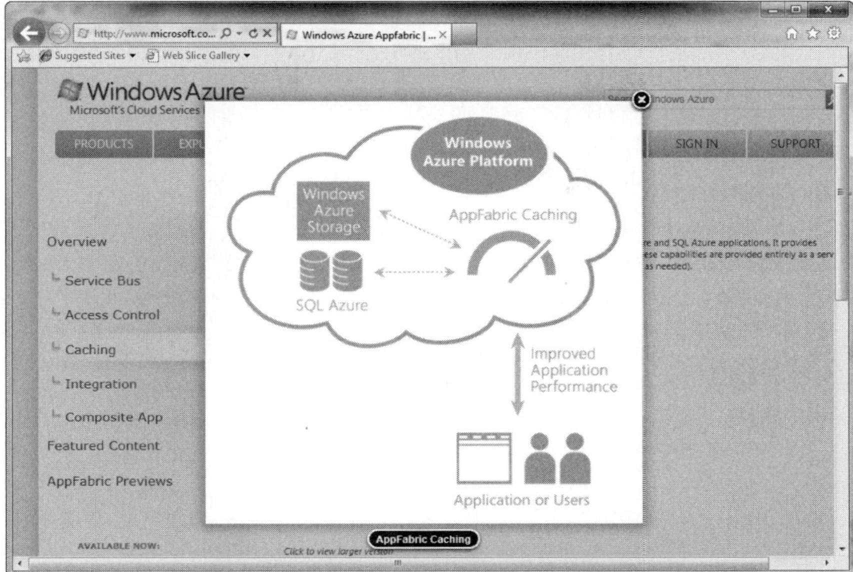

Hosted services code can use the Caching Service to cache remote resources on demand. You need to make only a few minor modifications to standard ASP.NET cache code to integrate with this new caching provider. You can secure the cache using the Access Control Service policy.

The Integration Service

The Integration Service component will be available as a CTP during 2011. At the time of this writing, Microsoft states the following about the Integration Service (Microsoft Corporation, Windows Azure website, 2011, *http://www.microsoft.com/windowsazure/appfabric/overview/default.aspx*):

> *...provides common BizTalk Server integration capabilities (e.g. pipeline, transforms, adapters) on Windows Azure, using out-of-box integration patterns to accelerate and simplify development. It also delivers higher level business user enablement capabilities, such as Business Activity Monitoring and Rules, as well as self-service trading partner community portal and provisioning of business-to-business pipelines.*

The idea is to ease the integration between applications hosted on the Windows Azure platform and third-party Software as a Service (SaaS) solutions. The Integration Service also extends the Service Bus service to ease integration with existing Line Of Business (LOB) applications. The official schema for this component is shown in the following figure.

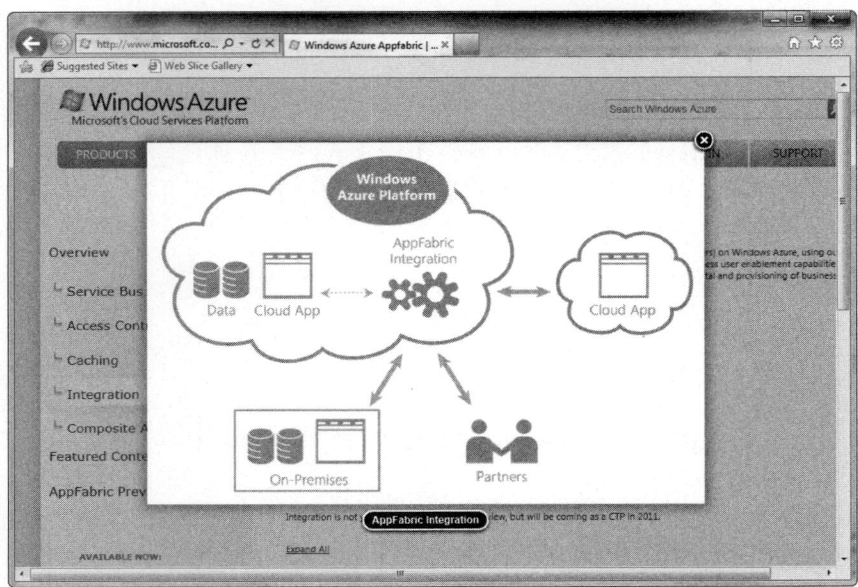

The Composite Application Service

Another new component, the Composite Application Service, is slated to ship as a CTP in 2011. Its goal is to simplify the deployment of a complex application that uses different Windows Azure services. You build Composite Applications by composing prebuilt components and services—both those developed in house and those purchased or licensed from third-party cloud services. These components and services might be distributed on on-premises hardware and/or on cloud machines.

The feature consists of a set of Microsoft .NET Framework extensions for composing applications, a visual designer directly integrated into Visual Studio to manage the creation and deployment of such applications, and a multitenant service that consumes the Composite Model definition and automates the deployment.

At the time of this writing, the Windows Azure website (Microsoft Corporation, 2011, *http://www.microsoft.com/windowsazure/appfabric/overview/default.aspx*) identifies the Composite Application as a Windows Azure platform feature that provides the following:

> *...a multi-tenant, managed service which consumes the .NET based AppFabric Composition Model definition and automates the deployment and management of the end to end application, eliminating manual steps needed by both developers and ITPros today. It directly executes application components to provide a high-performance runtime optimized for cloud-scale services and mid-tier components. It also delivers a complete hosting environment for web services built using Windows Communication Foundation (either natively developed or using WCF Data Services and WCF RIA Services) and workflows built using Windows Workflow Foundation.*

SQL Azure

The last (but not least) piece of the platform is the SQL Server cloud version, called SQL Azure. At the time of this writing, the official documentation presents SQL Azure with this statement (Microsoft Corporation, Windows Azure website, 2011, *http://www.microsoft.com/en-us/sqlazure/database.aspx*):

> *Microsoft® SQL Azure™ is a highly available, and scalable cloud database service built on SQL Server technologies. With SQL Azure, developers do not have to install, setup, patch or manage any software. High availability and fault tolerance is built-in and no physical administration is required. Additionally, developers can get productive on SQL Azure quickly by using the same familiar T-SQL based relational model and the same powerful development and management tools used for on-premises databases.*

The most important information you'll take away from Chapter 9, "Using SQL Azure," which covers SQL Azure in depth, is that the database service is built with the same concepts as the other components of the Windows Azure platform.

You can access a SQL Azure database using Tabular Data Stream (TDS) from the .NET Framework applications based on ADO.NET or any other programming environment in which a SQL Server ODBC driver is available (such as JDBC). The database is exposed through a virtual server name that you receive when you create your server on the portal. You can use the database feature from a cloud-based application or from a traditional on-premises application by adapting the connection string to the cloud format.

Summary

Windows Azure is the operating system for the Microsoft cloud platform. It is currently based on Windows Server 2008 R2 but completely removes the need for configuration and deployment, both for applications and the operating system. You don't need to apply patches or install any Windows components. Developers can deploy and manage an application using a simple-to-use web-based project portal. Windows Azure offers storage services with a storage account that can store blobs, tables, and queues.

In addition to the operating system, the Windows Azure platform offers comprehensive services that range from a cloud-based Service Bus to an Access Control Service.

SQL Azure is a cloud-based version of SQL Server that you use the same way as you would a traditional database application.

Chapter 3

Creating a Web Role Project

After completing this chapter, you will be able to

- Install and use the SDKs appropriate for the Windows Azure platform.
- Use the Web Role Project template.
- Build a Windows Azure Project.
- Deploy a project to Windows Azure.
- Configure and upgrade a deployed project.

The preceding chapters showed how Windows Azure provides a scalable and fault-tolerant environment that lets you create powerful applications without purchasing and configuring hardware and operating systems. Instead, you can rent what you need, following the Platform as a Service (PaaS) model.

This chapter translates PaaS into practice. You start by installing the SDK with Microsoft Visual Studio 2010, review some APIs and local development tools to help you understand the complete flow for building a Windows Azure project, and deploy a simple application in the cloud before moving on to Windows Azure storage in the next chapter.

Note Because URLs, UI names, and procedures may vary over time, some of them may be out of date by the time you read this. In that case, my best advice is to start looking for the information about the Windows Azure product on the Windows Azure home page (*http://www.azure.com*). Information included in this book was accurate at the time of writing.

Software Development Kits

To start developing Windows Azure projects, you need the relative SDKs and tools. Because Windows Azure is a multiplatform environment, you need to install the Windows Azure SDK or the tools for your development platform. Windows Azure also offers appropriate SDKs for other languages as well as tools for other development platforms.

To download the SDKs and tools, go to *http://www.azure.com*, the home page for the Windows Azure platform, and choose the Developers section. This section includes documentation about the components, a link to the Training Kit and to the SDK & Tools, which is what you should look at.

The SDK & Tools page (*http://www.microsoft.com/windowsazure/sdk/*) is divided into several sections: one is dedicated to Visual Studio and the Microsoft .NET Framework, a second to the SDK tools and AppFabric tools, and a third contains the Training Kit. Here is a brief explanation of each package.

- **Windows Azure Tools for Visual Studio** An add-in that extends both Visual Studio 2010 and Visual Studio 2008 to facilitate the creation, configuration, testing, debugging, and deploying of web applications and services on Windows Azure. This component includes the Windows Azure SDK, so this is the only tool you need to run the samples and complete the exercises in this chapter. To install it, follow exactly the steps provided in the installation section of this chapter.
- **Windows Azure SDK** The core component that provides the APIs you need in the sample projects in this book. It includes simulators for Windows Azure Compute and Windows Azure Storage so that you can test and debug applications locally, as well as a set of samples with which you can start testing the various components. This SDK is included in the Windows Azure Tools for Visual Studio.
- **Windows Azure AppFabric SDK** Related to both the Service Bus and the Access Control Service, as you will see in Chapter 7, "Building an AppFabric Solution." You don't need to download this component to complete the samples presented in this chapter.
- **Windows Azure Solution Accelerators** Provides a set of complete solutions for jump-starting applications.
- **Windows Azure Platform Training Kit** A comprehensive set of documentation, slides, and numerous hands-on labs and demonstration scripts.
- **Windows Azure Management Tools** Facilitates management operations, providing a remote, easy-to-use console.

A section of the Windows Azure home page is dedicated to the Interoperability SDKs and tools. In particular, the Windows Azure SDKs for Java and the Windows Azure SDK for PHP (Hypertext Preprocessor) are the equivalents of the Windows Azure SDK for the .NET Framework. Finally, the Windows Azure Tools for Eclipse is the counterpart of the Windows Azure Tools for Visual Studio.

Windows Azure Tools for Visual Studio

Before starting the installation, be sure to check the system requirements, especially verify that you have Internet Information Services (IIS) 7.*x* and the relevant components installed. To do that on computers running Windows Vista, Windows 7, and Windows Server 2008, open Control Panel, select Programs And Features, and then click the Turn Windows Features On Or Off link. Expand the Internet Information Services section and make sure that the following items are selected (if they aren't selected, select them): ASP.NET, CGI, WCF HTTP Activation, and Static Content. Selected items are shown in the next figure.

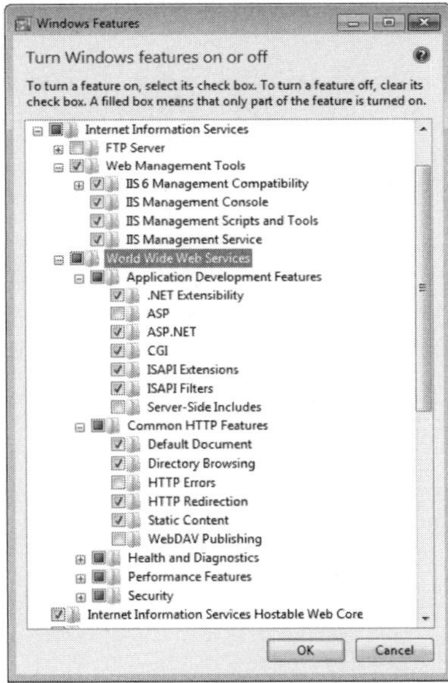

Note To install Windows Azure Tools for Visual Studio, you don't need the full Visual Studio 2010 version; you can download and install Microsoft Visual Web Developer 2010 Express Edition. Visit the page *http://msdn.microsoft.com/en-us/library/gg465715.aspx* to check the installation steps for your particular operating system.

Tip You'll find WCF Activation in the section named Microsoft .NET Framework 3.*x*, where *x* can be .0 or .5 based on which .NET Framework version you have installed.

Important Even though Microsoft SQL Server 2005 is not required for the examples used in this chapter because you don't use the Windows Azure storage account, the installation tool needs it. Therefore, if you don't have an instance of Microsoft SQL Server Express Edition on your machine, install it before continuing.

Note I strongly recommend that you double-check the system requirements as well as the instructions on the download page before downloading and installing any component. There are some differences between the requirements for 32-bit and 64-bit systems as well as some hotfixes that you might need to install before installing the SDK.

After completing the SDK installation, you are ready to begin your first project. Follow the step-by-step procedure in the next section to choose the right template and create the project.

Web Role Project Template

To debug and test your applications in the compute emulator (the local fabric that simulates the behavior of the real Windows Azure fabric), you need to run Visual Studio with administrative privileges.

Tip If you do not want to elevate your user account to an administrative level, you can just right-click Visual Studio from the Start menu or on the Taskbar, and select the Run As Administrator option.

Note It is beyond the scope of this book to introduce or discuss administrative accounts and their development ramifications.

Create the Project

The SDK and Tools setup process installed some new templates and wizards to facilitate the creation of a Windows Azure project. In Figure 3-2, under the Visual C# or Visual Basic project types, you can see a new section named Cloud that represents the entry point for a Windows Azure project. This new section exposes a single template named Windows Azure Cloud Service and this short description: A Project For Creating A Scalable Application Or Service That Runs On Windows Azure. Remember that "Windows Azure Service" just refers to an application; an application can consist of dynamic pages, static content, and/or services.

1. Create a new Windows Azure Project. To do that, open Visual Studio 2010, and from the File menu, select New Project. Choose Cloud from the list of installed templates, and then choose Windows Azure Project from the list of available projects.
2. Select version 4 as the .NET Framework version for your new project.
3. Name the new project **DevLeapCloudService**, and then choose a location on your file system and a solution name. You can assign any name you like, because there is no relationship between the cloud service name and the project name. When you're finished, click the OK button.

   If you use a source control system, you can select the Add To Source Control check box.

   The following figure shows the first step of the New Project wizard: I assigned the name DevLeapCloudService to both the project and solution.

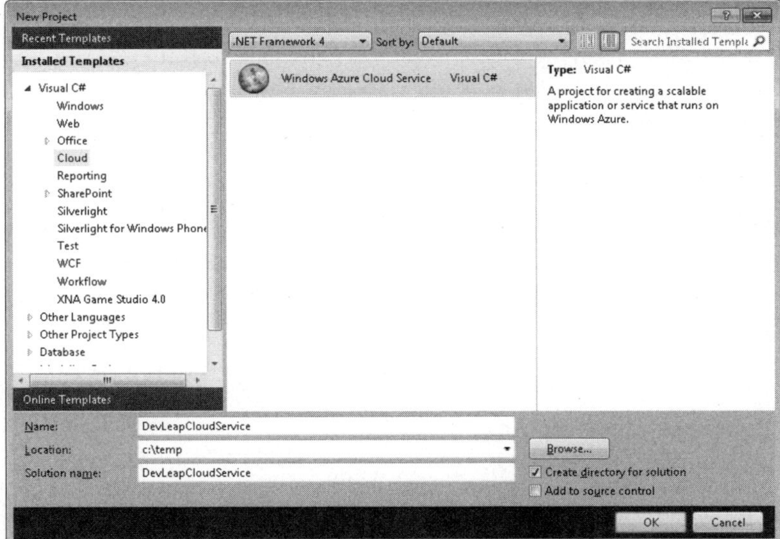

   At this stage, Visual Studio 2010 normally creates the solution folder, the project folder, and a project related to the chosen template. Because Windows Azure supports several different project types, the Cloud template starts the New Project wizard and asks what project type you want to create (as shown in the next figure). You can see that the wizard knows that this project uses Visual C#, and proposes various kinds of projects called roles.

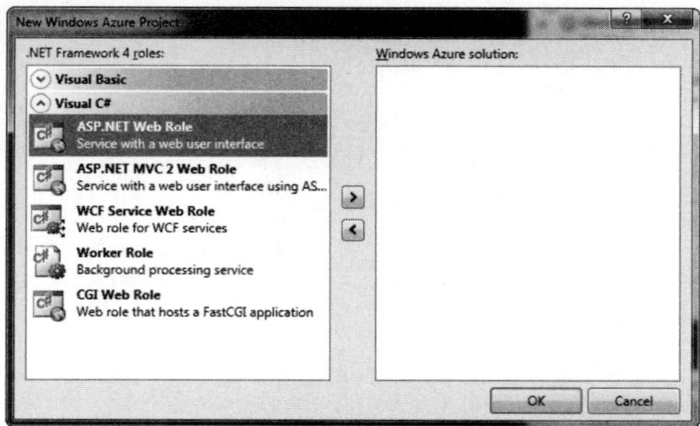

Note A role, as you learned in Chapter 2, "Introduction to the Windows Azure Platform," is not the correct term for the project type. The ASP.NET Web Role and CGI Web Role are both Web Roles, and the only different role type is the Worker Role.

Table 3-1 explains all the different project types.

TABLE 3-1 Cloud Service Project

Project Type	Description
ASP.NET Web Role	Classic ASP.NET project with a Default.aspx page that can be deployed on Windows Azure. This is the most common project template used for samples and classic Web Form application.
ASP.NET MVC 2 Web Role	ASP.NET project based on MVC 2 patterns introduced in .NET Framework 4.
WCF Service Web Role	ASP.NET project based on a WCF Service Project template.
CGI Web Role	FastCGI application hosted in a Web Role.
Worker Role	Template that creates a C# worker role project. (The Worker role is covered in Chapter 5, "Tables, Queues, and Work Roles."

Each project template is a starting point for building a project, which you can configure at a later time. For example, you could choose an ASP.NET MVC 2 Web Role and create a plain ASP.NET Web Forms Project instead, or vice versa.

Because this is your first example, and because it is beyond the scope of this book to examine the pros and cons of Web Forms vs. Model-View-Controller (MVC), you create a normal ASP.NET web application.

4. Choose the ASP.NET Web Role by clicking the Right Arrow button. An ASP.NET Web Role appears on the right in the Windows Azure Solution panel, meaning that your solution will contain one Web Role built with ASP.NET. You can also double-click an item in the left panel to add that item to the right panel.

Note You can add multiple Windows Azure projects to your solution.

You can rename your ASP.NET Web Role Project by selecting it in the right panel and clicking the pencil icon. The name automatically assigned by the system is used as the project name for the ASP.NET Web Role in this procedure (see the next figure). Do not change the name of your ASP.NET Web Role to follow this procedure.

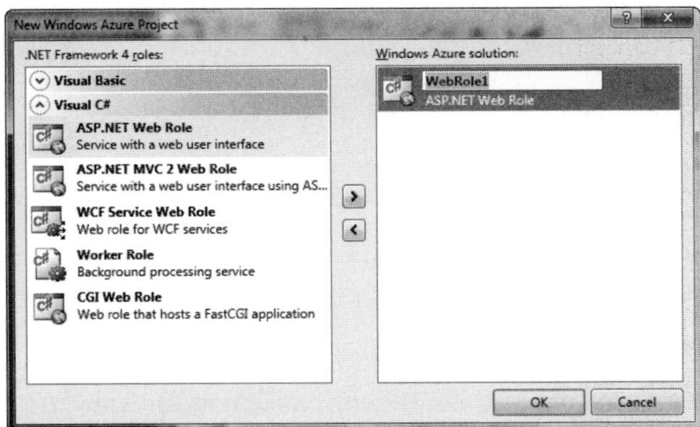

Visual Studio creates the solution folder and the classic solution file during the first phase of creating the project, using the name that you provided earlier. It then creates the ASP.NET project (or whatever project you chose in the wizard) and binds it to a Web Role in this second phase.

Because you selected the ASP.NET Web Role, Visual Studio uses a partially modified version of the classic ASP.NET template, which has added references to the Windows Azure APIs and a pre-created class named *WebRole.cs*. The rest of the project is identical to a standard ASP.NET web application. The project is hosted inside a normal Visual Studio solution that also contains a cloud project. Figure 3-1 shows the complete solution in Solution Explorer.

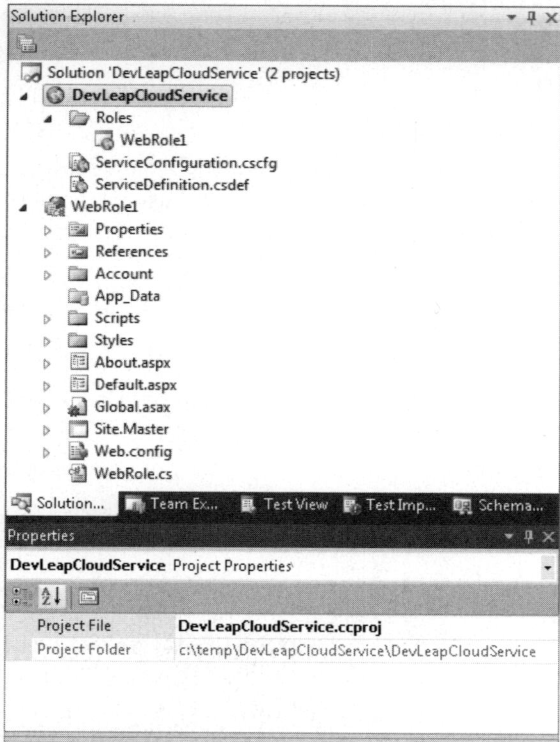

FIGURE 3-1 A complete cloud solution in Solution Explorer.

The lower part of Figure 3-1 shows the ASP.NET project files. Other than the WebRole.cs file, everything is identical to a classic ASP.NET Web Application project, including the ability to view the Default.aspx or About.aspx page in a browser by selecting the View In Browser option from the context menu.

Listing 3-1 shows the modified default page with the sample text removed and an added *Label* named *TimeLabel*.

LISTING 3-1 Modified Default.aspx page.

```
<%@ Page Title="Home Page" Language="C#" MasterPageFile="~/Site.master"
  AutoEventWireup="true" CodeBehind="Default.aspx.cs"
  Inherits="WebRole1._Default" %>

<asp:Content ID="HeaderContent" runat="server"
  ContentPlaceHolderID="HeadContent">
</asp:Content>
<asp:Content ID="BodyContent" runat="server" ContentPlaceHolderID="MainContent">
    <asp:Label ID="TimeLabel" runat="server" />
</asp:Content>
```

Listing 3-1 contains nothing special. It uses the master page feature as suggested by the template and contains a normal ASP.NET web control to render the content. There is nothing special in the code-behind file for this page either, because it doesn't use any features related to Windows Azure.

In the code-behind file, assign the current time to the *Label* (*TimeLabel*) within the *Page_Load* event, as shown in Listing 3-2.

LISTING 3-2 Code-behind file for Default page: Default.aspx.cs.

```
using System;
using System.Collections.Generic;
using System.Linq;
using System.Web;
using System.Web.UI;
using System.Web.UI.WebControls;
namespace WebRole1
{
    public partial class _Default : System.Web.UI.Page
    {
        protected void Page_Load(object sender, EventArgs e)
        {
            TimeLabel.Text = DateTime.Now.ToString();
        }
    }
}
```

Test the Solution

Follow these steps to modify and test the Default.aspx page in your new project.

1. Modify the Default.aspx file so that its contents are identical to Listing 3-1.
2. Open the code-behind file (Default.aspx.cs) and insert in the *Page_Load* method the boldface line in Listing 3-2.
3. To run the project, right-click the Default.aspx page and select View In Browser. Don't run the project by pressing F5 or Ctrl+F5.

Note Most ASP.NET developers test their applications in the local environment (ASP.NET Development Server) by using the debugger, and they ignore the View In Browser functionality. This shortcut menu compiles the web project, launches the ASP.NET Development Server if it is not running, and launches an instance of Windows Internet Explorer that navigates to the URL of the requested resource.

The following figure shows the results.

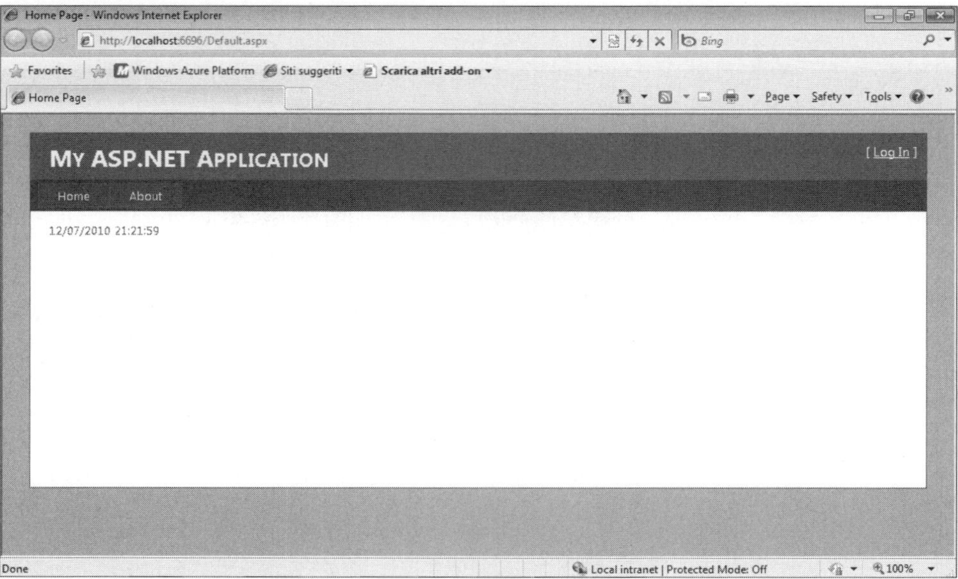

Now you have an ASP.NET application that runs on the ASP.NET Development Server, a classic Default.aspx page, a classic Web.config file, and a typical Global.asax file. To repeat, you don't need to do anything special to create a Windows Azure project in ASP.NET. You can use any web, HTML, or mobile control; bind the control to data sources as you normally do in ASP.NET; and use the Web.config file to configure authentication, authorization, tracing, caching, *HttpHandler*, modules, and so on.

The magic of Windows Azure lies not in what you can or can't do inside a project but in how you can leverage the deployment and scalability feature of the platform for the project.

The Cloud Project

So far, you created a cloud project as an ASP.NET web application, but you haven't used any cloud-specific APIs yet. In this section, you examine the cloud project inside the solution and explore some cloud APIs that you can use for your pages.

Notice the presence of a cloud project in your solution, shown earlier in Figure 3-1. Thanks to the property window, you can verify that the project has a .ccproj extension and that it is placed in a separate directory inside the solution like any Visual Studio project. Visual Studio represents the content of the .ccproj project as a root element with the same name as the project, a Roles folder, and two elements named ServiceConfiguration.cscfg and ServiceDefinition.csdef inside your WebRole1 project. Notice also that the cloud project is set as the startup project. You can test the project in a cloud-simulated environment by pressing F5.

When you run the project (unless you're running Visual Studio as an administrator), you will see a dialog box stating this error: The Compute Emulator Must Be Run Elevated. Please Restart Visual Studio In Elevated Administrator Mode In Order To Run The Project. This error contains an important message: Visual Studio is trying to communicate with the compute emulator (the local Windows Azure fabric simulator) to start the project. You've learned that you can start the project as an ASP.NET web application—even though it's contained in a cloud solution—by selecting View In Browser, but if you want to test the Windows Azure APIs or the application's real behavior in the cloud, you need to run the application in the compute emulator, and to do that, you need administrative privileges.

If you use an administrative account, you won't see the error dialog box, and both the result of the compilation and the execution will be exactly the same as in the previous example, which the next figure shows. However, this time, the application is running in a simulated cloud infrastructure in which Visual Studio deployed the solution that processes the URL request. If you look carefully at the address bar, you notice that this second example isn't using port 6696 as in the previous run. (This is the ASP.NET Development Server port on my development machine, but yours may differ.) Instead, it's using port 81.

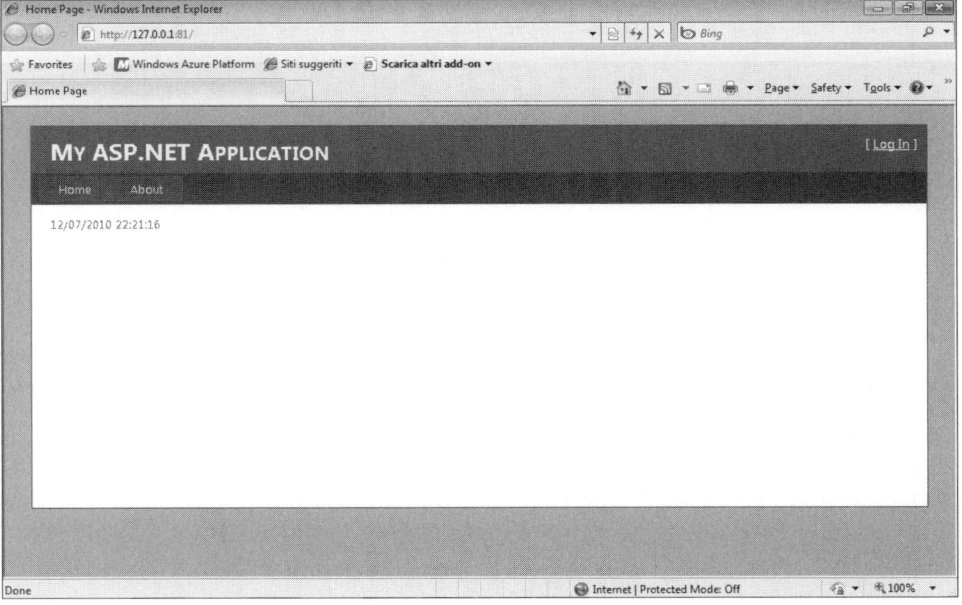

The difference isn't just the port number, but rather the entire environment in which the application is running. Go to the Notification Area of the Windows Taskbar and click the Windows Azure icon. When you click the icon, you receive a comforting message saying that everything is fine with the compute emulator and storage emulator.

If you right-click the icon and choose Show Compute Emulator UI, you end up with something similar to the following figure.

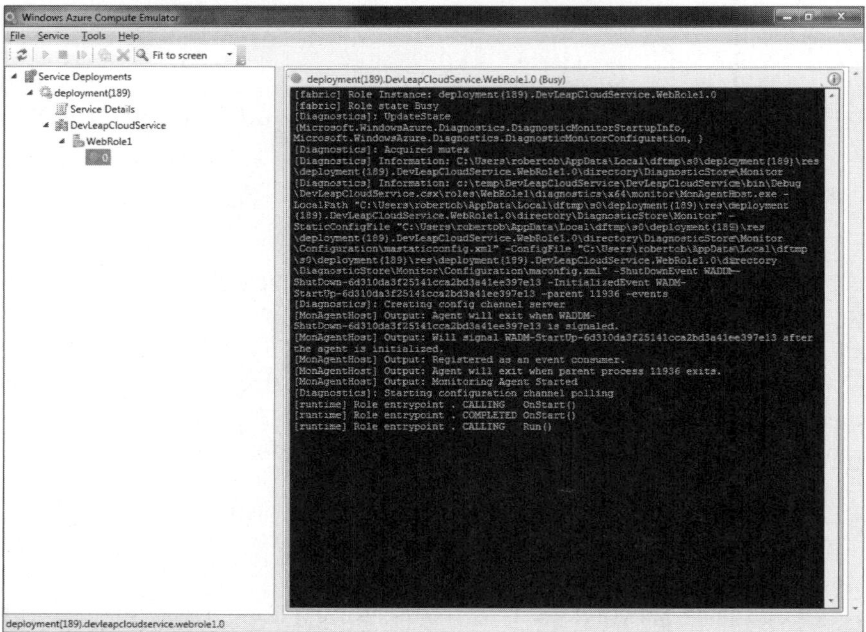

The tree in the left pane of the compute emulator window provides information about the local deployment of the sample project. The number adjacent to Deployment is an identity assigned to this deployment. (This is my 189th deployment on this machine since installing the Windows Azure SDK.) Every time you test an application by pressing F5 (or Ctrl+F5), Visual Studio asks the compute emulator to deploy the cloud solution, so it is pretty easy to reach high numbers.

In the user interface, you can see that the project named DevLeapCloudService contains a role named Web Role1 that has just one instance named 0. If you select this instance, the right pane of the window shows numerous trace messages. This pane reports all the events that the fabric has raised, together with some useful diagnostic information. I discuss these aspects in Chapter 6, "Windows Azure Operating System Details."

Service Details is useful for discovering how the fabric configured the service at run time, the port used by Web Roles, and other information about the service. Figure 3-2 shows the service detail for the sample project. On my machine, it uses port 81 on *localhost* (127.0.0.1), and there is an interface on *HttpIn* for *WebRole1* defined in the contract of the service, as well as the cloud-based infrastructure.

Now that you know the difference between running within an ASP.NET Development Server and running in the compute emulator simulator, let the beautiful part of this process begin.

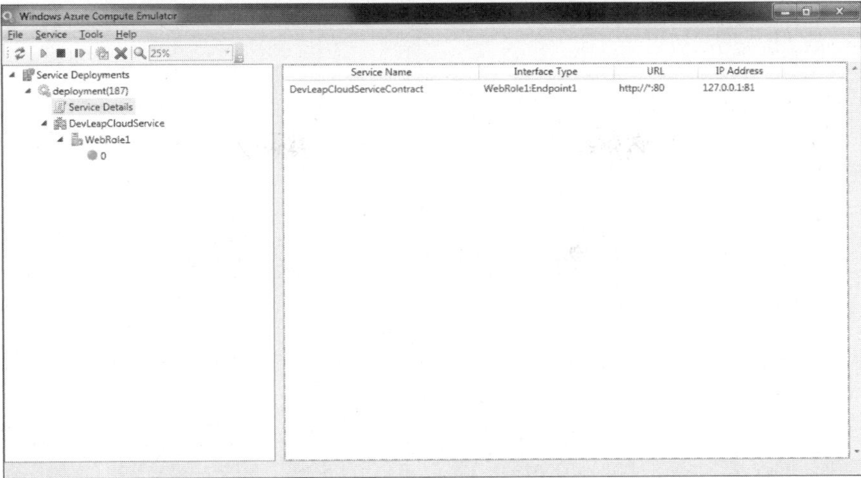

FIGURE 3-2 Compute emulator service detail.

Conduct a Multiple-Instance Test

1. Close the browser and return to the DevLeapCloudService project in your solution.
2. Double-click WebRole1 in the Roles folder of the cloud project. The result is shown in the following figure.

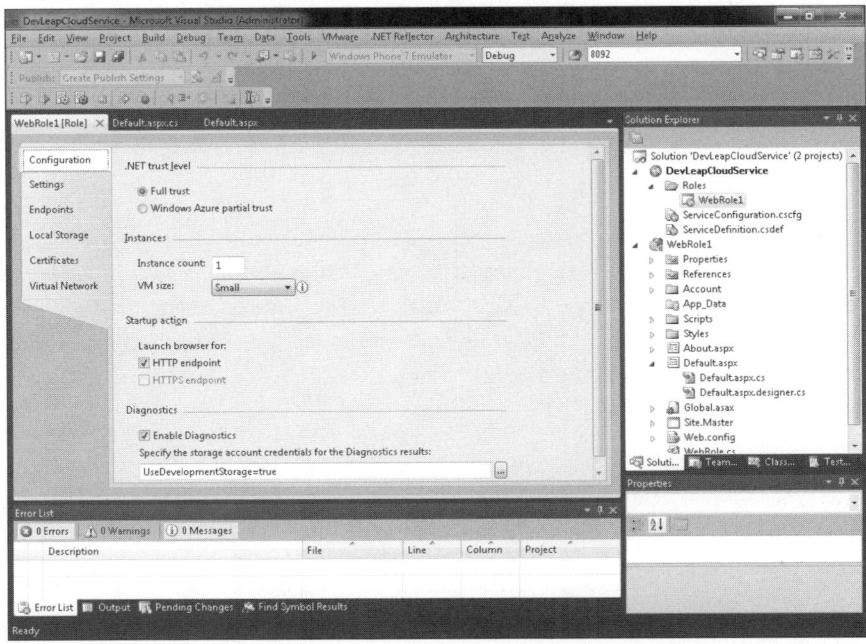

3. On the Configuration tab, in the Instances section, type the value 5 in the Instance Count text box.

4. Press F5 to run the project again.

   The response in the browser still looks the same, but if you now open the compute emulator UI, you notice a significant (and delightful!) difference, shown in the following figure.

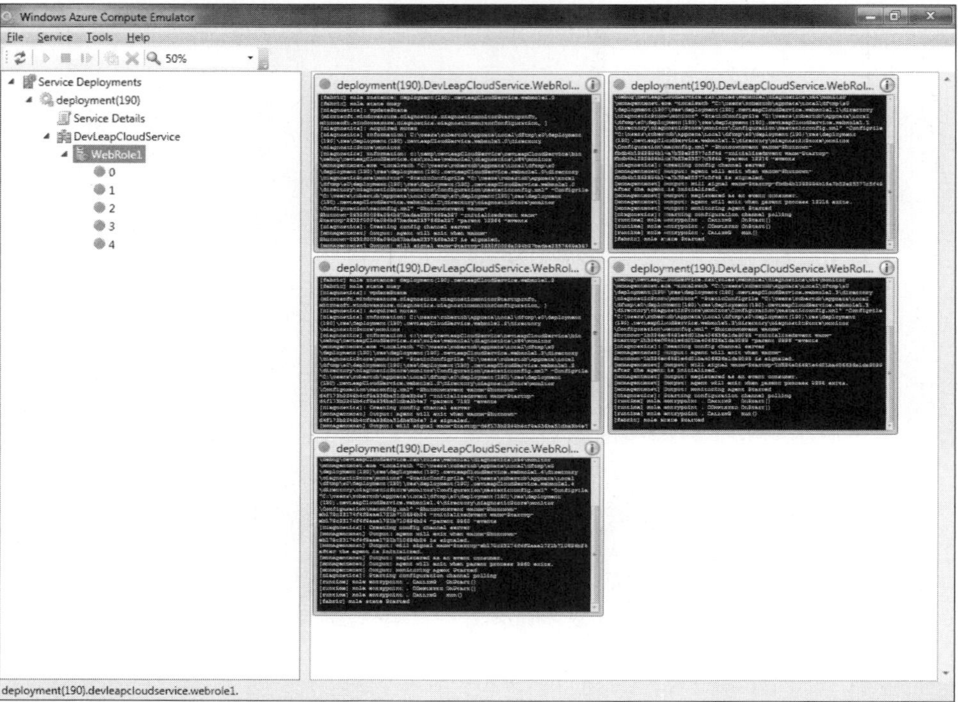

I hope this demo has proved the theory covered in Chapter 2—that with Windows Azure, you can forget installation steps, physical paths, all the aspects of transferring a configuration from machine to machine, and load-balancer configuration. Instead, you can just modify the instance count parameter, and Windows Azure takes care of upgrading or redeploying your application to the correct instances.

Locally, the compute emulator simulates instances using processes. In fact, if you open Task Manager, you see 10 processes named WaIISHost.exe, where *Wa* stands for Windows Azure, and *IISHost* means that the process is running inside IIS. The result in Task Manager looks similar to the following figure.

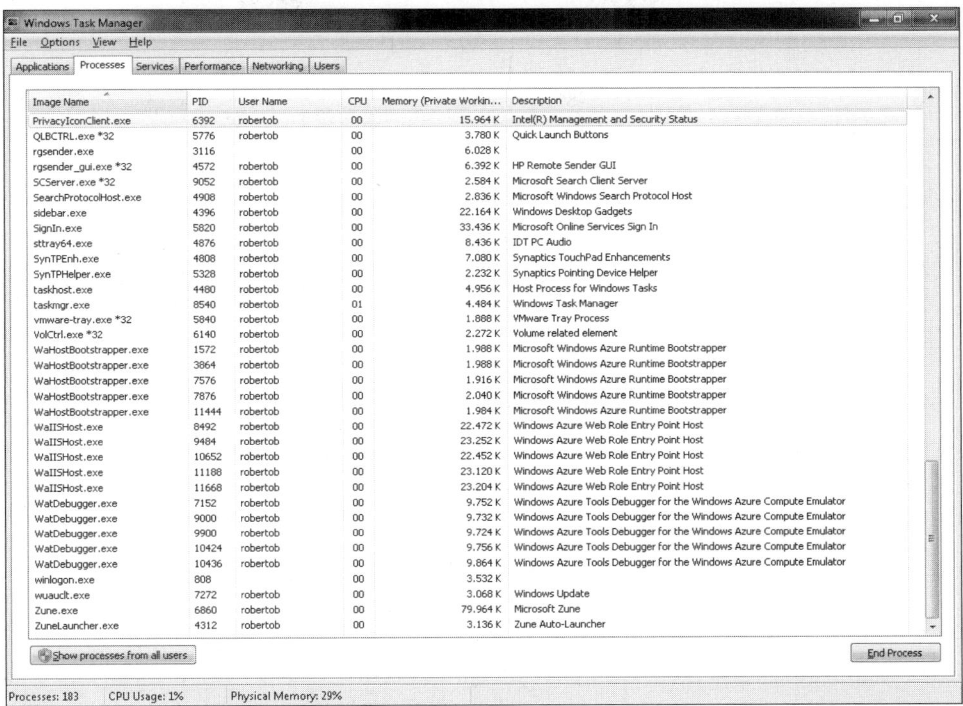

Every developer who sees Task Manager has the same thought: kill some processes! Go ahead! Kill whatever WaIISHost.exe you want. It doesn't matter, because the compute emulator restarts those processes when needed, just as Windows Azure would do with your Web Roles running in the actual cloud if something were to happen to them (such as a hardware failure or an application fault). Try adding the PID (process ID) column to the task manager to verify this behavior: as soon as you kill an Azure process, the same host returns under a different process ID.

Deployment to Windows Azure

As you saw in Chapter 2, managing projects and solutions in the cloud through the Windows Azure Portal is simple and straightforward. In this section, you deploy your sample to the cloud using Azure Services as a host. You follow the manual deployment process so that you can familiarize yourself with all the steps involved in the process.

> **Note** Since the June 2010 version of the Windows Azure SDK was released, Visual Studio 2010 can automate Azure Service deployment. Chapter 6 returns to this topic and delves into the details.

> **Note** Before trying to perform any operation on systems running Visual Studio or Windows Azure, verify that the project has just one instance in the configuration. Go back to the configuration tab and change the 5 to a 1.

Deploy Your Project Manually

To deploy a service, you need a package, a configuration file, and Windows Azure service.

1. Right-click the cloud project in your solution and select the Publish menu to activate the publication process.

   Because you're following a manual deployment procedure, choose the first option, Create Service Package Only. Windows Explorer opens the Publish subdirectory in the bin\Debug directory of the cloud project. If you are following the examples in this book, your path should be something like this:

   C:\temp\DevLeapCloudService\DevLeapCloudService\bin\Debug\Publish

   In the preceding path, the first DevLeapCloudService is the solution folder, and the second is the cloud project.

   Visual Studio creates two files in that folder. The file with the .cspkg extension is the cloud service package and contains every role in the solution. The file with the .cscfg extension is the configuration file.

2. You now have everything you need to deploy your solution. Open the portal using your Windows Live account, select your subscription, and create a new hosted service if you haven't already done so. (See Chapter 2 for information about creating a hosted service.)

For this simple demo, you are going to deploy the package to the production environment of your hosted service. Click New Production Deployment to access the upload form (called Create A New Deployment), which is shown in the next figure.

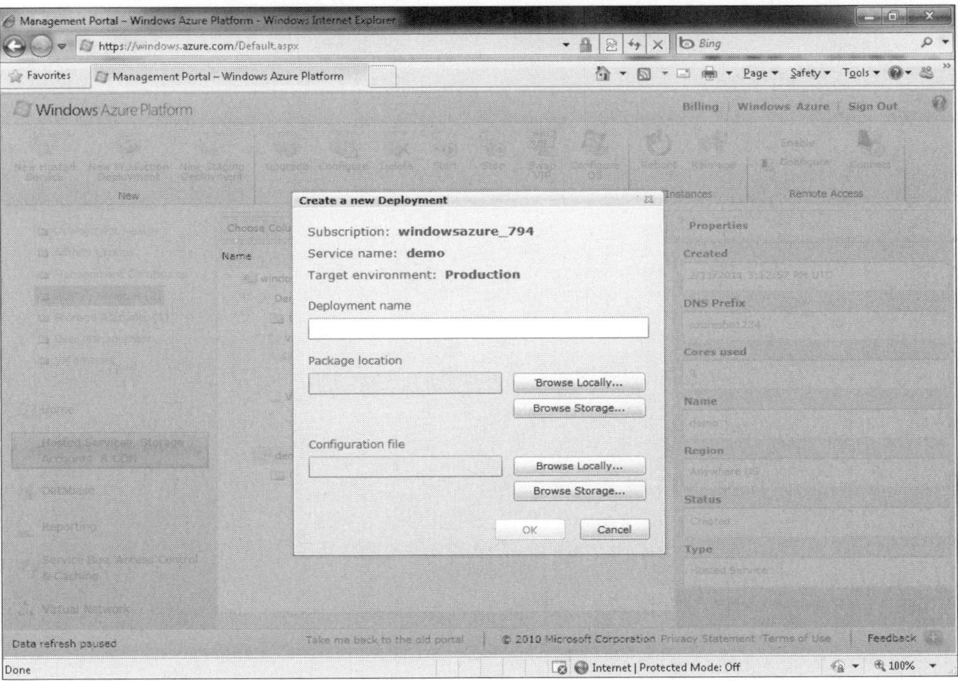

3. In the Package Location section of the user interface, click the Browse Locally button and select the application package created by Visual Studio that has the .cspkg extension. In the Configuration File section, click the Browse Locally button and select the file with the .cscfg extension.

4. In the Deployment Name text box, type a name for your deployment. The name you provide is completely useless to Windows Azure, but it will be crucial to you when identifying your deployment later. For example, the label you choose might indicate the iteration number of an Agile project, or it might include just a version number that allows you to quickly differentiate one deployment from another. The name you choose also has no direct connection with the software version or the .NET Framework assembly version.

5. Verify that you are using the correct Subscription and Service Name, because when you click the OK button, the application is deployed in the production environment and you are charged accordingly.

6. Click the OK button. At this point, you should see a warning message informing you that Windows Azure cannot guarantee the 99.95 percent uptime because you are deploying to just one instance, as shown in the following figure.

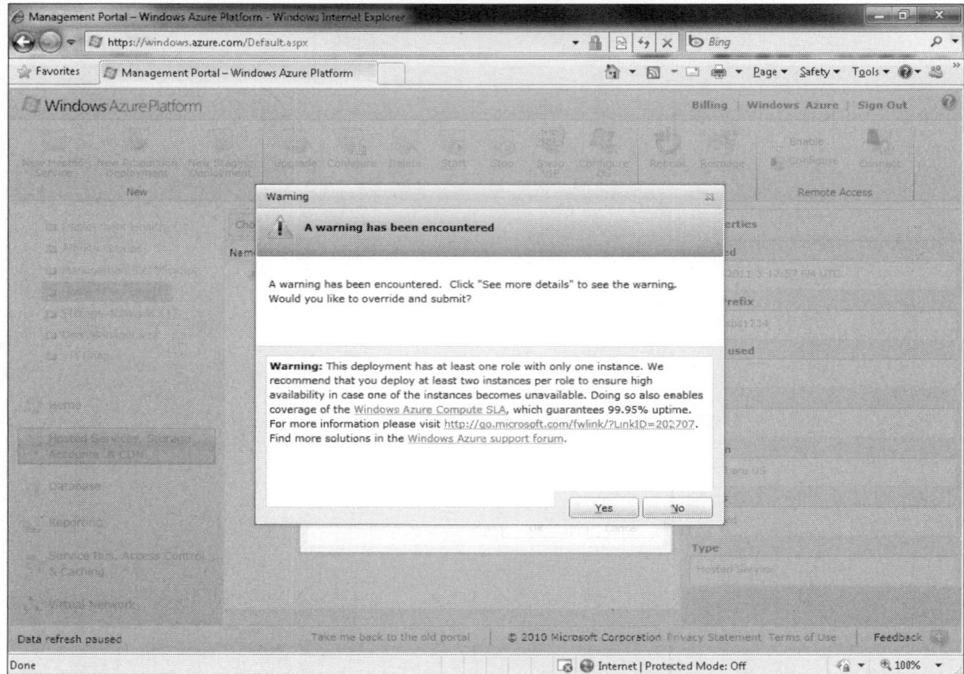

As soon as you return to the main screen, you can see the status of the deployment. Remember that you have started paying—every deployed hosted service begins accruing charges. Production and staging environments are identical from this point of view. The next figure shows the main screen. You can delete the deployment at any time to stop the payment system.

Note Your subscription can include some deployed time for free or at a discounted rate. If you don't exceed the included time, you won't pay anything.

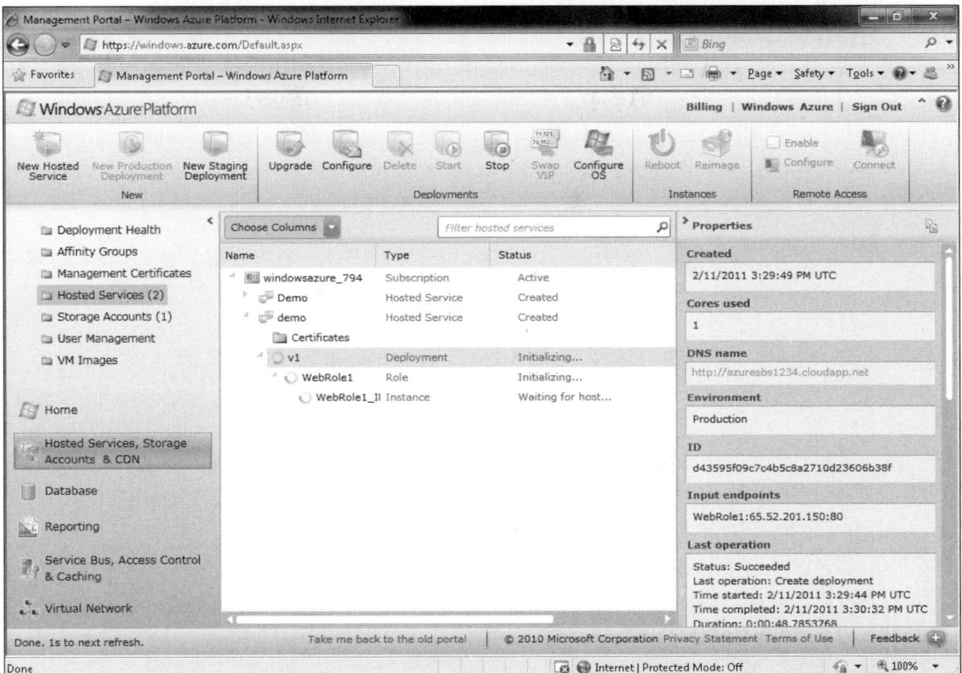

From this main screen, you can perform various operations on the deployed service. First, you should test the URL you chose in the Create A New Service wizard. The wizard responds with the message Internet Explorer Cannot Display The Webpage, because the service has not been deployed yet. Second, configure the application, which means modifying the configuration file you uploaded together with the application package, or just modifying the operating system version and upgrade policy. Third, configure the operating system, choosing which version of Windows Azure you want to use.

During the deployment, the status of the hosted service changes to reflect the internal operations. The underlying process involves three phases:

1. **Initializing** The virtual machine is created and the package is deployed.
2. **Busy** Windows Azure Fabric starts the roles involved.
3. **Ready** All roles in all instances are started, as shown in the next figure.

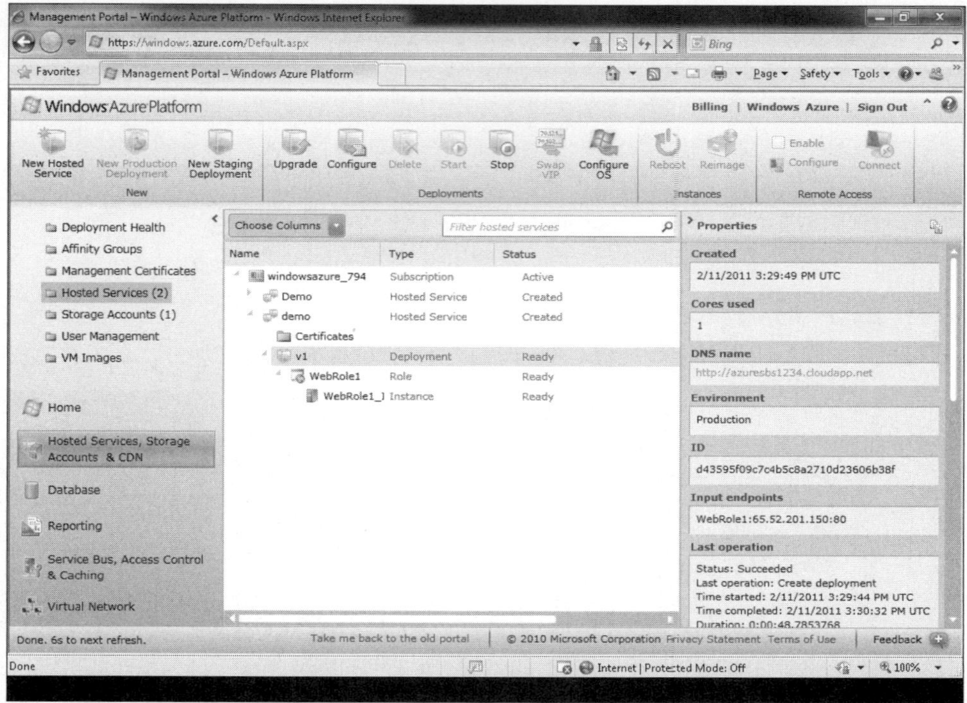

Do you want to know what time it is—in the cloud? Just click the link you chose for your service. The result is similar to the date and time stamp generated when running the program earlier in this chapter, but now the information is coming from the cloud. The time is based on UTC time; it does not reflect the time zone of the data center you choose. The following figure shows the URL and the page in Internet Explorer.

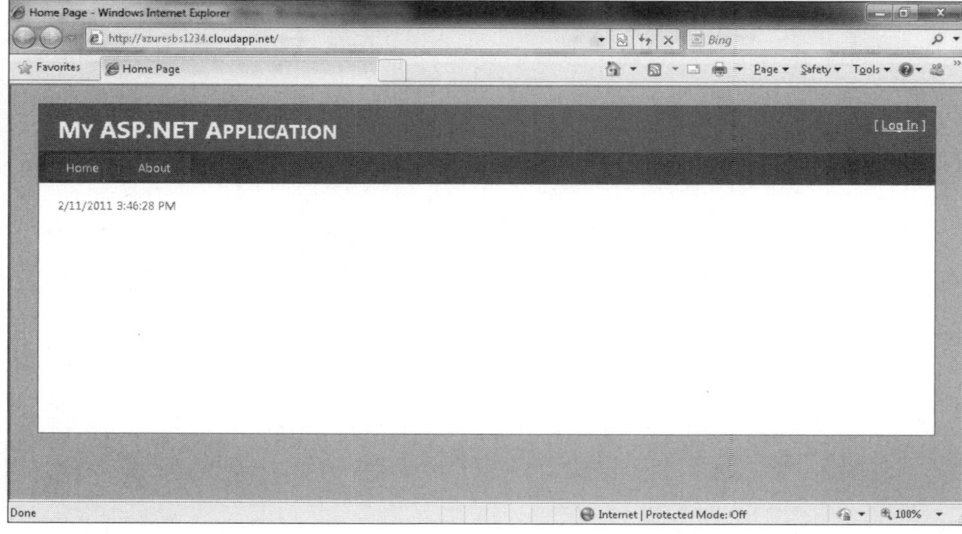

At any time, you can return to the configuration window to modify the number of instances, letting Windows Azure reconfigure the fabric to allocate more virtual machines and adjust the load-balancing policy.

You can also upgrade the production (or staging) environment at any time simply by uploading a newer version of the package. Now that you've learned the manual method, you can learn about a more efficient technique in the next section.

Configuration and Upgrading

The beauty of a PaaS environment and, in particular, of Windows Azure, is the complete isolation from the physical aspect of the file system as well as from the virtual directories and the load balancer. As you learned earlier, you can upload a package created by Visual Studio (or Eclipse) and then substitute a newer version of the running package in the cloud at any time, just by clicking the Upgrade button. However, this easy operation leads to a problem: what happens if the newer version of the package doesn't work in the cloud? What happens when you misspell a pathname or URL?

Ideally, you upload and test your solution in a separate environment and then move the solution to the real endpoint. In Windows Azure, there's no operation simpler than that—you deploy new applications or versions to the staging environment, use the given temporary URL to test the application, and then switch from the staging to the production environment. The switching operation is practically immediate, because Windows Azure Fabric doesn't move any physical components; it just switches DNS entries. At the time of the switch, the internal GUID-based URL gets switched to the real URL. You can package any update—pages, services, Global.asax, or Web.config created in Visual Studio—as a new version, upload it to staging, test it, and then move the application to production using this foolproof operation.

In on-premises, load-balanced solutions, even small configuration changes imply that you have to synchronize the Web.config file on each web server. In the cloud, this problem doesn't exist because Windows Azure manages the sync operations for you during the deployment. Nevertheless, a complete redeployment to staging or production in the cloud can be quite time consuming. The Web.config file is included in the application package, so any modification to application settings or connection strings would typically lead to a complete redeployment of the entire package.

Fortunately, Windows Azure proposes a new configuration file for these kinds of settings: the .cscfg file discussed earlier in this chapter. This file contains a special section for your configuration as well as important configuration information for Windows Azure fabric.

Configure a Cloud Service

Returning to the Visual Studio project, you can use the project properties dialog box to configure the application settings. This dialog box reads and writes values from the ServiceConfiguration.cscfg file.

1. Double click the Web Role Project named WebRole1 under the Roles section of the cloud project. The Settings tab contains a unique item named *Microsoft.WindowsAzure.Plugins.Diagnostics.ConnectionString.*

2. Add a new setting by clicking the Add Setting button in the Mini Toolbar. Type **EmailAdmin** as the new setting's name and type the value **roberto@devleap.com**. The following figure shows a setting named EmailAdmin with my email address as a value.

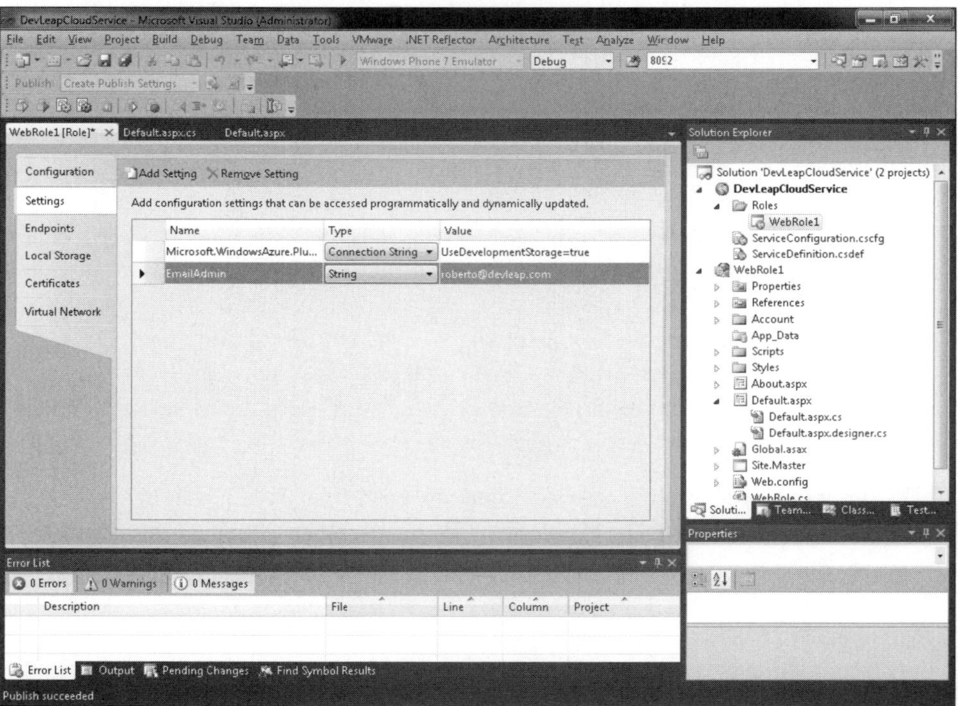

The Windows Azure SDK provides a new API called *RoleEnvironment* that exposes a simple method to read this value from the new configuration file. You don't need a reference because the modified ASP.NET project template used to create your project already contains it.

3. Test your configuration settings by adding a new *Label* to your default page. In the following code, the new *Label* is presented in boldface:

```
<%@ Page Title="Home Page" Language="C#" MasterPageFile="~/Site.master"
AutoEventWireup="true" CodeBehind="Default.aspx.cs" Inherits="WebRole1._Default" %>
<asp:Content ID="HeaderContent" runat="server" ContentPlaceHolderID="HeadContent">
</asp:Content>
<asp:Content ID="BodyContent" runat="server" ContentPlaceHolderID="MainContent">
    <p><asp:Label ID="TimeLabel" runat="server" /></p>
    <p><asp:Label ID="EmailAdminLabel" runat="server" /></p>
</asp:Content>
```

The code to read the configuration value uses the *GetConfigurationSettingValue(string)* static method exposed by the *RoleEnvironment* class, shown in boldface in the following code:

```
using System;
using System.Collections.Generic;
using System.Linq;
using System.Web;
using System.Web.UI;
using System.Web.UI.WebControls;
using Microsoft.WindowsAzure.ServiceRuntime;

namespace WebRole1
{
    public partial class _Default : System.Web.UI.Page
    {
        protected void Page_Load(object sender, EventArgs e)
        {
            TimeLabel.Text = DateTime.Now.ToString();
            EmailAdminLabel.Text =
                 RoleEnvironment.GetConfigurationSettingValue("EmailAdmin");
        }
    }
}
```

4. Add the code to your code-behind file, compile, and run the project.

RoleEnvironment is one of the APIs exposed by the *Microsoft.WindowsAzure.ServiceRuntime*, as you can see from the *using* statement in the preceding code. You do not need a reference to the assembly, because Visual Studio adds it automatically, together with *Microsoft.WindowsAzure.Diagnostics* (discussed in more detail in Chapter 6), and *Microsoft.WindowsAzure.StorageClient*, a helper class to manage the Azure Storage Account (discussed in Chapter 7).

Running your new service implementation locally sends a new package to the compute emulator, creates a new deployment directory on disk, and spins up a new process. The result is shown in the following figure.

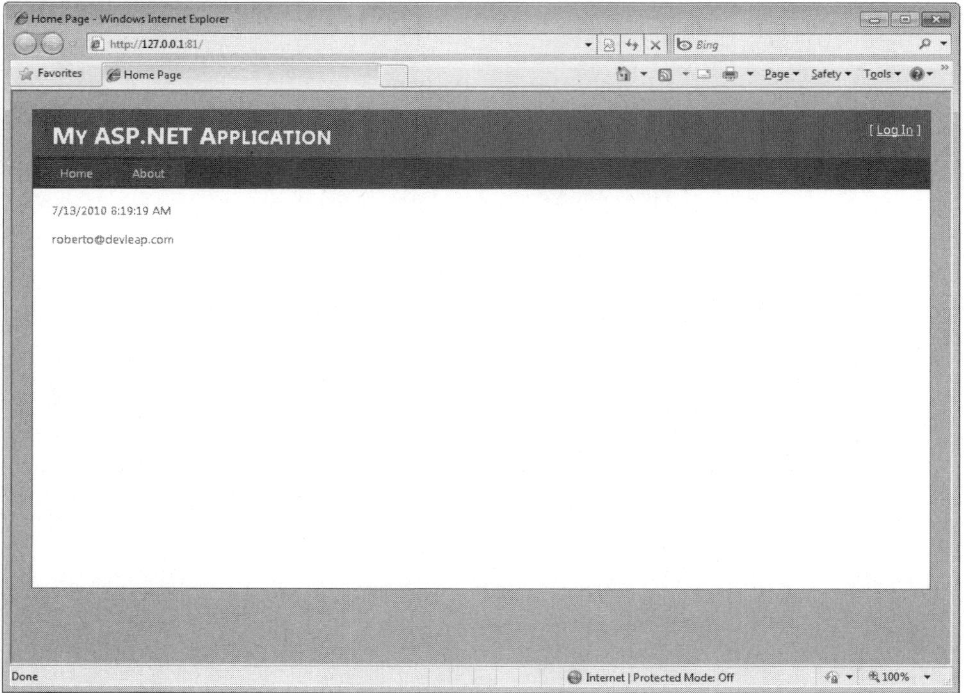

Before upgrading your live service with these new lines of code so that you can learn how to modify live settings, it is important to understand that the *GetConfigurationSettings Value* static method searches for configuration values both in Web.config and in ServiceConfiguration.cscfg—and in that sequence. This means that when your solution has a configuration value in Web.config, you can read it with the new API as well.

To test whether your service is running in the compute emulator or in a classic web server environment, you can check the value of the *IsAvailable* property. The value *true* means that the infrastructure provided a *RoleEnviroment*, so you know that the service is running in a Windows Azure fabric, either local or live. A value of *false* means that your service is running in a traditional web server environment.

The complete code for a solution that can be hosted on-premises or in the cloud looks something like Listing 3-5.

LISTING 3-5 Code-behind file for Default.aspx.

```
using System;
using System.Collections.Generic;
using System.Linq;
using System.Web;
using System.Web.UI;
using System.Web.UI.WebControls;
using Microsoft.WindowsAzure.ServiceRuntime;
using System.Configuration;
namespace WebRole1
{
    public partial class _Default : System.Web.UI.Page
    {
        protected void Page_load(object sender, EventArgs e)
        {
            TimeLabel.Text = DateTime.Now.ToString();

            if (RoleEnvironment.IsAvailable)
                EmailAdminLabel.Text =
                   RoleEnvironment.GetConfigurationSettingValue("EmailAdmin");
            else
                EmailAdminLabel.Text =
                   ConfigurationManager.AppSettings["EmailAdmin"];

        }
    }
}
```

To try this new behavior, you can add a configuration setting named *EmailAdmin* in the Web.config file and then choose View In Browser for your default page without launching the compute emulator—just close the browser and launch the application in the compute emulator using F5. As you learned in the previous chapter, you can deploy your solution to the staging environment to test it, and then easily move it to production. You can also upgrade your solution in place, where it was originally deployed. (You examine the various upgrade options in more detail in Chapter 6.) For now, publish manually by following the procedure described in this chapter, in the section "Deploy Your Project Manually," and upgrade the production environment by clicking the Upgrade button. The Upgrade Deployment form looks like the following figure.

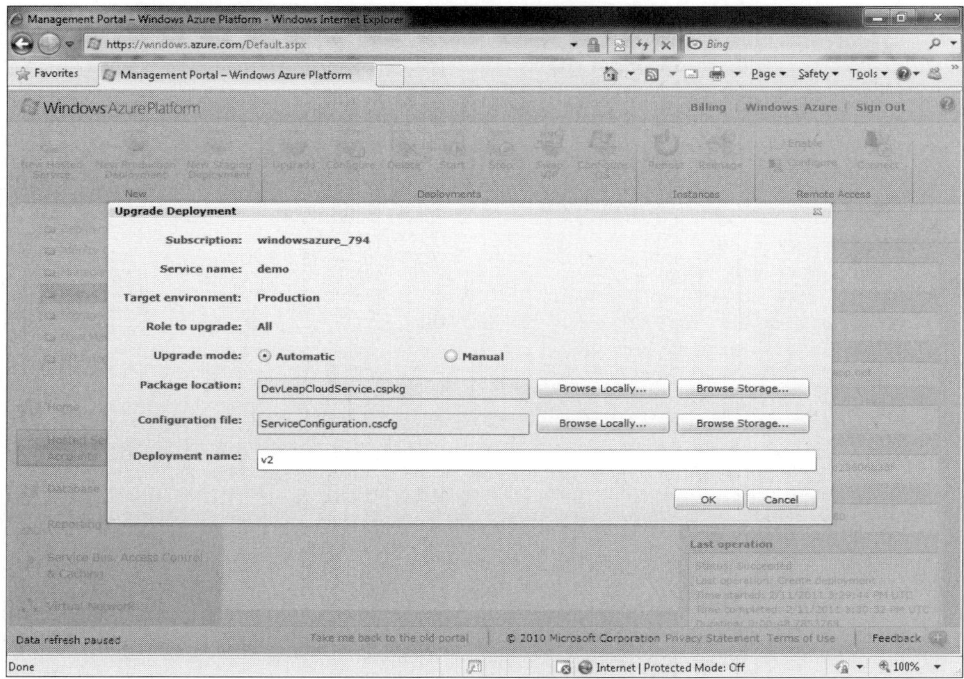

Select the application package and the new ServiceConfiguration.cscfg file, name the deployment **v2**, and click the OK button.

When the service instances are shown as Ready, you receive an error message (shown in the next figure) informing you that one or more configuration settings defined in the service definition file were not specified in the service configuration file. The error occurs because the service definition changed as a result of the new *EmailAdmin* setting. As you learn in Chapter 6, you can change the values of the configuration settings without redeploying, but when you introduce something new in the definition, the service needs to be redeployed, not just upgraded. You can create a new staging deployment to host the new version of the service and then swap the environment.

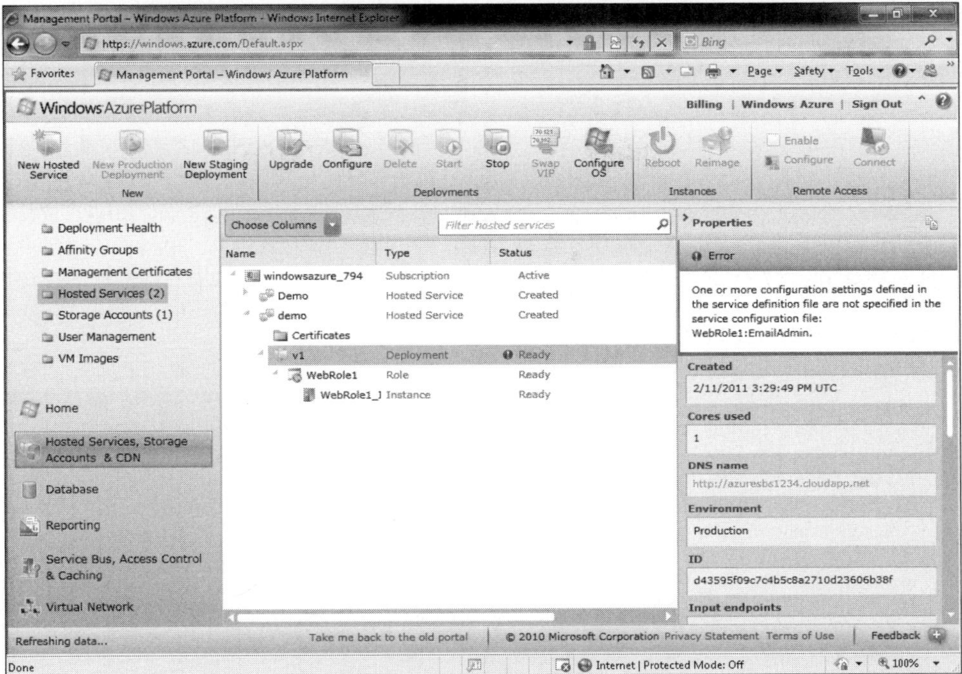

To continue this exercise, delete the current deployment, and then create a new production deployment.

You can modify the live configuration in ServiceConfiguration.cscfg whenever you want, either by uploading a new configuration file or by modifying that file directly on the portal. In the former case, you can also use the editor provided by Visual Studio to modify the file locally, and then upload the updated file. Using Visual Studio is simpler, and reduces the risk of a misspelled XML element or tag, but you have to use it carefully because some editor settings also modify the ServiceDefinition.csdef file and, as you learned, a modification of the definition file requires a new deployment. For this reason, it's best to use only the Settings tab to avoid unexpected effects on the overall configuration. You explore the ServiceDefinition.csdef file in the next section.

The process to upload a new ServiceConfiguration.cscfg file or modify it live on the portal is straightforward: just click the Configure button in the production or staging environment to open the configuration web form.

Note You can also copy the text in the configuration from the project portal and paste it to the Visual Studio editor or any other XML editor, modify it, and then copy it back to the portal.

You still haven't seen a description of one more important file in the WebRole1 project, which is a classic ASP.NET web application project that has three important modifications: the three references to the Windows Azure APIs, a new trace listener configuration (explained in Chapter 6), and a class named *WebRole*, defined in the WebRole.cs file. Listing 3-6 shows the class definition.

LISTING 3-6 WebRole definition.

```
using System;
using System.Collections.Generic;
using System.Linq;
using Microsoft.WindowsAzure;
using Microsoft.WindowsAzure.Diagnostics;
using Microsoft.WindowsAzure.ServiceRuntime;

namespace WebRole1
{
    public class WebRole : RoleEntryPoint
    {
        public override bool OnStart()
        {
            // For information on handling configuration changes
            // see the MSDN topic at
            // http://go.microsoft.com/fwlink/?LinkId=166357.

            return base.OnStart();
        }
    }
}
```

As you can see from Listing 3-6, the class derives from the *RoleEntryPoint* class, defined in the *Microsoft.WindowsAzure.ServiceRuntime* namespace. *WebRole* overrides the *RoleEntryPoint* class's *OnStart* method to provide an entry point when Windows Azure fabric starts the service. That method fires every time you choose to run a suspended service or increment the number of instances. Remember that the package is deployed on a varying number of virtual machines based on the ServiceConfiguration.cscfg setting.

During the execution of the *OnStart* method, your service is placed in a *Busy* state, as described in the previous section. You can use this method to initialize variables or handle other housekeeping chores. In the Windows Azure SDK 1.2, by default, the template uses this method to initialize the Diagnostic engine, passing the string you set in the ServiceConfiguration.cscfg file. The *DiagnosticsConnectionString* setting provides a location where the engine can store diagnostics information. (You learn more about this topic in Chapter 6.) In the Windows Azure SDK 1.3, the configuration for the diagnostic engine was moved from code to the service configuration.

A classic WebRole.cs file might look like Listing 3-7.

LISTING 3-7 A classic WebRole definition.

```
using System;
using System.Collections.Generic;
using System.Linq;
using Microsoft.WindowsAzure;
using Microsoft.WindowsAzure.Diagnostics;
using Microsoft.WindowsAzure.ServiceRuntime;

namespace WebRole1
{
    public class WebRole : RoleEntryPoint
    {
        public override bool OnStart()
        {
            RoleEnvironment.Changing += RoleEnvironmentChanging;

            base.OnStart();
        }

        private void RoleEnvironmentChanging(object sender,
           RoleEnvironmentChangingEventArgs e)
        {
            // If a configuration setting is changing
            if (e.Changes.Any(change => change is
               RoleEnvironmentConfigurationSettingChange))
            {
                // Set e.Cancel to true to restart this role instance
                e.Cancel = true;
            }
        }
    }
}
```

In Listing 3-7, the first line of the *OnStart* method informs the *RoleEnvironment* that there's an event handler for the *Changing* event. This event occurs before any change to the service configuration gets applied to the running instances of the role. The event handler receives an instance of the *RoleEnvironmentConfigurationSettingChange* class. This class exposes two interesting properties: *Cancel* and *Changes*. You use the *Cancel* property to signal to the fabric that you want to restart the instance. The read-only *Changes* property contains a collection of *RoleEnvironmentChange* instances that are to be applied to the role instance.

The code uses LINQ query syntax to inspect the collection and find any change that represents a configuration settings change (a *RoleEnvironmentConfigurationTopologyChange* class that derives from *RoleEnvironmentChange*). If the query returns *true*, the code sets *e.Cancel* to *true* to force a role instance restart.

From the code in Listing 3-7, you can see that, by default, a Visual Studio Web Role Project forces every instance to restart when you modify any setting in the ServiceConfiguration.cscfg file. However, if you modify only the instance number or other settings, the role instances are not restarted.

You can change this behavior as needed. For example, if you use static variables that depend on some configuration setting, you can choose to restart the instance, or just destroy your static value; if you use the *System.Cache* classes to cache a remote resource pointed to by a URL placed in the configuration file, you can remove the item from the cache, querying for the name of the URL setting.

In Chapter 4, "Windows Azure Storage," you use the *StorageClient* library to access the Windows Azure storage account. This library caches the URL for accessing the account and, by default, places these URLs in ServiceConfiguration.cscfg. You would need to modify the code in Listing 3-6 to respond to this type of change.

Service Definition File

Another topic to examine in this basic introduction to Web Roles is the ServiceDefinition.csdef file that the New Project wizard placed in the Cloud Service Project.

If you open ServiceDefinition.csdef, you see something similar to Listing 3-7. After the classic XML declaration, the definition continues with an XML element named *ServiceDefinition* that provides a name for it. This definition name is used by the compute emulator and the Windows Azure fabric to define a contract for a service.

LISTING 3-7 ServiceDefinition.csdef.

```
<?xml version="1.0" encoding="utf-8"?>
<ServiceDefinition name="DevLeapCloudService"
  xmlns="http://schemas.microsoft.com/ServiceHosting/2008/10/ServiceDefinition">
  <WebRole name="WebRole1">
    <Sites>
       <Site name="Web">
          <Bindings>
              <Binding name="Endpoint1" endpointName="Endpoint1">
          </Bindings>
       </Site>
    </Sites>
    <Endpoints>
      <InputEndpoint name="Endpoint1" protocol="http" port="80" />
    </Endpoints>
    <Imports>
        <Import moduleName="Diagnostics" />
    </Imports>
    <ConfigurationSettings>
      <Setting name="EmailAdmin" />
    </ConfigurationSettings>
  </WebRole>
</ServiceDefinition>
```

The service definition includes a *WebRole* element containing the name of the ASP.NET Web Role Project, and an *InputEndpoint* definition that lets the fabric configure ports and protocols for the service. In Figure 3-9, you can see these settings in the compute emulator user interface. Note that port 80 is configured in the definition file, but port 81 is used by the compute emulator. This behavior derives from the presence of IIS on my machine, which reserved port 80.

Note The compute emulator will use the first free port above the configured port.

The *ConfigurationSettings* element is somewhat strange because it seems like a duplication of that setting in the ServiceConfiguration.cscfg file. However, *ServiceDefinition* defines the existence of a setting, not a value, whereas the *ServiceConfiguration* setting assigns a value to each setting. You cannot assign a value to a setting in the ServiceConfiguration.cscfg file that hasn't been defined in the service definition file. The service definition file is packaged together with the roles code and deployed to every instance of the service in the cloud. This definition informs each instance that a setting with that precise name will exist. As you learned in the preceding section, from the Windows Azure portal, you can assign or modify the value of a setting.

Last but not least is the *Site* element, introduced with the Windows Azure SDK 1.3, which lets you configure multiple sites on the same Web Role. The Visual Studio template includes three XML attributes you can use to configure the *InputEndpoint* element: *name* is just a mnemonic element to identify the endpoint (and it is referenced by the *Binding* element), *protocol* identifies the protocol used to reach the endpoint, and *port* is the port where the endpoint listens for requests (and the port to be opened automatically by the firewall). You can also associate a digital certificate to enable the SSL protocol.

Role Properties

The cloud project has many other configuration settings that you can adjust, depending on the project type. Many of these are defined in the ServiceDefinition.csdef file, but some require that you modify the ServiceConfiguration.cscfg file as well

Visual Studio 2010 has a convenient editor for modifying these configuration files in a single place (the role properties page), but you can always modify these files manually, too. The first tab of this editor contains the general configuration and is shown in the following figure.

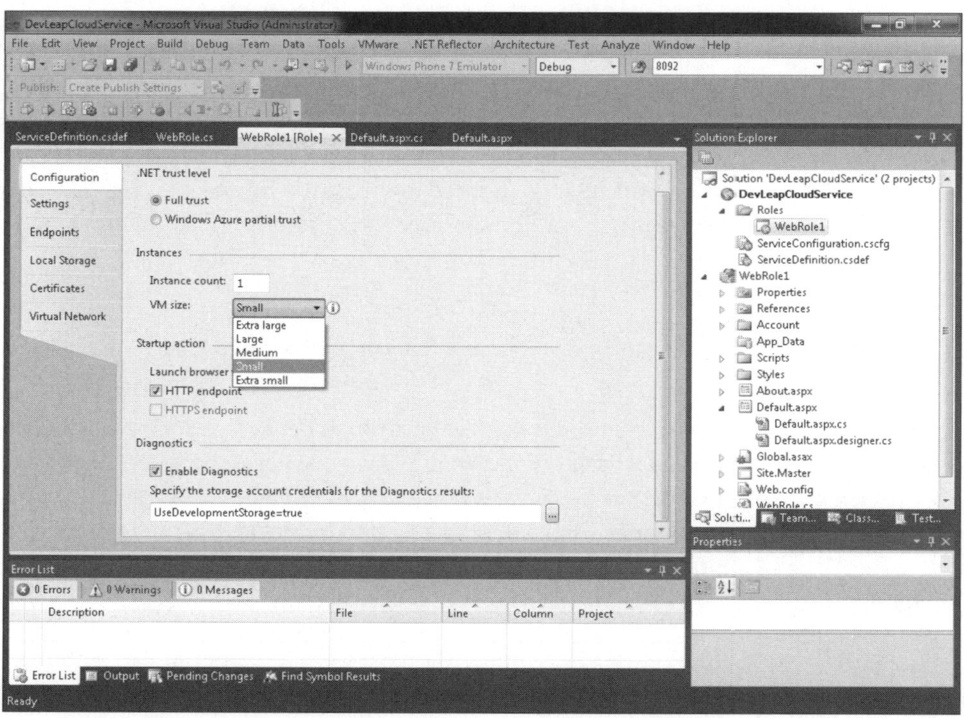

In this form, you can opt for Full Trust or Windows Azure Partial Trust. The Windows Azure Partial Trust setting means that you cannot execute native code. It corresponds to *enable-NativeExecutionCode* in ServiceDefinition.csdef, so changing it requires a complete redeploy.

The Instances section is dedicated to the virtual machine. You already saw the Instance Count setting at work in various sections of this chapter. The VM Size setting is related to your subscription, and you can choose among different sizes for the virtual machine instances. The Extra Large size differs from the Small size in the number of cores and gigabytes of RAM per instance. Check the documentation to discover the currently available configurations, because they can change over time.

The Startup Action section has options that identify the protocol passed to Internet Explorer by Visual Studio when you press F5 or Ctrl+F5. You haven't assigned any digital certificate to enable SSL, so you would select HTTP Endpoint.

The Diagnostics section lets you enable the diagnostic feature and specify the related Storage Account where the diagnostic engine will persist this kind of information.

In the next figure, you can see the Endpoints tab, where you configure the input endpoint of the service. An *input endpoint* is the port and the protocol that the fabric (local or in the cloud) has to configure to let requests come in.

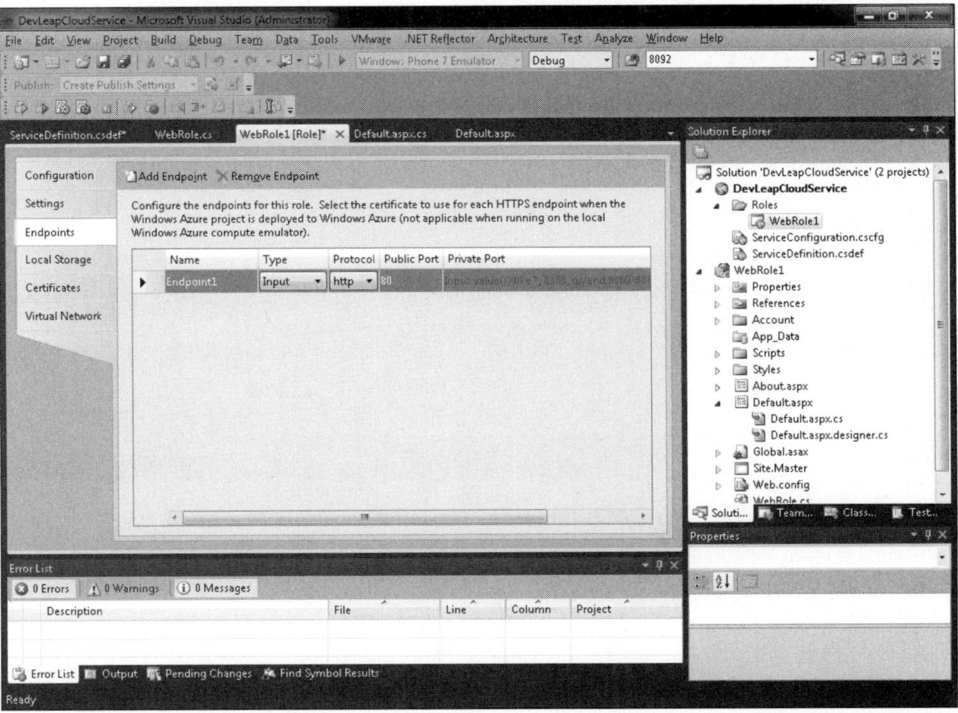

You can configure other endpoints manually in the ServiceDefinition.csdef file or at run time using the *RoleEnvironment* class. You return to this topic in Chapter 6.

The Local Storage settings, shown in the next figure, inform the fabric that your application needs some space in the virtual machine to cache resources. These settings ensure that the fabric will configure every instance with the necessary disk space. You can request different locations in which to cache data on the local file system by adding more settings. Each requested storage resource can be organized into different folders as needed. You learn about this in more detail in Chapter 4.

Warning Do not use local storage to maintain run-time data or application state, because—as in any on-premises solution—each instance can be recycled or can crash.

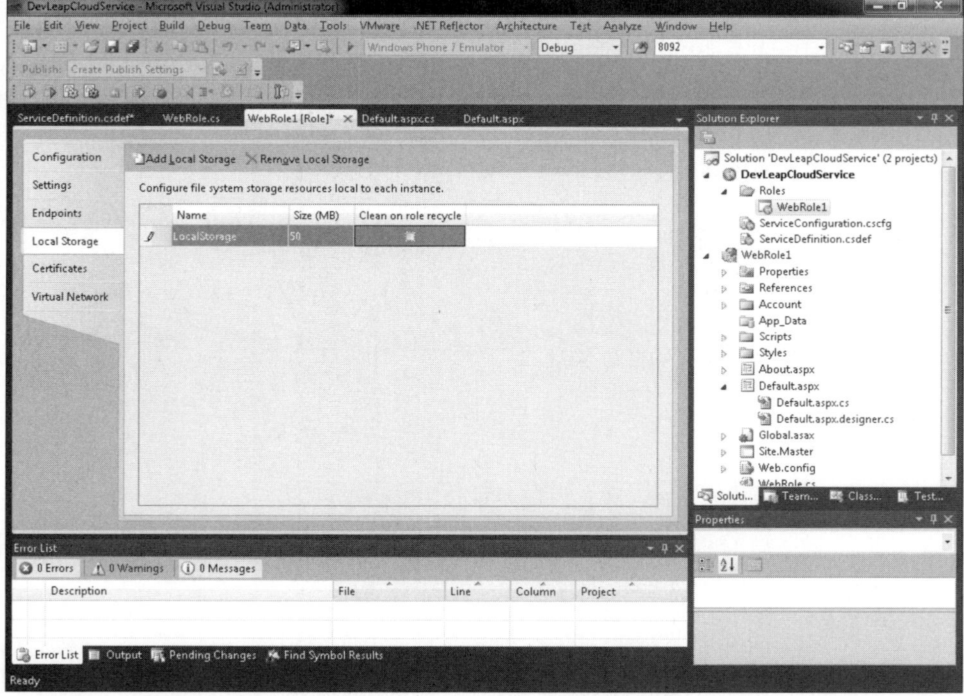

The Certificates configuration tab is reserved for digital certificates management. Using this form, you can assign different X.509 certificates to your services. You must upload any configured certificate to Windows Azure manually using the Developer Portal to use that particular certificate in your service. The upload operation is mandatory, because Visual Studio doesn't package certificates during the publishing process.

When you add a certificate in this form, you can use it in the Endpoints tab. Try adding a fake certificate and return to the Endpoints tab to understand the configuration without having to use a real certificate. You'll find that you cannot use a fake certificate; it breaks the security principles. In the following figure, I tried to add a certificate named Certificate1.

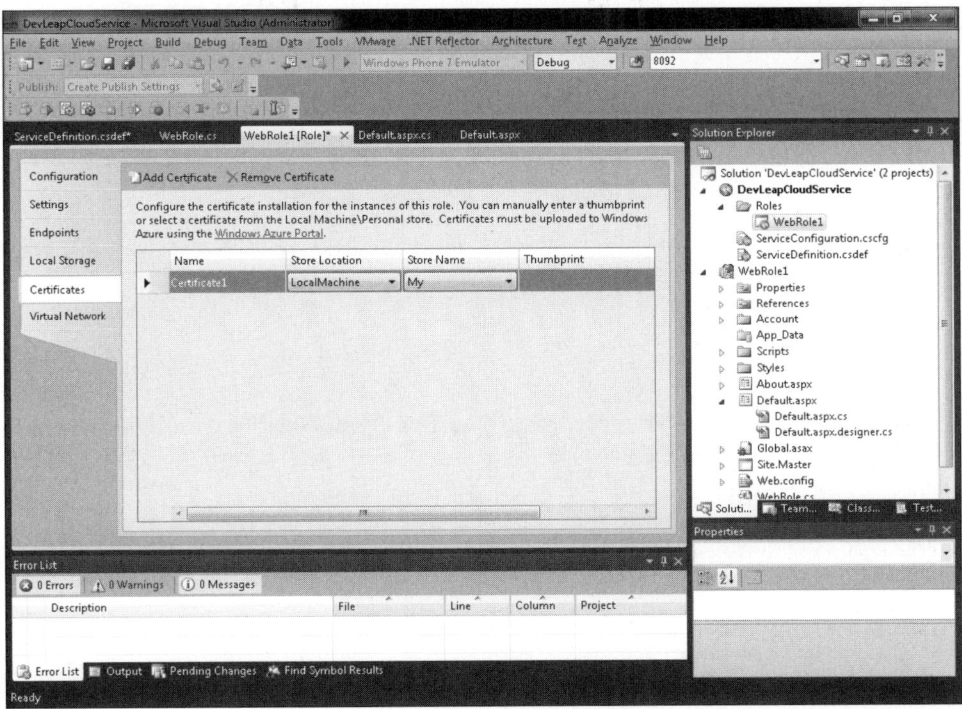

If you followed all the steps presented in this chapter, you should end up with the Service Definition file in Listing 3-8 and the Service Configuration file in Listing 3-9.

LISTING 3-8 ServiceDefinition.csdef.

```
<?xml version="1.0" encoding="utf-8"?>
<ServiceDefinition name="DevLeapCloudService" xmlns="http://schemas.microsoft.com/
ServiceHosting/2008/10/ServiceDefinition">
  <WebRole name="WebRole1" enableNativeCodeExecution="true">
    <Sites>
      <Site name="Web">
        <Bindings>
          <Binding name="Endpoint1" endpointName="Endpoint1" />
          <Binding name="Endpoint2" endpointName="Endpoint2" />
        </Bindings>
      </Site>
    </Sites>
    <Endpoints>
```

```
      <InputEndpoint name="Endpoint1" protocol="http" port="80" />
      <InputEndpoint name="Endpoint2" protocol="https" port="443" />
    </Endpoints>
    <Imports>
      <Import moduleName="Diagnostics" />
    </Imports>
    <ConfigurationSettings>
      <Setting name="EmailAdmin" />
    </ConfigurationSettings>
    <LocalResources>
      <LocalStorage name="LocalStorage" cleanOnRoleRecycle="false"
        sizeInMB="50" />
    </LocalResources>
    <Certificates>
      <Certificate name="Certificate1" storeLocation="LocalMachine"
        storeName="My" />
    </Certificates>
  </WebRole>
</ServiceDefinition>
```

The ServiceDefinition.csdef file now has two input endpoints for ports 80 and 443, a request for 50 MB of disk space that will survive to role recycle, and a partially configured certificate.

The ServiceConfiguration.cscfg contains a certificate section with a single certificate that corresponds to the definition in the ServiceDefinition.csdef file. The thumbprint is blank because the real certificate has not been chosen yet.

LISTING 3-9 ServiceConfiguration.cscfg.

```
<?xml version="1.0" encoding="utf-8"?>
<ServiceConfiguration serviceName="DevLeapCloudService" xmlns=
  "http://schemas.microsoft.com/ServiceHosting/2008/10/ServiceConfiguration">
  <Role name="WebRole1">
    <Instances count="1" />
    <ConfigurationSettings>
     <Setting name="Microsoft.WindowsAzure.Plugins.Diagnostics.ConnectionString"
       value="UseDevelopmentStorage=true" />
     <Setting name="EmailAdmin" value="roberto@devleap.com" />
    </ConfigurationSettings>
    <Certificates>
      <Certificate name="Certificate1" thumbprint=""
        thumbprintAlgorithm="sha1" />
    </Certificates>
  </Role>
</ServiceConfiguration>
```

Summary

In this chapter, you saw the complete cycle for creating and upgrading a simple but effective Windows Azure service. You learned about the SDK installation and the various pieces of the platform, and then you created a project. After a local test in the compute emulator, you deployed a solution in Windows Azure using the Developer Portal. You modified the project and followed the upgrade procedure. You saw every definition and configuration for the cloud project in Visual Studio.

The next chapter is dedicated to the Windows Azure storage account. You learn how to use it from cloud and on-premises solutions.

Quick Reference

To	Do this
Download the Azure SDK and tools	Go to *http://www.azure.com*.
Run your application in a web server context	In Visual Studio, right-click the page you want to run and select View In Browser from the pop-up menu.
Debug and test your applications in the compute emulator	In Visual Studio, press F5.
See the running instance	Open the compute emulator user interface and expand the node below the cloud projects.
Modify the number of instances	Open ServiceConfiguration.cscfg or right click the Role project, select Properties, and choose the Settings section.

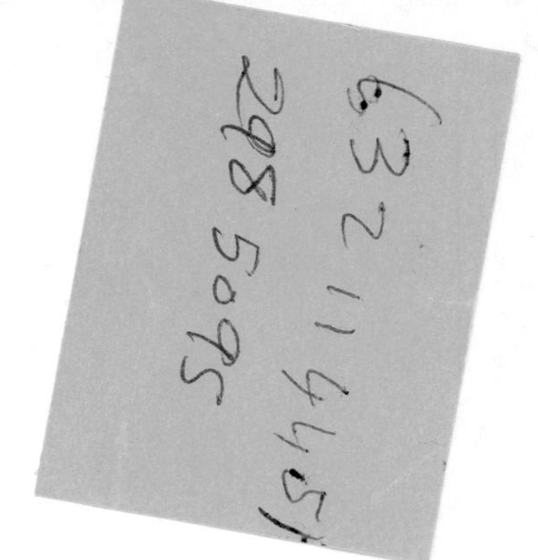

Chapter 4

Windows Azure Storage

After completing this chapter, you will be able to

- Use local storage.
- Understand the Storage Account Portal settings.
- Use the Windows Azure Management Tool to manage blobs.
- Use the Blob Storage APIs.

In the last chapter, you built a simple Windows Azure service using the Windows Azure Tools for Microsoft Visual Studio and the local debugging environment called the Windows Azure compute emulator. Then you deployed the solution in the cloud using the portal and upgraded it using the upgrade feature for production and staging. You saw a brief mention of the local storage feature when you configured the application.

This chapter focuses on a more complete introduction to the storage features exposed by Windows Azure. You learn how to use local storage to cache resources locally, and then you walk through exercises that show you how to use the various endpoints for storing and managing blobs, tables, and queues, both locally (for testing purposes), and in the live Storage Account Project.

Note Because URLs, UI names, and procedures may vary over time, some of them may be out of date by the time you read this. In that case, my best advice is to start looking for the information about the Windows Azure product on the Windows Azure home page (*http://www.azure.com*). Information included in this book was accurate at the time of writing.

Local Storage

As you learned at the end of Chapter 3, "Creating a Web Role Project," every Windows Azure Cloud Service has a service definition file (with a .csdef extension) that lets you request features, services, endpoints, and so on from the Windows Azure fabric. You also learned that this file, in conjunction with the service configuration file (which has a .cscfg extension), can hold application settings that you can read through the *RoleEnvironment* class.

Local storage is a feature exposed by the operating system to provide a space where an application can store and read data. It is somewhat like a traditional hard drive, although, as with every Windows Azure feature, it is exposed as a logical resource, not a physical one: it has neither a disk drive letter nor a normal path. To use it, you request some space, and then use the *RoleEnviroment* class to obtain the starting place to store your data. You can then create subfolders and files as you normally would with the Microsoft .NET Framework *System.IO* classes, read the files, update them, and delete them. The only difference is the way you reach the root of this space. You can also request multiple local storage if you prefer to store data in different places rather than in different folders.

The Windows Azure compute emulator tool simulates the local storage feature on your development machine so that you can test and debug the application's behavior locally, without having to deploy the application to the cloud.

Request Local Storage

1. Create a new Windows Azure Project, and name the project **ThinkAheadAzureStorage**.

Note To refresh your memory about how to do this, see Chapter 3.

2. In the New Windows Azure Project, add an ASP.NET Web Role to the Windows Azure Solution. Leave its name set to the default, WebRole1.
3. When Visual Studio is finished creating the project infrastructure, in the cloud project, under Roles, double-click the WebRole1 node to open the Role Configuration screen.
4. Click the Local Storage tab in the left pane and, in the Mini Toolbar in the right pane, click the Add Local Storage button.
5. Name this new local storage **MyStorage** and type **50** into the Size text box.
6. Do not select the Clean On Role Recycle check box (by default, it's not selected). Save the WebRole1 configuration.

   Figure 4-1 shows the result of your work.

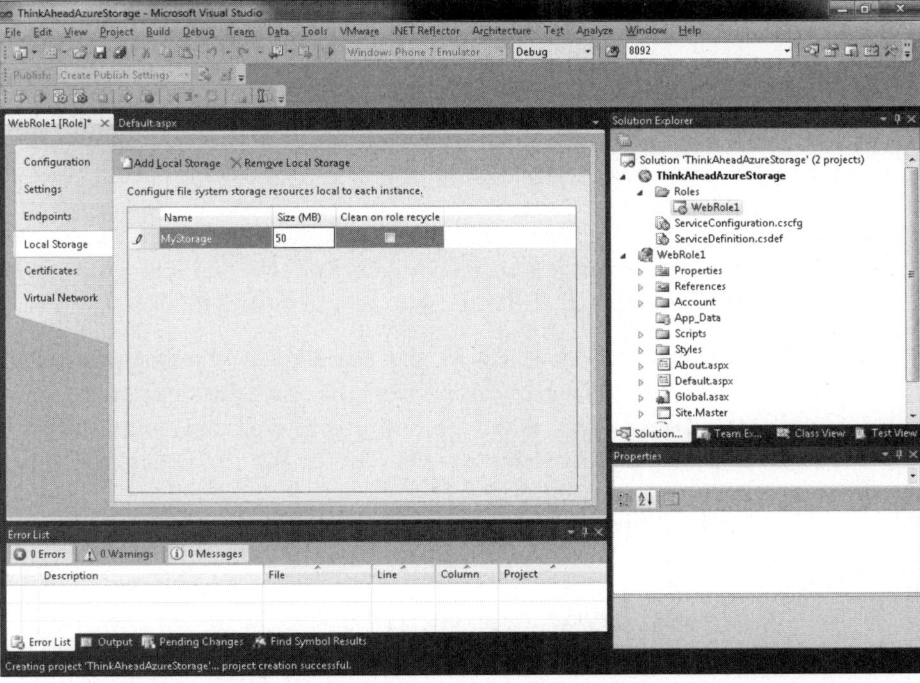

FIGURE 4-1 Request for local storage space.

After saving this configuration, the Visual Studio integrated development environment (IDE) modifies the ServiceDefinition.csdef file to request the required disk space to the Windows Azure fabric during the deployment of the hosted service, as shown in the following code.

```
<?xml version="1.0" encoding="utf-8"?>
<ServiceDefinition name="ThinkAheadAzureStorage" xmlns="http://schemas.microsoft.com/
ServiceHosting/2008/10/ServiceDefinition">
  <WebRole name="WebRole1">
    <Sites>
      <Site name="Web">
        <Bindings>
          <Binding name="Endpoint1" endpointName="Endpoint1" />
        </Bindings>
      </Site>
    </Sites>
    <Endpoints>
      <InputEndpoint name="Endpoint1" protocol="http" port="80" />
    </Endpoints>
    <Imports>
      <Import moduleName="Diagnostics" />
    </Imports>
    <LocalResources>
      <LocalStorage name="MyStorage" cleanOnRoleRecycle="false" sizeInMB="50" />
    </LocalResources>
  </WebRole>
</ServiceDefinition>
```

In the preceding XML, the *LocalResources* tag contains the *LocalStorage* element, which requests the specified amount of space from the fabric. Remember that when you deploy the service on Windows Azure or in the Windows Azure compute emulator, part of that deployment involves inspecting the configuration files to create the appropriate virtual machine. In this case, Windows Azure fabric creates a virtual machine with at least 50 MB of free disk space and exposes it under the name *MyStorage*.

You can read most of the settings by using the classes in the *Microsoft.WindowsAzure.ServiceRuntime* namespace and assembly, and—because this library is referenced by default in the cloud project template—you can use those APIs directly.

Through the *RoleEnvironment* class, you can access the configured local resources using the *GetLocalResource* method, which takes a string parameter corresponding to the requested resource name. The method returns a *LocalResource* type that exposes a *Name* property, a *MaximumSizeInMegabytes* property, and the information you need to access the storage: a *RootPath* property.

Read the Configuration Value

1. Modify the default page by adding a *Label* control, named *localStorage*, that you will use to display the path of the configured Local Storage. The complete code for the Default.aspx page follows. I also modified the default heading content:

```
<%@ Page Title="Home Page" Language="C#" MasterPageFile="~/Site.master"
AutoEventWireup="true"
    CodeBehind="Default.aspx.cs" Inherits="WebRole1._Default" %>

<asp:Content ID="HeaderContent" runat="server" ContentPlaceHolderID="HeadContent">
</asp:Content>
<asp:Content ID="BodyContent" runat="server" ContentPlaceHolderID="MainContent">
    <h2>
        Welcome to ThinkAhead Azure Storage
    </h2>
    <p>
        <asp:Label ID="localStorage" runat="server" />
    </p>
</asp:Content>
```

2. Modify the code-behind file, Default.aspx.cs, so that it calls the *GetLocalResource* method, which asks the fabric for a configured resource. Use the returned *LocalResource* instance to set the label's *Text* to the *RootPath* property, as shown in the following code:

```
using System;
using System.Collections.Generic;
using System.Linq;
using System.Web;
using System.Web.UI;
using System.Web.UI.WebControls;
using Microsoft.WindowsAzure.ServiceRuntime;

namespace WebRole1
```

```
{
    public partial class _Default : System.Web.UI.Page
    {
        protected void Page_PreRender(object sender, EventArgs e)
        {
            LocalResource resource = RoleEnvironment.GetLocalResource("MyStorage");

            localStorage.Text = resource.RootPath;
        }
    }
}
```

3. Run the project to see the local path assigned to your *MyStorage* local storage. (Remember that you have to start Visual Studio with administrative privileges.) The result should look similar to the following figure.

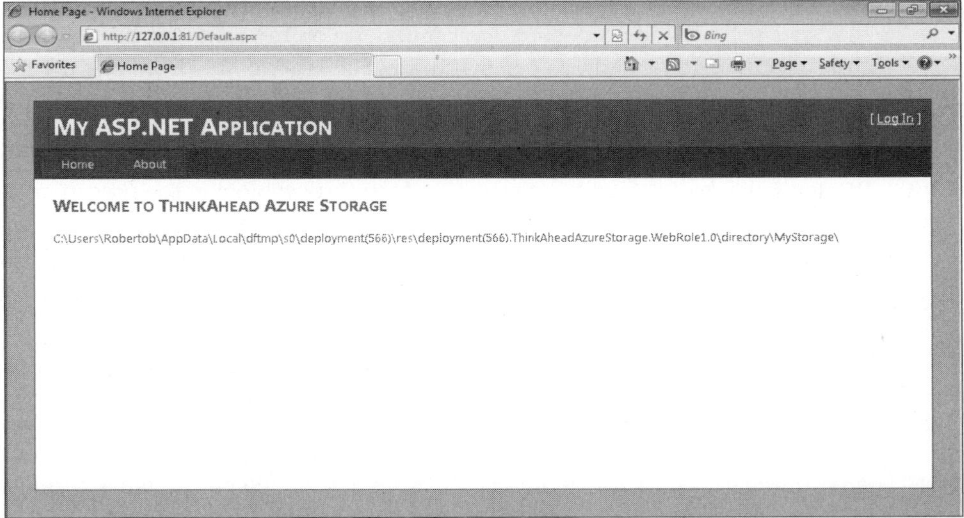

As you may remember from the previous chapter, the first part of the local storage path shown in the preceding screen is where the Windows Azure compute emulator deploys the solution; the number follows a progressive sequence of deployment on the machine. Each instance is uniquely referenced by the name of the project followed by a number starting from zero (for example, *WebRole1.0*). The local resource you specified in the configuration becomes a subdirectory of the directory root. You can perform whatever file or folder operations you want using this path.

Now that you know how to configure and use local storage, it's time to point out three different aspects:

- Local deployment
- Fault tolerance
- Scalability

The first aspect, local deployment, concerns the local environment. Every time you deploy a solution locally, the Windows Azure compute emulator creates a new deployment folder and assigns it a different number, which means that you will end up with many local folders, one for each debugging session. This behavior, apart from wasting some of your disk space, doesn't let you reuse the local storage from previous debugging sessions. If you modify files or folders during a debug session, you will need to copy the local storage content to the new deployment manually. For example, you can create a file in local storage and try to read its content in a single debug session, but if you stop the debugger and rerun the application, your deployment folder will be different, so the previously created file will no longer exist in the new deployment folder. You can either copy the file from the previous deployment folder, or you can adopt a completely different approach, similar to that imposed by the unit test practice approach, in which every test should be autonomous. So, if you are testing a procedure that reads a file, the test run has to copy the file during the initialization phase. That way, the reading procedure doesn't depend on the writing procedure or other previously executed code, and you can test the two independently from one another. Another benefit conferred by this approach is that you can test the reading procedure even when the writing procedure doesn't work, or even when it isn't developed yet.

The second aspect is fault-tolerance. I covered this problem in the preceding paragraph. You need to redeploy whenever the application is updated to include a new feature or to fix bugs—and every new deployment can deploy the solution to a different virtual machine. From this perspective, storing application or state information in local storage is not a good idea; every time you redeploy the solution, you lose everything in the previous local storage. Nevertheless, local storage is local to the machine and any machine-change operation that Windows Azure performs disregards your existing local storage.

The third aspect, scalability, is along the same lines as the second aspect: one of the advantages of the Windows Azure operating system is that you can increment the number of instances of a running service as needed. Multiple instances cannot share the local disk and, as I said before, every attempt to create a synchronization engine is a dangerous practice. Fortunately, as you see in the next section, Windows Azure gives you a shared storage environment, called a *storage account*, where you can store and retrieve application information and state across multiple instances.

So why does Windows Azure expose another, similar, type of storage? The answer is simple: to cache data in the location nearest to the application. If you think about a cloud solution, you realize that a virtual machine could conceivably be very distant from the data it needs. A Microsoft SQL Azure database, for example, might be many nodes away from the virtual machine, or when the solution needs some on-premises data, the path to reach that data for every external request might be too long.

The purpose of local storage is to cache data locally, in the nearest possible location to the code. The local disk serves this purpose perfectly. Because local storage is a sort of run-time cache, you should plan to use it by following the cache pattern: before using a resource, always check first whether it exists locally. If the resource does not exist, get it from the original source, store it in the local cache, and *then* use it. By following that pattern, you can leverage a very efficient local disk to cache whatever resource might be far from the solution or would be too time-consuming to recreate each time.

An option called Clean On Role Recycle is not selected by default (see Figure 4-1). This flag tells Windows Azure fabric whether to preserve local storage during a role recycle. For example, if you modify some important settings in a solution, you can request a role recycle to clear in-memory data and refresh your application entirely, just as you can in a traditional Internet Information Services (IIS) application. If you cached some resources based on those settings, you probably want to clean up your cache, too. If you cached a resource independently from the configuration settings, you can leave the option cleared, which will maintain the existing local storage content during the recycle operation. Remember that this option *cannot* ensure that your content will be available at any time. If your role crashes, for example, Windows Azure creates a new virtual machine as needed to restart a fresh, new copy of your service that cannot access the same local storage.

The Windows Azure Storage Account

You can compare local storage to the local file system on an on-premises server. SQL Azure can be the relational store for an application in the cloud, but its current version has some limitations regarding space and features. Also, you have to pay for it separately from your Windows Azure subscription. In addition, Microsoft Silverlight applications and AJAX/jQuery clients cannot access SQL Azure unless you build a service in the middle of the communication protocol that acts as a proxy to get the data for them.

A valid alternative for storing data in the cloud is a Windows Azure storage account. It's a perfect place to store blobs (even the biggest ones) and application entities (such as business entities), and it provides a queued mechanism to decouple applications or application components. Future versions of the Windows Azure storage account will provide a distributed cache and a store for file streams.

Note Remember that typically, your Windows Azure storage account accrues charges based on transactions and space consumed, but there are other subscription types available in which you can specify some fixed amount of disk space and/or number of transactions.

You can either create a storage account for each application or create different containers inside one storage account for different applications. I usually prefer the first method because every application can have a different permission set and can be administered by different users. For every operation you want to perform on the store, you must include the key provided by the storage account. There is only one key per storage account, so the first approach—creating a storage account for each application—should be more suitable for different scenarios.

The resources stored in the Windows Azure storage account are always available because Windows Azure replicates them on different nodes to guarantee both fault tolerance and scalability. If a node crashes, the fabric elevates a backup node to become the primary. If the response from a node becomes too slow, the fabric can allocate some resources on a different node to improve the overall efficiency.

You can access your Windows Azure storage account resources via REST and HTTP, so any application running on any platform can store, retrieve, and manipulate data in the cloud. You can decide to make these standard requests using the classes exposed by the technology of your choice, or you can use the wrapper classes in the SDK for the appropriate platform. These wrapper classes help in creating the code, because they make most of the details required to create REST requests and analyze HTTP responses transparent to developers.

The Windows Azure storage account is publicly available on the Internet, and you access it only via HTTP/HTTPS. From a protocol point of view, there is no difference between accessing the storage in the cloud using a cloud-based application or using an on-premises solution—except for the latency price when the solution is far away from the data center.

Create a Storage Account Project

1. To create a project, you need a subscription to Windows Azure services. (This can be the same subscription you used in the previous chapter to build the Windows Azure service.) Open the Windows Azure website (*http://www.azure.com*) and click the sign-in menu.
2. Sign in using your account to open the Management Portal, shown in the following figure.

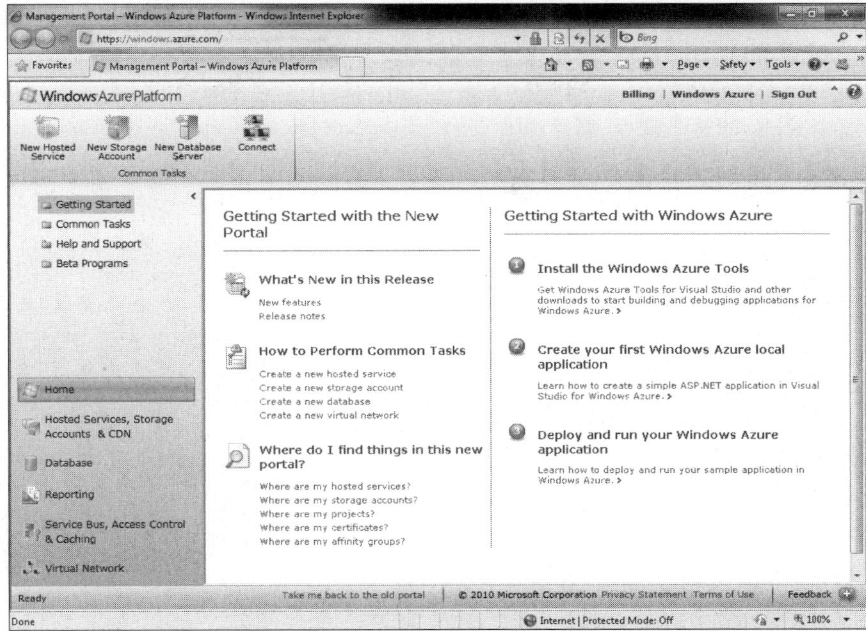

3. Click the Hosted Services, Storage Accounts & CDN button to open the summary page.
4. Click Storage Account (0) on the left side of the screen to show the summary page for the storage accounts. If you have not yet created a storage account, you see only the subscription name in the central pane, as shown in the following figure.

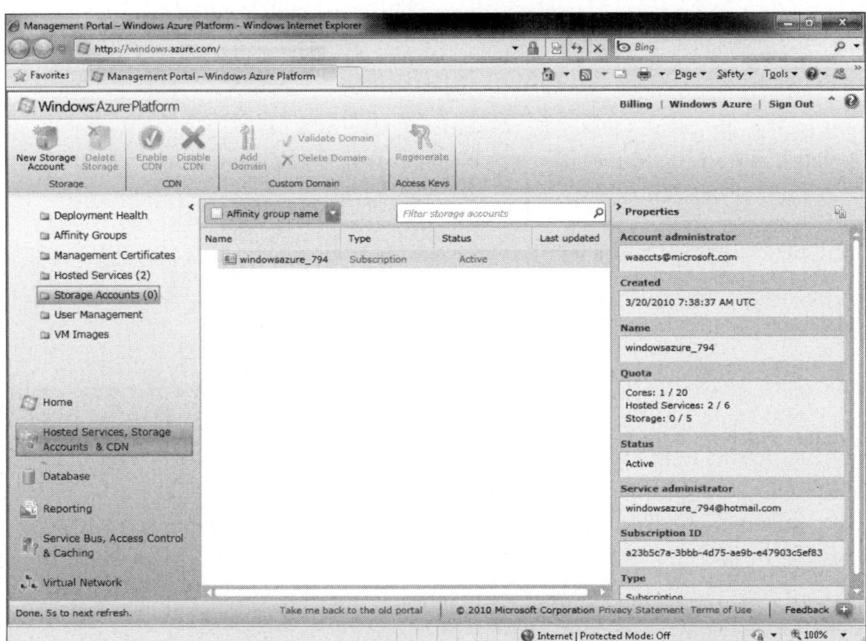

5. Click the New Storage Account button on the toolbar to open the Create A New Storage Account dialog box, shown in the following screen.

6. Type a unique name in the Enter A URL text box. Choose the public name for your service yourself, because it must be unique and meaningful to you. For example, if I were creating a site for this book, I might choose the name *azuresbs* ("sbs" stands for "step by step") as the prefix for the complete path, as shown in the following dialog box.

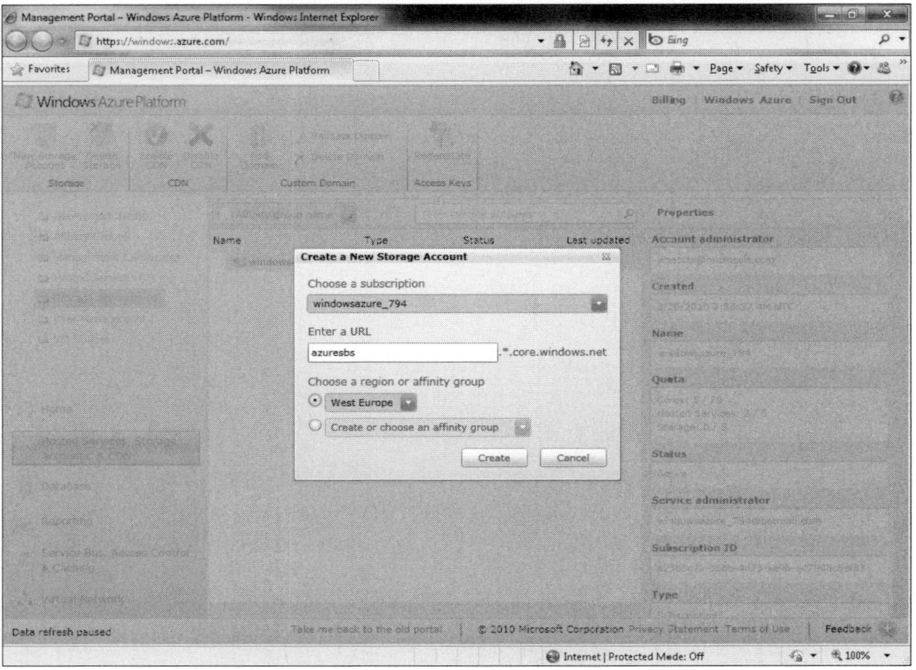

7. In the the dialog box, you choose a region or an affinity group where you want to create the storage account space for blobs, tables, and queues. Select the region you prefer. I chose West Europe.

8. Click the Create button to create the storage account.

You created your storage account, choosing a region to store your data as well as a public URL that every application will use to access the store.

Figure 4-2 shows the end result of the storage account creation filled with my own information. From this summary page, you can view the service details. First, notice that your new service appears in the list of services together with other storage accounts and cloud services—a good reminder of the importance of choosing a meaningful label for every project. In a production environment, I normally use the project name as the name of the cloud service project and the suffix "storage" for the storage account project. This way, the list, which is ordered alphabetically, shows me the various cloud projects together with the storage project, as shown in Figure 4-2.

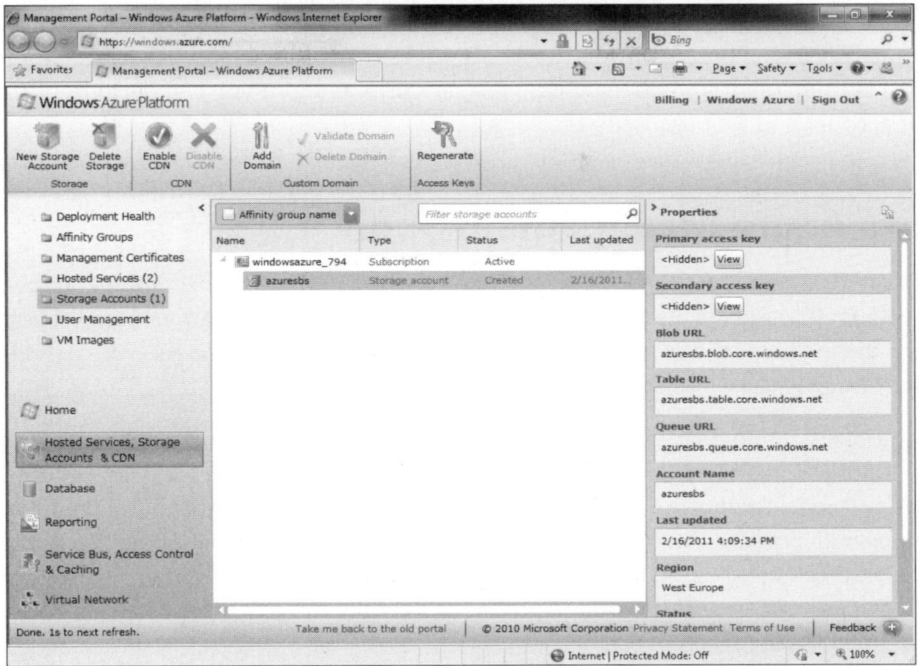

FIGURE 4-2 Result of creating the storage account.

The public name selected in the last wizard step becomes the root for the URLs of all kinds of resources. For example, to request a blob in the storage account, you would make an HTTP *GET* request to the following URI: *http://azuresbs.blob.core.windows.net*.

The Region box in Figure 4-2 shows that the service is hosted in West Europe and has no affinity group with other services. Affinity groups and the other options that appear in the service summary page are discussed more in Chapter 6, "Windows Azure Operating System Details."

Note the two hidden keys on the page: a primary key and a secondary key. You must include one of these in every request you make to the storage account resources—unless you decide to create a public section of the storage. You can use either the primary or the secondary key because both are valid. If one of them becomes compromised, you can use the other key in applications while you regenerate the compromised key. To regenerate a key, click the Regenerate button in the user interface.

You can view a key by clicking the View button next to it. In the View Storage Access Keys dialog box, you can also copy the keys to the Clipboard to reuse them in your code or some other management tool, as shown in the next section.

Before using the APIs to manage blobs and tables in the storage account, you should know about a useful tool for managing resources: a management console snap-in, called the Windows Azure Management Tool, that lets you manage the content of a storage account using the same APIs you will employ in code in the next sections of this chapter. This tool is particularly useful because Windows Azure does not provide a blob or table explorer. It is a good starting point for understanding the various operations you can perform on your storage account and for organizing resources.

Windows Azure Management Tool

You can download the Windows Azure Management Tool for free from the Windows Azure developer home page. Because URLs and pages can change over time, I suggest you start from the main page, *http://www.azure.com,* navigate to the developers' SDK section, and find the Windows Azure Management Tools link.

This tool lets you manage blobs, tables, and queues directly on your storage account (or in the Windows Azure storage emulator) so it is a perfect companion for every project that uses a storage account. You can also perform many other cloud project operations, such as deploying, upgrading, and managing the hosted service state; configuring the storage service; and managing digital certificates for Windows Azure Service. Almost every operation you can perform is available on the portal for storage accounts and hosted services, as you can see in the following figure.

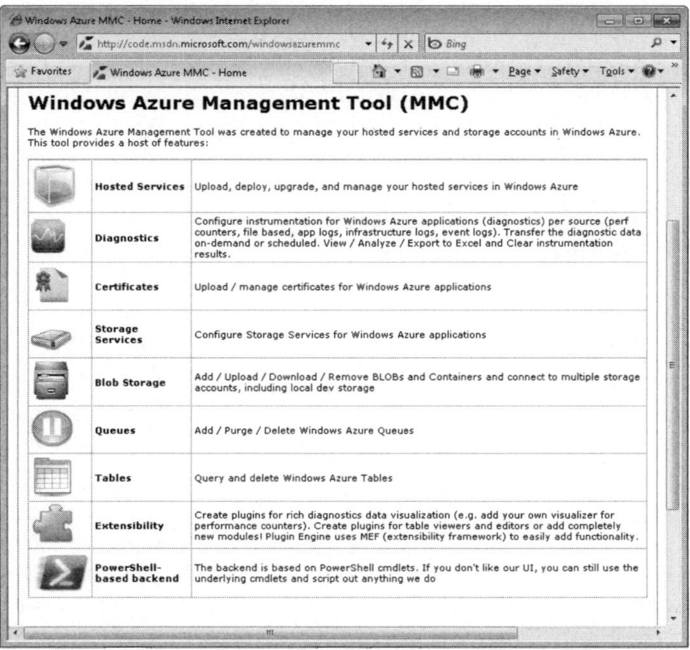

The next procedure shows how you can use the Windows Azure Management Tool to manage some blobs in the storage account azuresbs by using the primary key and the URL you saw earlier.

Manage Blobs with the Windows Azure Management Tool

You need to provide the information the tool needs to connect to your Windows Azure storage account, that is, the public name to construct the URLs and the key (primary or secondary, it doesn't make any difference) that will be used for every request. If you do not have a storage account, you can follow the next set of steps by connecting the tool to your local Windows Azure storage emulator, which is the simulated environment installed by the Windows Azure SDK to locally simulate storage account behavior.

1. Expand all the nodes in the management console.
2. Right click Storage Explorer, and select New Connection to create a new connection to the storage account.

   As you can see from the following figure, the shortcut menu provides options for managing the connection to the storage account. The Connect option lets you select an already-defined connection, whereas Connect Local defines a connection to the local emulator. The Delete Connection option deletes an existing connection.

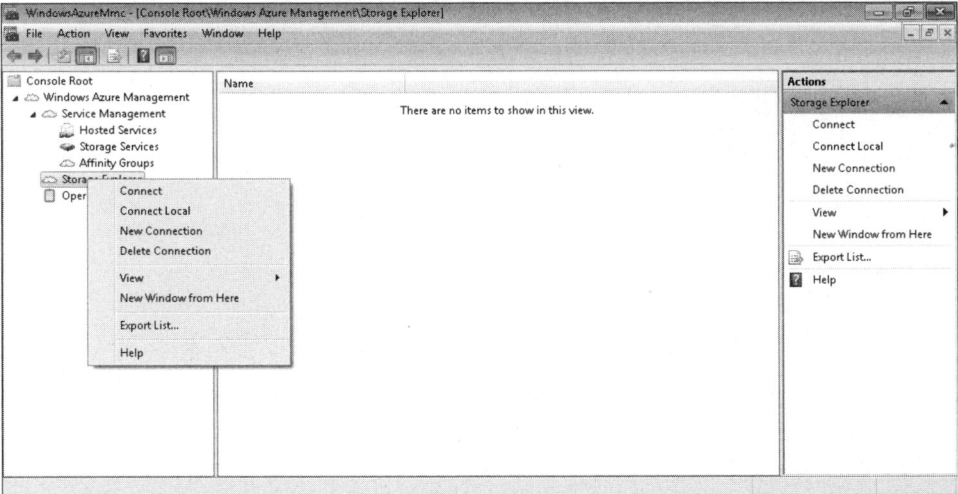

Note The term "connection" is somewhat misleading. When you select New Connection, you are not opening a connection; instead, you are simply defining the information the tool needs to make a connection. The same concept applies to Connect and Connect Locally; these menu items read the connection information and let you open and close the connection.

3. Type the account name that corresponds to the public name you chose when creating the storage account, and then copy and paste the primary (or secondary) key from the storage account summary page.

   As you can see in the next figure, I used azuresbs as the account name, and copied the primary key for that account. You don't have to fill in the URL fields, because the tool infers them from the account name.

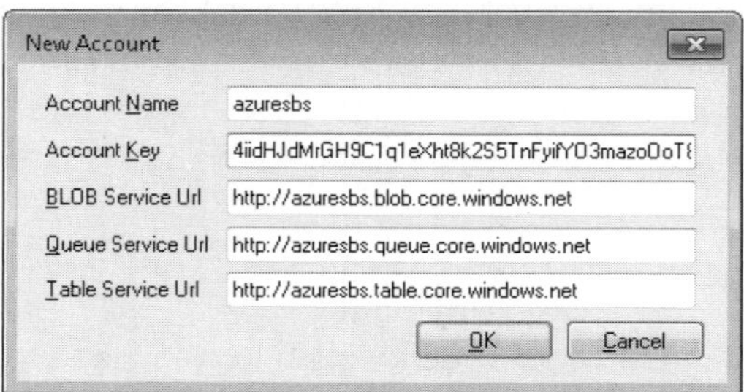

4. Verify the account and the key, and then click the OK button to store the connection information in the tool. You can define different connections for different storage accounts. A new node appears in the panel on the left, as you can see in Figure 4-3.
5. Expand the new node that has the same label as the account name (azuresbs in this case) to view the three resource types you can manage from this tool.
6. Click BLOB Containers to open the BLOB management window, shown in Figure 4-3.

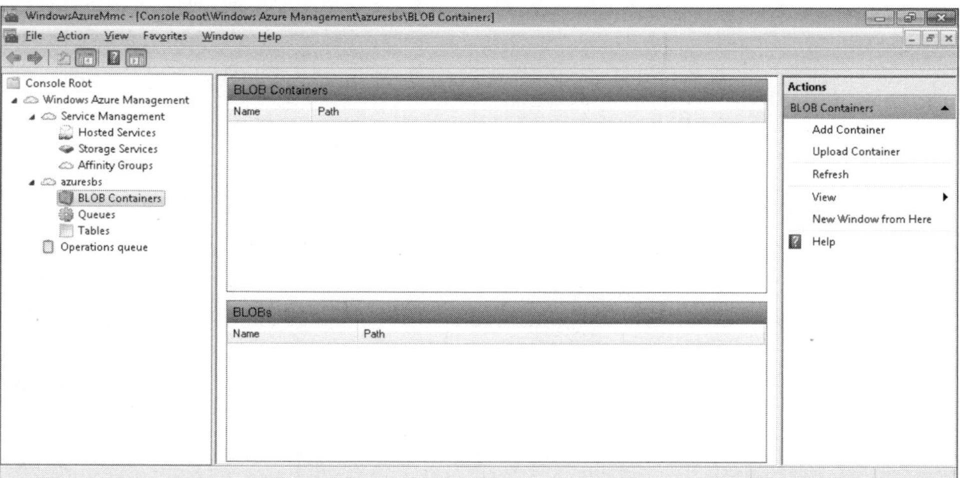

FIGURE 4-3 Blob management window.

Blobs are organized by containers, just as files in a traditional file system are organized by folders. You can define different containers to organize your blob however you like; the container name contributes to form a URL for REST operations. For instance, if I defined a container named *images* in this example, the URL for a *PUT* operation would be *http://azuresbs.blob.core.windows.net/images*.

7. Click the Add Container button in the far-right pane of the window to open the Add BLOB Container dialog box, where you can define the container name and the access type that will be applied to the container itself. Type **images** as the container name, and select Public for the access type, as shown in the following figure.

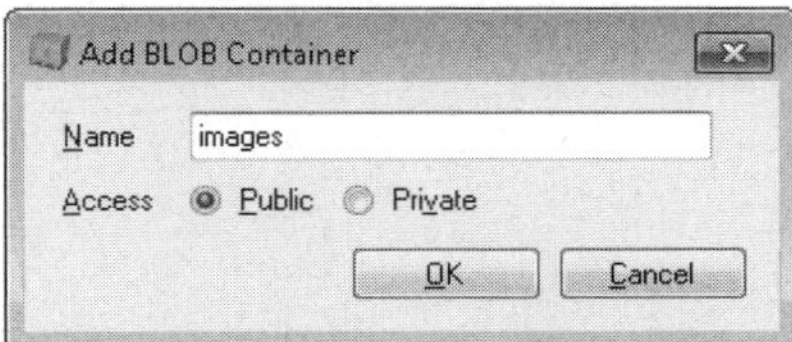

Every container can be either public or private. A public container is accessible for *GET* operations without the key being specified. In other words, any application or client can read information in a public container, but nonread operations, such as Create, Update, or Delete (CUD) requests, are possible only when made by authorized clients and applications. In contrast, a private container requires an access key for every operation.

8. Click the OK button to create the container. So far, no request has been made to the storage account, but now the tool connects to the account to request the new container. At the end of the creation procedure, you can see the new container in the list of containers.

When you click the OK button, the tool uses the underlying APIs to create an HTTP request with the *PUT* method, digitally signs the request, and sends the request to the URL assigned to the connection. You could perform this operation manually by issuing the same request. Remember that the Windows Azure storage account uses standard protocols (HTTP and REST) and that every operation is just a request to the public URL exposed by the service. The Windows Azure Management Tool also demonstrates what I pointed out earlier in this chapter—that you can access the storage account from anywhere, not just through a hosted service. In this case, I'm using an on-premises application that runs on my machine to access the storage account I created earlier.

To better understand the interaction between an application and the storage account, in the last step of the preceding procedure, I used an HTTP tracer to show you the underlying request. Almost every platform on planet Earth can make the request shown in Figure 4-4. The same concept applies when you want to upload a single blob file to the storage.

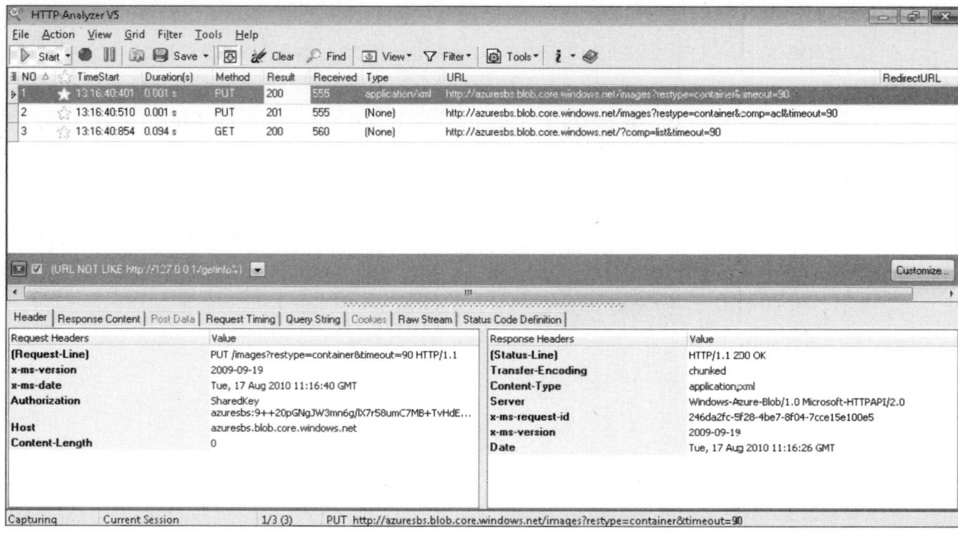

FIGURE 4-4 HTTP request for container creation.

As you can see in Figure 4-4, the first request uses the *PUT* method to ask the storage account service to create a container. The content type is XML, and the URL to which the request was sent includes the name of my storage account, the standard URI to the service, and the new container name. In practice, the tool asks the storage account to create this URI, and informs the underlying service that the *PUT* operation is for a container with a 90-second time-out period in the query string. The result code of the response is *200*, meaning that the service has successfully completed the request.

The trace shows three other important things. The first is the host value of the request, which contains the storage account path. The second is that the server value of the response headers tells you the server service version.

The third (and most important) item to note is the *Authorization* element of the request's header. As mentioned earlier, storage account management requests can be performed only by authorized applications. The management tool uses the provided key to pass an authorization header to the server that, in turn, checks its value to authorize or deny the incoming request.

Figure 4-4 shows two other requests: the first request is the continuation of the preceding one and contains the HTTP status code of *201 – Created*, telling the management tool that the container was created. The last request is made by the tool to ask for the list of containers during the refresh of the user interface. As you can deduce from the URL in the last request, the tool requested a *comp=list* value in the query string to get the list of containers.

Add Blobs to the Container

To complete the container and blob introductory tour, and before you learn about the APIs you will have to use in your code, try to add some images into the new blob container.

1. From the Windows Azure Management Tool, select the new container in the BLOB Containers window. A second window named BLOBs appears in the bottom of the main screen, and a new menu appears on the toolbar on the right side of the screen.
2. Click Upload Blob on that toolbar to open the Upload BLOB To Images dialog box. The term Images in the dialog box title is the container name, so this name varies for each container.
3. In the dialog box, choose the file you want to upload from your local hard drive by clicking the Browse button and selecting the appropriate image.

   By default, the blob inherits its name from the selected file name. I chose my company's logo, but regardless of the image you select, change the Blob Name to **ThinkAhead Logo**.

> **Note** If you want to follow this example exactly, you can download the logo from *http://thinkahead.cloudapp.net*.

   The Content Type is inferred from the file extension, as shown in the following figure.

   The Blob Name you enter is the identifier for this blob inside the storage account container. You need it for every subsequent operation with this blob.

4. Click the OK button to upload the blob into the container. As before, the request operation via HTTP occurs only after you press the OK button.
5. At the end of the upload operation, nothing seems to happen! That's because you're using an HTTP tool, so you have to ask for a refresh of the blob list to see the result. Double-click the container name to refresh it.
6. Repeat the upload operation procedure for another image, but giving this one the name **DevLeap Logo** (again, which image you select isn't important, but if you want to use the same one as the example, you can download it from *http://www.devleap.com*).

7. Refresh the interface by double-clicking the images container in the BLOB Containers window.

The result is straightforward: the BLOBs list pane shows you the two new blobs, as shown in the following figure.

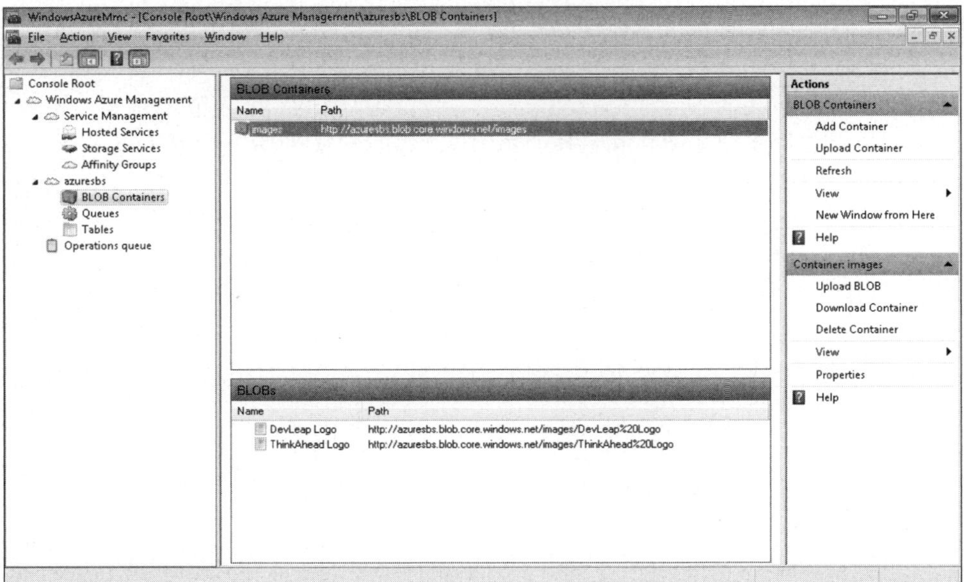

The two images in the *Images* container have names that represent the resource inside the storage. Each name must be unique inside its container, because the name contributes to form the URI for REST operations on each storage item. As you can see, the path (that is, the URI) for subsequent requests is composed of the name of the storage account followed by the standard URI, the container name, and the blob name. If you want to further separate the blobs in a container, use a forward slash (/) in the name of the blob you are uploading.

In the interface, you can also delete a container, download every blob to a local folder (or upload every file in a local folder to a single container), and upload a new blob to overwrite an existing blob in a container. You can activate a shortcut menu for each blob that provides options to download it, delete it, or ask the browser to request it. Every operation corresponds to an HTTP request that includes the authorization header.

The next figure shows the complete set of HTTP operations that the Windows Azure Management Tool performed behind the scenes during the preceding steps.

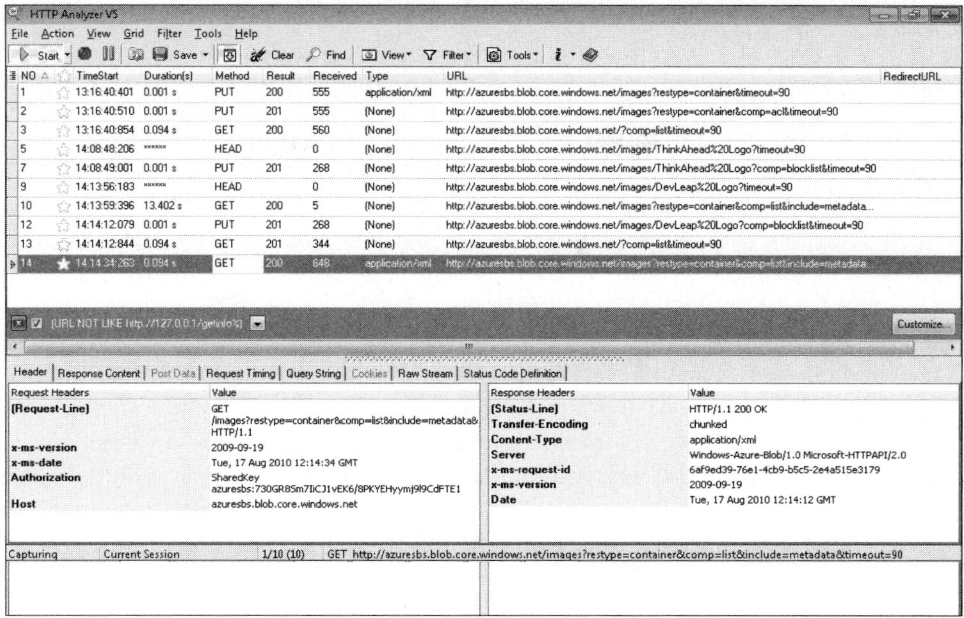

Because the *images* container is public, any client—even one with no key—can request a *GET* operation on the blobs it contains. For instance, open the browser of your choice and type the URI of one of the uploaded blobs. Because the browser receives a content type header of *image/jpeg*, the result is just the image, as you can see from the next figure. Look at the URL in the address bar of the browser. It refers directly to the uploaded blob at *http://azuresbs.blob.core.windows.net/images/ThinkAhead Logo*.

Blob APIs

I recommend that you experiment with the Windows Azure Management Tool, uploading, downloading, and deleting blobs and containers until you feel comfortable with these operations. This next section introduces the APIs that developers use to perform the same Create, Read, Update, Delete (CRUD) operations in code.

List the Blobs in a Container

The steps for listing the blob in a container are similar to the steps you followed using the Windows Azure Management Tool. You first obtain the connection information to build the URL so that you can make a *REST* request, and then you need to provide the authorization header and add it to every request. It can be useful to include this information in the Service Configuration file just as you would include any other configuration information (as you learned in Chapter 3). You can obtain a container reference easily by adding the container name to the URL. If you want to list the container's content, you need to append a *comp=list* query string. Finally, you can specify a time-out for every query operation.

The Windows Azure SDK, installed with the Windows Azure Tools for Visual Studio, contains a library that takes care of all of these details.

1. Open the project ThinkAheadAzureStorage you created at the beginning of this chapter.
2. Verify that the project contains a reference to the *Microsoft.WindowsAzure.StorageClient* library.

   A Visual Studio Windows Azure Project has the reference to this library, as well as to the *Microsoft.WindowsAzure.ServiceRuntime* that you used in the previous chapter.
3. Create a new setting in the Web Role configuration to store the account and the key information. Double-click WebRole1 in the Roles section of your cloud project, and then click Add Setting in the Settings section. Name the new setting **DataConnectionString**, and select Connection String as its type.
4. Click the ellipsis (...) button to open the Storage Connection String dialog box. You can also type the information directly in the text box near the button, but the dialog box helps you fill the information correctly.

5. As you did for the Windows Azure Management Tool, copy and paste this information from your Storage Accounts detail page. Follow the syntax shown in the following figure to reference your storage account. If you don't have a subscription, leave the Use The Windows Azure Storage Emulator option button selected. If you uploaded two images to the Windows Azure storage emulator in the earlier procedure, you will list those instead of any online images.

Note Remember to use your own information and not the information presented in this book, because it points to *my* storage account. You can choose HTTPS to protect the request made by an application to the store.

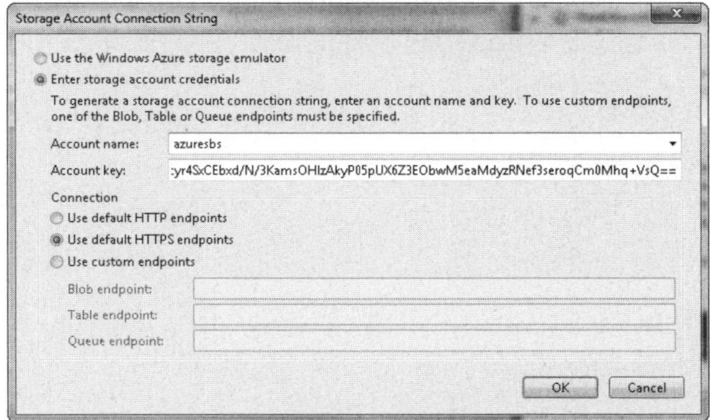

6. Add a new Web Form item to your project and name it **StorageAccountBlobs**.

   Insert a *Repeater* control in the page and name it **gridBlob**. Place an ItemTemplate inside it to show the *Uri* property of the blobs you are going to retrieve from the storage account.

   The resulting StorageAccountBlob.aspx page code is shown in Listing 4-1.

LISTING 4-1 Web Form for testing blobs.

```
<%@ Page Language="C#" AutoEventWireup="true"
CodeBehind="StorageAccountBlobs.aspx.cs"
    Inherits="WebRole1.StorageAccountBlobs" %>

<!DOCTYPE html PUBLIC "-//W3C//DTD XHTML 1.0 Transitional//EN"
http://www.w3.org/TR/xhtml1/DTD/xhtml1-transitional.dtd">
<html xmlns="http://www.w3.org/1999/xhtml">
<head runat="server">
    <title></title>
</head>
<body>
    <form id="form1" runat="server">
    <div>
        <p>
            <asp:Repeater ID="gridBlob" runat="server">
                <ItemTemplate>
                    <p>
                        <%# Eval("Uri") %></p>
                </ItemTemplate>
            </asp:Repeater>

        </p>
    </div>
    </form>
</body>
</html>
```

7. In the code-behind file, StorageAccountBlobs.aspx.cs, use the following code to bind the blobs contained in the *images* container of your storage account to the *GridView* control:

```
using System;
using System.Collections.Generic;
using System.Linq;
using System.Web;
using System.Web.UI;
using System.Web.UI.WebControls;
using Microsoft.WindowsAzure;
using Microsoft.WindowsAzure.StorageClient;

namespace WebRole1
{
    public partial class StorageAccountBlobs : System.Web.UI.Page
    {
        protected void Page_PreRender(object sender, EventArgs e)
        {
            CloudStorageAccount account =
```

```
                CloudStorageAccount.FromConfigurationSetting("DataConnectionString");

            CloudBlobClient blobClient = account.CreateCloudBlobClient();

            CloudBlobContainer container =
               blobClient.GetContainerReference("images");

            gridBlob.DataSource = container.ListBlobs();
            gridBlob.DataBind();
        }
    }
}
```

The first line of the *Page_PreRender* method in the preceding code retrieves the information you entered in the configuration setting in step 5. The *FromConfigurationSettings* static method of the *CloudStorageAccount* class reads the information in the ServiceConfiguration.cscfg file and returns an instance of the *CloudStorageAccount* type. This instance contains all the information necessary to build a proxy to the Storage Account Service exposed by Windows Azure in the cloud or to the local Windows Azure storage emulator. The *CreateCloudBlobClient* method creates the proxy you need to perform any operation on blobs and containers.

As you can see, the proxy has a method to get a reference to the container, named *GetContainerReference*, that accepts the container name as the only parameter. With that container reference, you can ask for the blobs it contains using the simple *ListBlobs* method. This method returns a type implementing *IEnumerable<IListBlobItem>* that you can bind to any control that supports data binding.

8. The code is almost complete, but the *CloudStorageAccount* class needs another little step in the configuration. Type the following code in the *Application_Start* method of your Global.asax.cs file to assure the class that every change in the configuration values of the storage account causes a recycle of the role to update the cached values. The following code comes directly from MSDN (Microsoft Developers Network) and is commented directly by the Azure team. Add the relative *using* clause for every class that needs it:

```
#region Setup CloudStorageAccount Configuration Setting Publisher

// This code sets up a handler to update CloudStorageAccount
// instances when their corresponding configuration settings change
// in the service configuration file.
 CloudStorageAccount.SetConfigurationSettingPublisher(
    (configName, configSetter) =>
    {
       // Provide the configSetter with the initial value
       configSetter(RoleEnvironment.GetConfigurationSettingValue(configName));
       RoleEnvironment.Changed += (s, arg) =>
       {
          if (arg.Changes.OfType<RoleEnvironmentConfigurationSettingChange>()
             .Any((change) => (change.ConfigurationSettingName == configName)))
          {
```

```
                    // The corresponding configuration setting has changed,
                    // propagate the value
                    if (!configSetter(RoleEnvironment.GetConfigurationSettingValue(
                          configName)))
                       // In this case, the change to the storage account credentials
                       // in the service configuration is significant enough that the
                       // role needs to be recycled in order to use the latest settings.
                       // (for example, the endpoint has changed)
                       RoleEnvironment.RequestRecycle();
                  }
               }
            };
         });
       #endregion
```

9. Set StorageAccountBlob.aspx as the default page by right-clicking it and selecting the Set As Start Page option.
10. Press F5 to start your project. If you pointed the connection string to your online storage account, be sure that you're connected to the Internet.

When you browse to the new StorageAccountBlobs.aspx page, you see the list of the URIs for each blob in the selected storage account. In the following figure, you can see the URIs for the two files I uploaded using the Windows Azure Management Tool in the previous section.

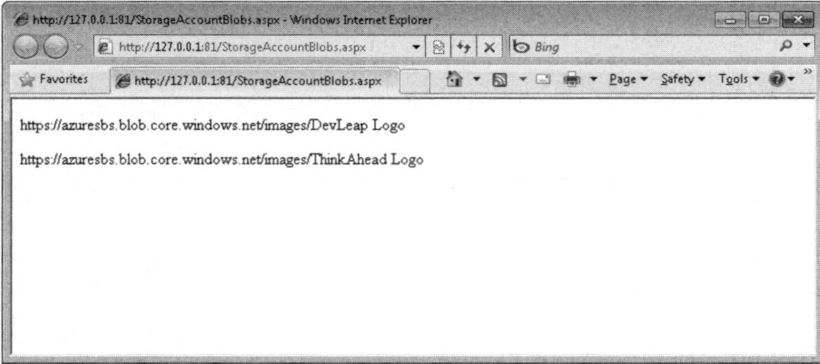

Because the URI points to a blob of the *type* image, you can replace the paragraph in the *ItemTemplate* inside the *Repeater* control with an *<img>* tag, as in the following code:

```
<asp:Repeater ID="gridBlob" runat="server">
   <ItemTemplate>
      <img src='<%# Eval("Uri") %>' />
   </ItemTemplate>
</asp:Repeater>
```

The result is straightforward, as you can see from the next figure, but this simple example unveils the power of a REST-based storage service.

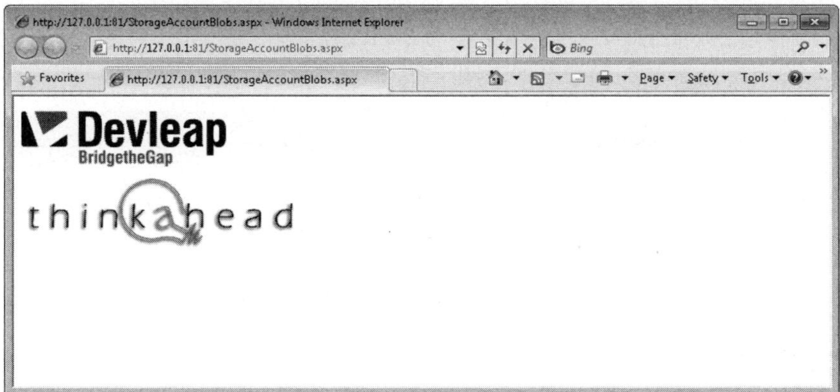

Note The *Eval* method is simple to use but it doesn't perform as you might think. It uses Reflection to figure out the underlying type that your code has set as the data source for the control. A better approach is to manually cast the data to the underlying type: such code not only executes more quickly, but the compiler can verify the type safety of the code, which it cannot do when using the *Eval* method. Listing 4-2 shows better code to perform this operation. (You can also find this listing in the downloadable sample code. See the book's "Introduction" for the download link.) Please note the use of the *Import Namespace* directive at the top of the page.

LISTING 4-2 Web Form for testing blobs with direct cast.

```
<%@ Page Language="C#" AutoEventWireup="true" CodeBehind="StorageAccountBlobs.aspx.cs"
   Inherits="WebRole1.StorageAccountBlobs" %>
<%@ Import Namespace="Microsoft.WindowsAzure.StorageClient" %>
<!DOCTYPE html PUBLIC "-//W3C//DTD XHTML 1.0 Transitional//EN"
http://www.w3.org/TR/xhtml1/DTD/xhtml1-transitional.dtd">
<html xmlns="http://www.w3.org/1999/xhtml">
  <head runat="server">
    <title></title>
  </head>
  <body>
    <form id="form1" runat="server">
      <div>
        <p>
          <asp:Repeater ID="gridBlob" runat="server">
           <ItemTemplate>
            <img src='<%# ((IListBlobItem)Container.DataItem).Uri %>' />
           </ItemTemplate>
          </asp:Repeater>
        </p>
      </div>
    </form>
  </body>
</html>
```

Upload New Blobs

This procedure demonstrates how you can use the *StorageClient* classes to add a new image in your storage account. You leverage the classic ASP.NET *FileUpload* control to upload the image to the hosted service, which in turn adds the image to the storage account as a blob.

1. Create a new paragraph *<p>* tag inside the top *<div>* of the *StorageAccountBlobs* page.
2. Add a *FileUpload* ASP.NET control in the new paragraph.
3. Add a *Button* control immediately after the *FileUpload* control in the same paragraph.

   The code for the page should be similar to the following; the new controls added are in boldface:

```
<%@ Page Language="C#" AutoEventWireup="true" CodeBehind="StorageAccountBlobs.aspx.cs"
    Inherits="WebRole1.StorageAccountBlobs" %>

<%@ Import Namespace="Microsoft.WindowsAzure.StorageClient" %>

<!DOCTYPE html PUBLIC "-//W3C//DTD XHTML 1.0 Transitional//EN" "http://www.w3.org/TR/
xhtml1/DTD/xhtml1-transitional.dtd">
<html xmlns="http://www.w3.org/1999/xhtml">
<head runat="server">
    <title></title>
</head>
<body>
    <form id="form1" runat="server">
    <div>
        <p>
            <asp:FileUpload id="imageUpload" runat="server" />
            <asp:Button Text="Upload" runat="server" onClick="upload_Click" />
        </p>
        <p>
            <asp:Repeater ID="gridBlob" runat="server">
                <ItemTemplate>
                    <img src='<%# ((IListBlobItem)Container.DataItem).Uri %>' />
                </ItemTemplate>
            </asp:Repeater>
        </p>
    </div>
    </form>
</body>
</html>
```

4. When a user clicks the button, the button fires the *upload_Click* event handler. Therefore, you need to obtain a container reference and use one of the upload methods provided by the *CloudBlob* class. Type the following code into the code-behind file:

```
protected void upload_Click(object sender, EventArgs e)
{
   CloudStorageAccount account =
     CloudStorageAccount.FromConfigurationSetting("DataConnectionString");
   CloudBlobClient blobClient = account.CreateCloudBlobClient();
```

```
        CloudBlobContainer container = blobClient.GetContainerReference("images");

        CloudBlob blob = container.GetBlobReference(imageUpload.FileName);

        blob.UploadFromStream(imageUpload.FileContent);

    }
```

The first part of the code contains nothing new compared to the *Page_PreRender* method you used in the preceding example. The next-to-last line of code asks the container for a *CloudBlob* instance by passing the desired blob name to the *GetBlobReference* method. This method does not create anything, nor does it connect to the storage account; it just constructs a new *CloudBlob* class with a complete URI, starting from the container URI. The last line of code creates the new blob by passing the content of the received file to the service.

If you run the sample and upload a new image (for example, another logo), you would end up with something like the following page.

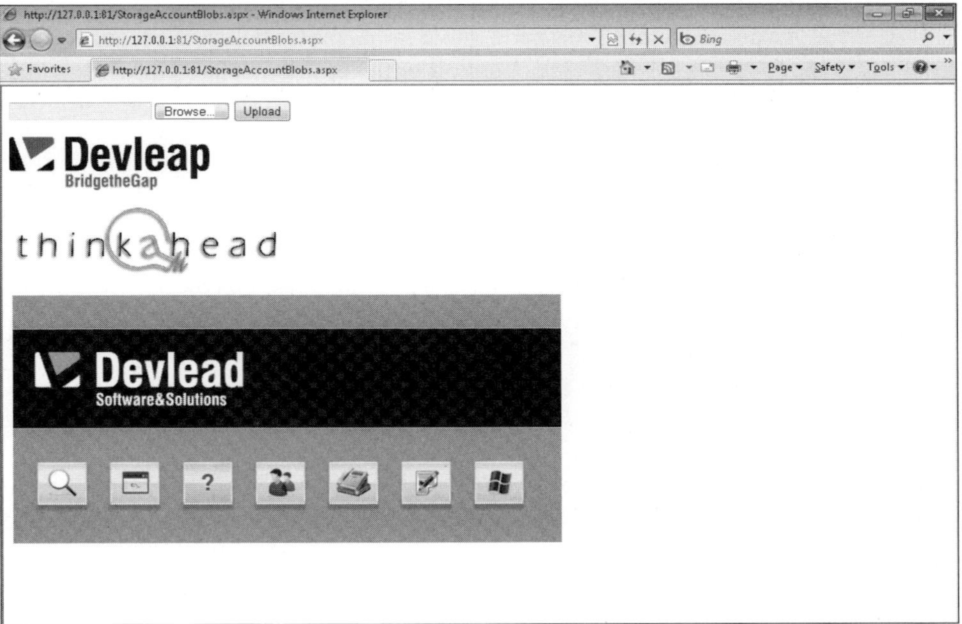

You can refine this code by refactoring the first three lines of code in the last example into a single method that you can call from the *Page_PreRender* method. The second improvement you should make before using this code is to add a *try/catch* block around each method call that invokes a service operation. Remember that the *CreateCloudBlobClient* method and the *GetReference* method do not invoke service operations, but the *UploadFromStream* and the *ListBlobs* methods do make a call to the service. The exceptions you can catch are based on the *StorageException* class, which represents every exception thrown by the library during a failed service call. To be more specific, you can use one of the two derived classes, *StorageClientException* or *StorageServerException*, which represent a problem in the request (such as an incorrect parameter) and a problem with the service itself, respectively.

Create a Container from Code

To complete your example, you need to add the code to create a container. The perfect place to do that is during application initialization. Because the application is a classic ASP.NET application, you can place this code in the *Application_Start* pipeline event.

1. Open the Global.asax.cs file and find the *Application_Start* method.

   Just below the Setup CloudStorageAccount Configuration Setting Publisher region you added in the previous procedure, call the *CreateIfNotExist* method on an instance of *CloudBlobContainer*. To create the *CloudBlobContainer* instance, use the same code you reviewed in the previous two procedures.

2. If you haven't refactored this code into a single method, add the following code before the call to the *Application_Start* method of the base class. Remember that because the new container must be publicly available, you have to assign proper permissions to it:

```
CloudStorageAccount account =
   CloudStorageAccount.FromConfigurationSetting("DataConnectionString");

CloudBlobClient blobClient = account.CreateCloudBlobClient();

CloudBlobContainer container = blobClient.GetContainerReference("images");

container.CreateIfNotExist();

BlobContainerPermissions permissions = container.GetPermissions();
permissions.PublicAccess = BlobContainerPublicAccessType.Container;
container.SetPermissions(permissions);
```

Before moving to the next chapter, in which you analyze tables, queues, and the Worker Role, test the completed code in your local environment. The test demonstrates that you can create a container from code, showing the usefulness of the Storage Client API. By making a small change in the configuration file, you can adapt the solution so that you can test it locally or use the live storage account.

To make that change to the configuration file, to use the local emulator, open the configuration settings for your Web Role and choose the Use Development Storage option for the *DataConnectionString* setting. You can do that in the Storage Configuration dialog box, or you can do it directly in the *TextBox* in the Configuration Settings, by typing **UseDevelopmentStorage=true**, as shown in the following figure.

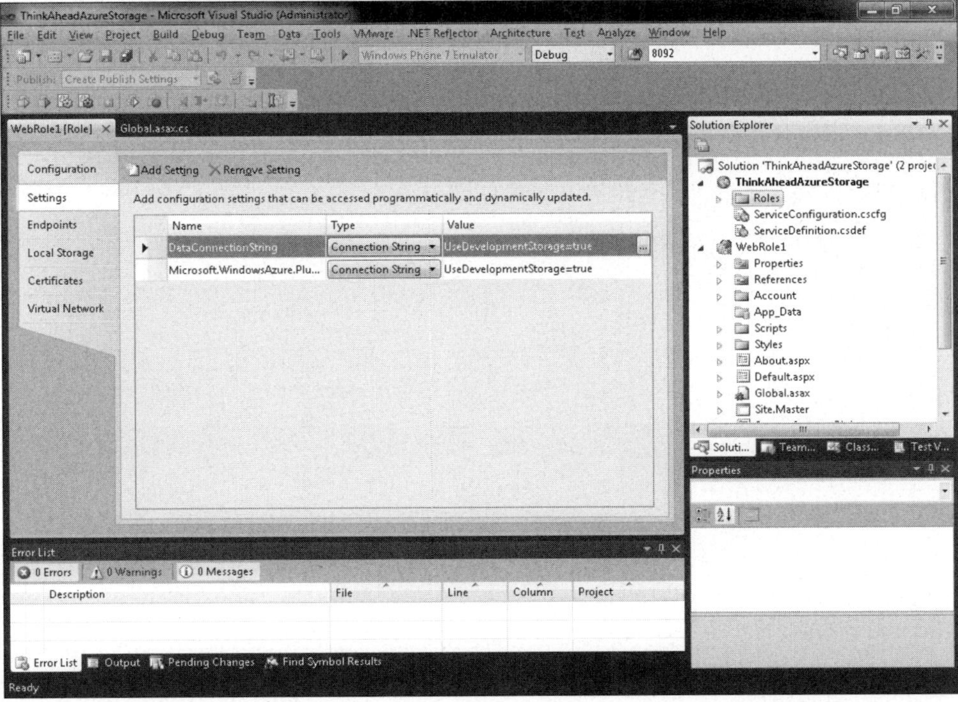

You can now test the solution by adding new images to the container created by the Windows Azure compute emulator using the code you placed in the *Application_Start* method. You can switch back to the live storage account whenever you want—but be very careful during the deploy operation; if you are testing the solution using the Windows Azure storage emulator storage and you deploy the ServiceConfiguration.cscfg file to Windows Azure, your role will fail, because there is no Windows Azure storage emulator in the cloud.

You can use the Windows Azure storage emulator interface to start and stop the service, reset the service instances, or shut down the entire service, as shown in the following figure.

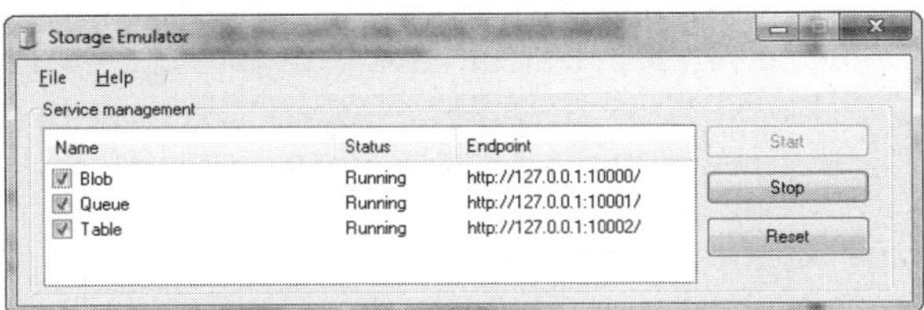

The emulator is a Windows process (DSService.exe) that simulates the various endpoints exposed for blobs, tables, and queues using different ports on the local machine. In the previous figure, for example, port 10000 is reserved for exposing the blob service. A request to the local service has a different URI scheme compared to the real cloud service, but the storage client library takes care of this difference for you. If you want to work at a lower level and compose the HTTP/REST request manually, make sure you form the correct URI.

Running the proposed code against the emulator and uploading two images results in the following underlying requests to *localhost*, shown with the HTTP trace in the following figure.

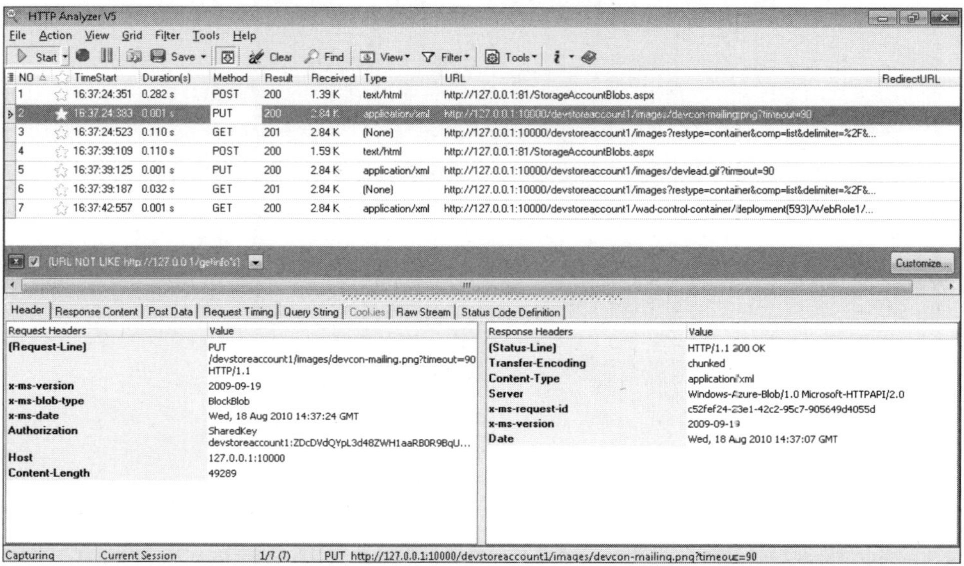

As you can see, the first request is simply a *POST* to the ASP.NET page. The page code asks for a *PUT* to create the image in the local storage. The third request is made by the *Page_PreRender* method when it asks for the list of blobs in the *images* container. The next *POST/PUT/GET* sequence occurs during the second upload operation, and the last *GET* is a diagnostic *ping* operation performed by the fabric (which you learn more about in Chapter 6).

Summary

In this chapter, you used the local Windows Azure compute emulator to explore your first Web Role project structure and behavior, and then deployed the solution to Windows Azure using the portal.

You were introduced to local storage for caching remote resources, and a more complete introduction to an Windows Azure storage account using live development accounts. You were introduced to the Windows Azure Management Tool and the API from a cloud project, and then shown how to test your solutions using the local emulator.

Quick Reference

To	Do this
Download the Windows Azure Management Tool	Go to *http://www.azure.com*, select the developers section, and then choose the Tools subsection.
Access blobs in the Storage Account	Make an HTTP/REST request or use the Windows Azure Storage Account library.
Debug and test your applications in the compute emulator	In Visual Studio, press F5. You can debug locally and use the live Storage Account.
See the content of a Storage Account	Use the Windows Azure Management Tool or the Visual Studio Server Explorer.

Chapter 5

Tables, Queues, and Worker Roles

After completing this chapter, you will be able to

- Use the API to store and retrieve application entities in storage account tables.
- Use the storage emulator to test the application locally.
- Use queues to decouple applications.
- Create a Worker Role project to perform background processes.

In Chapter 4, "Windows Azure Storage," you saw how to work with the Windows Azure storage account and used the project portal to create a new storage account. Then you were introduced to the Windows Azure Management Tool to gain experience with the features for managing blobs and containers. At the end of the chapter, you developed a simple application that uses the *StorageClient* API to store blobs both in the local simulated environment and the live account.

This chapter extends to both tables and queues the same concepts applied to blobs. It also introduces the Worker Role project type.

> **Note** Because URLs, UI names, and procedures may vary over time, some of them may be out of date by the time you read this. In that case, my best advice is to start looking for the information about the Windows Azure product on the Windows Azure home page (*http://www.azure.com*). Information included in this book was accurate at the time of writing.

The Table Service

As discussed at the beginning of Chapter 4, a Windows Azure storage account is a perfect place to store blobs (even large ones) and application entities (such as business entities) in tables, and it provides a queued mechanism that helps to decouple an application's front end from its back-end logic. The official definition for this feature at the time of this writing is as follows (Microsoft Corporation, Windows Azure website, 2011, *http://www.microsoft.com/windowsazure/*):

> *The Table Service offers structured storage in the form of tables. Tables store data as [a] collection of entities. Entities are similar to rows. An entity has a primary key and a set of properties. A property is a name, typed-value pair, similar to a column.*

The Table Service is exposed via the REST API for working with tables and their data.

Note In this section, you also use some APIs that leverage the Open Data Protocol (OData) and Windows Communication Foundation (WCF) Data Services (formerly named ADO.NET Data Services). If you need an introduction to these concepts, you can jump to Chapter 8, "OData, WCF Data Services, and Astoria Offline," read at least the first section, and then come back to this chapter to proceed with the storage concepts. You don't have to have a complete understanding of OData to follow the information in this chapter. All you need is a basic understanding of the REST protocol.

More Info For more information about the REST protocol, review the Wikipedia site at *http://en.wikipedia.org/wiki/REST*. For more information about OData, refer to *http://www.odata.org*. Note that sites and links change, and these were current at the time of this writing.

Local storage is not suitable for storing permanent or temporary application data, because the data is local to the specific virtual machine running your application. To store permanent application data that can survive application and node crashes and be shared among different nodes, you can use the Blob Service, which can also be exposed to outside clients.

The same storage concepts that apply to the Blob Service apply to the Table Service. The store is exposed via HTTP and can be accessed by any application on any platform because it uses the standard REST protocol. Access to the data occurs via an assigned shared key. The *StorageClient* library has classes and methods that simplify the code needed to manage data you store with the Blob Service. The data itself is replicated to different nodes to guarantee fault tolerance.

However, despite the few similarities shared by the Blob Service and the Table Service, the Table Service is really quite different in these ways:

- It organizes data in tables rather than in containers.
- Each table is represented by a flexible structured set of properties. A container contains files.
- Each table is composed of rows. Each row represents an entity, not a file.
- Developers have control over table data storage. For example, you can partition a table by using a specified key and can spread a table across several nodes. In contrast, blob management is automatic.
- Each table row has a primary key that represents the entity it contains. A blob is represented by the file and its file name.

Remember that the storage services are independent from the application hosted in the cloud. In other words, any client can access the storage service by using the HTTP protocol, and there are no differences in the code you would use to access a cloud-hosted application or an on-premises client except latency: an on-premises application pays a penalty, because it is probably several nodes away from the storage service.

To use the Table Service, you have to create a storage account on the Windows Azure portal. If you didn't create a storage account in Chapter 4, you can do it now.

When you create a Windows Azure storage account, the operating system allocates some space in some of the nodes in the selected data center to store your data, and gives you the URL to use in your REST query to manage the data. In this section, you use the URL *http://* account.*table.core.windows.net,* where *account* represents the name you chose for your public storage account name.

The following figure shows the portal displaying the result of the New Service wizard.

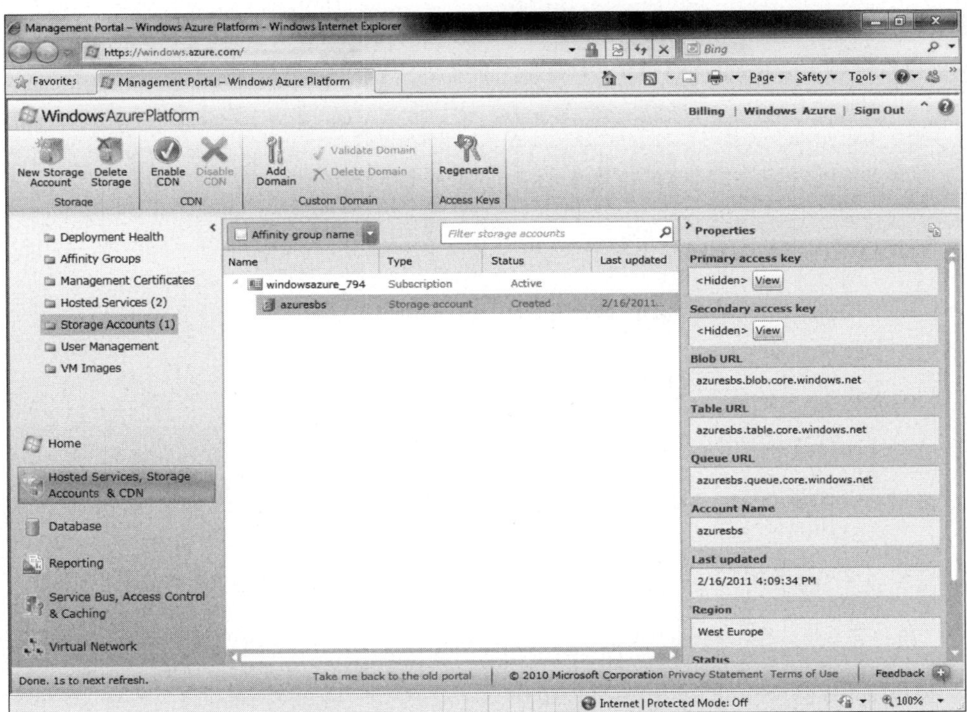

You have what you need to store an entity in table rows in your live cloud-based storage.

Use the Table Service APIs

To use the Table Service APIs in this procedure, you can either create a new Microsoft Visual Studio Web Role project, or use the same project you created in the previous chapter. The page name will be different from the example either way, so proceed as you prefer.

1. Open the project that you created at the beginning of Chapter 4. If you did not create the project, create a new Windows Azure Project using a Microsoft ASP.NET Web Role template.
2. Verify that the project contains a reference to the *Microsoft.WindowsAzure.StorageClient* library. A Visual Studio Windows Azure Project needs the reference to this library to use the storage account service, as well as to the *Microsoft.WindowsAzure.ServiceRuntime*.
3. If you chose to create a new project, add a new setting in the Web Role configuration to store the account and key information. To do so, double-click the name *WebRole1* in the Roles section of your cloud project, and then click the Add Setting button in the Settings section of the configuration. Name this new setting **DataConnectionString** and select Connection String as its type.
4. Click the ellipsis (...) button to open the Storage Account Connection String dialog box shown in the following figure. Type your account name and the related key. If you don't have an Internet connection, you can select the Use The Windows Azure Storage Emulator option.

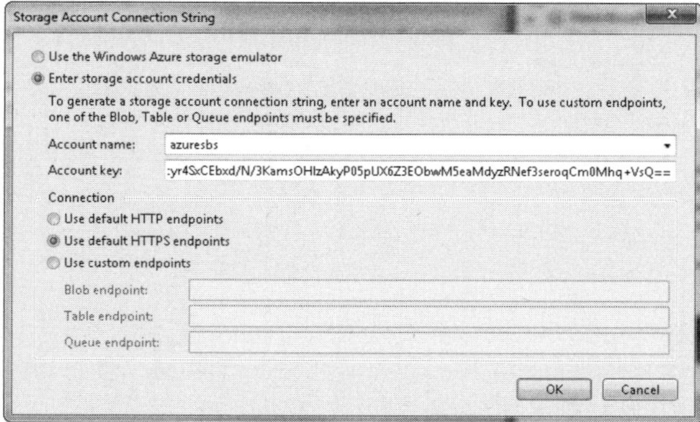

5. Click the OK button to build the storage connection string and return to the Settings page.

The storage emulator simulates the Table Service the same way it simulates the Blob Service. The Table Service responds to requests to *localhost* using the port 10002 (the Blob Service reserves the port 10001).

After this procedure, your project contains everything you need to use the StorageClient API to access your storage account. Before you can manage entities using the Table Service, you have to define the structure of the row you want to use for save or read operations. A table can contain heterogeneous entities—and each entity can have a completely different structure from the others. In this way, you can use the same table to store customers and orders. If you prefer, you can define a Customers table to store customer data and an Orders table to store orders, or, if you prefer yet a third way of structuring data, you can partition a table using a partition key of your choice to divide customers from orders.

In common scenarios, you might prefer different tables to store different types of entities as you normally would in a classic database, but you should take into account that the Table Service stores data in a nonrelational store. The service cannot enforce a constraint on an entity: you have to do that in your code. If you think about the storage from this point of view, there is no difference between storing different entities in different tables and storing them all in the same table.

You should also take performance considerations into account when you define your storage structure. Entities in the same table by default belong to the same partition, and every partition is guaranteed to be stored in the same physical node. If the number of data access operations grows up, the node might respond slowly. To achieve better performance, you can split the table into different partitions. Splitting data in different partitions allows the load balancer to store each partition in different nodes, increasing the scalability of the table. The first possibility that comes to mind is to divide a table by entity type—let's say Orders and Customers.

However, doing so does not exclude the possibility of ending up with a stressed node anyway, because Windows Azure cannot use the load balancer to serve the query on Orders by multiple nodes. In these scenarios, you can use the partition key to split the same entity type in the same table (for example, by order year), to achieve better scaling. The presented options are just examples, and unfortunately, there is no unique solution, but don't worry—you learn more about these issues in upcoming chapters.

The partition key is one of the three required fields for each table. Every row needs a *RowKey* field that, in tandem with the *PartitionKey* field, forms what is considered to be the primary key of that entity inside the store. The third field is a self-generated time stamp called *Timestamp*. The *StorageClient* library exposes a base class called *TableServiceEntity* that contains these three fields. The *PartitionKey* and *RowKey* are represented by two strings, whereas the *Timestamp* is exposed by a .NET *DateTime* type. Listing 5-1 shows the decompiled code for this class.

LISTING 5-1 TableServiceEntity definition.

```
[CLSCompliant(false), DataServiceKey(new string[] { "PartitionKey", "RowKey" })]
public abstract class TableServiceEntity
{
    // Fields
    [CompilerGenerated]
    private string <PartitionKey>k__BackingField;
    [CompilerGenerated]
    private string <RowKey>k__BackingField;
    [CompilerGenerated]
    private DateTime <Timestamp>k__BackingField;

    // Methods
    protected TableServiceEntity();
    protected TableServiceEntity(string partitionKey, string rowKey);

    // Properties
    public virtual string PartitionKey { [CompilerGenerated] get;
        [CompilerGenerated] set; }
    public virtual string RowKey { [CompilerGenerated] get;
        [CompilerGenerated] set; }
    public DateTime Timestamp { [CompilerGenerated] get;
        [CompilerGenerated] set; }
}
```

The code, taken directly from Reflector, shows the properties just mentioned as well as a constructor that takes the primary key composed by the two strings.

You can derive from this class to build your entities and use the *TableServiceContext* class to manage the entity. This class encapsulates the complexity of serializing and deserializing *TableServiceEntity* instances into REST format, and translates the *Add*, *Update*, and *Delete* operations in HTTP requests to the configured Table Service. Each request handled by the *TableServiceContext* class contains the shared key header, just like the *CloudBlobClient* example you saw in the previous chapter.

The suffix *Context* might remind you of LINQ to SQL, Entity Framework, or ADO.NET/WCF Data Services. In fact, the class *TableServiceContext* derives from the WCF Data Service *DataServiceContext* class, and extends it to expose the *StorageCredential* property used to store the account name and properties. These values can be inferred from the configuration and are used in every request to build the URL (local or live) and the authentication header.

Define an Entity

To begin working with the Table Service, you need to define an entity.

1. Add a new class to your project and name it **Message**.
2. Give the class a public accessor and derive it from *TableServiceEntity*, as shown in the code in step 4 of this procedure.

3. Place the *using* statements, as shown in the code in step 4.

4. Expose a simple property called *Body* with *public* scope.

```
using System;
using System.Collections.Generic;
using System.Linq;
using System.Web;
using Microsoft.WindowsAzure.StorageClient;

namespace WebRole1
{
    public class Message : TableServiceEntity
    {
        public String Body { get; set; }
    }
}
```

You use this *Message* class to store the body of the message that a user inserts in a page (which you create soon). Before creating the page, you create the context that encapsulates every request to the Table Service.

Create the Client-Side Context

1. Add a new class to the project and name it **MessageServiceContext**.
2. Derive your class from *TableServiceContext*.
3. Place the *using* statements, as shown in the code at the end of this procedure.
4. Add a constructor that calls the constructor of the base class to pass it the storage credentials and the base address. There is nothing special to do in the constructor, because the constructor of the base class will take care of that information by reading it from the configuration file.
5. Add a reference to *System.Data.Services.Client*. This reference is important because the class *TableServiceContext* derives from *DataServiceContext*, which is defined in this assembly.
6. To avoid complex code in the calling page, you can expose some methods that encapsulate the lines of code needed to instantiate the *Message* class, assign a *PartitionKey* and a *RowKey* automatically to it, and add the instance to the *Messages* table.

The following code is the complete code for the class described in this procedure:

```
using System;
using System.Collections.Generic;
using System.Linq;
using System.Web;
using Microsoft.WindowsAzure.StorageClient;
using Microsoft.WindowsAzure;

namespace WebRole1
```

```
{
    public class MessageServiceContext : TableServiceContext
    {
        public MessageServiceContext(string baseAddress,
                StorageCredentials credentials) : base(baseAddress, credentials)
        {
        }

        public void AddMessage(string body)
        {
            Message m = new Message();
            m.PartitionKey = "A";
            m.RowKey = Guid.NewGuid().ToString();

            m.Body = body;

            this.AddObject("Messages", m);
            this.SaveChanges();
        }
    }
}
```

The class constructor takes two parameters and passes them directly to the base class constructor. The *AddMessage* method takes the string that represents the message text and constructs one instance of the *Message* class. This method is useful for avoiding duplication of the assignment of the partition key, the row key, and the name of the corresponding table.

You've completed the complex part. Using these classes is straightforward, as shown in the next procedure. You now have everything you need to create an ASP.NET page that takes a message by the user, creates a new *Message* entity, and adds it to the context, asking the latter to save the message to the Table Service.

Use the Table Service

The client-side context represented by the *AzureStorageServiceContext* you created in the previous procedure lets you perform almost every Create, Read, Update, Delete (CRUD) operation that the OData standard defines. In this procedure, you create a simple chat application. Users can enter a message in the ASP.NET page, and the context saves the message to a row in the *Messages* table. The page also presents the list of saved messages by requesting them from the Table Service.

1. Create a new ASP.NET Web Form and name it **StorageAccountTable**.
2. Insert a *TextBox* control where users will insert a message. Name it ***messageTextBox***.
3. Insert a *Button* control under the *TextBox* and name it **addButton**.
4. Set the *OnClick* attribute of the *Button* control to ***addButton_Click*** to bind the click to the corresponding event handler. The following shows the complete code for the ASP.NET Web Form:

```
<%@ Page Language="C#" AutoEventWireup="true" CodeBehind="StorageAccountTable.aspx.cs"
Inherits="WebRole1.StorageAccountTable" %>

<!DOCTYPE html PUBLIC "-//W3C//DTD XHTML 1.0 Transitional//EN" "http://www.w3.org/TR/
xhtml1/DTD/xhtml1-transitional.dtd">

<html xmlns="http://www.w3.org/1999/xhtml">
<head runat="server">
    <title></title>
</head>
<body>
    <form id="form1" runat="server">
    <div>
    <p>
     <asp:TextBox ID="messageTextBox" runat="server" />
    </p>
    <p>
     <asp:Button Text="Add" ID="addButton" runat="server" onclick="addButton_Click" />
    </p>
    </div>
    </form>
</body>
</html>
```

5. In the code-behind file, StorageAccounTable.aspx.cs, retrieve the account information from the *CloudStorageAccount* class and pass it to the constructor of the *MessageServiceContext* class you created in the previous procedure.

   Because you already encapsulated the data access logic in the *MessageServiceContext* class, the code-behind file is very simple—just the following code:

```
using System;
using System.Collections.Generic;
using System.Linq;
using System.Web;
using System.Web.UI;
using System.Web.UI.WebControls;
using Microsoft.WindowsAzure.ServiceRuntime;
using Microsoft.WindowsAzure;

namespace WebRole1
{
    public partial class StorageAccountTable : System.Web.UI.Page
    {
        protected void Page_Load(object sender, EventArgs e)
        {

        }

        protected void addButton_Click(object sender, EventArgs e)
        {
            var account = CloudStorageAccount.
                 FromConfigurationSetting("DataConnectionString");
            var context = new MessageServiceContext(
```

```
                    account.TableEndpoint.ToString(), account.Credentials);

                    context.AddMessage(messageTextBox.Text);
            }
        }
    }
```

The first line of code in the *addButton_Click* event handler reads the value of the *DataConnectionString* setting using the built-in *CloudStorageAccount* class, just as it did in the previous chapter to access the Blob Service.

The second line of code calls the *AddMessage* method, which performs the operation to add the message to the storage.

6. Before you can compile and run this code, you need to add a reference to the *System.Data.Services.Client* assembly because the base class you implemented in this sample uses the types defined in that assembly.
7. If you started a new project in this chapter, you also need to add the *CloudStorageAccount* region into your Global.asax.cs *Application_Start* method. Just copy the following code to your *Application_Start* method:

```
#region Setup CloudStorageAccount Configuration Setting Publisher

// This code sets up a handler to update CloudStorageAccount instances when their
// corresponding configuration settings change in the service configuration file.
CloudStorageAccount.SetConfigurationSettingPublisher((configName, configSetter) =>
{
    // Provide the configSetter with the initial value
    configSetter(RoleEnvironment.GetConfigurationSettingValue(configName));

    RoleEnvironment.Changed += (sender, arg) =>
    {
        if (arg.Changes.OfType<RoleEnvironmentConfigurationSettingChange>()
            .Any((change) => (change.ConfigurationSettingName == configName)))
        {
            // The corresponding configuration setting has changed,
            // propagate the value
            if (!configSetter(RoleEnvironment.
                    GetConfigurationSettingValue(configName)))
            {
                // In this case, the change to the storage account credentials in the
                // service configuration is significant enough that the role needs
                // to be recycled in order to use the latest settings. (for example,
                // the endpoint has changed)
                RoleEnvironment.RequestRecycle();
            }
        }
    };
});
#endregion
```

8. Last but not least, you must create the table that will contain the messages. Just as you did in the previous chapter, you can create the container for these rows in the *Application_Start* method of your Global.asax.cs file, as shown in the following code. Before using this code, add a *using* statement for *Microsoft.WindowsAzure* and *Microsoft.WindowsAzure.StorageAccount:*

```
CloudStorageAccount account =
    CloudStorageAccount.FromConfigurationSetting("DataConnectionString");
CloudTableClient tableClient = account.CreateCloudTableClient();
tableClient.CreateTableIfNotExist("Messages");
```

You can now test your solution. (If you chose to use your live account, remember that you need an Internet connection.) Before testing your solution, remember to set the StorageAccountTable.aspx page as the start page for the project. The code used in this sample so far does not include any exception handling.

If you followed the procedure, you end up with a plain webpage that has a single field in which a user can enter a message and click the Add button, as shown in the following figure. After typing some text, for example, "hello everyone," the page simply presents a new copy of the insert form.

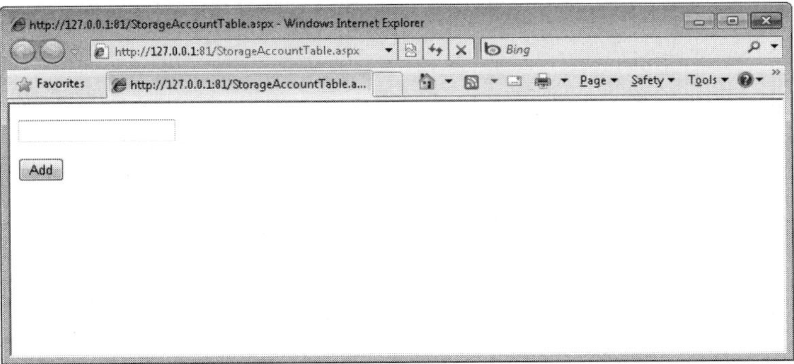

Query the Table Services

Now you can add a query to the page that requests—and even filters—the messages the page saves in the storage account. The procedure to perform these operations is very similar to the previous procedure; you need to add a public property to expose a query that encapsulates the logic to ask the service for the messages, and then call that method from the page *Load* event to present the list of stored messages to the user.

1. Add a new public property to the *MessageServiceContext* class. Name it **Messages** and type **IQueryable<Message>** as the return type.
2. In the *get* accessor, call the *CreateQuery* method inherited from the *DataServiceContext* base class, and pass the value *Messages* as a parameter.

The complete code for *MessageDataServiceContext* must be identical to the following:

```
using System;
using System.Collections.Generic;
using System.Linq;
using System.Web;
using Microsoft.WindowsAzure.StorageClient;
using Microsoft.WindowsAzure;

namespace WebRole1
{
    public class MessageServiceContext : TableServiceContext
    {
        public MessageServiceContext(string baseAddress, StorageCredentials
            credentials) : base(baseAddress, credentials)
        {
        }

        public IQueryable<Message> Messages
        {
            get
            {
                return this.CreateQuery<Message>("Messages");
            }
        }

        public void AddMessage(string body)
        {
            Message m = new Message();
            m.PartitionKey = "A";
            m.RowKey = Guid.NewGuid().ToString();

            m.Body = body;

            this.AddObject("Messages", m);
            this.SaveChanges();
        }
    }
}
```

The *CreateQuery<T>* method is inherited from the *DataServiceContext* class from which the base class *TableServiceDataServiceContext* derives. The method returns the *IQueryable* interface that represents the expression tree from which the code can construct a query. The *CreateQuery* method needs the name of the defined table so that it can store the entity. The purpose of all this work is to encapsulate the name of the table and the query-building operation inside a class, to free your page code from having to repeatedly perform this task. This way, from a page, you just need to ask for the *Messages* property whenever you want to build a query to the Table Service to get *Message* entities.

3. In the *Page_Render* event, create an instance of the *CloudStorageAccount* using the *FromConfigurationSetting* static method.

4. Use the *CloudStorageAccount* instance to pass the parameter to the *MessgeServiceDataContext* constructor, as you did in the previous procedure.

5. Add a *Repeater* control to the StorageAccountTable.aspx page:

```
<%@ Page Language="C#" AutoEventWireup="true" CodeBehind="StorageAccountTable.aspx.cs"
Inherits="WebRole1.StorageAccountTable" %>

<!DOCTYPE html PUBLIC "-//W3C//DTD XHTML 1.0 Transitional//EN"
   "http://www.w3.org/TR/xhtml1/DTD/xhtml1-transitional.dtd">

<html xmlns="http://www.w3.org/1999/xhtml">
<head runat="server">
    <title></title>
</head>
<body>
    <form id="form1" runat="server">
    <div>
       <p>
        <asp:TextBox ID="messageTextBox" runat="server" />
       </p>
       <p>
        <asp:Button Text="Add" ID="addButton" runat="server"
           onclick="addButton_Click" />
       </p>
       <p>
        <asp:Repeater ID="gridTable" runat="server">
            <ItemTemplate>
       <p>
                <%# ((WebRole1.Message)Container.DataItem).Body %></p>
            </ItemTemplate>
        </asp:Repeater>

       </p>

    </div>
    </form>
</body>
```

6. Bind the *Messages* property you built in step 2 to the *Repeater* control in the *Page_PreRender* event, as shown in the following excerpt:

```
public partial class StorageAccountTable : System.Web.UI.Page
{
     protected void Page_PreRender(object sender, EventArgs e)
     {
        var account = CloudStorageAccount.FromConfigurationSetting(
           "DataConnectionString");
        var context = new MessageServiceContext(
           account.TableEndpoint.ToString(), account.Credentials);
        gridTable.DataSource = context.Messages;
        gridTable.DataBind();
     }
```

7. Run the project by pressing F5.

The code you created in this procedure produces the result shown in the following figure. (I added some random messages using the interface to create the message list below the Add button.)

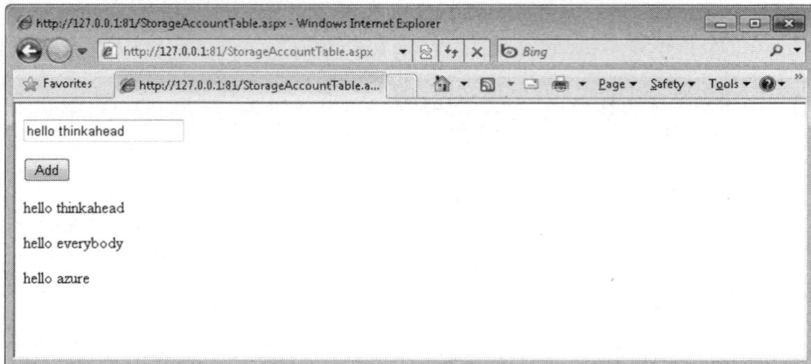

Looking at the code more closely, you can see that the *TableServiceServiceContext* class constructs a REST query and sends it to the table service configured in the ServiceConfiguration.cscfg file by using the authorization header with the shared key value.

Using an HTTP tracer, you can view the underlying REST query, shown in the following tracer output.

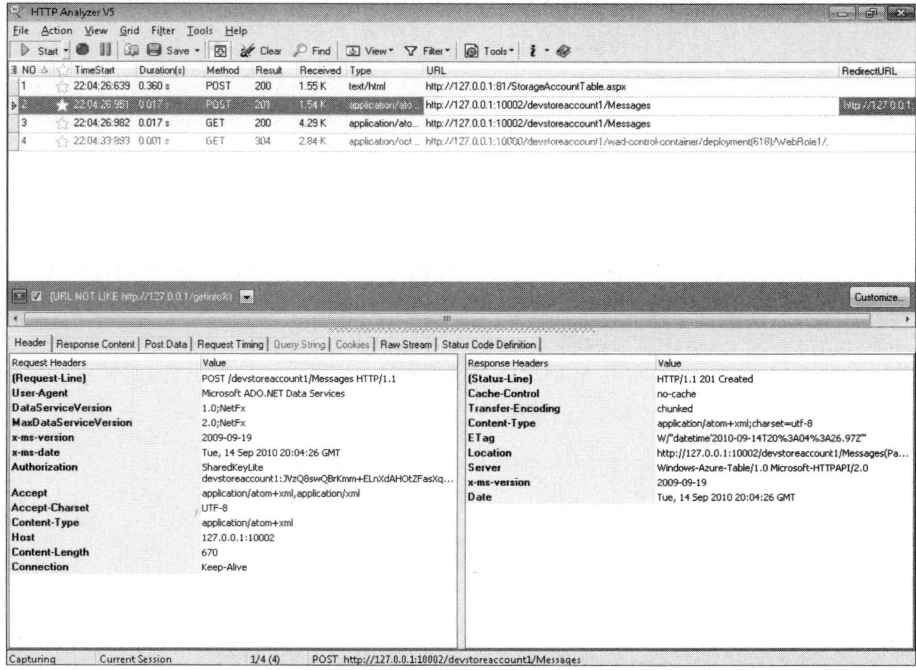

The first traced request is the *POST* directed to the StorageAccountTable.aspx page running in the compute emulator I am using to test the code on my machine. The request is straightforward: it posts the input field with the message I entered.

The second traced *POST* is more interesting. As you can see in the preceding image, the request URL is *http://127.0.0.1:10002/StorageAccount1/Messages*, which represents a REST request to the storage emulator that simulates the table service. If I change my ServiceConfiguration.cscfg to point to the live storage account, the *TableServiceContext* class adjusts the URL accordingly.

As you learned in the previous chapter, local URLs differ from live URLs in the order of the suffix and prefix. For a live URL, the storage account is the first element, but for a local URL, the storage account (*devstoreaccount1* is the default value) follows the socket indication.

The header shows you that the authorization was done via the *SharedKey* derived from the one configured in ServiceConfiguration.cscfg.

The third request is a *GET* performed by the *PreRender* method of the page, which requests the list of messages. The last request is not related to the current example; it's just a check performed by the compute emulator to the deployed service to verify that it is up and running.

You can expose the *Messages* properties as *IQueryable* because the *CreateQuery<T>* method of the *DataServiceContext* base class returns that type of interface. This also means that you can leverage the remote query functionality of the LINQ to the data service provider to request the messages filtered by one or more properties, or to take only a few elements. As you learn in Chapter 8, the provider is smart enough to build the REST query syntax based on the clause you specified for the *IQueryable* interface and implemented in the provider. For example, you can request a sorting clause using the following code:

```
context.Messages.Take(2)
```

That limits the message list to just two items, shown in the following figure.

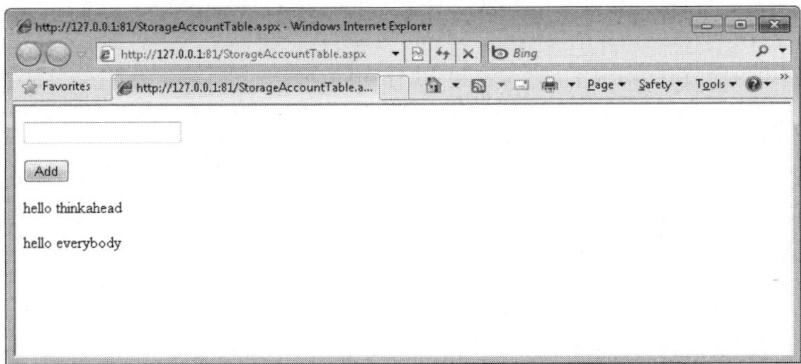

Please remember that each LINQ provider can implement only a subset of the *IQueryable* interface's defined methods—and the compiler cannot help you during the compilation because it cannot discover whether an implemented method throws a *NotImplementedException*. Check the documentation of the underlying provider or try the query directly in a unit test to make sure no errors occur. The provider throws an exception every time a method is not supported. Specifically, the *DataServiceContext* class throws a *DataServiceException* exception.

The resulting REST query created by the underlying data service provider will adhere to OData syntax. In this case, the URL contains a query string with the keyword *top* equal to the number of requested elements. You can try this query directly in your browser; the response will be similar to that shown in the Response Content tab in the following figure.

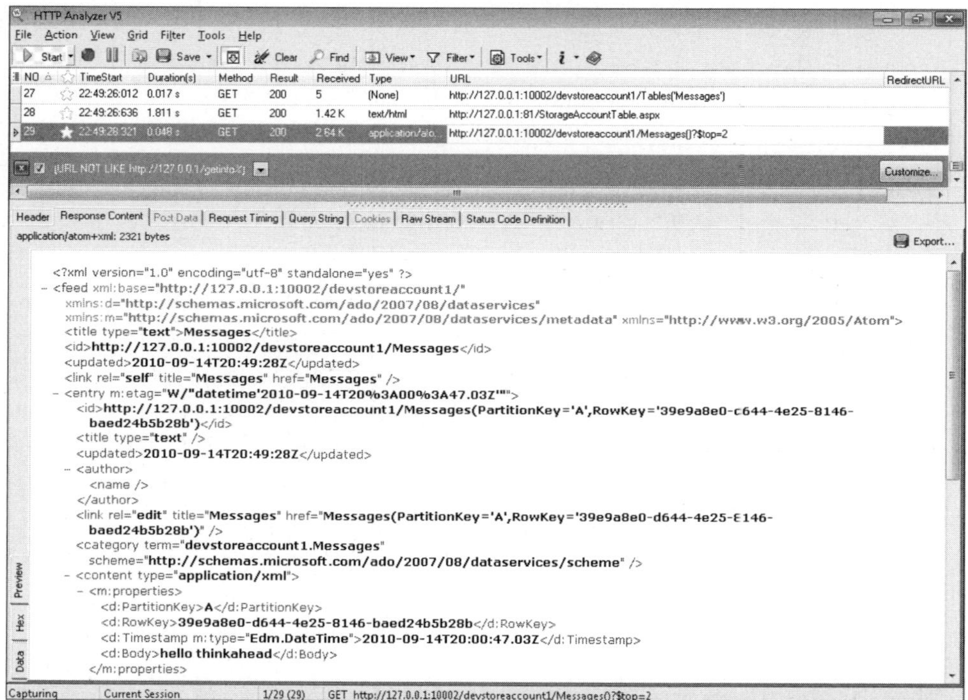

If you are using the storage emulator, all the tables and entities are stored in your local Microsoft SQL Server or local SQL Express database, so you can inspect the data inside the relative tables or even create new entities directly in the local database. This is advantageous when you practice test-driven development or you use unit tests, because a unit test usually needs some data to work with. You can use common tools (such as Visual Studio Ultimate) to generate sample data automatically that you can test against.

The last image that I want to show you before moving to the Queue Service and the Worker Role is of the Windows Azure Management Tool. This tool can query the Table Service in either the local or live storage account, and it can request the contained entities for each existing table. Because the entities in a table can be heterogeneous, the resulting grid may be confusing. Bear in mind that the tool cannot create tables or entities from scratch.

The next figure shows the Windows Azure Management Tool with an open query that requests all data from the message table you built and used in this section. Each row contains the assigned partition and row key, an autogenerated time stamp column, and a button that deletes the entire record. From the right pane, you can refresh the view or delete the entire table.

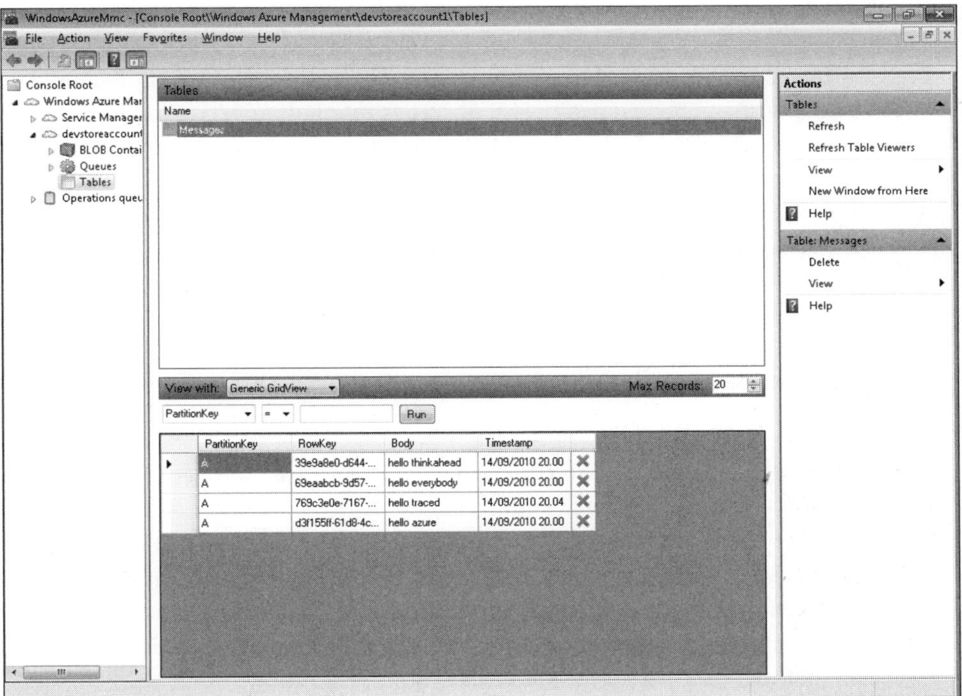

The Queue Service

Chapter 4 discussed how to use the Blob Service to store and retrieve files from the storage account. So far in this chapter, you've been introduced to the Table Service, which can manage application entities. But you can store another type of data in the storage account as well: a message. Just as a blob resides in a container and an entity in a table, a message resides in a queue.

As the name implies, a *queue* is not a store in which a software solution inserts, modifies, and/or reads application data; a queue is a place where an application can store messages that usually represent a yet-to-be-completed operation. The same application can retrieve these messages to process them later. The messages can also be dequeued by a different application that's responsible for taking care of the process.

You could use a table to achieve a similar result. For example, an application could insert an entity in a table, and another application could read the row and process it, but in the same way a database table isn't best suited for this kind of operation in an on-premises solution, the database table isn't the most suitable approach for a cloud solution. In the Microsoft world, you use Microsoft Message Queuing (MSMQ)—the message queue mechanism exposed directly by the operating system since 1996—or you opt for the SQL Server Message Broker that appeared for the first time in SQL Server 2005.

The cloud storage account exposes a smart queue service that serves to decouple one application from another. The first example that comes to mind is decoupling the front end of Azure, the Web Role, from the back end, called the Worker Role. A *Worker Role* is simply a role that, by default, is not exposed to the outside and is dedicated to performing some operations in the back end. A Worker Role project example is an order processing application that receives orders as messages created by the front end. In this approach, the front end is free to do other work immediately after inserting the message in the queue. If each order coming from the users had to be processed immediately by the page (or the business layer) on the front end, the Web Role could not be so scalable. Indeed, if a thread is processing the order, it cannot serve other requests, as it could do if the whole process were moved to the back end.

The decoupling practice has been common in enterprise solutions since the 1990s because it's a powerful way to serve more requests (and consequently orders) than a single front-end server could normally satisfy. If you think about the Windows Azure instances, this technique becomes even more powerful, because you can adjust the number of instances of the back end and the front end independently. If you want to accept more orders, you increase the number of instances for the front end. If the queue length is increasing, you can adjust the number of instances of the Worker Role accordingly.

The Worker Role project can access the local storage you learned about in the previous chapter, as well as the storage account blobs, tables, and queues; it can also access the Internet and use a Microsoft SQL Azure database, and it can use the Windows Azure AppFabric. There are no differences in what a Worker Role can do versus a Web Role. The main difference between these two roles is that the Worker Role starts with the corresponding staging or production environment, and loops continuously to perform its actions, whereas a Web Role sits behind the HTTP/HTTPS protocol and receives requests from the Internet or other roles in the cloud.

You learn how to put a message in the queue by using the Web Role and then consume that message using the Worker Role. The example in this section uses a message that contains just a string with the order to pass from the front end to the back end. You can use this approach to send a serialized order class.

Create the Message

In this procedure, you create the queue and then create a new page in the Web Role project that inserts the message in the queue. You add a new Worker Role project to the solution to dequeue the message.

1. Create a new ASP.NET page and name it **StorageAccountQueue**.
2. Add a *TextBox* control into which the user will type a message. Name it **orderTextBox**.
3. Insert a *Button* control under the *TextBox* control and name it **addButton**.
4. Set the *OnClick* attribute of the *Button* control to **addButton_Click** to bind the click to the corresponding event handler. The complete code for the ASP.NET page is shown here:

```
<%@ Page Language="C#" AutoEventWireup="true" CodeBehind="StorageAccountQueue.aspx.cs"
Inherits="WebRole1.StorageAccountQueue" %>

<!DOCTYPE html PUBLIC "-//W3C//DTD XHTML 1.0 Transitional//EN" "http://www.w3.org/TR
/xhtml1/DTD/xhtml1-transitional.dtd">

<html xmlns="http://www.w3.org/1999/xhtml">
<head runat="server">
    <title></title>
</head>
<body>
    <form id="form1" runat="server">
    <div>
    <p>
     <asp:TextBox ID="orderTextBox" runat="server" />
    </p>
    <p>
     <asp:Button Text="Add" ID="addButton" runat="server"
         onclick="addButton_Click" />
    </p>
    </div>
    </form>
</body>
</html>
```

5. In the code-behind file, create the *addButton_Click* event handler.
6. Copy the following code into the *addButton_Click* event handler:

```
using System;
using System.Collections.Generic;
using System.Linq;
using System.Web;
using System.Web.UI;
using System.Web.UI.WebControls;
using Microsoft.WindowsAzure;
using Microsoft.WindowsAzure.StorageClient;

namespace WebRole1
```

```
{
    public partial class StorageAccountQueue : System.Web.UI.Page
    {
        protected void addButton_Click(object sender, EventArgs e)
        {
            var account =
               CloudStorageAccount.FromConfigurationSetting("DataConnectionString");

            CloudQueueClient queueClient = account.CreateCloudQueueClient();

            CloudQueue queue = queueClient.GetQueueReference("orders");

            CloudQueueMessage m = new CloudQueueMessage(orderTextBox.Text);

            queue.AddMessage(m);
        }

    }
}
```

This code is very similar to the one used for the Blob Service; you must obtain a service proxy to begin working with the storage account. The *CloudStorageAccount* class provides a method called *CreateCloudQueueClient* that serves this purpose. The method returns a *CloudQueueClient* that represents the proxy for the Queue Service. You can call *GetQueueReference*("queuename") to obtain a reference to a queue, and then use the *CloudQueue* class to insert messages into or read messages from the queue.

The *CloudQueueMessage* class represents a message that will be serialized automatically to pass the content in the underline REST request.

7. Create the queue in the same place you created the table in the previous section. The *Application_Start* method of the *Global* class (in Global.asax.cs) is a good place to put this code, as you can see in the following excerpt:

```
CloudQueueClient queueClient = account.CreateCloudQueueClient();
CloudQueue queue = queueClient.GetQueueReference("orders");
queue.CreateIfNotExist();
```

Note The *CreateIfNotExist* method asks the service to create the queue if it does not exist yet, so the method makes a request to the service anyway.

8. Set this new StorageAccountQueue.aspx as the start page, and run the project. The page looks similar to the following figure.

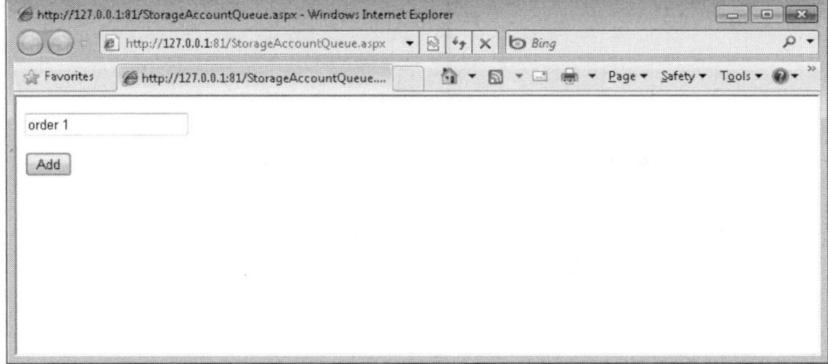

9. Type **order 1** into the text box and click the Add button to insert a new order into the queue.

You can verify the presence of the message in the queue by using the Windows Azure Management Tool, as shown in the next figure. Double-click the Queues item in the left pane to see the queues defined in the storage that is referenced by the specified connection. If you double-click the single existing queue, you can see the messages you inserted from the page. To each message, the service (local development storage in this example) assigns a unique GUID and an insertion date. (My personal computer has the date presented using the Italian convention: the day is 15 and month is September.)

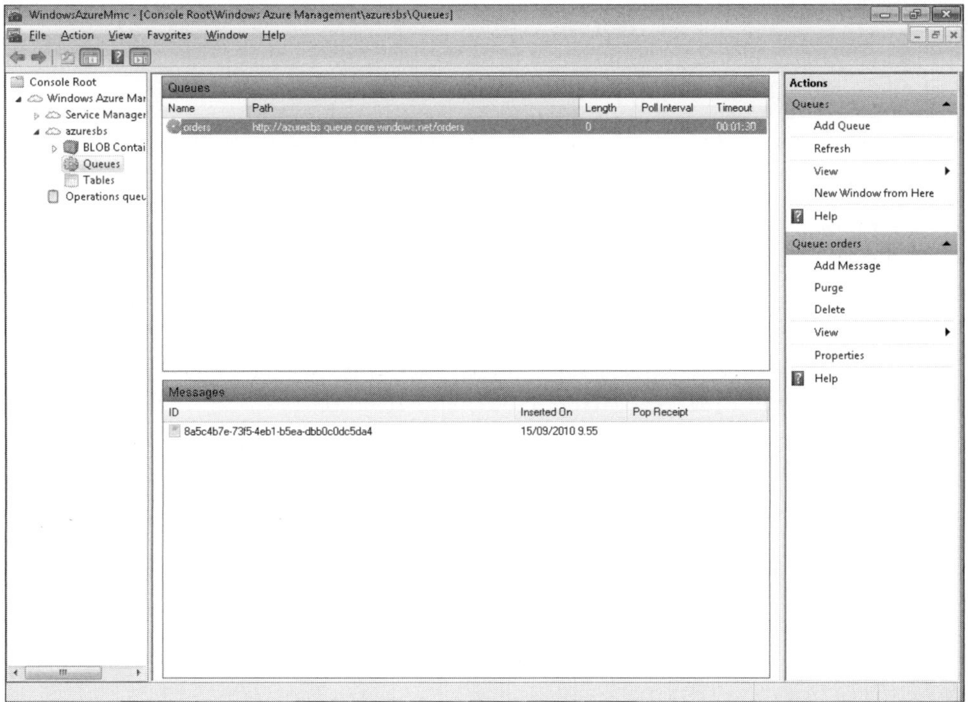

Create the Worker Role Project

In this procedure, you create the Worker Role project. After configuring the role so that it points to the same storage account as the WebRole project, you write the code to dequeue the messages from the orders queue.

1. In the Solution Explorer window, expand the cloud project, and right-click the Roles folder.
2. In the shortcut menu, choose Add, and then select New Worker Role Project.
3. In the left pane, verify that the language selected is C#, and in the right pane, verify that the Worker Role is the selected template.
4. Leave the default name set to WorkerRole1. (In a production environment, you should assign a more meaningful name to your project.)
5. Click the Add button to add the WorkerRole1 project to the solution.

The solution now contains two projects and two roles in the Roles folder in the cloud project. Visual Studio added a new configuration section for the new project. The first task you want to complete is opening the ServiceConfiguration.cscfg file or the visual editor provided by the IDE to configure this new project with the information for the storage account.

Configure the Worker Role Project

You can copy the configuration value from the *WebRole1* configuration to the *WorkerRole1* configuration, as you saw how to do in the previous chapter.

1. Open the configuration window by double-clicking the WebRole1 node in the Roles folder of the cloud project.
2. Go to the Setting tab and copy the text inside the *DataConnectionString*.
3. Open the configuration window for the WorkerRole1 project.
4. Go to the Setting tab and click the Add Setting button to add a new configuration element.
5. Type **DataConnectionString** in the name text box.
6. Paste the value you copied into the value text box.

Now your new Worker Role project has a pointer to the storage account you used to store the message.

As you might remember from the previous section, a project needs the Configuration Setting Publisher code before it can use the *CloudStorageAccount* class.

Configure the Setting Publisher

Because you already inserted the code to configure the Configuration Setting Publisher in the WebRole1 project, you can copy it from that project to this new one.

1. Open the Global.asax.cs file in the WebRole1 project.
2. Find the code region named Setup CloudStorageAccount Configuration Setting Publisher in the *Application_Start* method and copy it to the Clipboard.
3. Open the WorkerRole.cs file in the WorkerRole1 project.
4. Find the *OnStart* method and paste the code inside it before the return statement.

Now you have everything you need to dequeue an order from the orders queue.

A Worker Role project does not have a user interface, because its job is to process requests continuously or at scheduled intervals. You have to override the *Run* method of the base class to build your own loop (or timers) and insert the code inside the loop. The Visual Studio template provides the following default code:

```
using System;
using System.Collections.Generic;
using System.Diagnostics;
using System.Linq;
using System.Net;
using System.Threading;
using Microsoft.WindowsAzure;
using Microsoft.WindowsAzure.Diagnostics;
using Microsoft.WindowsAzure.ServiceRuntime;
using Microsoft.WindowsAzure.StorageClient;

namespace WorkerRole1
{
    public class WorkerRole : RoleEntryPoint
    {
        public override void Run()
        {
            // This is a sample worker implementation. Replace with your logic.
            Trace.WriteLine("WorkerRole1 entry point called", "Information");

            while (true)
            {
                Thread.Sleep(10000);
                Trace.WriteLine("Working", "Information");
            }
        }
    }
}
```

As you can see, the template proposes an infinite loop with a delay of 10 seconds between two consecutive operations. You can do whatever you want inside this method: call external web services, access the Table or Blob Service, use SQL Azure—or, as in the next procedure, dequeue and process a message.

Dequeue Messages from the Worker Role

You need to obtain a reference to the queue using the same code used in your WebRole1 project, and then dequeue a message using the Queue Service proxy. When you receive a message, you can process the order accordingly. The purpose of this example is to show you how to dequeue a message and send its content to the trace infrastructure.

1. Create an instance of the *CloudStorageAccount* class using the *FromConfigurationSetting* static method.
2. Create the Queue Service proxy by calling the *CreateCloudQueueClient* method of the *CloudStorageAccount* class.
3. Get a *CloudQueue* object by using the *GetQueueReference* method of the created proxy.
4. Inside the proposed loop, use the *CloudQueue.GetMessage* method to obtain a *CloudQueueMessage*.
5. Test whether you obtained a message by comparing the result to *null* before calling the *AsString* method to analyze its content. Make sure you always do this.
6. Delete the retrieved message from the queue.

The resulting code is shown in the following listing:

```
public override void Run()
{
   // This is a sample worker implementation. Replace with your logic.
   Trace.WriteLine("WorkerRole1 entry point called", "Information");

   CloudStorageAccount account =
       CloudStorageAccount.FromConfigurationSetting("DataConnectionString");
   CloudQueueClient queueClient = account.CreateCloudQueueClient();
   CloudQueue queue = queueClient.GetQueueReference("orders");


   while (true)
   {
      CloudQueueMessage m = queue.GetMessage();
      if (m != null)
      {
         queue.DeleteMessage(m);

         Trace.WriteLine(m.AsString, "Information");
      }
      Thread.Sleep(2000);
   }
}
```

Assuming you didn't delete the existing message in the queue using the Windows Azure Management Tool, if you run this code, you end up with the compute emulator trace shown in the following figure.

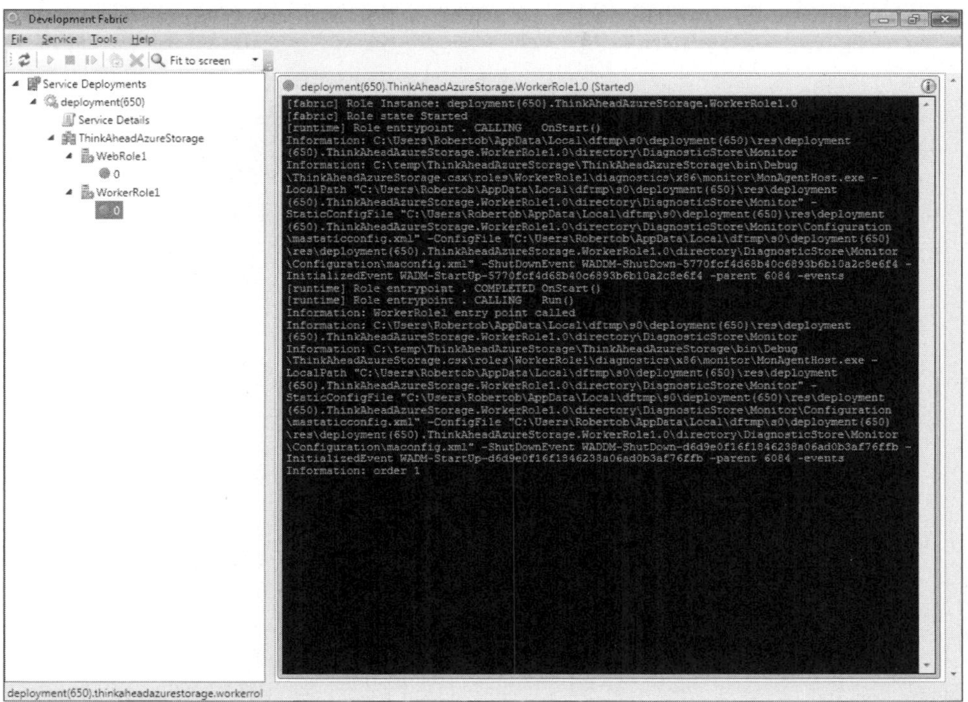

You can see the *order 1* information message at the end of the trace. With this process in place, you can insert new orders from the webpage and verify the process in the compute emulator trace. You can also change the *DataConnectionString* setting value to your live or local storage account.

Summary

This chapter provided a complete introduction to the Table Service, explaining how to use it in your solutions to store and retrieve entities. You saw how to use the Queue Service exposed by the storage account to decouple an application's front end from its back end. The queue service is a cloud-based queue system similar to the familiar Microsoft Message Queue you would use in an on-premises solution. In the last part of the chapter, you saw how a Worker Role project functions in a solution that built a simple order-processing system in the back end.

Quick Reference

To	Do this
Visually manage table entities	Use the Windows Azure Management Tool.
To create a storage account	Use the Windows Azure project portal and select New Service, choosing Storage Account as the project type.
Test the solution locally	Use the storage emulator.
Use a unit test to test the solution locally	Use the tables created by the storage emulator in the configured SQL instance.
Configure SQL Server instead of SQL Express	Use *DSInit.exe* /sqlinstance:<namedinstance>.

Chapter 6

Windows Azure Operating System Details

After completing this chapter, you will be able to

- Understand the billing section of the portal.
- Configure Affinity Groups to avoid latency.
- Configure the Content Delivery Network.
- Deploy developer certificates to Windows Azure to simplify deployment.
- Configure diagnostics and logging.

The last two chapters showed the Windows Azure storage account at work. You used the project portal to create a storage account, and then used the Windows Azure Management Tool to understand the client interaction process for managing blobs, tables, and queues. At the end of the previous chapter, you developed a Worker Role to build a simple back end that dequeues order messages sent from the front-end Web Role.

This chapter provides you with some important details about the Windows Azure operating system.

Note Because URLs, UI names, and procedures may vary over time, some of them may be out of date by the time you read this. In that case, my best advice is to start looking for the information about the Windows Azure product on the Windows Azure home page (*http://www.azure.com*). Information included in this book was accurate at the time of writing.

Live ID, Subscriptions, and Billing

It's important to understand the relationship among your Windows Live ID account, subscriptions, and services. As you learned in previous chapters, you must have a Windows Live ID account to access the Windows Azure portal, Windows Azure AppFabric, and the Microsoft SQL Azure portal. In the portals, the term *subscription* refers to a group of services that shares a common billing account. You have to choose a subscription each time you want to create a new hosted service or a new storage account. You can also switch from one subscription to another in the Create A New Hosted Service dialog box. The Choose A Subscription drop-down list is visible in the following figure.

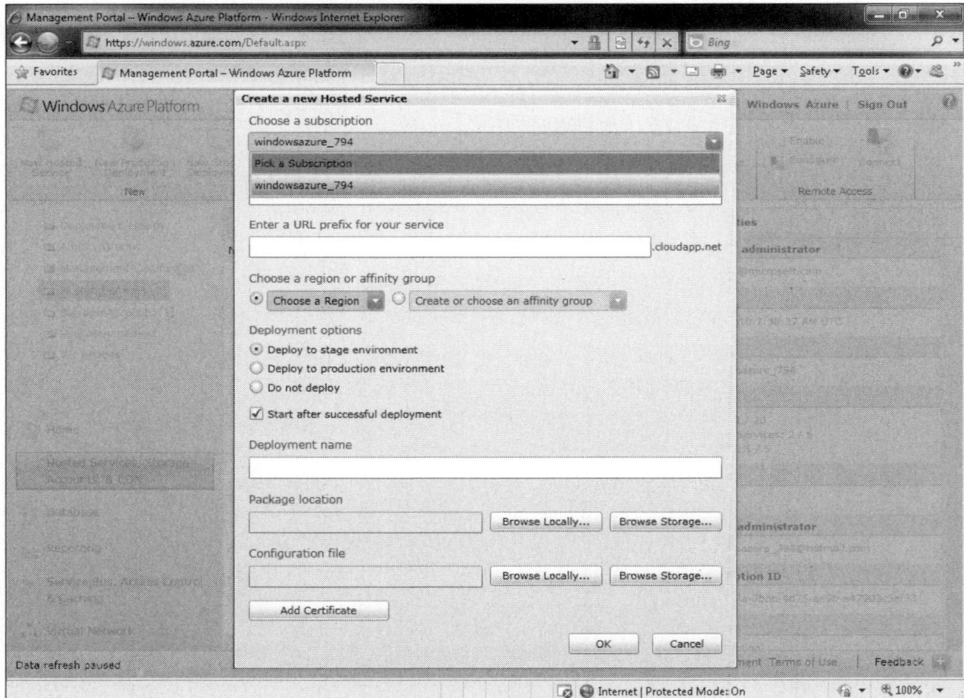

Recall from Chapter 3, "Creating a Web Role Project," that every subscription can contain multiple services. You can view and manage all subscriptions connected to your Windows Live ID account on the home page of the Management Portal, as shown in Figure 6-1.

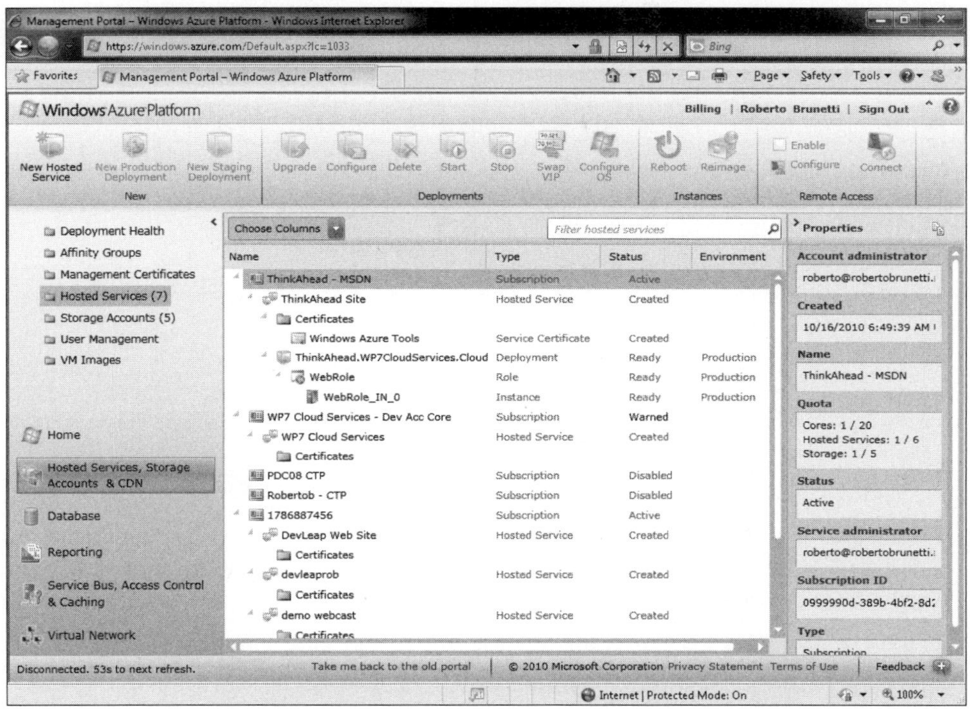

FIGURE 6-1 Windows Azure Management Portal.

At the top of the page, on the right side, is a link named Billing that takes you to the Billing section of the portal. That link leads to the Microsoft Online Services Customer Portal—the public website for the Business Online Productivity Suite (BPOS) services. The first time you use the platform, you must obtain an account. The link for creating a new account is on the Windows Azure Account page. You can reach this page by clicking the Get Your Account or the Buy or the Try links on the Windows Azure portal home page, shown in the following figure.

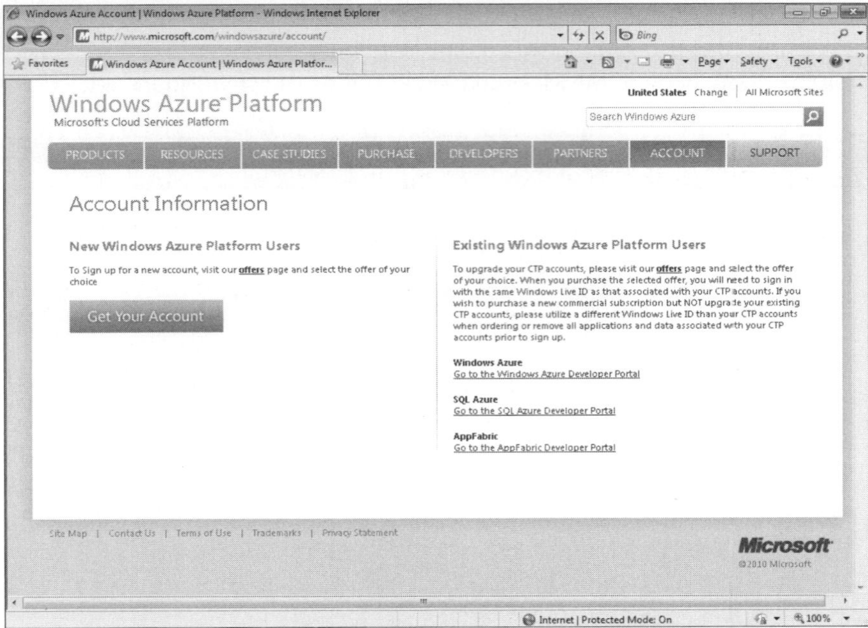

After obtaining an account, you can access the billing system to add one or more subscriptions to the account (and pay for them, too). Figure 6-2 shows the home page for the Microsoft Online Services Customer Portal.

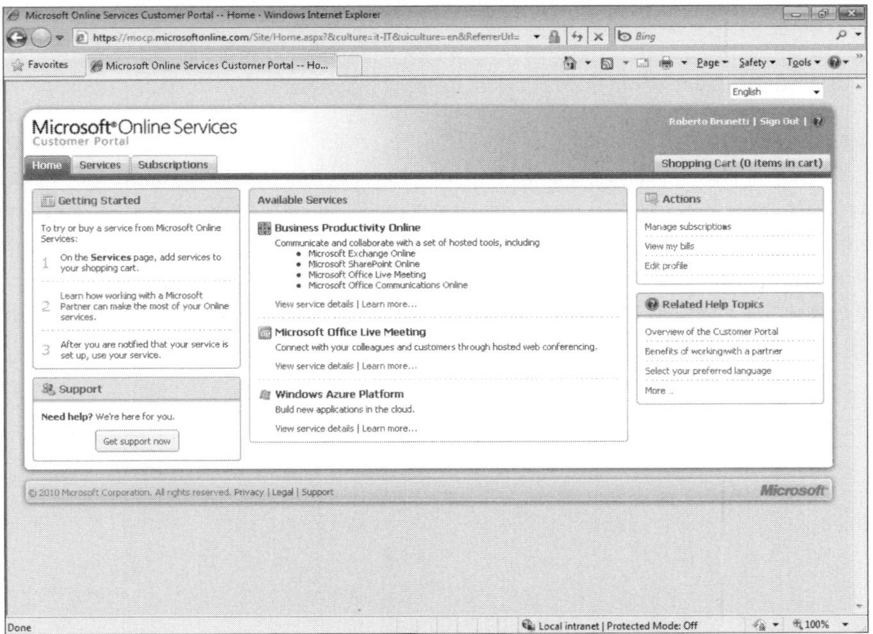

FIGURE 6-2 Microsoft Online Services Customer Portal home page.

From the Customer Portal, you can buy and associate various services that run the gamut from Microsoft Exchange Online to Microsoft Office Communication Online, and from Microsoft Office Live Meeting to Windows Azure platform services.

When you click an option, detailed prices and quotas are provided (as shown in the following figure). Every option provides detailed prices and quotas.

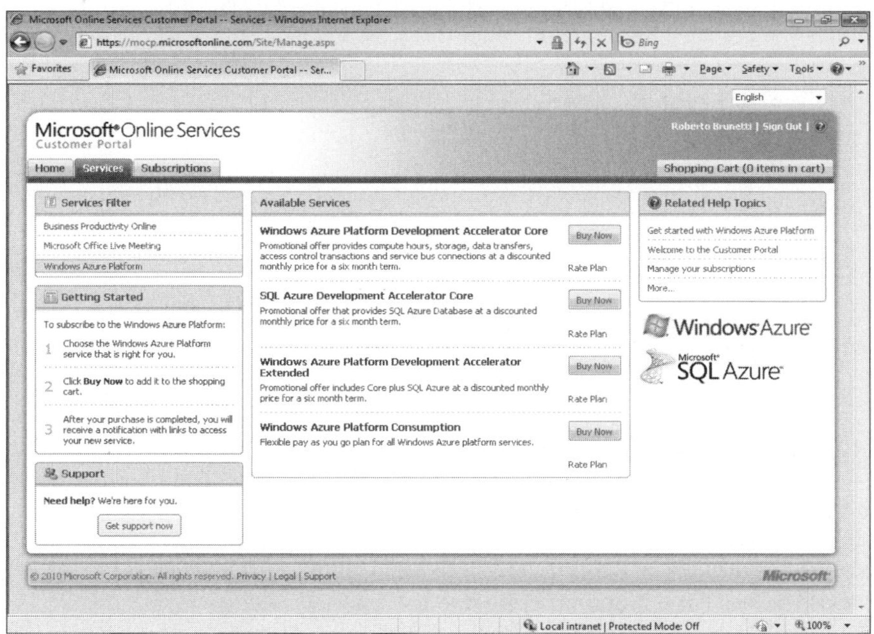

To purchase a service, you must provide your credit card information and have your card validated. The term *subscription* is synonymous with *project* in the Windows Azure portal. If you compare the subscription names shown in Figure 6-1 with the subscription names in Figure 6-3, you can see they match. The first match is for the project 1786887456, which corresponds to the Windows Azure Platform Introductory Special subscription shown in the Figure 6-3. The Exchange Online Standard subscription that you can see in the billing system is not displayed in the Windows Azure Management Portal because it is related to Microsoft Exchange Online.

Each subscription also has a numeric identifier. For every subscription except the Introductory Special, you can assign a meaningful name in the subscription detail page. Because a BPOS subscription corresponds to a subscription in the Windows Azure portal, you will find the assigned name in the Windows Azure portal as well.

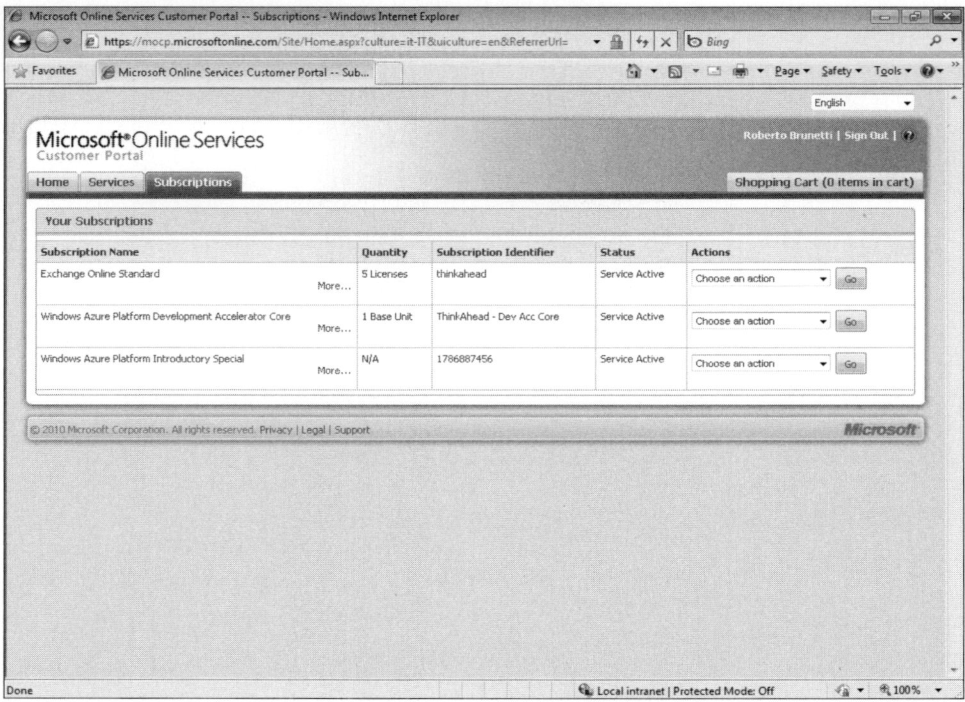

FIGURE 6-3 Subscription list in the Customer Portal.

As Figure 6-3 reveals, my account also includes an Exchange Online Standard subscription that does *not* have a corresponding project in the Windows Azure portal.

To download invoices or consult your current month's billing charges, use the View My Bills link (see Figure 6-2) to access the information for each service. In the same section of the page, you can choose the Subscription ID and see the details. You can also see detailed daily usage information that provides a complete list of every billable service. Each entry in this list shows the related service, the type of service (for instance, SQL Azure Web Edition), the region of the data center, the resource charged (computing power in numbers of hours, the database, or data transfer), the relative consumption value, the type of services, and their name. Figure 6-4 shows you one of my real subscriptions: the Development Accelerated Core project with one SQL Azure database showing charges for August and September 2010.

Figure 6-4 shows that I have two active instances, one for the Web Role, and another for the Worker Role. The total computed hours for a single day (the Windows Azure Compute line) is 48 (24 hours for each instance). The subscription is the test environment for a production web service that uses SQL Azure as the database for a Windows Phone 7 application called Save the Planet.

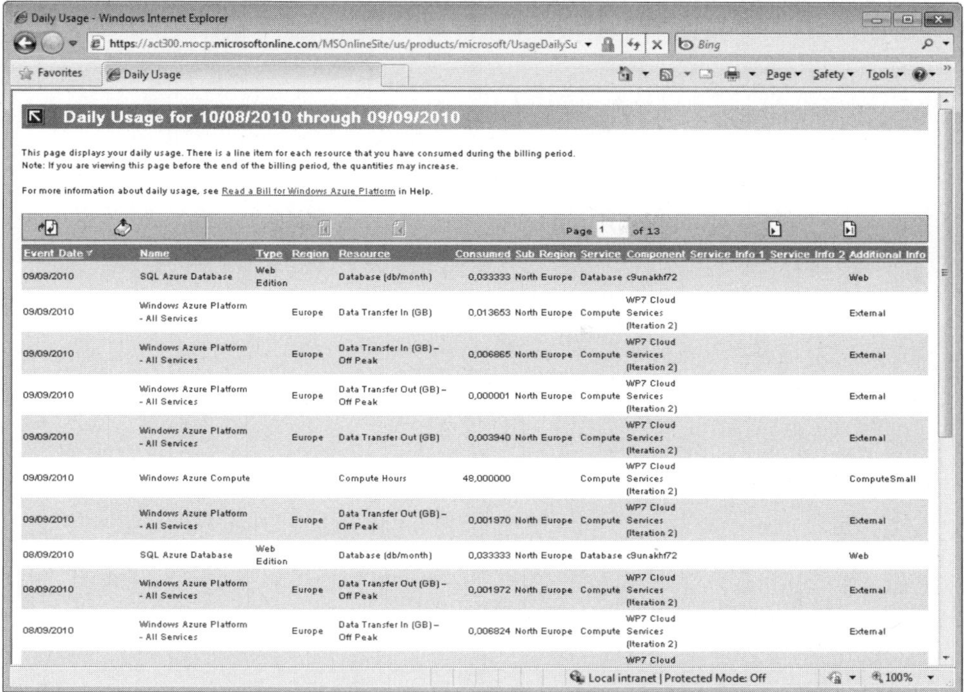

FIGURE 6-4 Daily Usage report.

Affinity Group

An *affinity group* is a group of nodes you can create to host different services in the same data center. The location is independent from the charges applied to the solution, so you can create as many affinity groups as you want.

You can create a new affinity group whenever you create a new hosted service or a new storage account as you learned in Chapter 4, "Windows Azure Storage," and you can fully manage these types of groups from the Account tab of a project in the Windows Azure portal.

Figure 6-5 shows the Create A New Hosted Service wizard.

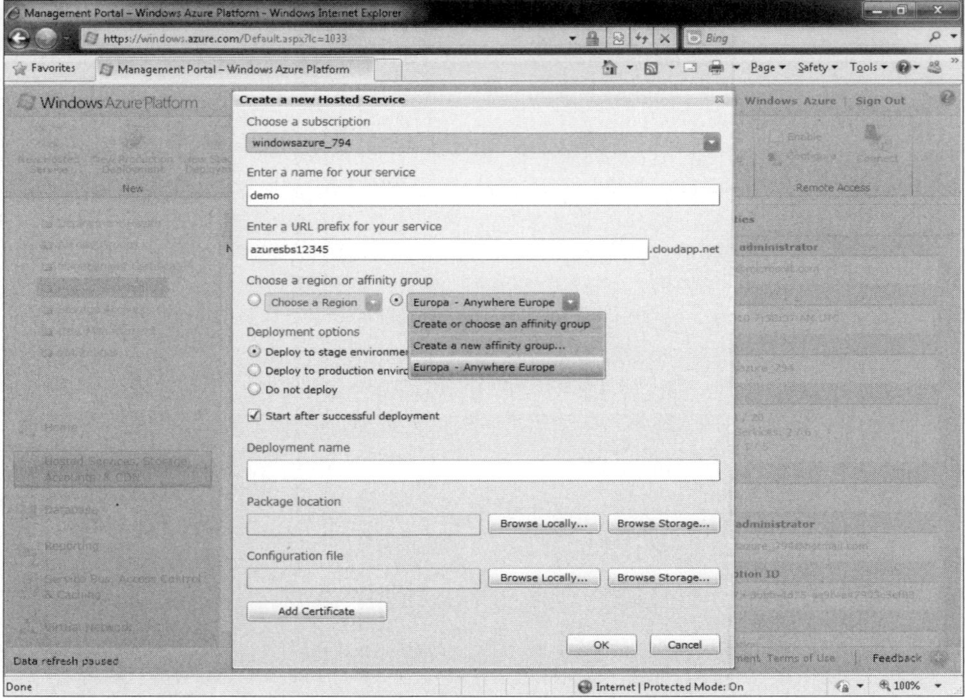

FIGURE 6-5 Affinity group selection.

As you learned in Chapter 2, "Introduction to the Windows Azure Platform," when you create a new service, you can select a region from the Choose A Region drop-down list box. Choosing a region creates the nodes for your service in the selected region, but it does not use any affinity group; the node can be anywhere in the region you choose. Two nodes in the same region are located in the same area of the world, but without any affinity group, one node might be very far away from other nodes in the same region. For instance, if you chose Europe – Anywhere Europe, one node might be placed in a German data center and another node in an Italian data center. There is no guarantee that two services in the same region belong to the same data center. The region parameter just means that the physical location of a service is within the selected region.

However, services in the same affinity group reside in nodes located in the *same* data center in the selected region. As you might have noticed in Figure 6-5, I created an affinity group called Europa (the Italian word for Europe) that resides in the Anywhere Europe region. This selection means that the new service I'm going to create will be placed in the same data center as the other nodes included in the Europa affinity group.

From the same page, you can create a new affinity group to store the new service and then associate that affinity group to other services. To manage the affinity group and see which services belong to which affinity groups, you have to click the Hosted Service, Storage

Accounts & CDN option on the portal home page and then click Affinity Groups, as shown in the following figure. The management page shows every affinity group in your subscription, the region it belongs to, and the relative status.

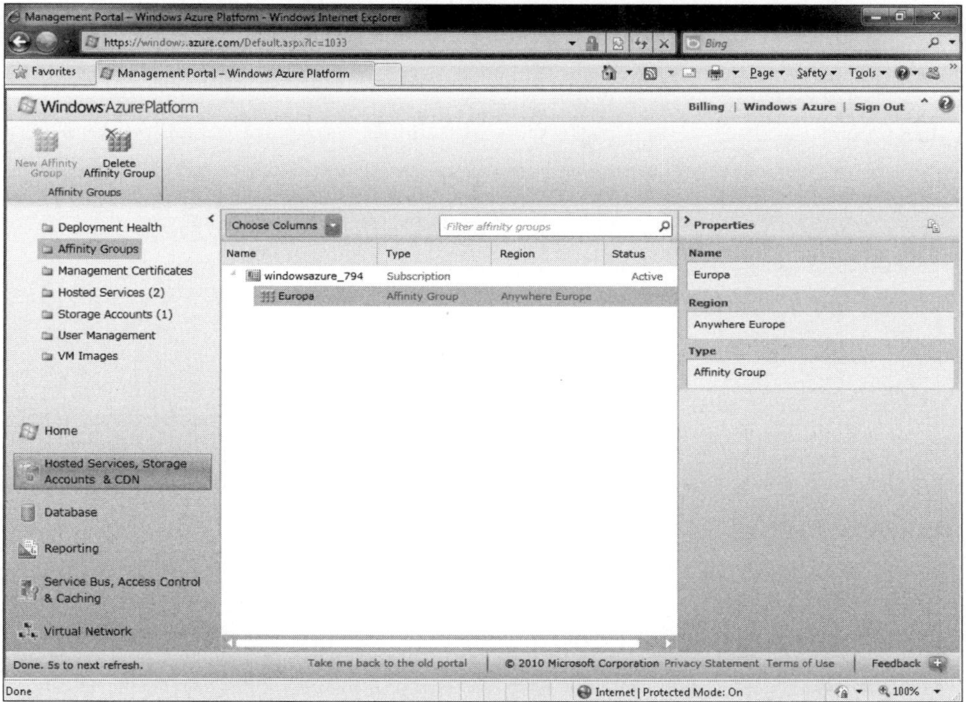

This affinity group keeps the Windows Phone 7 cloud services together (the service that hosts the WCF Data Services for the Windows Phone 7 application you saw in the billing section and the Storage Account service that manages the data associated with it). You can delete an affinity group using the Delete Affinity Group button.

Content Delivery Network

Now that you're familiar with the Affinity Group Service, you may have anticipated the following problem: when you create international applications or international websites, services within the same affinity group reside in the same data center, thus lowering the latency for calls between them. This technique works well inside the application, but what about the user? Suppose you chose the North Europe data center to host an application and services. Requests made by the application to storage would occur as quickly as possible to avoid the high latency that intradata center nodes might incur. However, consider an Australian user, who is pretty far away from the service and the storage. Remote users (those not located near the data center) would pay substantial latency costs to download data from the application or the storage, even when the application has no internal latency.

To avoid this user latency problem, you need to reduce the number of hops the request has to make. Fortunately, you can do that with the Content Delivery Network (CDN) Service. This service provides a convenient way to minimize latency, because it caches data in various geographic locations across the globe.

The CDN is tightly integrated with Azure Storage, as shown in Figure 6-6. To use it, you enable the CDN Service.

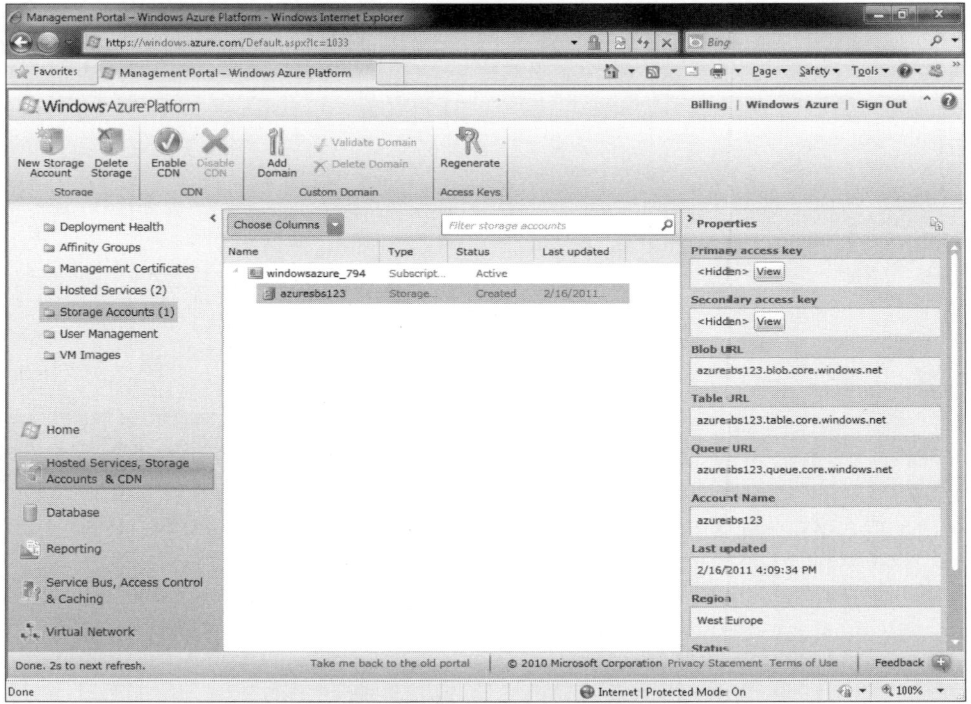

FIGURE 6-6 Storage account management.

Clicking the Enable CDN button in the toolbar turns on the CDN for that particular storage account—a process that requires up to 60 minutes to take effect. The delay occurs because the service distributes files and containers around the world. After the CDN is active, you must change the URL from which your blobs are accessible. The URL will be in the following format: *http://*<guid>*.vo.msecnd.net/*. The *guid* is autogenerated by the system.

The following figure shows the Enable CDN dialog box warning about the timeframe for activation as well as the link to the CDN billing plan.

Important Different charges apply when using the CDN, so before you activate it, read the billing information referenced in the dialog box carefully.

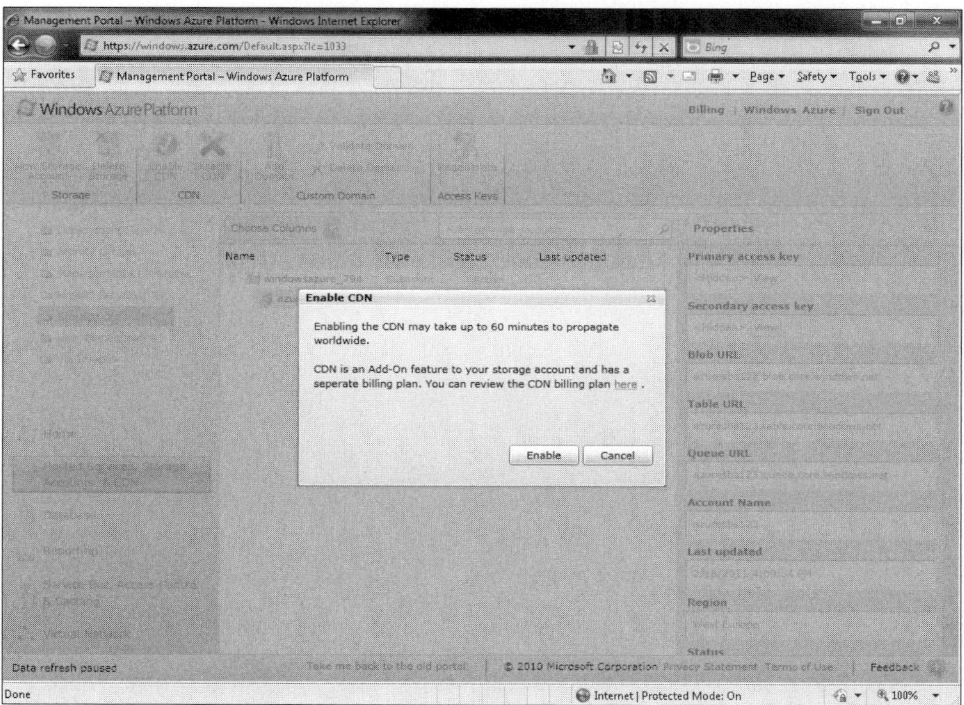

When using a CDN, you must consider an important issue concerning blobs. If you update a blob in the storage account, the new version will not be accessible by remote users until the Time To Live (TTL) setting on the previous version of the file expires. The default time interval for a Windows storage account is 72 hours; to adjust the TTL, you can set the *CacheControl* metadata property of the *CloudBlob* instance. Reducing this interval too much will make the CDN less effective. In practice, every operation on an existing blob, such as updating it, deleting it, or modifying some of its metadata, requires the system to propagate a fresh copy of that blob to all the CDN nodes around the world immediately after the TTL expires.

Certificates

Windows Azure can host and use two certificate types. The first type is the classic Secure Socket Layer (SSL) certificate that enables a Web Role to respond to HTTPS requests.

You can assign the SSL certificate to a single service, because it contains the HTTPS common names that correspond to the URLs. You can use your DNS name as an alias of the chosen service name. The upload procedure for a certificate is straightforward. To add a certificate, in the portal, click the Hosted Services, Storage Account & CDN button, click Hosted Services in the left toolbar, and select the Certificates item from the tree view that is related to the service you want to assign the certificate to. Click the Add Certificate button in the upper toolbar and upload the certificate from your machine. You have to type the password assigned to the certificate you want to upload in the following dialog box.

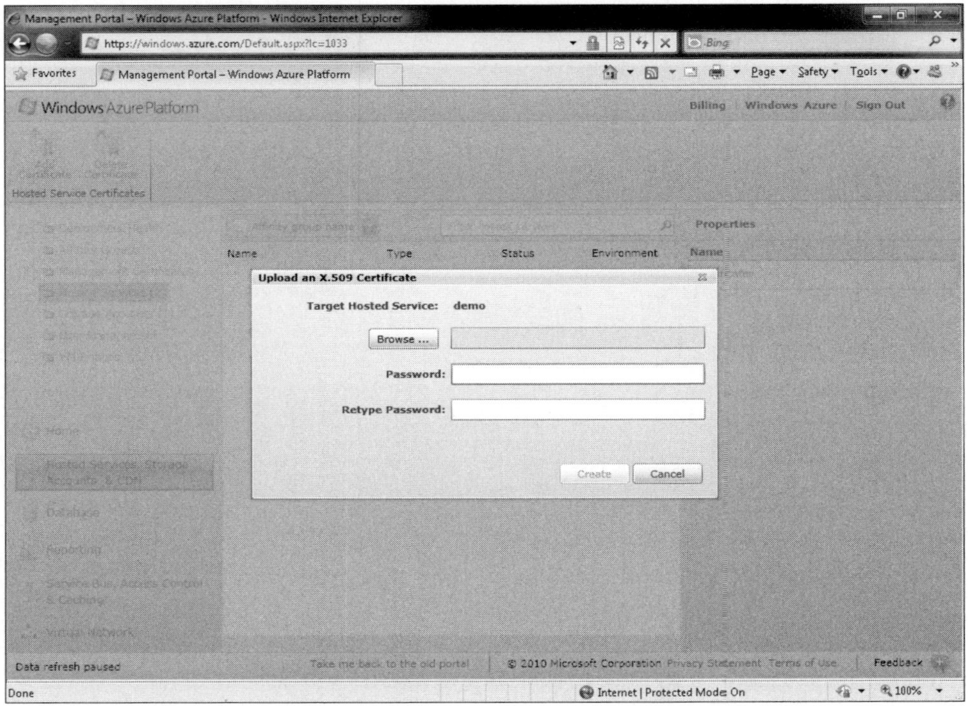

After you upload a certificate file (remember to upload a PFX file, which is a certificate that contains the private key), you can use the certificate in the service configuration file to enable the HTTPS connection, as you can see in the following code excerpt:

```
<?xml version="1.0" encoding="utf-8"?>
<ServiceDefinition name="ThinkAheadAzureStorage" xmlns="http://schemas.microsoft.com/
ServiceHosting/2008/10/ServiceDefinition">
  <WebRole name="WebRole1">
    <Sites>
      <Site name="Web">
        <Bindings>
          <Binding name="Endpoint1" endpointName="Endpoint1" />
          <Binding name="Endpoint2" endpointName="Endpoint2" />
        </Bindings>
      </Site>
```

```
    </Sites>
    <Endpoints>
      <InputEndpoint name="Endpoint1" protocol="http" port="80" />
      <InputEndpoint name="Endpoint2" protocol="https" port="443"
         certificate="ThinkAhead" />
    </Endpoints>
    <Imports>
    </Imports>
    <LocalResources>
    </LocalResources>
    <ConfigurationSettings>
    </ConfigurationSettings>
    <Certificates>
      <Certificate name="ThinkAhead" storeLocation="LocalMachine" storeName="My" ... />
    </Certificates>
  </WebRole>
</ServiceDefinition>
```

To simplify this configuration procedure, you can use the Microsoft Visual Studio Configuration Designer, shown in the next figure, to select a local certificate and assign it to the Web Role. (I removed my thumbprint in the screen.)

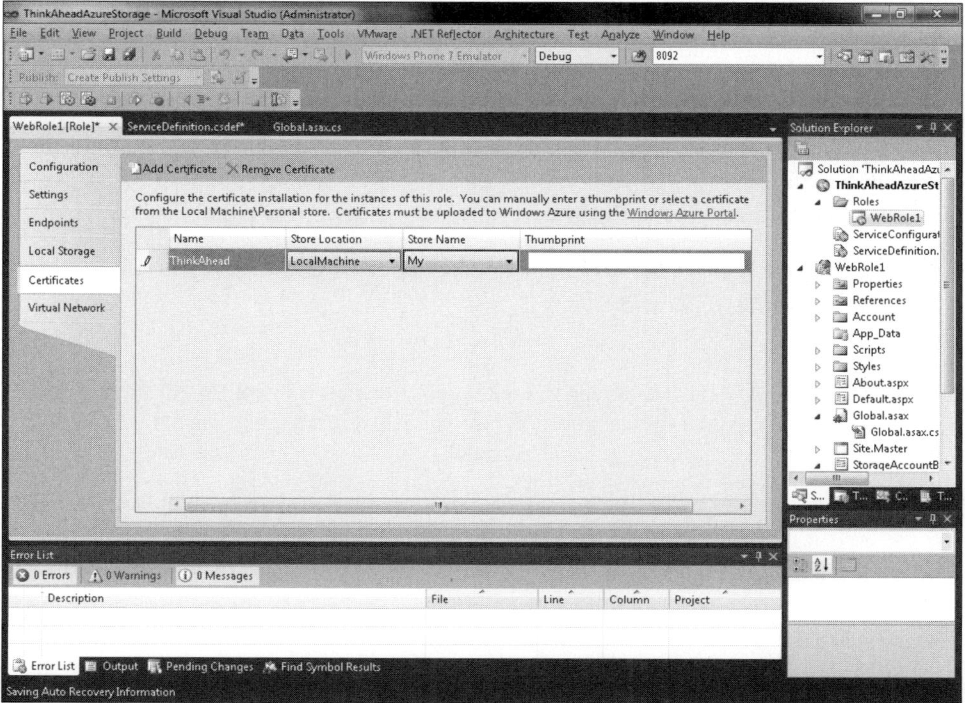

After this operation, you need to configure the endpoint to use the HTTPS protocol. You can do this from the Endpoints configuration tab of the Visual Studio Configuration Designer, which is shown in the following figure.

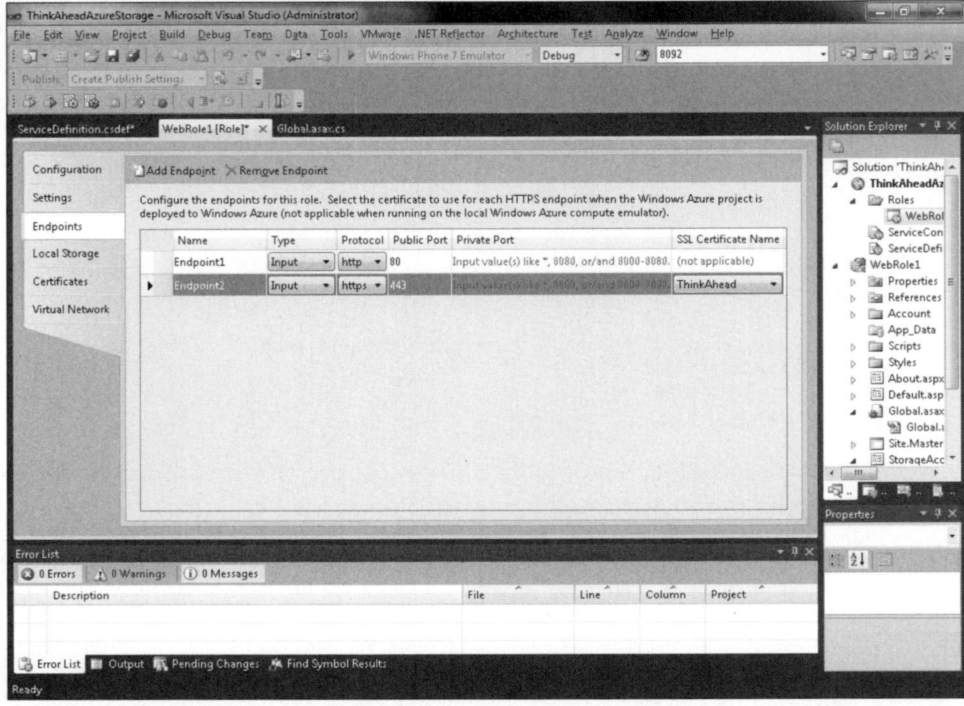

If you want to try this configuration in the compute emulator, you can create a self-signed certificate using the tool of your choice—Internet Information Services (IIS) is perfect—and assign the certificate on the Certificate tab of the service configuration.

The second certificate type, with the .cer extension, is useful when you want to use the portal API from a remote application.

> **Note** This kind of certificate type has nothing in common with the SSL certificate discussed previously; the purpose of the .cer certificate is to enable remote use of the Management API.

Each action exposed by the portal uses an underlying API. Remote applications can access these APIs if the request is signed with a private key contained in a certificate that has been uploaded to the portal. This scheme lets Windows Azure verify the identity of the requesting application by using the public key contained in the uploaded certificate to decrypt the request signed by the corresponding private key.

Visual Studio and the Windows Azure Management Tool can use a certificate to let developers take some actions without having to use the portal. You can also use this feature to build your own remote tool that uses the Management API.

First, you need to upload a developer certificate to the portal on the Manage API Certificates page, which is on the Account tab of the portal. The certificate lets authorized requests perform management operations for all the services created using the corresponding account.

As you can see in the following dialog box, all you have to do is upload a .cer certificate file (the default file extension for X.509 certificates) to the portal. To complete this task, click the Hosted Services, Storage Accounts & CND button, and then in the portal, select the Management Certificates menu item in the left toolbar.

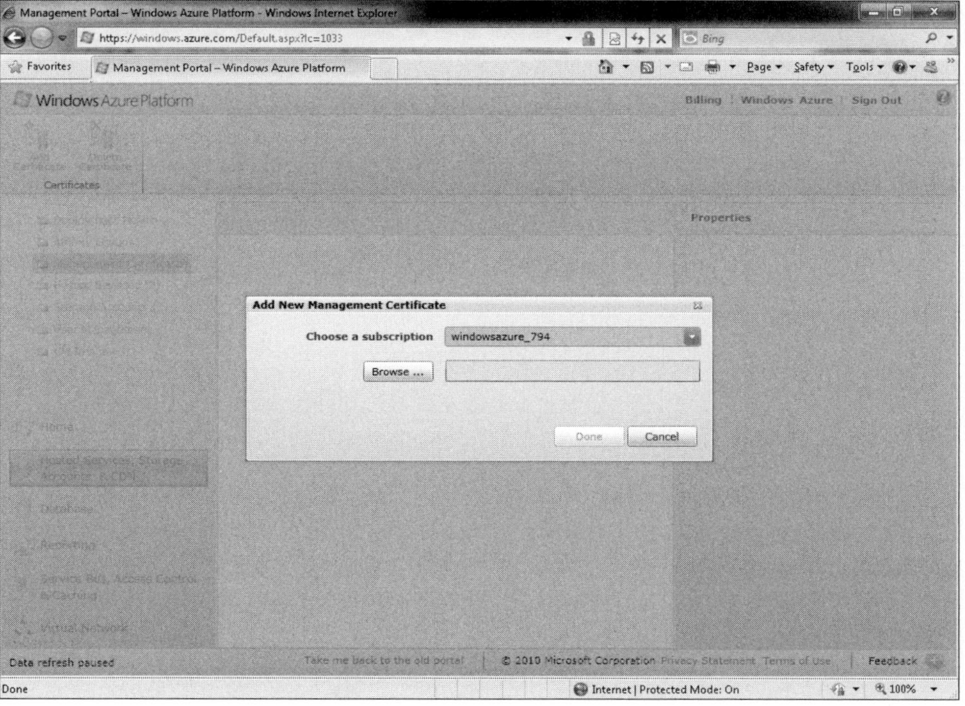

After uploading the certificate, you can verify or delete it at any time using the provided interface, shown in Figure 6-7.

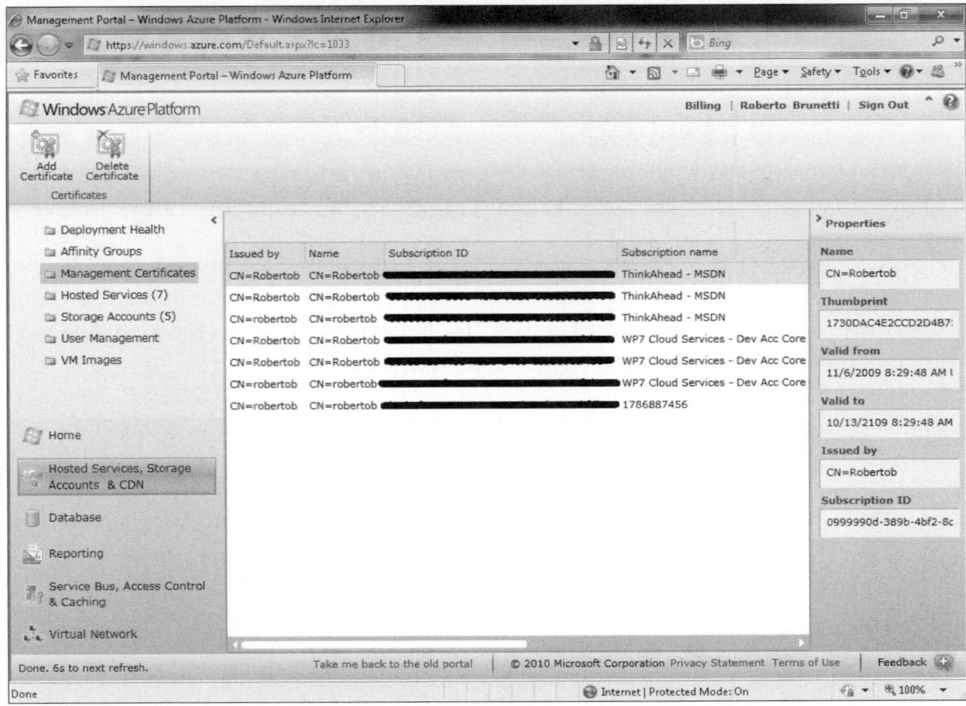

FIGURE 6-7 Management Certificate page.

As Figure 6-7 shows, my account (Roberto Brunetti) has many certificates associated with different subscriptions. I uploaded the Windows 7 default certificate associated with my account from three different computers to all my subscriptions.

Having uploaded my certificate, I can publish my applications directly from the Visual Studio 2010 Publish dialog box. The only remaining task is to associate the same certificate with the publish operation, and Visual Studio will do the rest, asking the remote management API to publish the cloud project by signing the request with the provided certificate.

Figure 6-8 shows the Publish Cloud Service dialog box with the Deploy Your Cloud Service To Windows Azure option selected (instead of with the package option selected, as in the previous chapters). I chose the certificate from the Credentials combo box (you can create different configurations and certificates to publish to different accounts), selected the staging environment as the deployment target, and selected the storage account that serves as temporary storage during the upload and deploy operations. You can also assign the standard Deployment Label.

FIGURE 6-8 Publish Cloud Service dialog box.

After deploying a certificate to your account, you can perform some other operations directly from Visual Studio as well, such as checking the status of the live production or staging environments using Visual Studio Server Explorer, shown in the next figure.

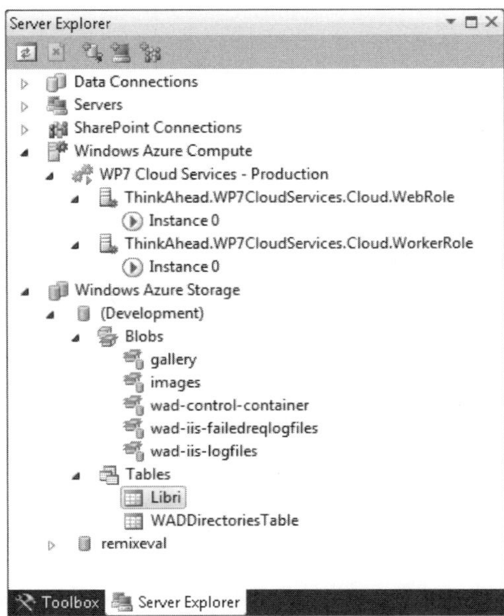

Note You can also view a Storage Account from Visual Studio Server Explorer as shown in the preceding image. This feature does not need a published certificate.

Also, the Windows Azure Management Tool can use the Management APIs. You have to use the same certificate you uploaded to the portal and bind it to the Subscription ID you typed in the Connection page. Take a look at the following figure.

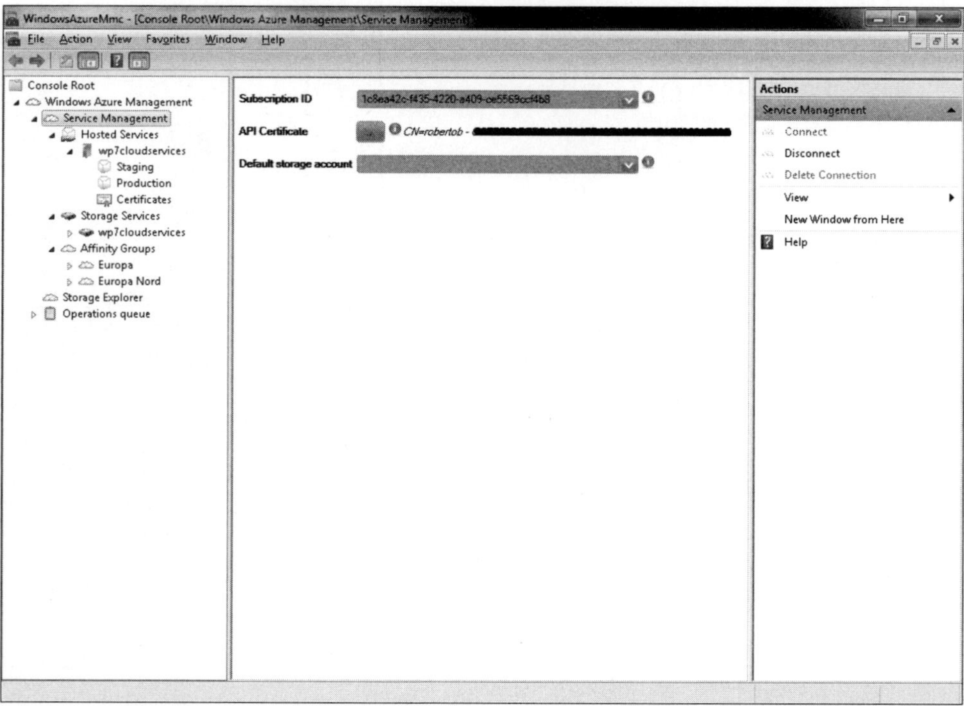

When you associate the subscription with the certificate, you can manage the services remotely. The following figure shows a real configuration for a production environment.

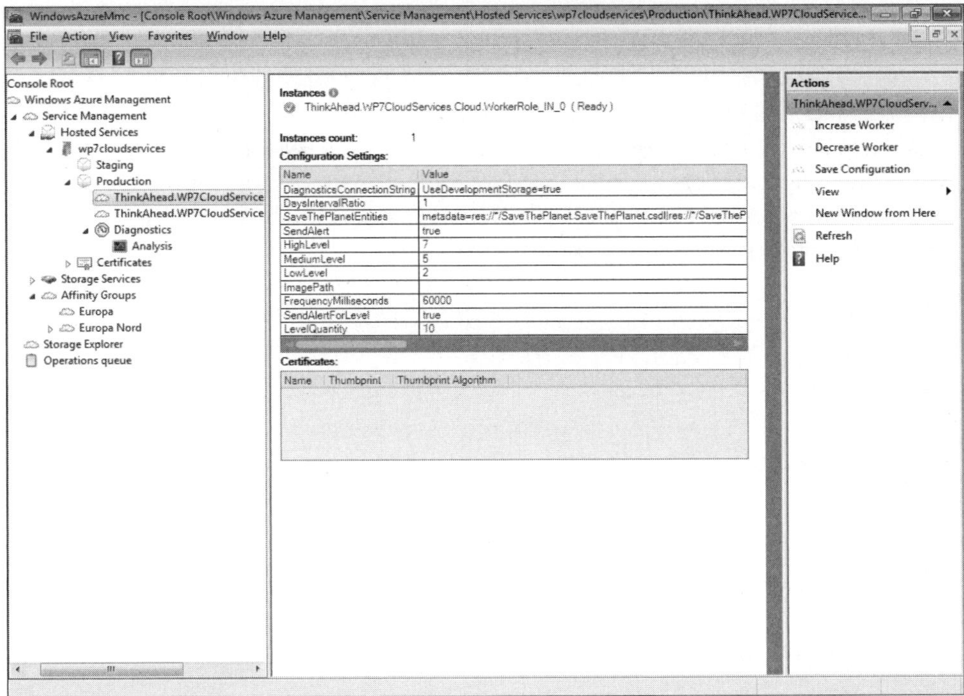

You have both role status and complete configuration settings in a simple but effective data grid. You can change values and click the Save Configuration link in the upper-right section of the Actions pane. You can also increase or decrease the number of instances at a moment's notice using the corresponding links. And you can view any installed certificates for the role or change them.

Another useful feature is Diagnostics, shown in the tree in the left pane, just below the Production item. The next section introduces Diagnostics, but you'll come back to the MMC at the end of the chapter.

Diagnostics

One issue that a cloud-based solution must address is collecting and analyzing diagnostic information. Because the application is in the cloud, traditional ways to collect logs (for instance, IIS logs) are not suitable. Log files are stored in the local file system, and that type of storage is inaccessible from the outside. Application traces are also normally stored in the local file system, as well as IIS 7 FREB (Failed Request Tracing) XML files and related XSLT (Extensible Stylesheet Language Transformations).

The Diagnostic APIs are the core of the diagnostic infrastructure. The related assembly is referenced by default for every Windows Azure role, so you don't have to do anything special to use it.

The primary goal of the APIs is to transfer diagnostic data in a manual or scheduled way from local storage to the storage account so that logged messages are available to external tools for analysis. Some types of logged data get stored in a blob container, and other types to a table, depending on the data structures involved.

Using the Web Role Configuration designer, developers can enable the diagnostic feature and configure the storage account where the native APIs store the related information. The following figure shows the Configuration tab of the designer.

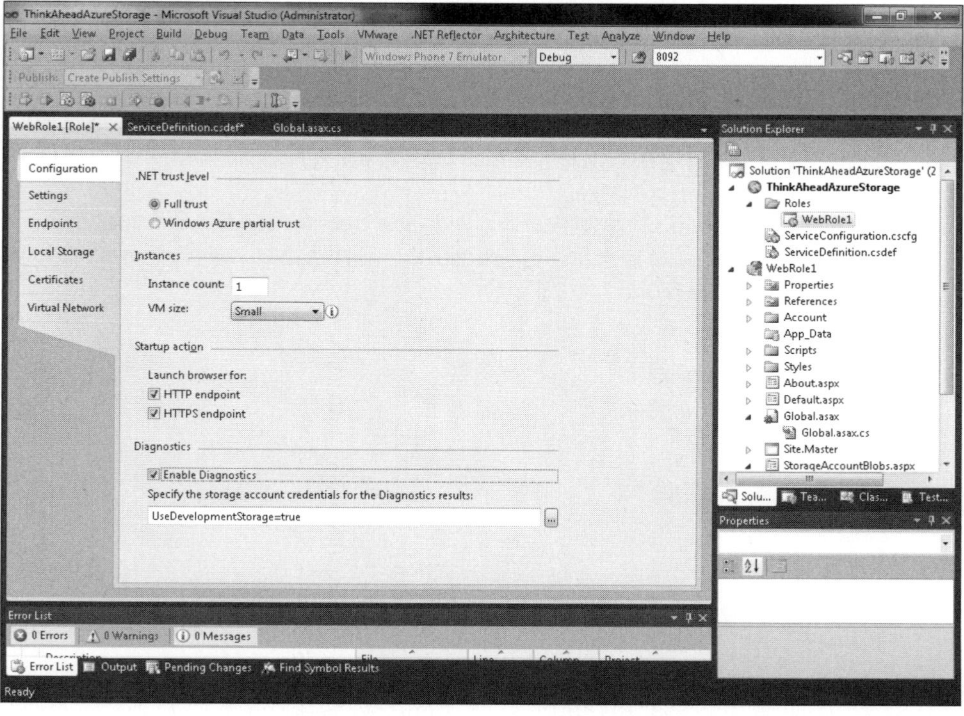

The diagnostics feature can also be enabled by code in the *OnStart* method of a Web Role. The *OnStart* method is the best place to configure this service, because as you saw in previous chapters, this method gets called during startup for every role instance. The following code contains a comment line before each setting to indicate the relative storage:

```
using System.Linq;
using Microsoft.WindowsAzure.Diagnostics;
using Microsoft.WindowsAzure.ServiceRuntime;
using System;

namespace WebRole1
{
    public class WebRole : RoleEntryPoint
    {
        public override bool OnStart()
        {
            // Get factory from config
            DiagnosticMonitorConfiguration diaConfig =
               DiagnosticMonitor.GetDefaultInitialConfiguration();

            // Transfer Infrastructure Log

            //  TABLE WADDiagnosticsInfrastructureLogsTable
            diaConfig.DiagnosticInfrastructureLogs.ScheduledTransferPeriod =
                TimeSpan.FromSeconds(5);
            diaConfig.DiagnosticInfrastructureLogs.ScheduledTransferLogLevelFilter
                = LogLevel.Information;

            // Transfer Directory Log
            //  TABLE WADDirectoriesTable
            //      FREB - Log IIS
            //  Container
            //      wad-iis-failedreqlogfiles
            //      wad-iis-logfiles

            diaConfig.Directories.ScheduledTransferPeriod = TimeSpan.FromSeconds(5);

            // Tranfer User Log
            //  TABLE WADLogTable
            //  Trace ASP.NET + Trace.Write/Warn
            diaConfig.Logs.ScheduledTransferPeriod = TimeSpan.FromSeconds(5);
            diaConfig.Logs.ScheduledTransferLogLevelFilter = LogLevel.Information;


            // Start with a connection string
            DiagnosticMonitor.Start("DiagnosticsConnectionString", diaConfig);

            // For information on handling configuration changes
            // see the MSDN topic at http://go.microsoft.com/fwlink/?LinkId=166357.
            RoleEnvironment.Changing += RoleEnvironmentChanging;

            return base.OnStart();
```

```
        }

        private void RoleEnvironmentChanging(object sender,
            RoleEnvironmentChangingEventArgs e)
        {
            // If a configuration setting is changing
            if (e.Changes.Any(change => change is
                RoleEnvironmentConfigurationSettingChange))
            {
                // Set e.Cancel to true to restart this role instance
                e.Cancel = true;
            }
        }
    }
}
```

Note Every class referenced in the preceding code is included in the *Microsoft.WindowsAzure.Diagnostics* namespace, so I inserted a *using* statement at the beginning of the stub code that is inserted by the Visual Studio template.

In the *OnStart* method, the first line of code reads the default configuration and creates a new instance of the *DiagnosticMonitorConfiguration* class. This class contains all you need to configure the diagnostic monitor.

The second and third lines of the *OnStart* method are related to the Infrastructure Log, which is scheduled to be transferred to the storage account every five seconds. Information sent to the storage account can be filtered by type; this example moves only the trace of the "informational" level to the storage. The Infrastructure Log gets transferred to the *WADDiagnosticsInfrastructureLogsTable* table in the storage account.

The second code block schedules the transfer of directories. The term *Directory*, to the Diagnostics APIs, refers to the directories where IIS produces logs as well as FREB files. These types of resources are moved to two blob containers named, respectively, *wad-iis-failedreqlogfiles* and *wad-iis-logfiles*. As you saw in the previous code, the *WADDirectoryTable* does not contain logged data; it serves solely as a reference to know which container is used for every resource.

The third code block schedules the transfer of the ASP.NET/IIS trace listener data. Every *Trace.Warn* or *Trace.Write* message, as well as the trace outputs produced by the ASP.NET runtime that are informational in nature, are moved every five seconds to the *WADLogTable* table in the storage.

The last line of code before the default code produced by the Visual Studio template is the most important line. Without the *Start* method call, any modification in the configuration would produce no effect. The *Start* method takes the name of the configuration setting (which by default is called *DiagnosticsConnectionString*) configured with the storage account information. As you saw in Chapter 5, "Tables, Queues, and Worker Roles," this kind of connection string can refer to either the development storage local simulated environment or to the live account.

If you elected to use the Windows Azure Management Tool to manage your Windows Azure services, you will be happy to know that the tool can export diagnostic data to Microsoft Excel, as shown in the following figure.

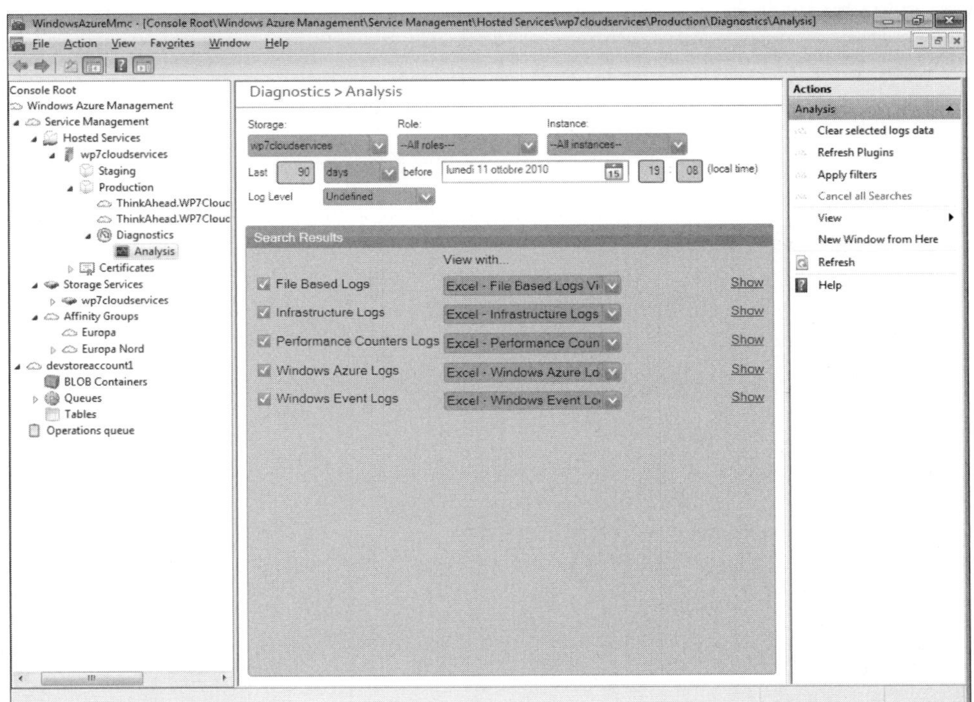

This tool is useful because it can filter data directly using the simple user interface shown in the preceding figure. If you want to build your own tool, you could do that as well, because at this point you have acquired sufficient knowledge to access the storage account programmatically.

Summary

In this chapter, you learned about the operating system. The chapter began by introducing the relationships between projects and subscriptions, and then drilled down a bit to the billing system. Next, you explored the role of the two types of certificates that you can use to open an HTTPS endpoint and use the management API for administration tasks on your roles. Finally, you saw how to use the Windows Azure Management Tool and the Visual Studio Server Explorer to manage deployed solutions. The chapter ended with an introduction to the native diagnostics features and APIs.

Quick Reference

To	Do this
Check your billing status	Go to *http://www.azure.com*, log on with your Windows Live ID, and select Billing.
Configure an affinity group	From the project portal, go to the account section and choose Affinity Group.
Enable the Content Delivery Network	Go to the storage account you want to deliver and configure the related section.
Use Visual Studio to automatically deploy a cloud project	Upload a certificate in the portal and set the same certificate in the Publish wizard.
Read diagnostics information	Use the Windows Azure Management Tool or use the APIs to retrieve information from the storage account.

Chapter 7

Building an AppFabric Solution

After completing this chapter, you will be able to

- Understand the components exposed by Windows Azure AppFabric.
- Install and use the Windows Azure AppFabric Software Development Kit (SDK).
- Build a simple solution that leverages the Service Bus feature to connect two applications.
- Understand the Access Control Service.
- Build a claims-based authentication mechanism in the cloud.

This chapter is dedicated to one of the most important components of the Windows Azure Platform: Windows Azure AppFabric. AppFabric consists of an Internet Service Bus and a claims-based Access Control Service. This chapter describes these components and then guides you through the process of creating a simple application that uses them.

According to Microsoft, during 2011, Windows Azure AppFabric will expose three other important components, which were discussed in Chapter 2 "Introduction to the Windows Azure Platform." The goal of this chapter is to explore the released features so that you will not work with any beta component.

Note Because URLs, UI names, and procedures may vary over time, some of them may be out of date by the time you read this. In that case, my best advice is to start looking for the information about the Windows Azure product on the Windows Azure home page (*http://www.azure.com*). Information included in this book was accurate at the time of writing.

Windows Azure AppFabric Components

Windows Azure exposes the base services for the entire platform. The operating system provides the basic layer for every Windows Azure Platform component. Microsoft also provides other services built on top of the Windows Azure operating system. One of these services is the Microsoft Push Notification Service for Windows Phone 7. which developers can use to register and send notifications to client applications. Because this service is hosted by Windows Azure, Microsoft can adjust the scalability switches you learned about in the preceding chapters to adapt the system to support the continually growing numbers of Windows Phone 7 customers.

Windows Azure AppFabric is another set of services hosted on top of the operating system. It provides a comprehensive middleware platform. Developers use Windows Azure AppFabric to connect application components together, manage identity, define access control rules, cache remote resources, and create composite applications. At the time of this writing, the first page of the documentation that addresses Windows Azure AppFabric (Microsoft Corporation, Windows Azure website, 2011, *http://www.microsoft.com/windowsazure/appfabric/overview/default.aspx*) describes AppFabric as a component that does the following:

> *provides a comprehensive cloud middleware platform for developing, deploying and managing applications on the Windows Azure Platform. It delivers additional developer productivity adding in higher-level Platform-as-a-Service (PaaS) capabilities on top of the familiar Windows Azure application model.*
>
> *It also enables bridging your existing applications to the cloud through secure connectivity across network and geographic boundaries, and by providing a consistent development model for both Windows Azure and Windows Server.*
>
> *Finally, it makes development more productive by providing higher abstraction for building end-to-end applications, and simplifies management and maintenance of the application as it takes advantage of advances in the underlying hardware and software infrastructure.*

The middleware services run with the same paradigms described in the preceding chapters. They are exposed as Platform as a Service (PaaS) components; are simple to deploy on the platform; you pay only for what you use; you can manage resources via the web portal or through the remote APIs; and the platform autoconfigures lower-level components such as load balancers as well as fault tolerance strategies.

Windows Azure AppFabric was released in April 2010 with two important initial services: Service Bus and Access Control. As understood at the time of this writing, other services will be released as Community Technical Previews (CTPs) during 2011.

To start developing Windows Azure AppFabric solutions, you need to download and install the related SDKs and tools. Because Windows Azure AppFabric can be used in many different environments and by different languages, install the specific SDK for your language and environment. The example in this chapter uses C# and Microsoft Visual Studio 2010 (the same concepts would apply to C# in Microsoft Visual Studio 2008), but Windows Azure AppFabric also offers appropriate SDKs for other languages, as well as tools for other development platforms.

The SDKs available at the time of this writing include the following:

- Windows Azure AppFabric SDK for Microsoft .NET Framework
- AppFabric SDK for Java Developers
- AppFabric SDK for PHP Developers
- AppFabric SDK for Ruby Developers

To download the SDK and tools, go to *http://www.microsoft.com/windowsazure/sdk/*, the home page for the Windows Azure platform, and choose the Developers section. The drop-down menu items include documentation about the components, a link to the Training Kit, and SDK & Tools. Select SDK & Tools.

Note Because URLs and names may vary over time, the preceding directions may be out of date by the time you read this. In that case, my best advice is to start looking for the Windows Azure components on the Windows Azure home page (*http://www.azure.com*). Information included in this book was accurate at the time of writing.

The SDK & Tools page is divided into several sections: the first one is dedicated to Windows Azure. You use this section to download the Windows Azure Tools for Visual Studio add-in and the Windows Azure SDK. The second section is dedicated to Windows Azure AppFabric and the Management Tools (the Windows Azure Management Tools you downloaded and used in Chapter 4, "Windows Azure Storage"). You also find the Windows Azure AppFabric SDK download in this section. Download and install it now.

You do not need the Windows Azure Tools for Visual Studio add-in or the Windows Azure SDK to use this SDK, because there are no relationships between the two. You do not need a Windows Azure project to use Windows Azure AppFabric components. If you do not want to deploy a solution to Windows Azure, you can use the Windows Azure AppFabric SDK by itself in on-premises solutions.

The first example you build in this chapter is a console application that leverages the Windows Communication Foundation (WCF) infrastructure and the Service Bus APIs to exchange some data with another console application.

Important You do not need Windows Azure to use the Windows Azure AppFabric SDK. As mentioned earlier, although Windows Azure AppFabric is built on top of the Windows Azure operating system, it completely hides the operating system itself; you see only a web portal that you use to configure and use Windows Azure AppFabric. In fact, you don't even need to know anything about Windows Azure.

I chose to use two console applications to demonstrate that there's nothing magical behind this technology. You will create a service, hosted in a console application on your personal computer, and—without doing anything special—you'll be able to receive operational calls from a client on the Internet. You do not have to configure Internet Information Services (IIS) to expose the service, nor do you have to open external firewall ports on your LAN for the Service Bus to be able to reach your computer. Your computer will contact the Service Bus, as you will learn soon.

Service Bus

The Service Bus Service provides secure connectivity and messaging capabilities through which distributed and disconnected applications can exchange data. The Service Bus is publicly hosted, so it's accessible by any application using an Internet connection. The infrastructure is secured by the Access Control Service, freeing the Service Bus itself from the logic and data required to validate users, map them to groups and roles, and discover permissions. The Access Control Service performs this job on behalf of the Service Bus.

The goal of the Service Bus is to facilitate the connection of applications that are behind firewalls, NATs (Network Access Translators), applications using dynamic DNS, or mobile applications that may have dynamic IPs. The Service Bus can interconnect these applications by creating a secure channel exposed on the Internet. Each application can register with this channel to receive messages. For example, an on-premises application has no problems talking with the Service Bus infrastructure, because the application can contact it using TCP or HTTP protocols. After registering with the Service Bus, an application receives a public URI on the Service Bus channel. When other authorized applications send a message to that URI, the Service Bus infrastructure relays the message to the on-premises application using the channel opened by the on-premises application itself. You can think of the Service Bus as a Windows Live Messenger Service for applications. You can talk with your friends through Windows Live Messenger even when you are hosted in a completely different network. The Windows Live Messenger Service works by relaying messages from your machine, which has no problem talking to the Internet, or to your friend's machine that has previously opened a channel to the same service.

Figure 7-1 describes the typical message flow I introduced. An on-premises application behind a firewall or a NAT registers itself on the Service Bus using a simple *POST* request to the service namespace URL (created in the portal). Subsequently, when authorized applications send messages to this public URL, the Service Bus acts as a relay; it forwards the messages to the on-premises application. This technique eliminates the need to expose the on-premises application to the outside world. It also enables new applications to become part of the message flow with minimal effort. Any new application that needs to receive the same messages can register itself in the service namespace.

The Service Bus can relay messages that contain text, XML, graphics, binary data, and streaming data.

To use the Service Bus, you follow the same pattern you have used throughout this book: create a new service using the portal and use some specific APIs to simplify your code. Then you can start exchanging messages via the Service Bus from any application and platform without any other complications.

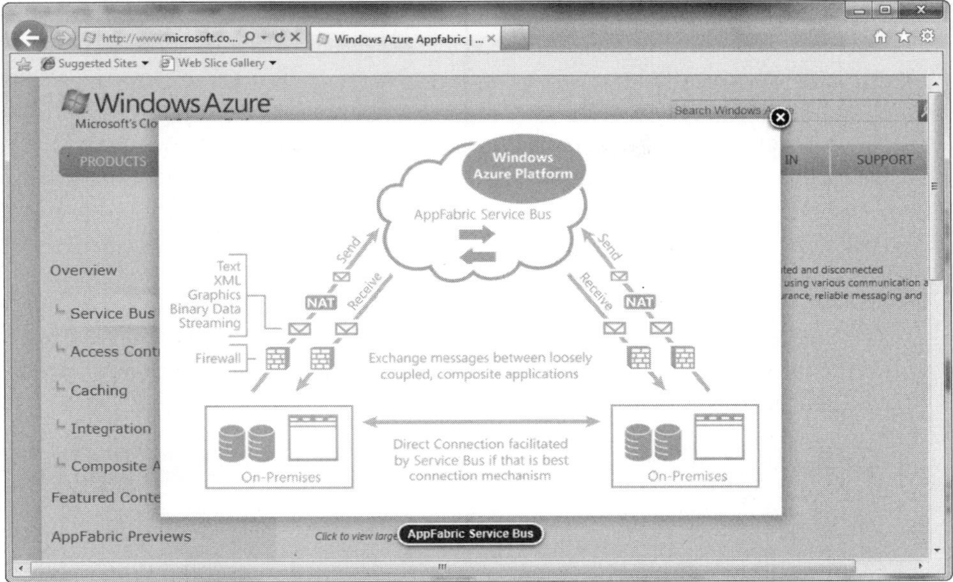

FIGURE 7-1 Service Bus message flow.

The service uses Internet standards such as HTTP and REST to create services and exchange messages so that you can use the service from any desktop and server platform without any SDK or specific tools. You can also use the service from such disparate programs as Windows Phone 7 applications, Apple iPhone, iPad, and Android mobile clients. If your service-oriented architecture (SOA) solution is based on WCF, adapting the solution to use the Service Bus involves only a few lines of code and some configuration settings.

At the time of this writing, Microsoft presents the Service Bus with this statement (Microsoft Corporation, Windows Azure website, 2011, *http://www.microsoft.com/windowsazure/appfabric/overview/default.aspx*):

> *The Service Bus provides secure messaging and connectivity capabilities that enable building distributed and disconnected applications in the cloud, as well as hybrid application across both on-premises and the cloud. It enables using various communication and messaging protocols and patterns, and saves the need for the developer to worry about delivery assurance, reliable messaging and scale.*

It's time to write some code that uses the Windows Azure AppFabric SDK to exchange some dates between two on-premises applications. Before doing that, you create the service namespace that will publicly expose the URI for the simple application.

Create the Service Namespace

In this procedure, you create a new Namespace for your service. The term *service namespace*, or simply *namespace*, refers to the prefix of the public URI that the Service Bus creates for you. Like Windows Azure, the Service Bus infrastructure has a fixed DNS domain in which you can create your private space using a globally unique name. The DNS for the Service Bus is *servicebus.windows.net*, and the default prefix you see in the portal is simply *sb*. As you will see in the next example, you can use also use HTTP as the default protocol to talk to the Service Bus infrastructure.

1. Sign in to the Windows Azure portal using your Windows Live ID. In the lower-left toolbar, choose the AppFabric section of the portal by clicking Service Bus, Access Control & Caching. This option is shown in the following figure.

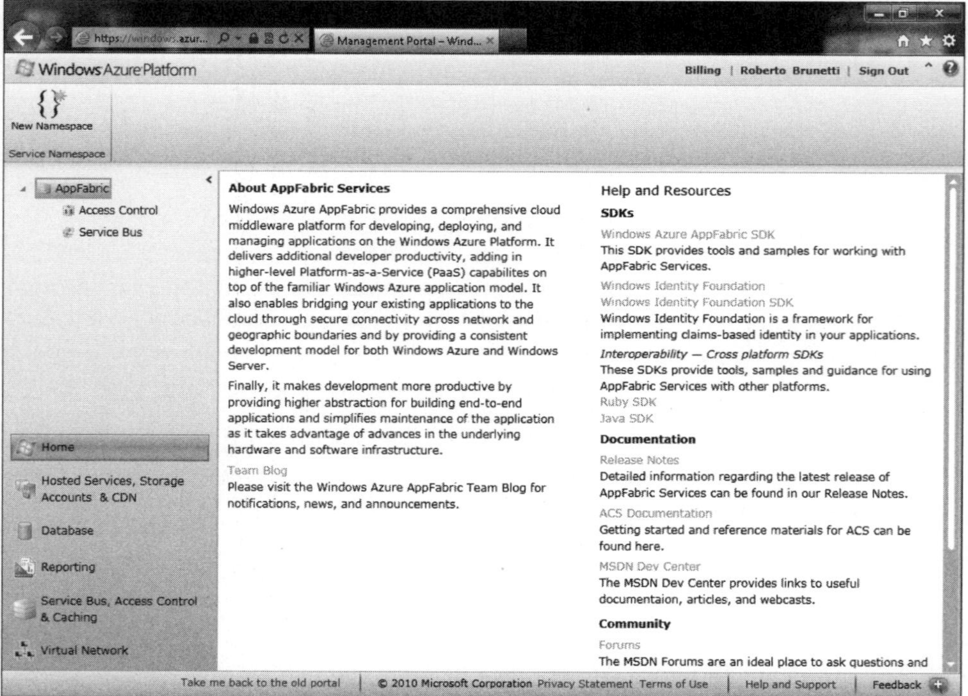

2. Click the New Namespace button. The Create A New Service Namespace dialog box, shown in the following figure, appears.

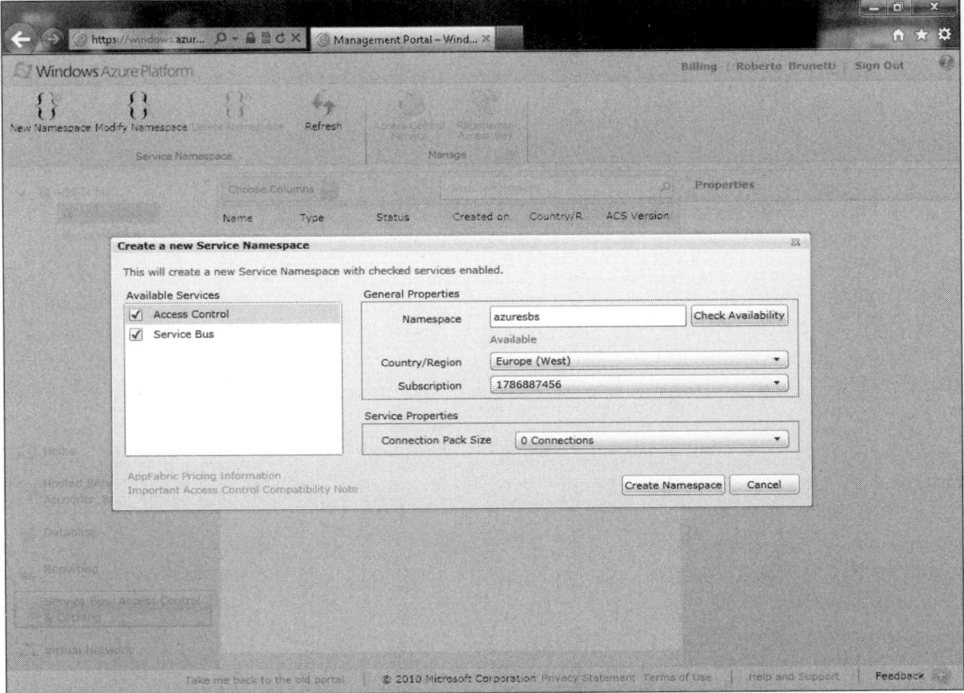

3. Enter a name of your choice in the Namespace text box and validate it. I chose azuresbs for this example. The name you choose must be unique, so validate it with the system to ensure that the name you select hasn't already been chosen by other users.

4. Choose the data center region that will host your service namespace. You cannot define an affinity group of services as you can with Windows Azure Hosted Service or Windows Azure storage account, so if you want to host the Service Bus as physically near your other cloud applications as possible, choose a data center in the same region.

5. Choose the subscription you want to use for this service as you did for every service you've created in this book.

6. Choose the Service Bus Connection Pack. You can choose 0 Connection if you prefer a complete pay-as-you-go billing arrangement, or you can select a pack of connections billed at a discounted but fixed rate. For now, leave the option set to its default value.

7. Click the Create Namespace button.

You can see your service in the list of service namespaces for your project. Clicking the service namespace lets you see all the details for your new namespace, as shown in the following figure.

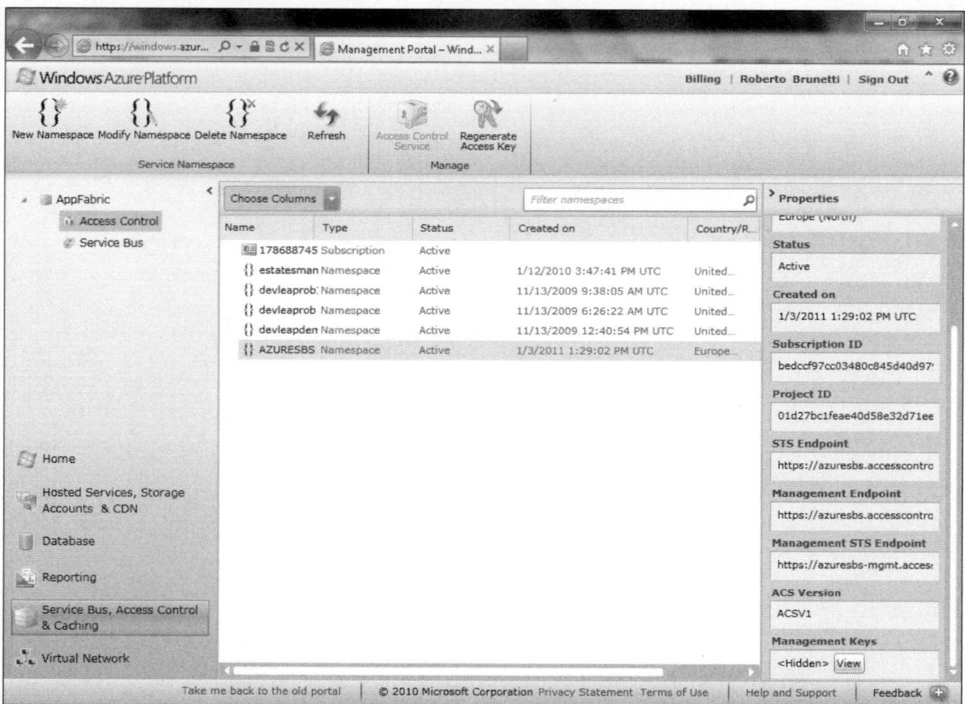

The most important thing to notice here is the URI created on your behalf. The URI is based on your globally unique name, and exposed using the HTTPS protocol. The infrastructure created a new digital certificate to secure the conversation between an application and the Service Bus. This is the address the application must use to register on the Service Bus, and it's also the address where other applications can send messages.

Also note the Secure Token Service (STS) Endpoint—another namespace on the Access Control Service address named *accesscontrol.windows.net*. As mentioned at the beginning of this chapter, the Service Bus does not expose a security mechanism by itself; instead, it relies on the claims-based infrastructure exposed and managed by the Access Control Service. An application that wants to register on the Service Bus has to request permission from the Access Control Service by providing a set of claims. The Access Control Service uses these claims to validate the request and produce a token representing the permission level the application has with the Service Bus. This token is sent to the requesting application, which, in turn, can send the token to the Service Bus, which then verifies the claims (or permission) the token represents. Because the Service Bus has a trusted relationship with the Access Control Service, it trusts the permission token and lets the application either register to the Service Bus or send or receive a message.

> **Note** A *claim* is an assertion of truth made by someone to whom the counterparty has some kind of trusted relationship.

Finally, note that the last part of the STS Endpoint URI reveals the protocol used to authenticate the resource. Currently, it uses the Web Resource Access Protocol, version 0.9.

You use the Management STS Endpoint (also HTTPS) to configure permissions for this Service Bus namespace. To authenticate these HTTPS, requests you have to use the management key name and the current management key.

The Management Endpoint is the URI where an application can request registration to or deregistration from the Service Bus Namespace.

By default, the infrastructure creates a default issuer name and a default issuer key (called *credentials*) that correspond to a user. This set of credentials has complete control over the Service Bus namespace; it can request that the Management Endpoint register an application on the Internet Service Bus. In the following procedure, you use these credentials to access and manipulate the infrastructure.

You completed all the necessary operations to configure the service. To summarize, you create a new service namespace from the Windows Azure AppFabric Portal, choose a globally unique name, and then use the provided credentials to register an application.

As mentioned at the beginning of this section, you can use HTTP and REST to interact with the Service Bus infrastructure. These provide low-level control of the message flow and content. Alternatively, you can use the SDK to greatly simplify your code.

If you did not yet download and install the Windows Azure AppFabric SDK, you should do that now.

Create a WCF Service Application

In this procedure, you create a new console application that acts as the service for the sample application, using the Windows Azure AppFabric SDK that wraps WCF to simplify the service's registration with the Service Bus and the creation of a listening channel.

1. Open Visual Studio and create a new console application using the default template. Name the project **Service** and the solution **AppFabricDemo**, as shown in the following figure. Use two different names, because you will create another project inside the solution that represents a client for this service. Click the OK button.

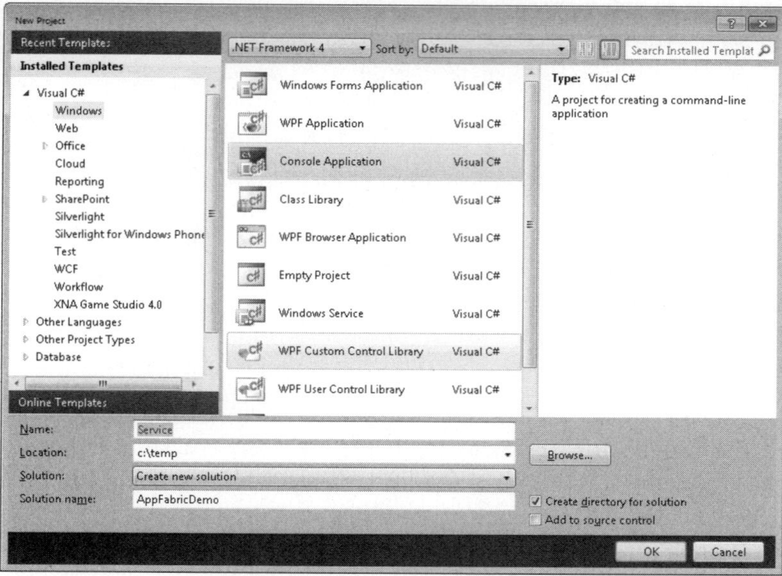

2. Create the WCF service interface, just as you would normally, to define the contract for the service. Add a new C# interface item to the project and name it **IHelloService.cs**. Open the file, delete all the file's default content, and type the following code.

```
using System.ServiceModel;
namespace Service
{
    [ServiceContract(Name = "HelloContract", Namespace =
       "http://samples.devleap.com/ServiceBus/")]
    public interface IHelloContract
    {
        [OperationContract]
        string SimpleHello(string text);
    }
}
```

As you can see, there is nothing special nor anything related to the Service Bus in this code. You defined a *ServiceContract* named *"HelloContract"* in a custom namespace. The contract indicates an operation called *SimpleHello* that receives a string and returns a string.

3. Add a reference to the *System.ServiceModel* assembly.

4. Implement the service as usual, and don't worry about the Service Bus. Create a new class item in the project and name it **HelloService**. Use the following code to build the class:

```
using System;
using System.ServiceModel;

namespace Service
{

    [ServiceBehavior(Name = "HelloService", Namespace =
        "http://samples.devleap.com/ServiceBus/")]
    public class HelloService : IHelloContract
    {
        public string SimpleHello(string text)
        {
            Console.WriteLine("{0} received", text);
            Console.WriteLine();
            return "I've received : " + text;
        }
    }
}
```

You created a traditional WCF service that implements a defined contract. The method that corresponds to the *SimpleHello* operation simply traces the received text to the console and replies with the same string, preceded by *"I've received : "*.

5. Add a new application configuration file. Accept the default name of the Service project to configure your service, and fill it with a *system.serviceModel* section that contains a traditional *netTcpBinding* for the *HelloService* service, shown in the following code:

```
<?xml version="1.0" encoding="utf-8" ?>
<configuration>
  <system.serviceModel>

    <bindings>
      <!-- Application Binding -->
      <netTcpBinding>
        <binding name="default" />
      </netTcpBinding>
    </bindings>

    <services>
      <service name="Service.HelloService">
        <endpoint name="RelayEndpoint"
                  contract="Service.IHelloContract"
                  binding="netTcpBinding"
                  bindingConfiguration="default"
                  address="" />
      </service>
    </services>
  </system.serviceModel>
</configuration>
```

The service tag contains the service name and an endpoint configured with the *netTcpBinding* that contains nothing but the default binding, without any particular configuration.

6. To expose the service from the simple console application, from the classic Program.cs file, use the *System.ServiceModel* class to build the *ServiceHost* on the defined service and open it. The following code uses the port *1234* using the *net.tcp* protocol, which corresponds to the *netTcpBinding* binding defined in the application configuration file:

```
using System;
using System.Collections.Generic;
using System.Linq;
using System.Text;
using System.ServiceModel;

namespace Service
{
    class Program
    {
        static void Main(string[] args)
        {

            Uri address = new Uri("net.tcp://localhost:1234");

            Console.WriteLine("Address : " + address);
            Console.WriteLine();

            ServiceHost host = new ServiceHost(typeof(HelloService), address);

            host.Open();


            Console.WriteLine("Press [Enter] to exit");
            Console.ReadLine();

            host.Close();
        }
    }
}
```

Note This is probably the simplest possible example to demonstrate how to modify the service that you built in the previous procedure for exposure on the cloud Service Bus and used by a remote client. When creating a real-world WCF service, you should consider defining the service, the contract, and the host in different projects, to decouple the pieces one from another.

You can now run the project. You should obtain a result similar to the following figure.

So far, you haven't done anything special. You can build a client application that uses *nct.tcp://localhost:1234* and run it on the same machine to call the *SimpleHello* operation and receive a result.

Next, you expose this service on the Service Bus by creating a channel that relays every message sent to the service's public address to the on-premises console service application.

Expose the Service to the Service Bus

In this procedure, you expose the traditional WCF service created in the preceding procedure on the Service Bus Namespace that you created at the beginning of this chapter.

1. Add a reference to the *Microsoft.ServiceBus* assembly. To do this, right-click the Service project and choose Add Reference. Click the Browse tab and navigate to the Windows Azure AppFabric installation folder. You can find the assembly in the Program Files \Windows Azure AppFabric SDK folder. Inside that folder is a directory representing the installed version (currently 1.0) and a separate directory for .NET Framework 3.5 and 4.0. Choose the 4.0 version and locate the Microsoft.ServiceBus.dll assembly file. You can see the complete default path in the following figure.

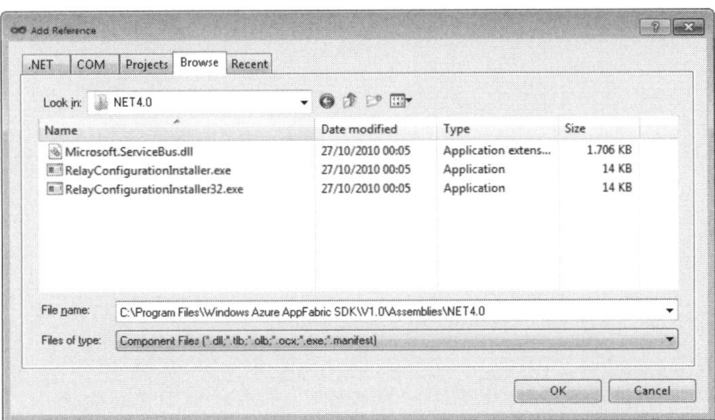

2. The *Microsoft.ServiceBus* assembly has a dependency on the *System.ServiceModel.Web*, assembly—which is not in the .NET Framework 4.0 Client Profile. A new console application created in Visual Studio 2010 defaults to the .NET Framework 4.0 Client Profile, making the application incompatible with the Service Bus. You have to retarget your application using the Service project's properties dialog box, as you can see in the next figure. Change the Target Framework to .NET Framework 4, and then click the Yes button to confirm the change.

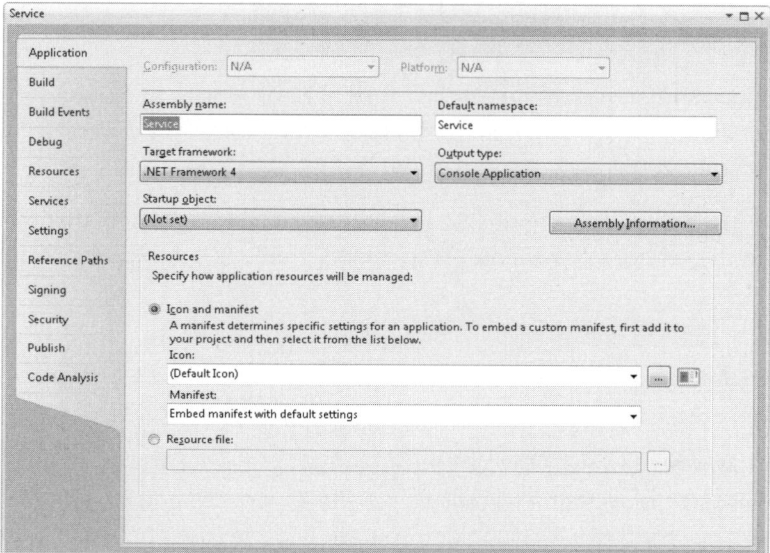

3. In the Program class's *Main* method, you have to modify the service URI. You can compose the Service Bus URI automatically using the Service Bus APIs. Comment out the first line and type the following boldface lines of code from this excerpt:

```
using System;
using System.Collections.Generic;
using System.Linq;
using System.Text;
using System.ServiceModel;
using Microsoft.ServiceBus;

namespace Service
{
    class Program
    {
        static void Main(string[] args)
        {
            //Uri address = new Uri("net.tcp://localhost:1234");
            Uri address = ServiceBusEnvironment.CreateServiceUri("sb", "azuresbs",
               "HelloService");

            Console.WriteLine("Address : " + address);
```

```
            Console.WriteLine();

            ServiceHost host = new ServiceHost(typeof(HelloService), address);

            host.Open();


            Console.WriteLine("Press [Enter] to exit");
            Console.ReadLine();

            host.Close();
        }
    }
}
```

The first parameter of the *CreateServiceUri* static method of the *ServiceBusEnvironment* is the protocol that the service uses to interact with the Service Bus. The *sb* protocol uses TCP on port 808 to send messages from the console application to the cloud Service Bus service. The second parameter must match the name of your service namespace. Type the name you chose in the first step of the Create New Service Namespace wizard in the previous section.

The last parameter is the name of the service. The *ServiceBusEnviroment* appends this parameter to the URI it constructs. The REST request that results from this method call will be *sb://azuresbs.servicebus.windows.net/HelloService*.

4. The only other required change before you can use the Service Bus infrastructure is to adapt the binding in the application configuration file. You need to change *netTcpBinding* to *netTcpRelayBinding* and provide (as you may remember from the previous section) the credentials required to use your service namespace. Following is the new application configuration file (the lines in boldface are the modified lines):

```
<?xml version="1.0"?>
<configuration>
  <system.serviceModel>

    <bindings>
      <!-- Application Binding -->
      <netTcpRelayBinding>
        <binding name="default" />
      </netTcpRelayBinding>
    </bindings>

    <services>
      <service name="Service.HelloService">
        <endpoint name="RelayEndpoint"
                  contract="Service.IHelloContract"
                  binding="netTcpRelayBinding"
                  bindingConfiguration="default"
                  behaviorConfiguration="sharedSecretClientCredentials"
                  address=""/>
      </service>
    </services>
```

```
        <behaviors>
          <endpointBehaviors>
            <behavior name="sharedSecretClientCredentials">
              <transportClientEndpointBehavior credentialType="SharedSecret">
                <clientCredentials>
                  <sharedSecret issuerName="owner"
                     issuerSecret="DZ9VqyGQkakohsbMuWoIzU=" />
                </clientCredentials>
              </transportClientEndpointBehavior>
            </behavior>
          </endpointBehaviors>
        </behaviors>
      </system.serviceModel>
      <startup>
        <supportedRuntime version="v4.0" sku=".NETFramework,Version=v4.0"/>
      </startup>
    </configuration>
```

First, note the new binding—the relayed version of the *net.tcp* classic binding. Second, note that the modification is the new *behaviorConfiguration* that uses the *issuerName* and the *issuerSecret* you received when you created the Service Namespace. Your *issuerSecret* is obviously different from the presented one.

You can press F5 to run the new service and, if you have used the correct *issuerSecret,* you end up with something similar to the following figure.

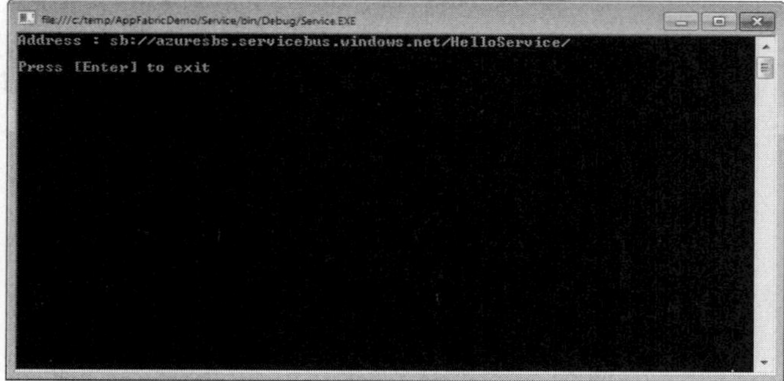

As you can see, your service is now publicly available on the Windows Azure AppFabric. It uses a Service Bus URI on the *sb* TCP/IP protocol. The service used port 808 to communicate with the Service Bus management service, and will use the relayed version of *netTcpBinding* (*netTcpRelayBinding*) as the binding to exchange data with service consumers.

Before you learn about other available bindings and messaging patterns (in which you learn how to use HTTP instead of TCP to communicate with the management infrastructure), you build a service consumer.

Create the Service Consumer

In this procedure, you create a service consumer that uses the same binding and address you created in the previous two procedures to exchange data via the Service Bus with the simple service.

1. Stop the debugger if you haven't done that yet.
2. Add a new project to the solution. Right-click the solution and choose Add New Project.
3. Choose the Console Application template, and type **Consumer** as the project name. You should see the following figure.

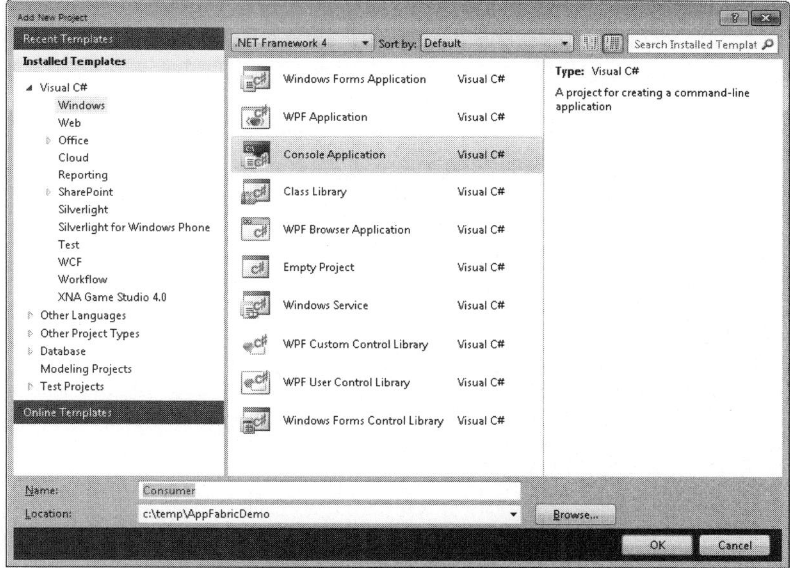

4. Add a reference to the *System.ServiceModel* and *Microsoft.ServiceBus* assemblies, just as you did in the Service project. Also, change the target configuration to .NET Framework 4.
5. Add a new class file and name it **HelloProxy**. Type the following code to create the client-side interface and the relative WCF channel, as you would for a non–Service Bus proxy:

```
using System.ServiceModel;
namespace Consumer
{
    [ServiceContract(Name = "HelloContract", Namespace =
        "http://samples.devleap.com/ServiceBus/")]
    public interface IHelloContract
```

```
        {
            [OperationContract]
            string SimpleHello(string text);
        }

        public interface IHelloChannel : IHelloContract, IClientChannel
        {
        }
    }
```

6. Add a new application configuration file to the Consumer project and use the *system.ServiceModel* configuration you worked with in the previous procedure, making sure you use the *Consumer* contract defined in the previous step:

```
<?xml version="1.0"?>
<configuration>
  <system.serviceModel>
    <behaviors>
      <endpointBehaviors>
        <behavior name="sharedSecretClientCredentials">
          <transportClientEndpointBehavior credentialType="SharedSecret">
            <clientCredentials>
              <sharedSecret issuerName="owner"
                issuerSecret="DZ9VqyGQkaNbL98upEX3WD7wGrcZCwcIohsbMuWoIzU="/>
            </clientCredentials>
          </transportClientEndpointBehavior>
        </behavior>
      </endpointBehaviors>
    </behaviors>
    <bindings>
      <!-- Application Binding -->
      <netTcpRelayBinding>
        <binding name="default"/>
      </netTcpRelayBinding>
    </bindings>

    <client>
      <!-- Application Endpoint -->
      <endpoint name="RelayEndpoint" contract="Consumer.IHelloContract"
                binding="netTcpRelayBinding"
                bindingConfiguration="default"
                behaviorConfiguration="sharedSecretClientCredentials"
                  address="http://AddressToBeReplacedInCode/"/>
    </client>

  </system.serviceModel>
  <startup>
    <supportedRuntime version="v4.0" sku=".NETFramework,Version=v4.0"/>
  </startup>
</configuration>
```

As you can see from the code in step 5, the configuration is almost identical to the previous one—in fact, this example uses the same *issuerName* and *issuerSecret* that the service does. The binding has to be identical to talk with the service as in traditional WCF configurations. As for the service, the code builds the address, as shown in the next step.

7. The code for the *Main* method in the *Program* class of the Consumer application is straightforward (the inserted line in the default template is in boldface):

```
using System;
using System.Collections.Generic;
using System.Linq;
using System.Text;
using Microsoft.ServiceBus;
using System.ServiceModel;

namespace Consumer
{
    class Program
    {
        static void Main(string[] args)
        {
            Uri serviceUri = ServiceBusEnvironment.CreateServiceUri(
               "sb", "azuresbs", "HelloService");

            Console.WriteLine("I will send messages to {0}", serviceUri);
            Console.WriteLine();

            ChannelFactory<IHelloChannel> channelFactory = new ChannelFactory
               <IHelloChannel>("RelayEndpoint", new EndpointAddress(serviceUri));
            IHelloChannel channel = channelFactory.CreateChannel();

            channel.Open();

            Console.WriteLine("Hello to be sent (or [Enter] to exit):");

            string input = Console.ReadLine();

            while (!String.IsNullOrEmpty(input))
            {
                try
                {
                    Console.WriteLine("Reply from the service : {0}",
                        channel.SimpleHello(input));
                    Console.WriteLine();
                }
                catch (Exception e)
                {
                    Console.WriteLine("Error: " + e.Message);
                }

                input = Console.ReadLine();
            }
```

```
                channel.Close();
                channel.Dispose();
                channelFactory.Close();
            }
        }
    }
```

The first line of code builds up the Service Bus URI used in the second line. Then the code creates a *ChannelFactory* instance using both the *IHelloChannel* interface that represents the contract and the composited URI. Finally, it creates the *Channel* and opens it to send the text read from the console.

There is nothing special in this procedure either except for the first line of code of the *Main* method and the binding configuration in the application configuration file. In practice, to use the Service Bus from an existing service, you need only to modify the URI construction and the service configuration. Service registration and data exchange is completely transparent, thanks to the new bindings. Remember to use the service namespace you chose at the beginning of this procedure.

Start the service by pressing F5 and wait for the console to show the "Press [Enter] to exit" message (at that point, the service has been registered on the Service Bus and is ready to receive messages). Then, right-click on the Consumer project and choose Debug | Start New Instance to start one instance of the consumer.

If everything worked, you will receive a prompt for sending messages to the Service Bus URI you configured, as shown in the following figure.

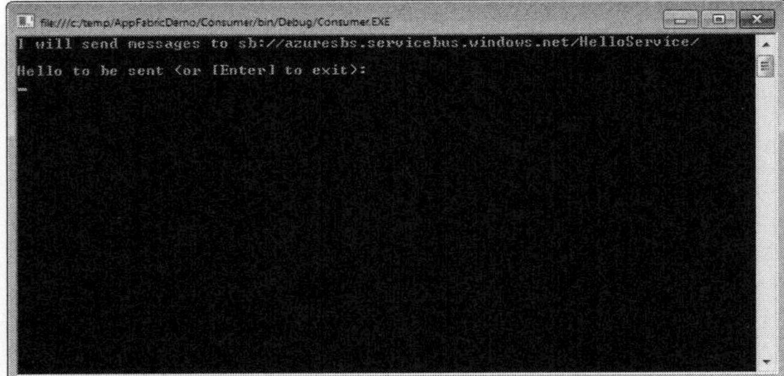

Type some random text in the console and press Enter to send the message to the service, which will reply according to the code you wrote. For instance, if you type **Hello Azure Step by Step Book !**, press Enter, and then type **Hello everyone** and press Enter again, you end up with the following output.

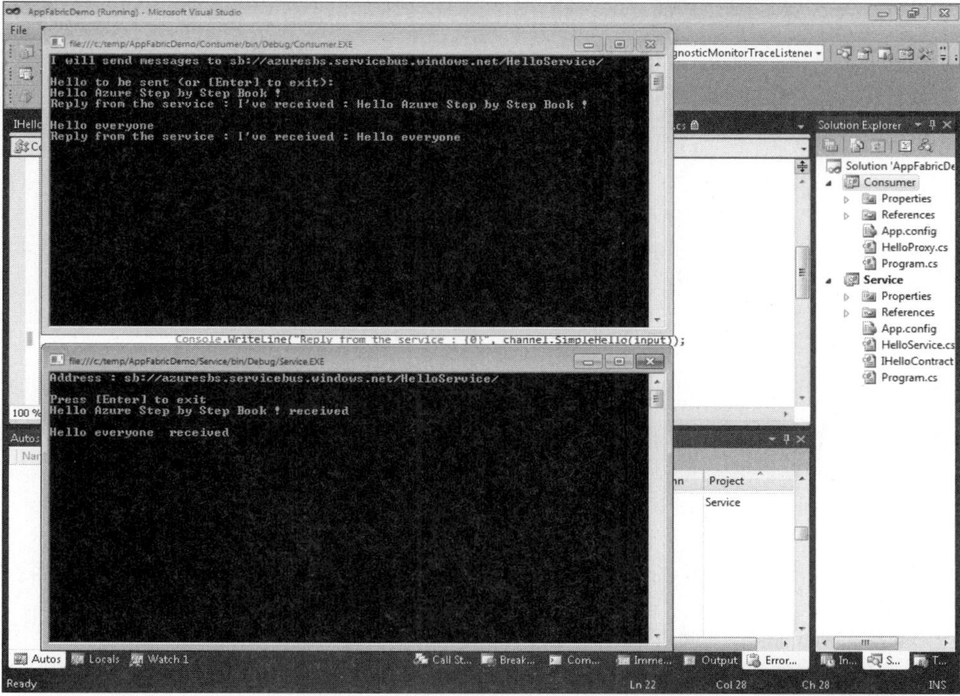

The requests are being relayed from the consumer client application up into the cloud, and then back down to the service application. They happen to be on my computer, but they could really be anywhere on the Internet.

You have seen how to create a new Service Bus namespace and how to exchange data between a consumer and a service using the relay feature of the Internet Service Bus provided by Windows Azure AppFabric. As with other Windows Azure Platform components, you can use the portal to configure the component you want to use without configuring anything else, and then you can start using it with the related APIs.

Remember that you can leverage the Service Bus infrastructure directly using REST and HTTP without an SDK. For example, if you want to register a service on the Service Bus, you can issue a *POST* to the management URI using the security token you have to request to the Access Control Service. If you want to send a message to a remote service, you can make a *POST* to the public URI of the service. If you use the SDK, these steps are performed by the provided infrastructure.

Before you move to a new example, try to start another instance of the consumer and use it to send messages to the same service. As you will discover, the Service Bus infrastructure can be used by more than one client to talk with a single endpoint.

Direct Connection

In the preceding section, you learned how to use the Service Bus to create a channel between two applications that can be hosted in totally different networks using the relay capabilities of the Windows Azure AppFabric Service Bus. You can connect an on-premises application with remote clients without having to open firewall ports or reduce the security of your network. For example, you can use this feature to connect remote notebooks with a service hosted on premises. But sometimes notebook owners work on the same network that hosts the on-premises service. In such cases, relaying messages through the Internet to talk to a service in the same LAN is not efficient. Fortunately, the Service Bus and the SDK provide a completely transparent algorithm that can make direct calls (provided that they are allowed) when appropriate, and still make remote calls when the consumer and service are on different LANs.

It is so transparent that, with the exception of the measurable speed difference, you don't really know which communication method the consumer and service are using. You configure this type of connection in the following procedure.

Use Direct Connection

1. Open the application configuration file for the consumer and change the binding element, adding the *connectionMode* attribute and the security element, as in the following code:

```
<bindings>

   <netTcpRelayBinding>
     <binding name="default" connectionMode="Hybrid">
       <security mode="None" />
     </binding>
   </netTcpRelayBinding>

</bindings>
```

2. Do the same for the service configuration file.
3. Run the sample by pressing F5 and then start a new *Consumer* instance. After some time, depending on the speed of your LAN, a Windows Security Alert might appear asking you if you want to allow direct communication. If you are using Windows 7, the alert will be similar to the following figure. (Depending on your firewall settings, this alert may not appear at all.)

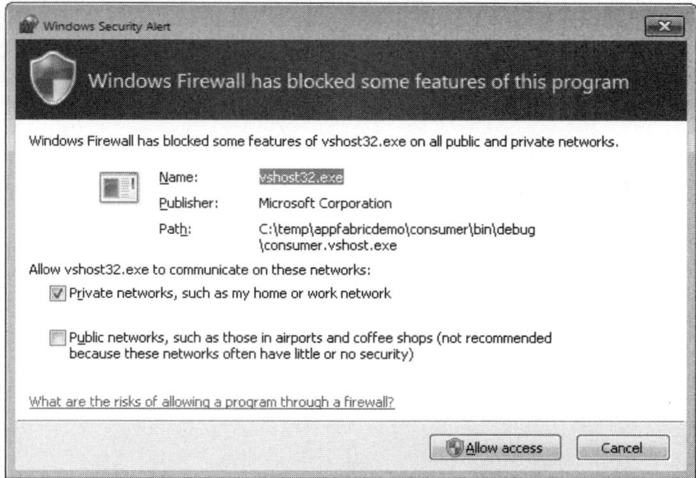

You have to select, at minimum, your private network, and then click Allow Access to create a direct connection between the consumer and the service. (Don't worry, you learn how to remove that permission pretty soon.) If you do not allow that kind of connection, the sample continues to work using the relayed connection. The term *hybrid*, in fact, means that a connection is created using the relayed binding and then, if possible, the connection is elevated to a direct connection. If something goes wrong with the direct connection, or if the client or the service moves to another network, the connection falls back to relay.

If you want to expose, or discover, the type of connection being used, the *Microsoft.ServiceBus* library provides an event that fires when the connection status changes. You can insert this code immediately after opening the channel:

```
IHybridConnectionStatus hybridConnectionStatus =
   channel.GetProperty<IHybridConnectionStatus>();

Console.WriteLine("Initial status : {0}",
   hybridConnectionStatus.ConnectionState);
Console.WriteLine();

if (hybridConnectionStatus != null)
{
    hybridConnectionStatus.ConnectionStateChanged += (o, e) =>
    {
        Console.WriteLine("Status changed to: {0}.", e.ConnectionState);
    };
}
```

To test the speed, you can insert this code inside the *while* loop:

```
while (!String.IsNullOrEmpty(input))
{
    try
    {
        Int32 start = Environment.TickCount;
        String response = channel.SimpleHello(input);
        Console.WriteLine("Response {0} - Time{1}", response,
            Environment.TickCount - start);
    }
    catch (Exception e)
    {
        Console.WriteLine("Error: " + e.Message);
    }
    input = Console.ReadLine();
}
```

If you run the sample and send different messages before and after the connection status changes, you observe that speed can vary significantly between a direct connection and a relayed connection, as shown in the following figure.

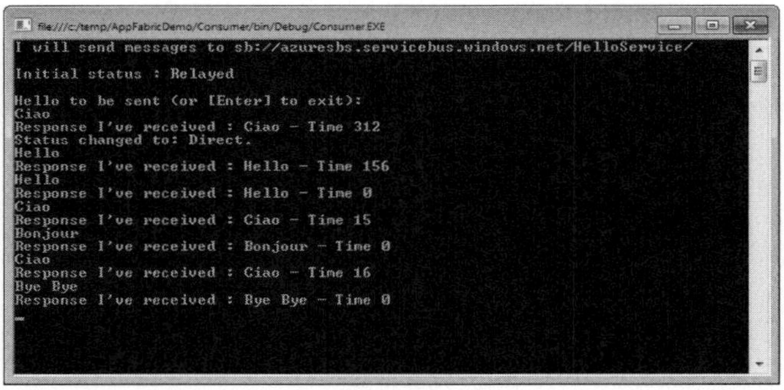

```
I will send messages to sb://azuresbs.servicebus.windows.net/HelloService/

Initial status : Relayed

Hello to be sent (or [Enter] to exit):
Ciao
Response I've received : Ciao - Time 312
Status changed to: Direct.
Hello
Response I've received : Hello - Time 156
Hello
Response I've received : Hello - Time 0
Ciao
Response I've received : Ciao - Time 15
Bonjour
Response I've received : Bonjour - Time 0
Ciao
Response I've received : Ciao - Time 16
Bye Bye
Response I've received : Bye Bye - Time 0
```

The first and second lines in the preceding figure show a relayed connection that is significantly slower than the others. The first message takes the longest amount of time because of DNS resolution. Note that the event is asynchronous, and was fired during the second operation call. This explains why the "status changed" line appears before the second call.

You can always remove the rule that the Windows Firewall creates when you select the Allow Access button in the security alert using the Allowed Programs list in Control Panel.

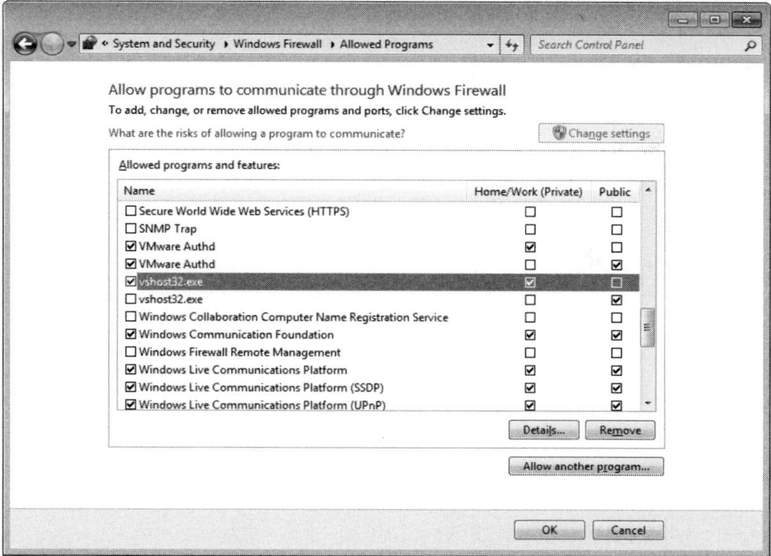

As you can see, the program vshost32.exe has permission to use Home/Work features—that is, the private network. You can remove that rule by selecting each of that program's two entries, and clicking the Remove button. If you have more entries, click the Details button to see what program they point to.

Bindings

The Windows Azure AppFabric SDK exposes many other bindings you can use to exchange data in direct or relayed connections. You can find detailed information about the different bindings in the official documentation on MSDN.

The complete list of bindings for the current version, created by using Reflector, appears in the following figure.

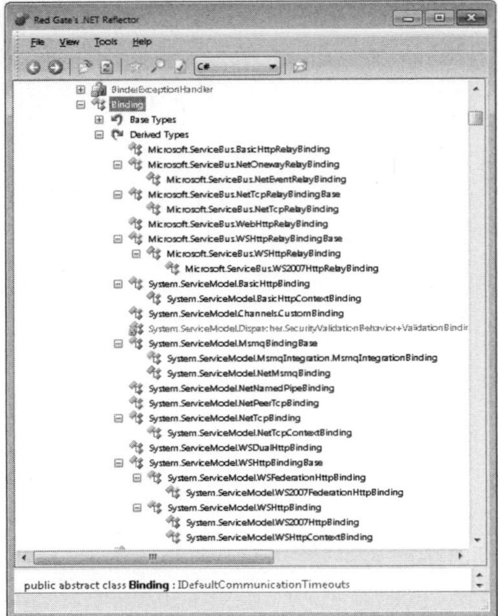

Many of the Service Bus bindings are simply relayed versions of the related WCF bindings. The *netEventRelayBinding* lets the infrastructure send the same message to many receivers.

In the near future, there will be many other bindings that allow round-robin scenarios, load balanced receivers, message filtering, queuing mechanisms, and so forth. If you are interested in building Service Bus solutions, keep an eye on the documentation.

In the next exercise, you switch bindings to use the *ws2007HttpBinding* instead of the *netTcpRelayBinding*.

Use a Different Binding

In this procedure, you use *ws2007HttpBinding*. This binding applies security to the transport protocol, exchanging data from the same consumer with the same service you built in the previous procedure.

1. Change the application configuration file for the service and the consumer so that their *<bindings>* sections specify the new binding, as shown in the following code:

```
<bindings>
  <!-- Application Binding -->
  <ws2007HttpRelayBinding>
    <binding name="default">
      <security mode="Transport"/>
    </binding>
  </ws2007HttpRelayBinding>
</bindings>
```

2. Change the endpoint configuration for both the consumer and the service that it points to the new binding:

```
<endpoint name="RelayEndpoint" ...
          binding="ws2007HttpRelayBinding"
          ... />
```

3. Change the parameter of the *CreateServiceUri* method in the *Main* method of the consumer and the service to use *https* instead of *sb*:

```
Uri serviceUri = ServiceBusEnvironment.CreateServiceUri(
    "https", "azuresbs", "HelloService");
```

Note The security mode of the binding states that any security has to be done at the transport level, so if you followed the procedure, make sure you use *https* and not *http* as the first parameter.

4. In the consumer *Main* method, remove the code to test the hybrid connection.
5. Run the sample using the same pattern you used in the previous procedure.

The result should be similar to the following image.

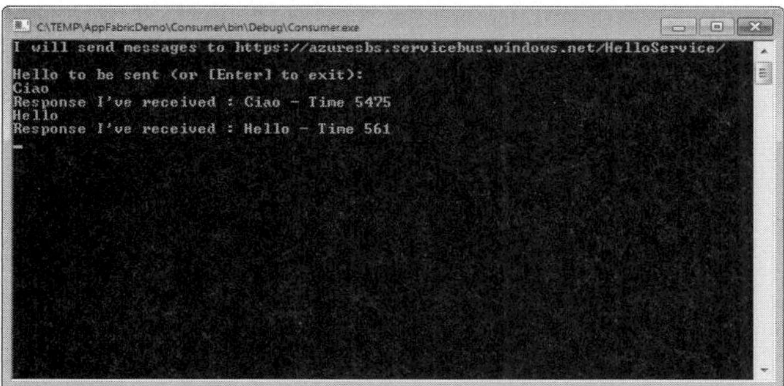

As you can see, the client uses an HTTPS endpoint to send messages, and the service is listening at the same address.

The following analyzer image shows the requests made by the two parties during this process.

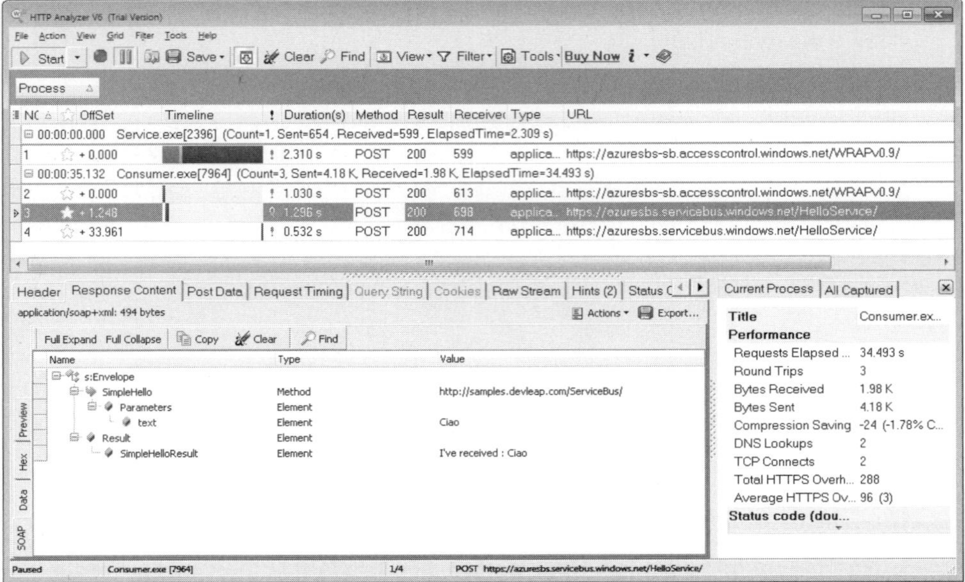

Look at the highlighted row. The underlying API uses the *POST* method over the HTTPS protocol to send something to the *azuresbs.servicebus.windows.net/HelloService* URI. The payload, shown in the bottom section of the preceding screen, shows the invoked operation, *SimpleHello*, the text Ciao, and the result as *SimpleHelloResult*. The last *POST* is the call to the "Hello" message.

The service makes the first *POST* request. It is also an HTTP POST, but it's directed to the Access Control Service that is responsible for authenticating the service to listen for Service Bus messages. The content of the response is a Web Resources Access Protocol (WRAP) access token that you can view. It looks something like the following text:

```
wrap_access_token=net.windows.servicebus.action%3dListen%252cSend%252cManage%26Issuer%3dhttp
s%253a%252f%252f
azuresbs-sb.accesscontrol.windows.net
%252f%26Audience%3dhttp%253a%252f%252f
azuresbs.servicebus.windows.net%252f
HelloService%26ExpiresOn%3d1294076696%26HMACSHA256%3dz5fHrxClp4L4ZHshE5x69PbofrnHKBUflqnpV4f
7TPk%253d&wrap_access_token_expires_in=1200
```

The token contains three encrypted permissions for Listen, Send, and Manage (shown in boldface in the code). I'm using, like you, the default Issuer that is the owner of the service namespace, so I have all the permissions. The second line states that the token was issued by *azuresbs-sb.accesscontrol.windows.net*, and the last part shows the intended audience, that is, *azuresbs.servicebus.windows.net* for the *HelloService*. Like any other token, this one also contains an expiration date and a Hash-based Message Authentication Code (HMAC) hash of the password.

The second post is similar to the first, but the consumer issues it. It contains the request for a token to the Access Control Service. Here's the payload:

```
wrap_scope=http%3a%2f%2fazuresbs.servicebus.windows.net%2fHelloService%2f&wrap_assertion_
format=SWT&wrap_assertion=Issuer%3downer%26HMACSHA256%3dgqoxIUAM5XrfFO4gevEmNehlnM5wRckfU8Vx
Ej0f564%253dwrap_scope=http%3a%2f%2fazuresbs.servicebus.windows.net%2fHelloService%2f&wrap_
assertion_format=SWT&wrap_assertion=Issuer%3downer%26HMACSHA256%3dgqoxIUAM5XrfFO4gevEmNehlnM
5wRckfU8VxEj0f564%253d
```

The request is not so difficult to understand; the consumer uses the *Issuer=owner* and the hashed password to request the permission for the URI *http://azuresbs.servicebus.windows.net/HelloService*.

Note The acronym SWT, shown in the preceding code, stands for *Simple Web Token*.

It is important to point out that modifying the binding changes the way the message is transported from the consumer to the server, but it does not modify the protocol that the two parties use to talk to the Service Bus management infrastructure. You can use *ws2007HttpRelayBinding* to exchange data and use TCP on port 808 or 828 (if you use SSL over TCP) to register the service to the Service Bus and establish the connection from a consumer.

HTTP for Management URI

As I just pointed out, changing the binding does not change the way the service and the consumer talk to the management infrastructure (also called the *control channel*). If the service or the consumer has problems using the output port for TCP/IP, either can switch to a complete HTTP-based connection.

To make the switch, you must modify the code of one of the presented examples slightly. You need to inform the infrastructure to use an HTTP connection instead of the default one.

The change is simple and is shown in the following code:

```
ServiceBusEnvironment.SystemConnectivity.Mode =
    ConnectivityMode.Http;
```

You have to set the *SystemConnectivity* before opening the channel. If you were to make this modification to both the consumer and the service, your connection would be completely based on HTTP.

That's a convenient change for teaching purposes, because using an HTTP-based connection lets me show you the complete HTTP trace for an end-to-end test, using the same code you used in the last procedure. The trace is shown in the following figure.

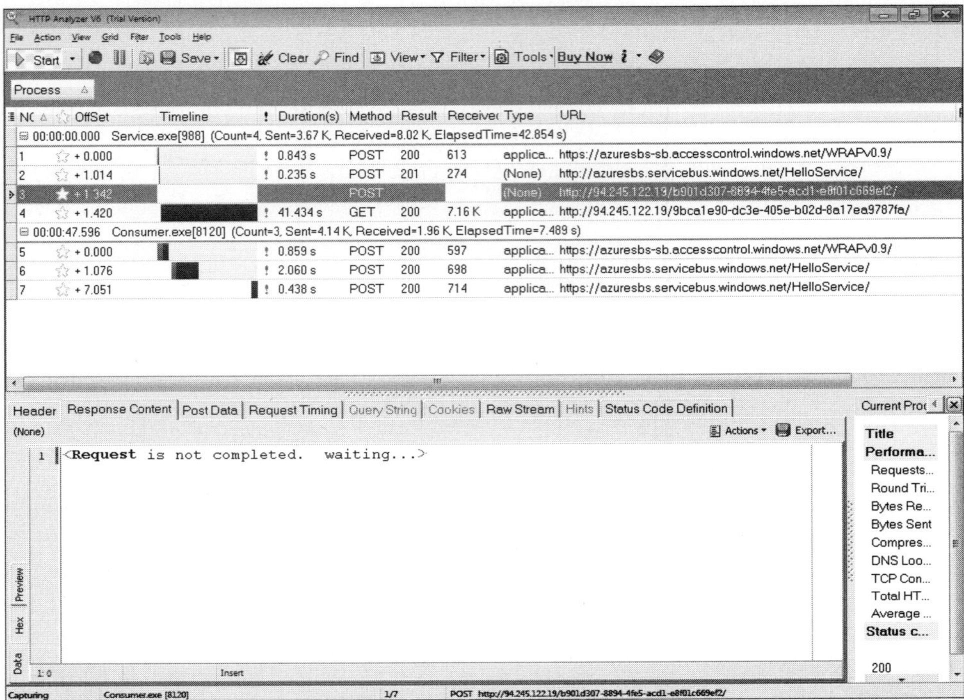

The analyzer shows that the service issues a *POST* to the Access Control Service (the first traced line) to request the simple web token that contains its permission for the service namespace. It then issues a *POST* to create the channel for the *HelloService* service. The response status code is *201 Created*, stating that the Service Bus management APIs successfully created the public endpoint. Next, the service issues another *POST* to a different address. This address represents the front-end node of the Service Bus selected to be the forwarder (the node that relays the message). As you can see in the bottom section of the screen, this request remains open to allow any further communication from the forwarder to the on-premises service. (Remember that this example uses the HTTP protocol and doesn't expose the service itself on the Internet.)

Summary

In this chapter, you examined a simple application that sends messages from a consumer to a service using the relay feature of the Windows Azure AppFabric Service Bus. The consumer code can be used by any .NET Framework client running on premises or in the cloud—just as the service code can. You saw how to configure both relayed and direct connections as well as how to configure using HTTP rather than TCP to manage the service namespace. The Windows Azure AppFabric Access Control Service manages the service access rules.

Quick Reference

To	Do this
Download the Windows Azure AppFabric SDK for a different platform	Go to *http://www.azure.com*.
Build the Service Bus URI	Use the *ServiceBusEnviroment* class.
Create a new Service Bus namespace	Use the Windows Azure AppFabric portal.
See the default Issuer Name and Issuer Secret for the management key	Use the Windows Azure AppFabric portal.
Use a direct connection	Use the *Hybrid* connection mode attribute in binding element of the configuration.
Allow a direct connection	Use the Windows Firewall rule.

Chapter 8
WCF Data Services and OData

After completing this chapter, you will be able to

- Understand Open Data Protocol (OData).
- Expose an Entity Data Model to REST/HTTP protocols.
- Use REST queries against an exposed model.
- Execute CRUD operations from a remote client.
- Build a WCF Data Service client application.

Open Data Protocol (OData) is an emerging protocol for querying and updating data across the web. It uses existing technologies such as HTTP, JSON (JavaScript Object Notation), and Atom Publishing Protocol (AtomPub) to provide abstract access to a variety of services, stores, applications, and data.

Microsoft supports OData in a growing list of products, including Microsoft SharePoint Server 2010, Microsoft SQL Server 2008 R2, Microsoft Visual Studio 2008 SP1 and Visual Studio 2010, and Microsoft Excel 2010 (via PowerPivot for Excel). OData is exposed natively by Windows Azure storage as well as Microsoft SQL Azure through Windows Communication Foundation (WCF) Data Services (that is, ADO.NET Data Services). Microsoft also provides client libraries for the Microsoft .NET Framework, Microsoft Silverlight, and Microsoft ASP.NET AJAX.

This chapter begins by reviewing the history of the Astoria project, which was the code name for what is now WCF Data Services, and presents the technologies that followed it by using procedures to help you understand the concepts.

Note Because URLs, UI names, and procedures may vary over time, some of them may be out of date by the time you read this. In that case, my best advice is to start looking for the information about the Windows Azure product on the Windows Azure home page (*http://www.azure.com*). Information included in this book was accurate at the time of writing.

The Astoria Project

Early in 2007, Microsoft presented a project with the code name Astoria. Astoria exposes data services that enable applications to access and manipulate data over HTTP connections, using URIs to identify pieces of information within these data services. The data values are represented in XML or JavaScript Object Notation (JSON) when transferred from client to server or from server to client.

The theory was interesting, because a number of scenarios and solutions, such as the emerging Web 2.0 applications, needed a simple and effective way to exchange data from the browser to the server. AJAX-based applications benefitted from Astoria because it helped separate data from its presentation; you could ask the server for some piece of data directly in JavaScript without requesting an entirely new page. JQuery and other emerging libraries also benefitted from this approach.

This separation was even more important in technologies such as Adobe Flash and Silverlight (which was at version 1.0 at that time), because their code is compiled before the browser plug-in downloads it. When the compiled code reaches the client, the client can request data from the server again using HTTP, XML, and/or JSON. Users can update various bits of information before sending back just the modified values.

The Astoria project was released officially in the .NET Framework 3.5 SP1 in August 2008 together with Visual Studio 2008 SP1. The .NET Framework 3.5 SP1 exposes the server and the client APIs, including an AJAX version for the major browsers, and Visual Studio 2008 SP1 provides sophisticated designers and data binding features.

In Visual Studio 2010 and the .NET Framework 4, this technology was renamed yet again—to WCF Data Services. This chapter uses the .NET Framework 4 and Visual Studio 2010, but almost every step is identical in Visual Studio 2008 SP1 and the .NET Framework 3.5.

WCF Data Services (ADO.NET Data Services)

There are two main goals of this changing-name technology. The first is to aid developers in defining data services that expose simple methods to query and update a behind-the-scenes data source in a standard way. The second is to provide libraries that can access these services from a variety of clients, including Silverlight, XNA, AJAX, jQuery, or any .NET Framework client.

If you have an existing Entity Data Model (EDM), you can build a WCF Data Service in about two minutes. If you don't have an existing EDM, but want to expose every table or view in a compatible database, it will take you about four minutes.

Data exchange between client and server is based on JSON, AtomPub, or XML. Data access requires only simple HTTP methods such as a *GET* to retrieve an entity, a *POST* to insert a new one, a *MERGE* to do an update operation, or a *DELETE* to remove an entire row of information.

Server-side ADO.NET Data Services is based on classes that derive from WCF classes: it is a specialized version of WCF, so renaming it in .NET Framework 4 was appropriate. These classes serve as base classes for custom data services and expose every operation for every entity defined in the EDM. The contracts for each operation are defined inside this class and provide common operations on the data exposed by the EDM.

In practice, all you need to do to get started with ADO.NET/WCF Data Services is to derive a class and let the library do its work. Next, you can adjust the behavior by adding security policy and query interceptors. You filter data based on user roles or remove an operation from the contract. Setting up most of these operations is very easy.

Behind these standard services, you can use LINQ to SQL to expose a model for data stored in SQL Server, or use the ADO.NET Entity Framework (both versions 3.5 and 4.0 are supported) to build a more complex model and to support other database servers.

In practice, the data service inspects the model and provides classic Create, Read, Update, and Delete (CRUD) operations, including filtering or sorting, join operations between entities defined in the model, and lazy or explicit loading via HTTP. Each query gets sent to the wire, inspected by the service, and then analyzed by the provider, letting the provider send optimized queries to the database for maximum performance and scalability. The service uses the *IQueryable* interface to pass the expression tree to the LINQ to SQL and ADO.NET Entity Framework providers. Because every query is based on the *IQueryable* interface, it is possible to expose your custom data source to WCF Data Services.

Because every service is exposed via HTTP/REST using XML, AtomPub, or JSON, essentially any client can access these services to query and update data. If you use any supported Microsoft technology to build the client, you can add a service reference to the service and let the WCF Data Services client library provide you with a data context so that you can query data, modify that data locally, and send only the modified entities back to the service using CUD (Create, Update, Delete) operations.

The next chapters examine application architectures that decouple your applications using three or more layers. The rest of this chapter takes a step-by-step approach using a simple example that ignores architectural considerations.

The Building Blocks

Create an ASP.NET Web Application

To begin, you need to create a simple ASP.NET Web Application that will serve as a container to expose data services. You don't need to choose any special project template—define the service wherever clients can reach it. An ASP.NET web application is perfect for achieving this result.

1. From Visual Studio 2010, create a normal ASP.NET web application without Model–view–controller (MVC) or Dynamic Data, and name the project and solution **DevLeap.WCFDataService**. Select the Create Directory For Solution check box, which is shown in the figure that follows. You can also create a Web Site project, because the resulting project is a fully functional website.

Note The ASP.NET Web Site Project template was introduced in Microsoft Visual Studio 2005 as a simpler model than the Visual Studio 2002/2003 ASP.NET Web Project. Autocompilation of code-behind files and other features were interesting, but developers soon faced numerous problems, so Microsoft proposed an add-in for Visual Studio 2005 to return to the classic model. In Visual Studio 2008 and Visual Studio 2010, I prefer the ASP.NET Web Application approach.

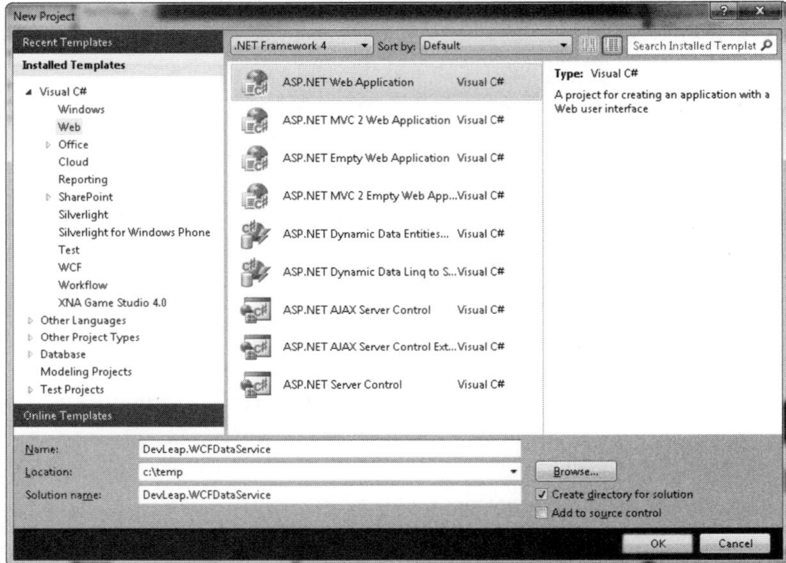

If you're using the .NET Framework 3.5, you end up with an ADO.NET Data Service. If you're using the .NET Framework 4, you end up with a WCF Data Service. Which one you end up with is not important, because WCF Data Services is just a new name for ADO.NET Data Services.

2. Check to make sure the element *compilation* in the Web.config file has a *debug* attribute with the value of *true*. Because the ASP.NET runtime compiles the .aspx pages and the .svc file, you want to compile them in debug mode during development so that you can obtain useful information if something goes wrong.

Next, you need to create an EDM that provides the query operation for the different entities and models the relations between them. You can choose a LINQ to SQL model, an Entity Framework 3.5 or 4.0 model, or any class that implements the *IQueryable* interface. If you haven't used Entity Framework, don't worry—you see how to use the basic functionality in this section.

This example uses a simple database called *EstatesManagement*, which has just five tables and the simple structure shown in the next figure. The first table is *tabSalesmen* and represents real estate salesmen. Every salesman has a number of assigned estates represented by the *tabEstates* table, so this table exposes an *idSalesman* field. Each estate has a particular type; the *tabEstateTypes* table is a lookup table for this data. The other two tables are not used in this example.

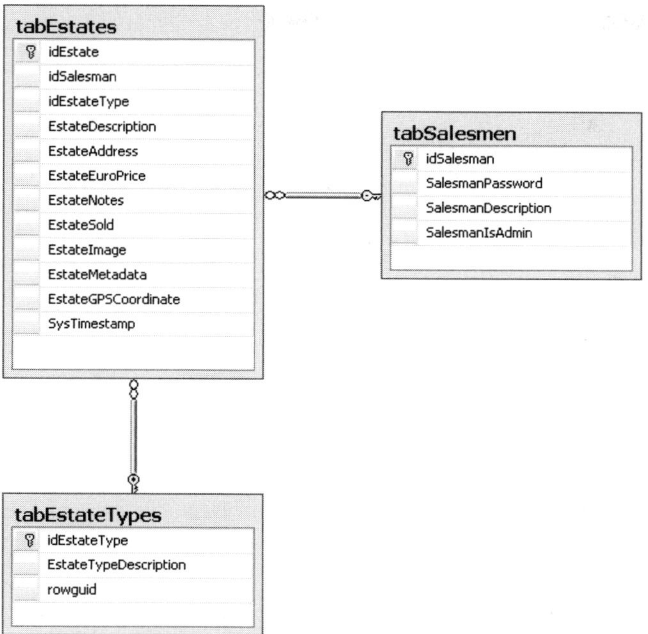

Create the Database

1. Create a new SQL Server Database called **DevLeap.EstatesMagement.DB.SQL2005** using SQL Server Management Studio.
2. Use the Database.sql file from the Chapter 8 Demo zip file to create the database structure and fill it with some sample data. (Please refer to this book's "Introduction," which contains the download link.)

You now have the database and the sample data you will look at in the pages that follow.

Create an Entity Data Model

1. To add an Entity Data Model to your project, right-click the project inside the solution and select the Add New Item menu. Then select the ADO.NET Entity Framework template. Remember to choose Data from the template types menu on the left side of the wizard, which is shown in the following figure.

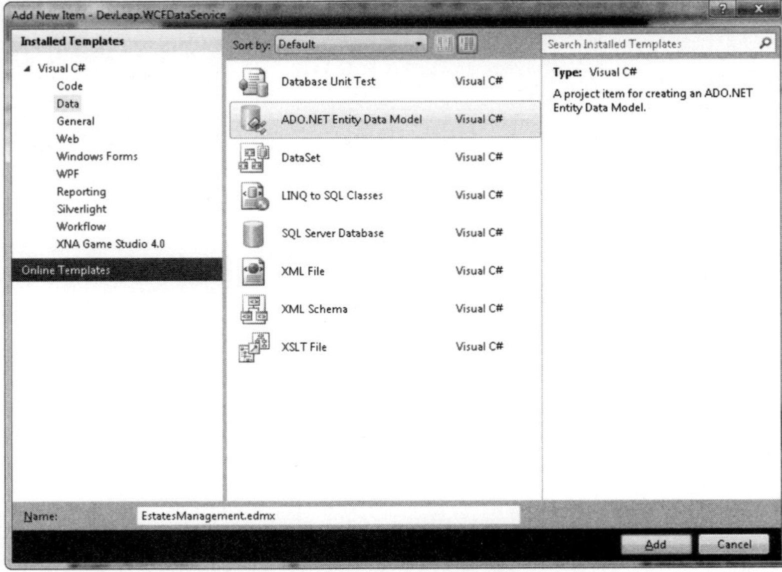

2. Name the model **EtatesManagement.edmx**, and then click the Add button. The template opens a new wizard that guides you through the process for creating the EDM.
3. You can elect to build a model from scratch or to generate the model from an existing database, as shown in the following figure. Because you already have the database in this case, choose the Generate From Database option, and then click Next.

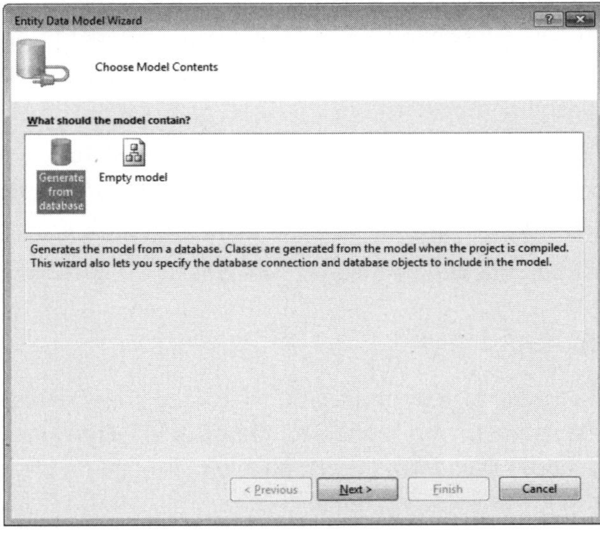

4. Choose a database connection. Because this is the first time you have used this database, the first list box does not display a connection. You need to click the New Connection button in the upper-right side of the wizard page to open a standard Connection Properties dialog box. Fill in the information based on your configuration, and then click the OK button to return to the Entity Data Model Wizard.

   Figure 8-1 shows the wizard page. Notice the following selected options and check boxes in the figure:

   - **Yes, Include The Sensitive Data In The Connection String** This being selected means that the connection string will include the password. You can avoid that by electing the option No, Exclude Sensitive Data From The Connection String. I Will Set It In My Application Code. Because the purpose of this chapter is to fully understand every piece needed to expose a WCF Data Service, for now, use the default option as shown in Figure 8-1. Note that if you are using a trusted connection, the option button will be dimmed.
   - **Entity Connection String box** In Figure 8-1, metadata values appear before the classic connection string. *Entities* is identified as the default name. The Entity Framework describes the model with three different languages, which are introduced in the next section of this chapter.
   - **Save Entity Connection Settings In Web.Config As check box** This is selected and indicates the name of the *connectionString* element created by the wizard to store the connection string. Leave it to the default proposed by the wizard, because it will be easier to use the model if you do.

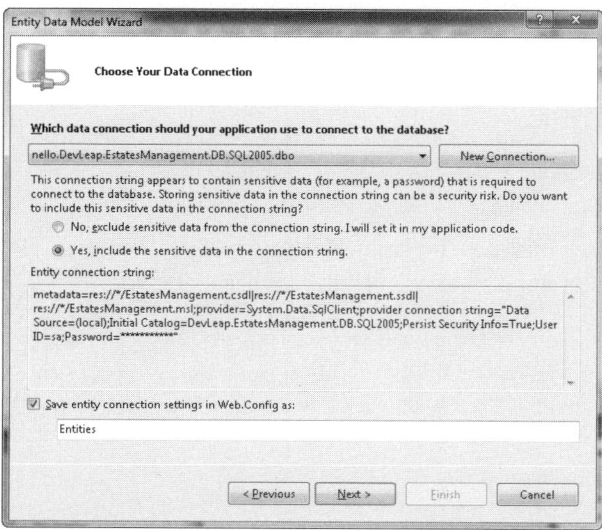

FIGURE 8-1 Entity Data Model connection information.

5. Choose which objects to include in the model. For instance, you could add just two tables and three views when your application doesn't care about other information stored in the database. As you can see in the next figure, you can also include stored procedures. In this case, the stored procedure will become a method of the model that you can call, just as you can call any other standard .NET Framework methods.

   Expand the Tables node, and select *tabEstates*, *tabEstateTypes*, and *tabSalesmen*, and then select the Pluralize Or Singularize Generated Object Names check box to let the designer adapt the collection of entity names to their plural forms. The option Include Foreign Key Columns In The Model is self-explanatory, and it is one of the new features (as well as the pluralizing) of Entity Framework 4.0.

   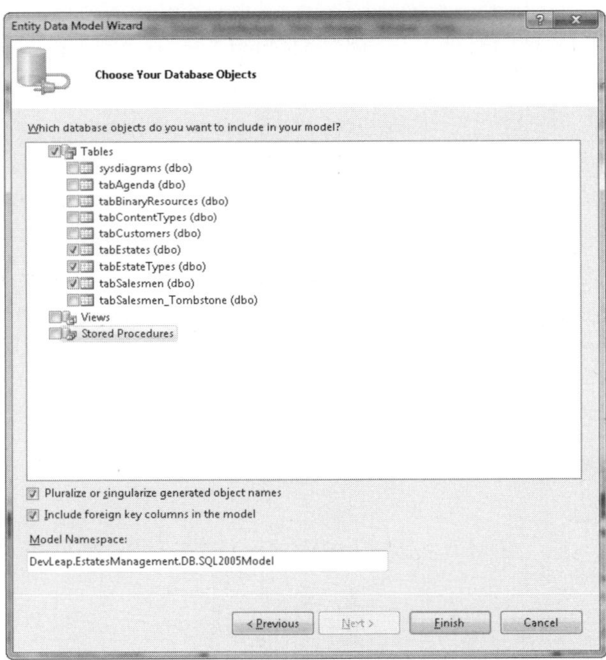

   The model namespace includes the defined entity, and you can change it at any time from the designer that appears after you click the Finish button.

The wizard adds some new references to the project required by the Entity Framework APIs; a new connection string in the Web.Config file, identical to the one you saw in the second wizard step; and a new file called EstatesManagement.edmx that represents the Entity Data Model.

The wizard also opens the designer for the new EDM included in the project, showing you the three entities inferred from the chosen database table. Each entity contains the exact set of fields as the underlying table and has the same relationship with other entities that the tables do in the database schema.

Each relation is represented by a navigation property that, by default, assumes the same name as the entity referenced. In some cases, the navigation property name is plural, meaning that the property represents the *N*-side of a 1:*N* relation. In this example, the *tabSalesman* has a navigation property called *tabEstates* that refers to all the estates assigned to that salesman. On the other hand, the *tabEstate* entity has a *tabSalesman* property, which refers to the salesman assigned to each estate.

Rename the Entity and Entity Set

1. Rename every entity, deleting the tab prefixes. You can do this in the properties window (press F4 in the designer with an entity selected) or directly from the design surface in the header of the entity. Entity Framework manages the mapping between the entity and the corresponding table.
2. Verify that the Entity Set Name is renamed, too. If it is not, rename it. The entity name represents a single entity, and the Entity Set Name represents the collection of entities.
3. Rename every navigation property as well, as shown in the next figure.

Note This is only a brief introduction to Entity Framework 4.0 A complete analysis of the methodology or of best practices for using Object Role Modeling (ORM) is beyond the scope of this book.

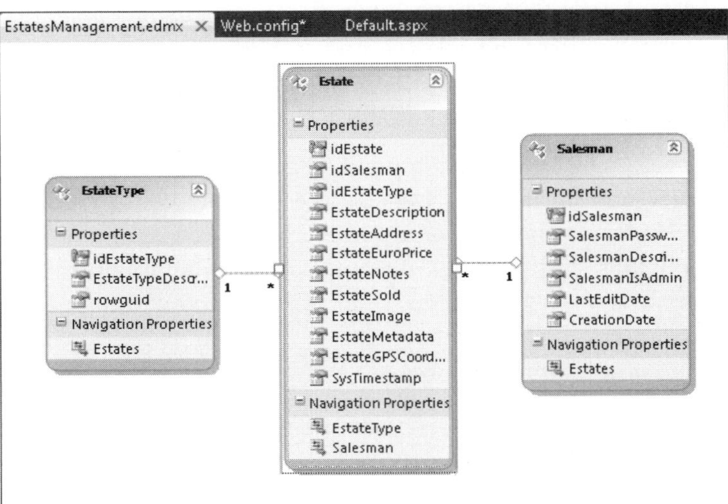

The renaming operation introduces an important concept: Entity Framework, or more precisely the Entity Framework Designer, uses different languages to describe the entity model, the underlying database, and the mapping between the two. The EDMX file is composed of three different sections that are also indicated in the connection string inserted automatically in the Web.config file, as you can see in Listing 8-1.

LISTING 8-1 Connection string.

```
metadata=
  res://*/EstatesManagement.csdl|
  res://*/EstatesManagement.ssdl|
  res://*/EstatesManagement.msl;
  provider=System.Data.SqlClient;provider
  connection string="Data Source=(local);Initial
      Catalog=DevLeap.EstatesManagement.DB.SQL2005;Persist Security
      Info=True;User ID=sa;Password=***********"
```

These three languages are described in the following list:

- **Conceptual Schema Definition Language (CSDL)** This represents the entity definitions as you want to use them in code. Each element inside an entity is a property exposed by the class that represents the entity. This means that the designer produces a class named *Estates* which includes, for instance, a public property named *EstatesDescription*. You can modify the property name using the designer.
- **Storage Schema Definition Language (SSDL)** This represents the database object definition. Because you used an existing database, the schema contains the name of the included tables and the definition of every table field. These definitions are partially visible in the designer.
- **Mapping Schema Language (MSL)** With this language, the framework is able to map an entity with the corresponding table, and each property with the corresponding field. The MSL is also used to convert the .NET Framework type to the database type and vice versa. It is important to note that I used SQL Server 2008, but Entity Framework is not limited to Microsoft databases.

Before exposing the model with a WCF Data Service, you can use the model from the Microsoft Visual C# code to query the entity and its relationships without having to remember field and table names. Entity Framework handles this tough job for you. You can express a query using LINQ to Entities, Entity SQL, or a mix of both.

Create a Simple Page to Show the Result

1. Place a *GridView* control named *salesmenGrid* in the Default.aspx page, as illustrated in Listing 8-2.

LISTING 8-2 Default.aspx.

```
<%@ Page Title="Home Page" Language="C#" MasterPageFile="~/Site.master"
AutoEventWireup="true"
    CodeBehind="Default.aspx.cs" Inherits="DevLeap.WCFDataService._Default" %>

<asp:Content ID="HeaderContent" runat="server" ContentPlaceHolderID="HeadContent">
</asp:Content>
<asp:Content ID="BodyContent" runat="server" ContentPlaceHolderID="MainContent">
    <h2>
        Welcome to ASP.NET!
    </h2>
    <p>
        <asp:GridView ID="salemenGrid" runat="server" AutoGenerateColumns="true"
/>
    </p>
</asp:Content>
```

2. In the code-behind file, in the *Page_Load* event, create a new data context, represented by the *Entity* class, and express a LINQ query on the *Estates* entity set.
3. Bind the result of the *ToList* method of the query object to the *GridView* control, and call the *DataBind* method on it, as illustrated in Listing 8-3.

LISTING 8-3 Default.aspx code-behind file.

```
using System;
using System.Collections.Generic;
using System.Linq;
using System.Web;
using System.Web.UI;
using System.Web.UI.WebControls;

namespace DevLeap.WCFDataService
{
    public partial class _Default : System.Web.UI.Page
    {
        protected void Page_Load(object sender, EventArgs e)
        {
            Entities context = new Entities();

            var query = from estate in context.Estates
                        where estate.EstateSold == true
                        select estate;

            salemenGrid.DataSource = query.ToList();
            salemenGrid.DataBind();
        }
    }
}
```

Note that the code in Listing 8-3 does not catch any exception. It is fundamental to put the code in a *try/catch* block before releasing the code in a production environment. The connection string is read automatically by the constructor of the *ObjectContext* class, from which the Entities model is derived.

After inserting some sample data with the tool of your choice (or manually, if you prefer), test the code by pressing F5. The result is straightforward and should look similar, apart from entity data, to the page shown in the next figure. I used Visual Studio 2010 Ultimate to populate sample data in the database.

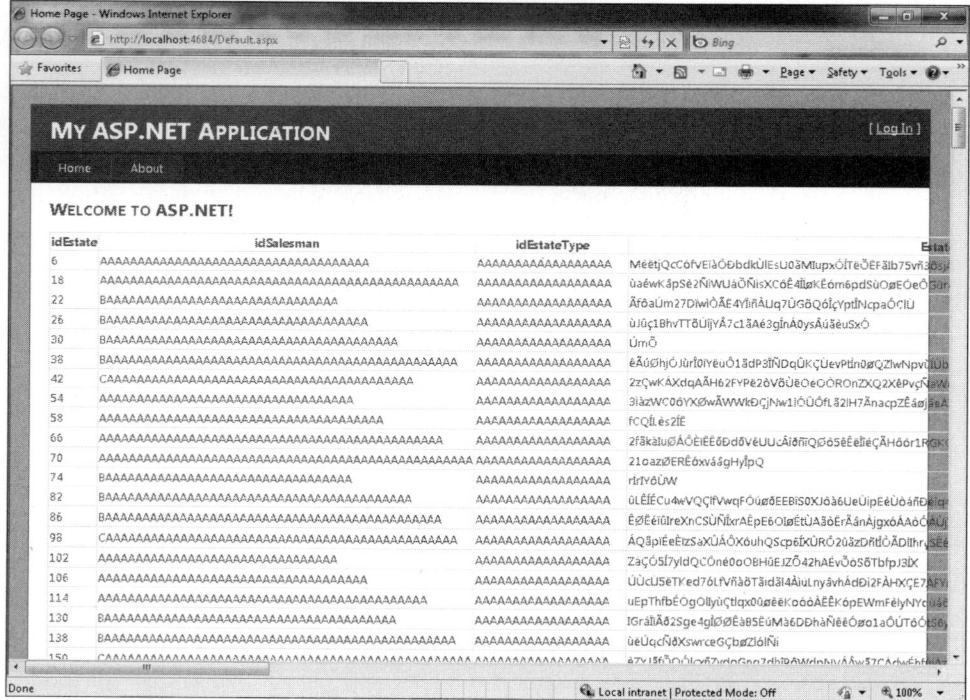

The layout and the fonts are far from perfect, but the example is very useful because it shows you how the foreign keys are used in the Entity Framework. The support for the foreign key is one of the new features of the Entity Framework 4.0.

You can try a different query to leverage the foreign key and navigation properties. Listing 8-4 shows a modified version of the previous query. This query extracts the value of the foreign key *idEstateType* of every estate that is already sold and has a salesman in the administrative role.

LISTING 8-4 Default.aspx code-behind file with Linq to Entities query.

```
using System;
using System.Collections.Generic;
using System.Linq;
using System.Web;
using System.Web.UI;
using System.Web.UI.WebControls;

namespace DevLeap.WCFDataService
{
    public partial class _Default : System.Web.UI.Page
    {
        protected void Page_Load(object sender, EventArgs e)
        {
            Entities context = new Entities();

            var query = from estate in context.Estates
                        where estate.EstateSold == true
                           && estate.Salesman.SalesmanIsAdmin == true
                        orderby estate.EstateType.EstateTypeDescription
                        select estate.idEstateType;

            salemenGrid.DataSource = query.ToList();
            salemenGrid.DataBind();
        }
    }
}
```

Entity Framework makes the best effort to optimize the query by leveraging the underlining data store engine. From a LINQ to Entities statement, the query is transformed in text using the data source dialect (T-SQL, in the case of a SQL Server) and it is arranged by the Entity Framework engine before it is passed to the database.

WCF Data Service

The underlying infrastructure is ready to be exposed by the service. If you are not familiar with Entity Framework or other ORMs, you might be amazed by what you did in the previous section. That was just the beginning! The most fun part is about to start.

Create a WCF Data Service

1. Use the Add New Item wizard to add a WCF Data Service. The template is in the web section of the screen and is shown as highlighted in the next figure. Assign the WCF Data Service a meaningful name in the Name text box such as **EstatesManagement.svc**, because this name is included in the path that the client has to use to reach the service.

2. Open the generated code-behind file and give a value to the generic type of *DataService* class from which your new *EstatesManagement* service derives. As you can see from the comment in Listing 8-4, the class needs your data source class, meaning the name of the class that represents your Entity Data Model. If you didn't change the default name shown in Figure 8-1, your class name should be *Entities*.

   Now your service is ready, although by default, it does not expose anything yet for security reasons. You have to explicitly give granular permission to every entity.

3. Modify the first uncommented line of the *InitilizeService* static method to open your service to the incoming request. For now, use an asterisk (*) as the first parameter of the *SetEntitySetAccessRule* method and modify the value of the *EntitySetRights* enumeration. The resulting code is shown in Listing 8-5.

   LISTING 8-5 Data Service code-behind file.

```
using System;
using System.Collections.Generic;
using System.Data.Services;
using System.Data.Services.Common;
using System.Linq;
using System.ServiceModel.Web;
using System.Web;

namespace DevLeap.WCFDataService
{
    public class EstatesManagement : DataService<Entities>
    {
        // This method is called only once to initialize service-wide policies.
```

```
        public static void InitializeService(DataServiceConfiguration config)
        {
            // TODO: set rules to indicate which entity sets and service
            operations are visible, updatable, etc.
            // Examples:
            config.SetEntitySetAccessRule("*", EntitySetRights.All);
            config.SetServiceOperationAccessRule("*",
                ServiceOperationRights.All);
            config.DataServiceBehavior.MaxProtocolVersion =
                DataServiceProtocolVersion.V2;
        }
    }
}
```

I introduce the *SetServiceOperationAccessRule* in the sections that follow. For now, leave it commented and forget about it.

To test your work, open the new service in a browser of your choice by selecting View In Browser from the shortcut menu that appears on the .svc file; or compile the solution, open a browser, and request EstatesManagement.svc.

The result of opening your browser should be similar to the response screen shown in Figure 8-2. If you don't see any XML but instead some beautiful representation similar to a feed, you have to configure your browser to show the real XML response. In Windows Internet Explorer, you can change this setting. From the Tools menu, open the Internet Options dialog box and select the Content tab. In the Feeds And Web Slices section of this tab, you can find a button named Settings. Click the Settings button and clear the Turn On Feed Reading View check box. You may have to restart your browser. The menu or tab position of this configuration changes from browser to browser, as well as changes depending on the version of a particular browser.

The service, during the browser call, inspects the model and requests the conceptual schema, showing the result in an AtomPub feed. From this feed, you can understand what collections (Entity Set) of entities are exposed by the service and can refine the request by selecting just what is wanted.

Each entity collection has an *atom:tile* XML element that represents the name of the entity as well as an *href* attribute of the *collection* element, which provides the path to inspect the entity set and query it.

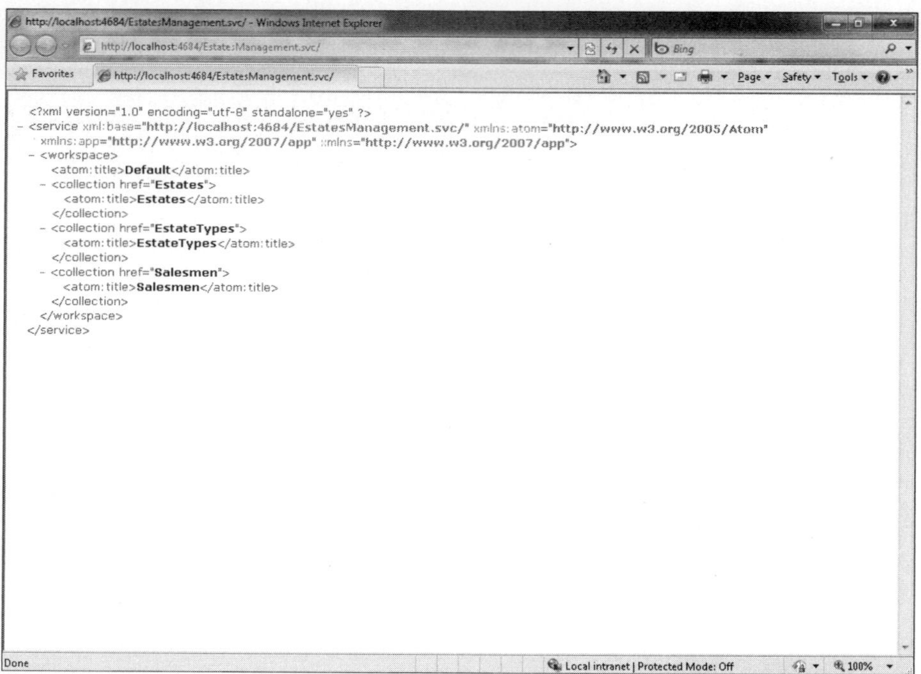

FIGURE 8-2 AtomPub result returned by a WCF Data Service call.

Try to change the URL of your request to include a specific request for the entity set named *Salesmen*. You have to use something like the following:

```
http://localhost:port/EstatesManagement.svc/Salesmen
```

The response shown in Figure 8-3 is created automatically from the service you wrote. As you can see, the *feed* XML element tells you that the infrastructure is using the standard way to provide a feed to a requesting client. The *xmlns* refers to *http://www.w3.org/2005/Atom* and confirms that you are using an OData-compatible protocol to represent the information. The *d* and *m* namespaces inform the requesting client that you are talking to a data service with a specification created by Microsoft for the ADO schema in August 2007.

The AtomPub feed contains a *title* element representing the name of the entity set, an *id* element that refers to the path of the service, and an *updated* element containing the processing date. After the feed definition, for each entity included in the entity set of the underlying model, the data service composed an *entry* element containing several bits of information.

The WCF Data Service queried the underlying ADO.NET Entity Framework model that, in turn, translated the salesmen request into a T-SQL statement and executed it against the underlying database.

The resulting query in the SQL Server Profiler is a common *SELECT* statement, which is shown in Listing 8-6.

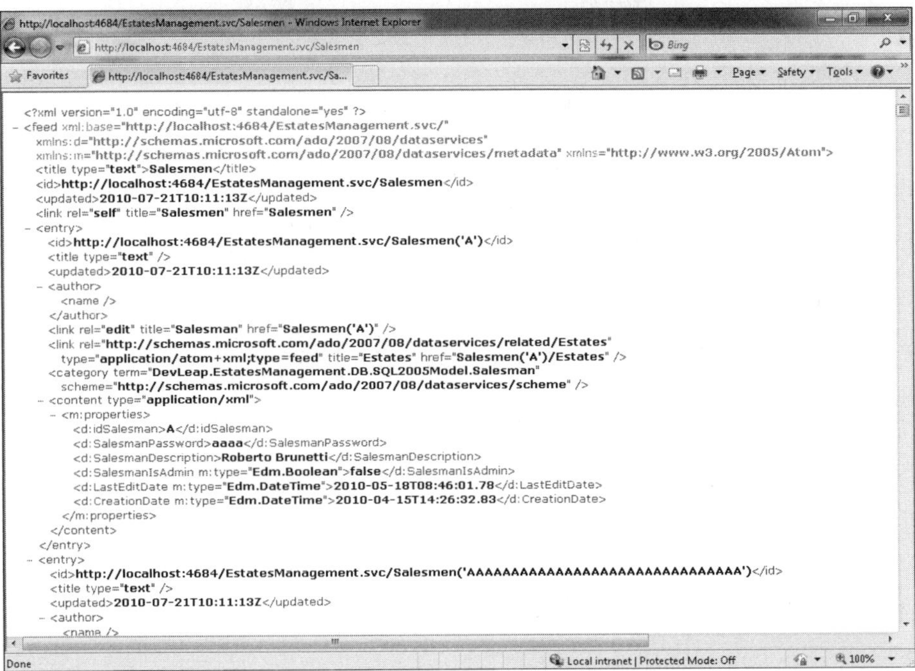

```
<?xml version="1.0" encoding="utf-8" standalone="yes" ?>
- <feed xml:base="http://localhost:4684/EstatesManagement.svc/"
  xmlns:d="http://schemas.microsoft.com/ado/2007/08/dataservices"
  xmlns:m="http://schemas.microsoft.com/ado/2007/08/dataservices/metadata" xmlns="http://www.w3.org/2005/Atom">
  <title type="text">Salesmen</title>
  <id>http://localhost:4684/EstatesManagement.svc/Salesmen</id>
  <updated>2010-07-21T10:11:13Z</updated>
  <link rel="self" title="Salesmen" href="Salesmen" />
- <entry>
    <id>http://localhost:4684/EstatesManagement.svc/Salesmen('A')</id>
    <title type="text" />
    <updated>2010-07-21T10:11:13Z</updated>
  - <author>
      <name />
    </author>
    <link rel="edit" title="Salesman" href="Salesmen('A')" />
    <link rel="http://schemas.microsoft.com/ado/2007/08/dataservices/related/Estates"
      type="application/atom+xml;type=feed" title="Estates" href="Salesmen('A')/Estates" />
    <category term="DevLeap.EstatesManagement.DB.SQL2005Model.Salesman"
      scheme="http://schemas.microsoft.com/ado/2007/08/dataservices/scheme" />
  - <content type="application/xml">
    - <m:properties>
        <d:idSalesman>A</d:idSalesman>
        <d:SalesmanPassword>aaaa</d:SalesmanPassword>
        <d:SalesmanDescription>Roberto Brunetti</d:SalesmanDescription>
        <d:SalesmanIsAdmin m:type="Edm.Boolean">false</d:SalesmanIsAdmin>
        <d:LastEditDate m:type="Edm.DateTime">2010-05-18T08:46:01.78</d:LastEditDate>
        <d:CreationDate m:type="Edm.DateTime">2010-04-15T14:26:32.83</d:CreationDate>
      </m:properties>
    </content>
  </entry>
- <entry>
    <id>http://localhost:4684/EstatesManagement.svc/Salesmen('AAAAAAAAAAAAAAAAAAAAAAAAAAAAAAA')</id>
    <title type="text" />
    <updated>2010-07-21T10:11:13Z</updated>
  - <author>
      <name />
```

FIGURE 8-3 Result from querying the *Salesmen* entity set.

LISTING 8-6 T-SQL statement for the salesmen entity set request.

```
SELECT
[Extent1].[idSalesman] AS [idSalesman],
[Extent1].[SalesmanPassword] AS [SalesmanPassword],
[Extent1].[SalesmanDescription] AS [SalesmanDescription],
[Extent1].[SalesmanIsAdmin] AS [SalesmanIsAdmin],
[Extent1].[LastEditDate] AS [LastEditDate],
[Extent1].[CreationDate] AS [CreationDate]
FROM [dbo].[tabSalesmen] AS [Extent1]
```

Each *entry* has some standard information coming from the AtomPub standard such as the *title type*, the author of the feed, and a core part represented by the *m:properties* element that shows every single property of the entity defined by EDM. By default, every entity property is exposed and can be used by the client.

An important piece of information is contained in the *id* element, because this element tells you how to reach the single entity from a URL. Try the URL *http://localhost:yourport/EstatesManagement.svc/Salesmen('A')* to request the single entity with key *A* or whatever key you have in your database.

If you try the link identified in the *id* element, the response should be similar to the figure shown in Figure 8-4. In this case, you executed a query to the service asking for a particular entity referenced by the key. The service queried the EDM that in turn executed the T-SQL statement shown in Listing 8-7.

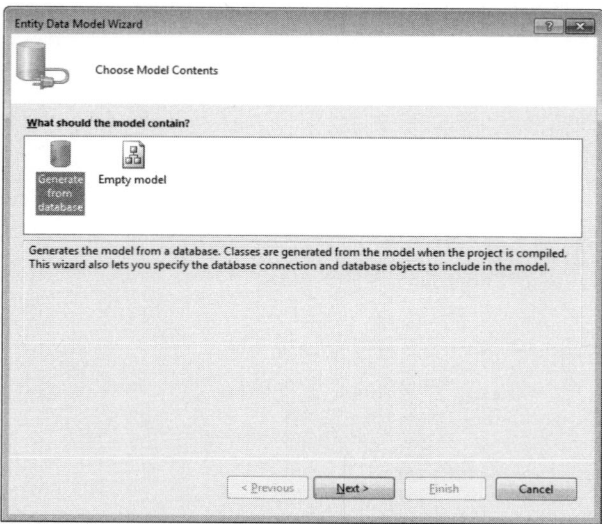

FIGURE 8-4 Request for a single *salesman* entity.

LISTING 8-7 T-SQL statement for a single *salesman* request.

```
SELECT
[Extent1].[idSalesman] AS [idSalesman],
[Extent1].[SalesmanPassword] AS [SalesmanPassword],
[Extent1].[SalesmanDescription] AS [SalesmanDescription],
[Extent1].[SalesmanIsAdmin] AS [SalesmanIsAdmin],
[Extent1].[LastEditDate] AS [LastEditDate],
[Extent1].[CreationDate] AS [CreationDate]
FROM [dbo].[tabSalesmen] AS [Extent1]
WHERE N'A' = [Extent1].[idSalesman]
```

Remember that you are requesting entities defined in the EDM, not from the underlying table. Every request uses an entity and an entity set name, and every response contains data that is serialized in entries. The translation to a T-SQL statement is not performed by the service, but rather from the Entity Framework engine.

Query and Relationship

The last two elements of an entry element that I haven't explained yet are link elements. You use the first in the next section dedicated to the CUD operation; and you use the second to reference the navigation properties of your entity. As you might remember from Figure 8-4, because the salesman entity has a single navigation property, the corresponding entry shows you that you can compose a URL to ask for the *Estates* of the *Salesman*.

The URL to compose is *http://localhost:port/EstatesManagement.svc/Salesmen('A')/Estates*, and the response will be a new feed with the title *Estates*, an *id* representing the URL you asked for, and an entry for every estate of the salesman with the key equal to *A*. Figure 8-5 shows the result.

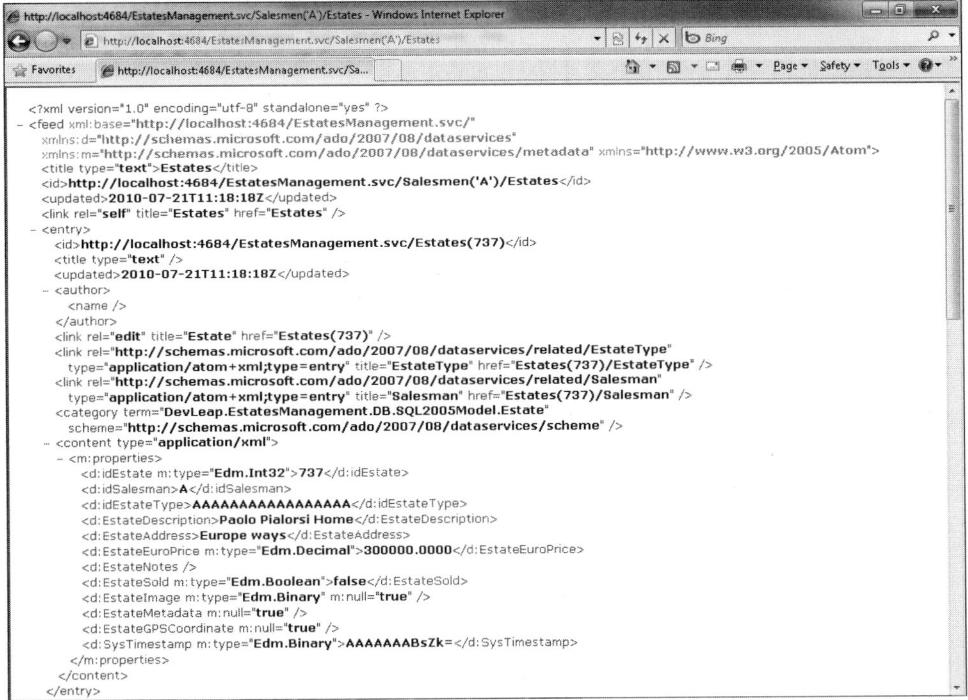

FIGURE 8-5 Query for the estates entity set for a single salesman.

In Listing 8-8, you can see how the Entity Framework engine has translated your request into an optimized T-SQL statement without doing any filter operation in memory. This approach is the best to maintain the scalability of your solution.

LISTING 8-8 T-SQL statement for navigation property request.

```
SELECT
[Extent1].[idEstate] AS [idEstate],
[Extent1].[idSalesman] AS [idSalesman],
[Extent1].[idEstateType] AS [idEstateType],
[Extent1].[EstateDescription] AS [EstateDescription],
[Extent1].[EstateAddress] AS [EstateAddress],
[Extent1].[EstateEuroPrice] AS [EstateEuroPrice],
[Extent1].[EstateNotes] AS [EstateNotes],
[Extent1].[EstateSold] AS [EstateSold],
[Extent1].[EstateImage] AS [EstateImage],
[Extent1].[EstateMetadata] AS [EstateMetadata],
[Extent1].[EstateGPSCoordinate] AS [EstateGPSCoordinate],
[Extent1].[SysTimestamp] AS [SysTimestamp]
FROM [dbo].[tabEstates] AS [Extent1]
WHERE N'A' = [Extent1].[idSalesman]
```

Every estate represented by entries in the resulting AtomPub feed has the same properties as the initial salesman, so you can ask for the salesman of every single estate, or for the *EstateType* navigation property that implies another join in the database.

For exampe, try this request:

```
http://localhost:port/EstatesManagement.svc/Salesmen('A')/Estates(737)/EstateType
```

This request receives the type of the first estate (with key 737) of your initial salesman (with key *A*), as shown in Listing 8-9.

LISTING 8-9 AtomPub response for a request to a single *EstateType*.

```
<?xml version="1.0" encoding="utf-8" standalone="yes" ?>
 <entry xml:base="http://localhost:4684/EstatesManagement.svc/"
        xmlns:d="http://schemas.microsoft.com/ado/2007/08/dataservices"
        xmlns:m="http://schemas.microsoft.com/ado/2007/08/dataservices/metadata"
        xmlns="http://www.w3.org/2005/Atom">
   <id>http://localhost:4684/EstatesManagement.svc/EstateTypes('AAAAAAAAAAAAAAA
     AA')</id>
   <title type="text" />
   <updated>2010-07-21T11:27:15Z</updated>
   <author>
     <name />
   </author>
   <link rel="edit" title="EstateType" href="EstateTypes('AAAAAAAAAAAAAAAAA')" />
   <link rel="http://schemas.microsoft.com/ado/2007/08/dataservices/related/Estates"
     type="application/atom+xml;type=feed" title="Estates"
     href="EstateTypes('AAAAAAAAAAAAAAAAA')/Estates" />
```

```
    <category term="DevLeap.EstatesManagement.DB.SQL2005Model.EstateType"
      scheme="http://schemas.microsoft.com/ado/2007/08/dataservices/scheme" />
    <content type="application/xml">
    <m:properties>
    <d:idEstateType>AAAAAAAAAAAAAAAAA</d:idEstateType>
    <d:EstateTypeDescription>KÒ4Ój fôïvËnWBôÑØÙ6õÂ</d:EstateTypeDescription>
    <d:rowguid m:type="Edm.Guid">49d08682-4097-e4a3-95cf-ff46699c73c4</d:rowguid>
    </m:properties>
    </content>
  </entry>
```

The underlying query that translated to T-SQL from the Entity Framework engine is listed in Listing 8-10.

LISTING 8-10 T-SQL for a double jump in the navigation property.

```
SELECT
[Extent2].[idEstateType] AS [idEstateType],
[Extent2].[EstateTypeDescription] AS [EstateTypeDescription],
[Extent2].[rowguid] AS [rowguid]
FROM  [dbo].[tabEstates] AS [Extent1]
INNER JOIN [dbo].[tabEstateTypes] AS [Extent2] ON [Extent1].[idEstateType] =
[Extent2].[idEstateType]
WHERE (N'A' = [Extent1].[idSalesman]) AND (737 = [Extent1].[idEstate])
```

At first glance, the T-SQL statement seems strange because it is not necessary to filter for *idSaleman* equals *A*; the query is already filtered by *idEstates*, which is the primary key of the underlying *tabEstates*. In any case, this is not a problem related to the WCF Data Service, because the translation from the EDM query to SQL is performed by the Entity Framework engine. But when you think about the problem and realize that *idEstate* might not be unique, the query becomes correct, and as a matter of fact, the query returns all the *EstateType* entities for estates with "*idEstate* equals 737 and *idSaleman* equals *A*".

You can also request a single property of a single entry and, as usual, obtain the response formatted in AtomPub. For example, try this request:

```
http://localhost:1185/EstatesManagement.svc/Salesmen('AAAAAAAAAAAAAAAAAAAAAAAAAAAAAAA')/
SalesmanDescription
```

The response is the description of the estate that has the key equal to 737 and is assigned to the salesman with key *A*, as you can see in Listing 8-11.

LISTING 8-11 AtomPub response for a single property and related T-SQL.

```
--- AtomPub---
<?xml version="1.0" encoding="UTF-8" standalone="true"?>

<SalesmanDescription xmlns="http://schemas.microsoft.com/ado/2007/08/dataservices">hÍg
YÈÙWÙÛçÉÛÑTQOÕqÇdúî1ké7pôpóXfÍñoëçSgçGëg0wÑAÒî</SalesmanDescription>
--- T-SQL Statement ---

SELECT

[Extent1].[idSalesman] AS [idSalesman],

[Extent1].[SalesmanPassword] AS [SalesmanPassword],

[Extent1].[SalesmanDescription] AS [SalesmanDescription],

[Extent1].[SalesmanIsAdmin] AS [SalesmanIsAdmin],

[Extent1].[LastEditDate] AS [LastEditDate],

[Extent1].[CreationDate] AS [CreationDate]

FROM [dbo].[tabSalesmen] AS [Extent1]

WHERE N'AAAAAAAAAAAAAAAAAAAAAAAAAAAAAAAA' = [Extent1].[idSalesman]
```

Before moving to the filtering and sorting section, I have to mention a useful technique. If your objective is to analyze the data of every estate of every salesman using the code shown in the previous examples, you will end up with a roundtrip for every estate: the code will work but you will pay the latency on every request.

The WCF Data Service has a keyword to request the full entry of a related entity instead of just the link. The keyword is *expand=entity set*, and it corresponds to the *Include* method of the LINQ to Entities syntax.

This is a query requesting the estate entries for every salesman:

```
http://localhost:port/EstatesManagement.svc/Salesmen?$expand=Estates
```

The resulting response and the generated T-SQL statement is something similar to Listings 8-12 and 8-13.

LISTING 8-12 AtomPub response for expanded related entity.

```
AtomPub

<entry>
  <id>http://localhost:9138/EstatesManagement.svc/Salesmen('A')</id>
  <title type="text" />
  <updated>2010-07-22T08:03:37Z</updated>
  <author>
  <name />
  </author>
  <link rel="edit" title="Salesman" href="Salesmen('A')" />
  <link rel="http://schemas.microsoft.com/ado/2007/08/dataservices/related/Estates"
    type="application/atom+xml;type=feed" title="Estates"
    href="Salesmen('A')/Estates">
  <m:inline>
  <feed>
  <title type="text">Estates</title>
  <id>http://localhost:9138/EstatesManagement.svc/Salesmen('A')/Estates</id>
  <updated>2010-07-22T08:03:37Z</updated>
  <link rel="self" title="Estates" href="Salesmen('A')/Estates" />
  <entry>
  <id>http://localhost:9138/EstatesManagement.svc/Estates(737)</id>
  <title type="text" />
  <updated>2010-07-22T08:03:37Z</updated>
  <author>
  <name />
  </author>
  <link rel="edit" title="Estate" href="Estates(737)" />
  <link rel="http://schemas.microsoft.com/ado/2007/08/dataservices/related/EstateType"
    type="application/atom+xml;type=entry" title="EstateType"
    href="Estates(737)/EstateType" />
  <link rel="http://schemas.microsoft.com/ado/2007/08/dataservices/related/Salesman"
    type="application/atom+xml;type=entry" title="Salesman"
    href="Estates(737)/Salesman" />
  <category term="DevLeap.EstatesManagement.DB.SQL2005Model.Estate" scheme="http://
schemas.microsoft.com/ado/2007/08/dataservices/scheme" />
  <content type="application/xml">
  <m:properties>
  <d:idEstate m:type="Edm.Int32">737</d:idEstate>
  <d:idSalesman>A</d:idSalesman>
  <d:idEstateType>AAAAAAAAAAAAAAAAA</d:idEstateType>
  <d:EstateDescription>Paolo Pialorsi Home</d:EstateDescription>
  <d:EstateAddress>Europe ways</d:EstateAddress>
  <d:EstateEuroPrice m:type="Edm.Decimal">300000.0000</d:EstateEuroPrice>
  <d:EstateNotes />
  <d:EstateSold m:type="Edm.Boolean">false</d:EstateSold>
  <d:EstateImage m:type="Edm.Binary" m:null="true" />
  <d:EstateMetadata m:null="true" />
  <d:EstateGPSCoordinate m:null="true" />
  <d:SysTimestamp m:type="Edm.Binary">AAAAAAABsZk=</d:SysTimestamp>
  </m:properties>
  </content>
  </entry>
```

LISTING 8-13 T-SQL for expanded related entity.

```
SELECT
[Project1].[C1] AS [C1],
[Project1].[idSalesman] AS [idSalesman],
[Project1].[SalesmanPassword] AS [SalesmanPassword],
[Project1].[SalesmanDescription] AS [SalesmanDescription],
[Project1].[SalesmanIsAdmin] AS [SalesmanIsAdmin],
[Project1].[LastEditDate] AS [LastEditDate],
[Project1].[CreationDate] AS [CreationDate],
[Project1].[C2] AS [C2],
[Project1].[idEstate] AS [idEstate],
[Project1].[idSalesman1] AS [idSalesman1],
[Project1].[idEstateType] AS [idEstateType],
[Project1].[EstateDescription] AS [EstateDescription],
[Project1].[EstateAddress] AS [EstateAddress],
[Project1].[EstateEuroPrice] AS [EstateEuroPrice],
[Project1].[EstateNotes] AS [EstateNotes],
[Project1].[EstateSold] AS [EstateSold],
[Project1].[EstateImage] AS [EstateImage],
[Project1].[EstateMetadata] AS [EstateMetadata],
[Project1].[EstateGPSCoordinate] AS [EstateGPSCoordinate],
[Project1].[SysTimestamp] AS [SysTimestamp]
FROM ( SELECT
     [Extent1].[idSalesman] AS [idSalesman],
     [Extent1].[SalesmanPassword] AS [SalesmanPassword],
     [Extent1].[SalesmanDescription] AS [SalesmanDescription],
     [Extent1].[SalesmanIsAdmin] AS [SalesmanIsAdmin],
     [Extent1].[LastEditDate] AS [LastEditDate],
     [Extent1].[CreationDate] AS [CreationDate],
     1 AS [C1],
     [Extent2].[idEstate] AS [idEstate],
     [Extent2].[idSalesman] AS [idSalesman1],
     [Extent2].[idEstateType] AS [idEstateType],
     [Extent2].[EstateDescription] AS [EstateDescription],
     [Extent2].[EstateAddress] AS [EstateAddress],
     [Extent2].[EstateEuroPrice] AS [EstateEuroPrice],
     [Extent2].[EstateNotes] AS [EstateNotes],
     [Extent2].[EstateSold] AS [EstateSold],
     [Extent2].[EstateImage] AS [EstateImage],
     [Extent2].[EstateMetadata] AS [EstateMetadata],
     [Extent2].[EstateGPSCoordinate] AS [EstateGPSCoordinate],
     [Extent2].[SysTimestamp] AS [SysTimestamp],
     CASE WHEN ([Extent2].[idEstate] IS NULL) THEN CAST(NULL AS int) ELSE 1 END AS
[C2]
     FROM  [dbo].[tabSalesmen] AS [Extent1]
     LEFT OUTER JOIN [dbo].[tabEstates] AS [Extent2] ON [Extent1].[idSalesman] =
[Extent2].[idSalesman]
)  AS [Project1]
ORDER BY [Project1].[idSalesman] ASC, [Project1].[C2] ASC
```

Filtering, Sorting, and Pagination

So far in this chapter, you tested your service by requesting the entire entity set as well as a particular entity by requesting its key, but the WCF Data Services allows more refined queries. You can ask the service to filter and sort data, and you can pass some parameters to paginate the data server-side. Remember that every request is based on the entities and properties of the EDM. The service translates the URL request to the Entity Framework queries and, in turn, the Entity Framework engine translates them to a T-SQL statement to leverage database capabilities.

For instance, you can ask for the estates of a particular salesman requesting an ordering clause on a field, such as *EstateEuroPrice*, as shown in the following:

```
http://localhost:port/EstatesManagement.svc/Salesmen('A')/Estates?$orderby=EstateEuroPrice
desc
```

First, you need to use the question mark to separate the query string of the URL and, only after that, express the query arrangement. The syntax to use is always defined by the WCF Data Services schema, and it is translated into a query on the EDM by the service.

The result of your ordering request is just a normal list of entries with the order specified, and the resulting T-SQL query is shown in Listing 8-14.

LISTING 8-14 T-SQL for an ordered request.

```
SELECT
[Extent1].[idEstate] AS [idEstate],
[Extent1].[idSalesman] AS [idSalesman],
[Extent1].[idEstateType] AS [idEstateType],
[Extent1].[EstateDescription] AS [EstateDescription],
[Extent1].[EstateAddress] AS [EstateAddress],
[Extent1].[EstateEuroPrice] AS [EstateEuroPrice],
[Extent1].[EstateNotes] AS [EstateNotes],
[Extent1].[EstateSold] AS [EstateSold],
[Extent1].[EstateImage] AS [EstateImage],
[Extent1].[EstateMetadata] AS [EstateMetadata],
[Extent1].[EstateGPSCoordinate] AS [EstateGPSCoordinate],
[Extent1].[SysTimestamp] AS [SysTimestamp]
FROM [dbo].[tabEstates] AS [Extent1]
WHERE N'A' = [Extent1].[idSalesman]
ORDER BY [Extent1].[EstateEuroPrice] DESC
```

Before analyzing how an application requests this data and how you can leverage the existing technologies (such as AJAX or LINQ) to request an OData to WCF Data Service, I want to show you one of the parameters that is particularly useful for paginating a query. The query can be any query that returns an entity set or a related entity set, with or without an *orderby* clause; it can also contain a *filter* or any clause you've encountered in this chapter.

llowing request that asks for page 3 of the *Estates* entity set, where every page is of 20 estates. The underlying T-SQL query is arranged, as you can see in Listing 8-15:

```
alhost:9138/EstatesManagement.svc/Estates?$orderby=EstateEuroPrice
0&$skip=40
```

T-SQL for a paginated request.

```
SELECT TOP (20)
[Extent1].[idEstate] AS [idEstate],
[Extent1].[idSalesman] AS [idSalesman],
[Extent1].[idEstateType] AS [idEstateType],
[Extent1].[EstateDescription] AS [EstateDescription],
[Extent1].[EstateAddress] AS [EstateAddress],
[Extent1].[EstateEuroPrice] AS [EstateEuroPrice],
[Extent1].[EstateNotes] AS [EstateNotes],
[Extent1].[EstateSold] AS [EstateSold],
[Extent1].[EstateImage] AS [EstateImage],
[Extent1].[EstateMetadata] AS [EstateMetadata],
[Extent1].[EstateGPSCoordinate] AS [EstateGPSCoordinate],
[Extent1].[SysTimestamp] AS [SysTimestamp]
FROM ( SELECT [Extent1].[idEstate] AS [idEstate], [Extent1].[idSalesman] AS
[idSalesman], [Extent1].[idEstateType] AS [idEstateType], [Extent1].[EstateDescription]
AS [EstateDescription], [Extent1].[EstateAddress] AS [EstateAddress], [Extent1].
[EstateEuroPrice] AS [EstateEuroPrice], [Extent1].[EstateNotes] AS [EstateNotes],
[Extent1].[EstateSold] AS [EstateSold], [Extent1].[EstateImage] AS [EstateImage],
[Extent1].[EstateMetadata] AS [EstateMetadata], [Extent1].[EstateGPSCoordinate] AS
[EstateGPSCoordinate], [Extent1].[SysTimestamp] AS [SysTimestamp], row_number() OVER
(ORDER BY [Extent1].[EstateEuroPrice] DESC, [Extent1].[idEstate] ASC) AS [row_number]
     FROM [dbo].[tabEstates] AS [Extent1]
)  AS [Extent1]
WHERE [Extent1].[row_number] > 40
ORDER BY [Extent1].[EstateEuroPrice] DESC, [Extent1].[idEstate] ASC
```

You can also use *$filter* to express a filter clause following the OData syntax. For instance, the following request asks for every salesman with the property *SalesmanIsAdmin* equal to *true*.

```
http://localhost:9138/EstatesManagement.svc/Salesmen?$filter=SalesmanIsAdmin eq true
```

The filter clause can contain the classic operator to check for not equal (*Ne*), greater than (*Gt*), and lower than (*Lt*), and it can express logical *and* and logical *or* operators.The OData proposal also contains string operators like *substringof*, *startswith*, *indexof*, and *replace*.

WCF Data Service Client

You used a browser to request OData from the simplest WCF Data Service. You also created an EDM to represent your domain model entities and then you created a new WCF Data Service using the template proposed by Visual Studio 2010, adjusting the generic type to be identical to the EDM class name.

In the preceding procedure, you saw that Internet Explorer is very useful when you want to understand the methods for requesting data by using the OData schema. Because every modern platform exposes a way to request data via HTTP at some URL, you can use the platform of your choice to build any query illustrated in this chapter.

For example, in the .NET Framework, you can use the *HttpWebRequest* class to ask something via HTTP and use *HttpWebResponse* to analyze the response.

In a simple .NET Client (let's say, a console application), you can use the standard class to build the query.

Create a Simple Client

1. Create a console application project in the same solution of your WCF Data Service.
2. Copy the code in Listing 8-16 inside the main method.
3. Change the port number to adapt it to your solution.
4. Verify that the ASP.NET Development Server is running. You can start it using the View In Browser option from the EstatesManagement.svc file.

As you can see in Listing 8-16, the *Main* method asks for the same result of the last query in the previous section. The query asks for page 3 of the estates ordered by the Euro price with a page size equal to 20 elements.

LISTING 8-16 Console application requesting raw data.

```
using System;
using System.Collections.Generic;
using System.Linq;
using System.Text;
using System.Net;
using System.IO;

namespace DevLeap.WCFDataService.ConsoleApp
{
    class Program
    {
        static void Main(string[] args)
        {
            HttpWebRequest request = (HttpWebRequest)WebRequest.Create(
              "http://localhost:9138/EstatesManagement.svc/Estates?
              $orderby=EstateEuroPrice desc&$top=20&$skip=40");

            request.Method = "GET";

            HttpWebResponse response = (HttpWebResponse)request.GetResponse();

            StreamReader reader = new StreamReader(response.GetResponseStream());
```

```
                StringBuilder output = new StringBuilder();

                output.Append(reader.ReadToEnd());

                Console.WriteLine(output.ToString());

                response.Close();


                Console.ReadLine();

            }
        }
    }
```

The response is shown in Figure 8-6.

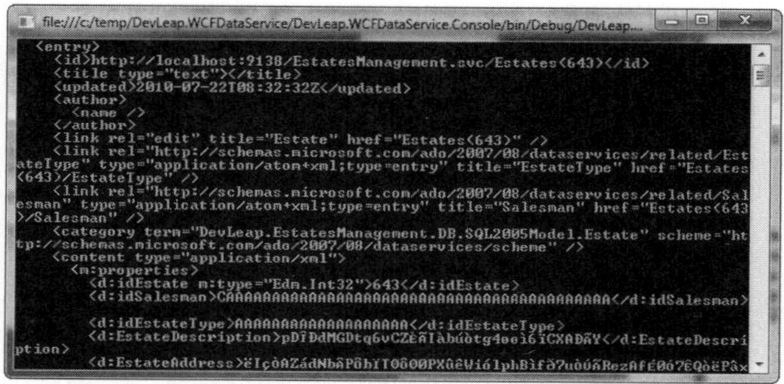

FIGURE 8-6 Console application requesting raw data.

You can also change the response format (asking for a JSON response) that tells the service what format you accept. Add the following line just after the *HttpWebRequest* method definition. The response is visible in Figure 8-7:

```
request.Method = "GET";
request.Accept = "application/json";
```

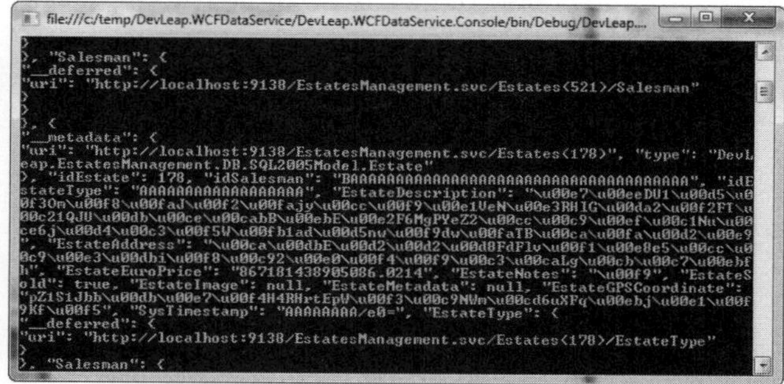

FIGURE 8-7 JSON response in a console application.

Using this technique, you can add a CUD operation to your console application. Because the WCF Data Service uses the common OData pattern, you can pass the payload for these operations as AtomPub, JSON, or XML, and choose the corresponding HTTP method. The *POST* method is for adding a new entity, the *MERGE* method is for an update operation, and *DELETE* is (not surprisingly) for deleting an entity.

You can modify the console application to update an estate entity, for instance, the 737 that you saw in the previous section. The code in Listing 8-17 shows your console application updating the address of an entity using a *MERGE* method. I included simple but effective error logging to simplify the test process in case there are errors. If everything goes fine, the response will be empty, otherwise, the *WebException* will provide the classic *Message* property with a status code. You can also inspect the HTTP status code and response to fully understand what happened during the service execution. Remember to change the port number to your actual port.

LISTING 8-17 Code to request and update an entity.

```
using System;
using System.Collections.Generic;
using System.Linq;
using System.Text;
using System.Net;
using System.IO;

namespace DevLeap.WCFDataService.ConsoleApp
{
    class Program
    {
        static void Main(string[] args)
        {
            HttpWebRequest request = (HttpWebRequest)WebRequest.Create("http://
                localhost:9138/EstatesManagement.svc/Estates(737)");

            // JSON payload
            string requestPayload = "{EstateAddress:'new highway'}";

            // HTTP MERGE to update
            request.Method = "MERGE";

            UTF8Encoding encoding = new UTF8Encoding();

            request.ContentLength = encoding.GetByteCount(requestPayload);

            request.Credentials = CredentialCache.DefaultCredentials;

            request.Accept = "application/json";
            request.ContentType = "application/json";
```

```
            using (Stream requestStream = request.GetRequestStream())
            {
                requestStream.Write(encoding.GetBytes(requestPayload), 0,
                    encoding.GetByteCount(requestPayload));
            }

            try
            {
                // Send the request
                HttpWebResponse response = request.GetResponse() as HttpWebResponse;
                string responseBody = "";

                // Analize the response
                using (Stream rspStm = response.GetResponseStream())
                {
                    using (StreamReader reader = new StreamReader(rspStm))
                    {
                        Console.WriteLine("Response Description: " +
                                response.StatusDescription);
                        Console.WriteLine("Response Status Code: " +
                                response.StatusCode);

                        responseBody = reader.ReadToEnd();

                        Console.WriteLine("Response Body: " +
                            responseBody);
                    }
                }


                Console.WriteLine("Status Code: " +
                    response.StatusCode.ToString());
            }
            catch (System.Net.WebException ex)
            {
                Console.WriteLine("Exception message: " + ex.Message);
                Console.WriteLine("Response Status Code: " + ex.Status);

                // Error details
                StreamReader reader =
                    new StreamReader(ex.Response.GetResponseStream());
                    Console.WriteLine(reader.ReadToEnd());
            }

            Console.ReadLine();
        }
    }
}
```

The code in Listing 8-17 requests the estates with a key equal to *737*, constructs the payload for updating the address in JSON format, and then requests the update with a *MERGE* operation to the service.

Listing 8-18 shows the query executed in SQL Server. The first query corresponds to the first request to the service, and the second query refers to the update operation.

LISTING 8-18 T-SQL code for a request and an update operation.

```
--- Request ---
SELECT
[Extent1].[idEstate] AS [idEstate],
[Extent1].[idSalesman] AS [idSalesman],
[Extent1].[idEstateType] AS [idEstateType],
[Extent1].[EstateDescription] AS [EstateDescription],
[Extent1].[EstateAddress] AS [EstateAddress],
[Extent1].[EstateEuroPrice] AS [EstateEuroPrice],
[Extent1].[EstateNotes] AS [EstateNotes],
[Extent1].[EstateSold] AS [EstateSold],
[Extent1].[EstateImage] AS [EstateImage],
[Extent1].[EstateMetadata] AS [EstateMetadata],
[Extent1].[EstateGPSCoordinate] AS [EstateGPSCoordinate],
[Extent1].[SysTimestamp] AS [SysTimestamp]
FROM [dbo].[tabEstates] AS [Extent1]
WHERE 737 = [Extent1].[idEstate]

--- Update ---
exec sp_executesql N'update [dbo].[tabEstates]
set [EstateAddress] = @0
where ([idEstate] = @1)
select [SysTimestamp]
from [dbo].[tabEstates]
where @@ROWCOUNT > 0 and [idEstate] = @1',N'@0 nvarchar(200),@1 int',@0=N'new
highway',@1=737
```

The presented examples in this chapter show you how to interact with the OData provided by WCF Data Services in a standard and easy way. You can choose any platform that supports HTTP to build a client for your service. All platforms can be used as clients for your OData/WCF Service.

The .NET Framework Client

If your client is based on the .NET Framework, you can leverage the WCF client tools and APIs to simplify the communication with the service.

Because a WCF Data Service is a specialized version of a classic WCF Service, you can just add a service reference (using the Add Service Reference dialog box) to your service and forget every detail about requests and responses, such as formatting the payload or analyzing error codes.

With a classic service reference, you have a proxy that lets you create service requests and inspect service responses in a simpler way. But this kind of service doesn't expose the classic methods and input/output parameters. A WCF Data Service can receive a query directly in the URL, and the response is formatted accordingly. There are no fixed methods with fixed responses. Thus, a classic WCF proxy is not very useful for wrapping this kind of request, because the request itself does not have a fixed schema. The response is very difficult to analyze because the service can reply with different entities based on the query sent to it.

Visual Studio 2008 SP1 and Visual Studio 2010 have a modified version of the Add Service Reference functionality that creates a special proxy to request a client version of the EDM to the service. The dialog box is very similar to the one you are familiar with, as you can see in Figure 8-8. You have to change the port number to reflect your development environment.

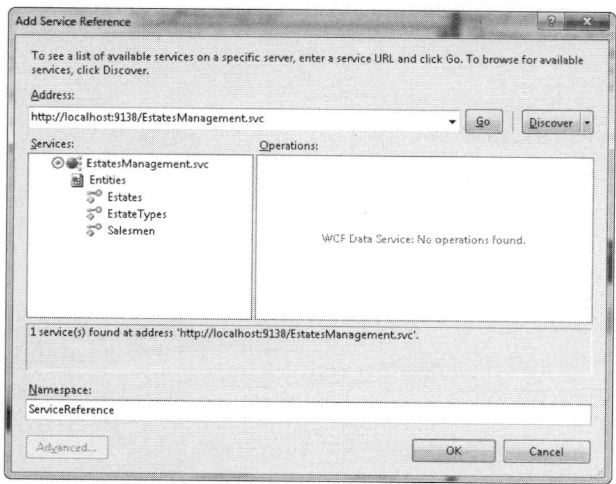

FIGURE 8-8 WCF Data Service Add Service Reference dialog box.

You can simulate the same request using a special query string that contains the text */$metadata*. The service asks the Entity Framework for the conceptual model and creates a response with entries that describe the model. The client receives just the conceptual model, because the SSDL is completely useless without a connection to the database. Remember that the client talks to the service via HTTP and cannot talk directly to the database or to the server-side Entity Framework engine.

The same concept applies to the command-line tool. You cannot use SvcUtil.exe to create the client proxy. Instead you have to use the WCF Data Service version called DataSvcUtil.exe. This tool asks for the conceptual model and creates a local version of every entity exposed by the service (remember that you can expose a subset of entities) as well as a class that represents the client data context. Visual Studio uses this utility behind the scenes.

The client version of the EDM is a file with the .edmx extension and is downloaded in the Service Reference folder of the client project, as shown in the next figure. In the solution, I added a new project to differentiate it from the previous example in which I used the HTTP classes directly from code.

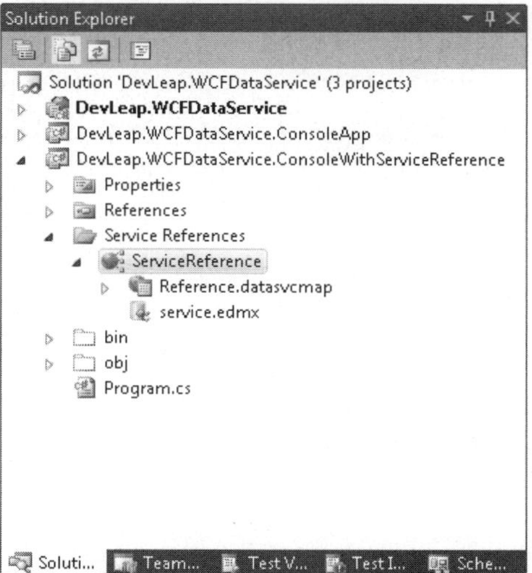

The first task you can accomplish with your new proxy is use the *DataServiceQuery* class to build queries against the service, leaving all the details about protocol and communication to this class. You have to manually add a reference to the assembly named *System.Data.Service.Client,* which contains everything a client needs to talk to a WCF Data Service.

Listing 8-19 contains the code for a new console application that requests the list of salesmen and shows using the client *DataContext* class and *DataServiceQuery* class. Before running this code, change the port number.

LISTING 8-19 DataContext and DataServiceQuery classes.

```
using System;
using System.Collections.Generic;
using System.Linq;
using System.Text;
using System.Data.Services.Client;
using DevLeap.WCFDataService.ConsoleWithServiceReference.ServiceReference;

namespace DevLeap.WCFDataService.ConsoleWithServiceReference
{
    class Program
    {
        static void Main(string[] args)
        {
            Entities ctx = new Entities(new Uri("http://localhost:9138/
                EstatesManagement.svc"));

            DataServiceQuery<Salesman> query = ctx.CreateQuery<Salesman>("Salesmen");

            foreach(Salesman s in query)
```

```
            {
                Console.WriteLine(s.SalesmanDescription);
            }

            Console.ReadLine();

        }
    }
}
```

You can express the OData *Include* behavior using a safer method exposed by *DataServiceQuery* to prefetch a related instance instead of making too many roundtrips. For instance, you can ask the service to include an entry for every single estate of each salesman by using the code in Listing 8-20.

LISTING 8-20 Expand/Include to avoid a deferred query.

```
DataServiceQuery<Salesman> queryInclude =
ctx.CreateQuery<Salesman>("Salesmen").Expand("Estates");

foreach (Salesman s in query)
{
    Console.WriteLine(s.SalesmanDescription);
    foreach (Estate e in s.Estates)
    {
        Console.WriteLine(e.EstateDescription);
    }
}

Console.ReadLine();
```

Updating an entry with the classes exposed by the proxy is very simple and does not require a full understanding of the underlying protocol. The *DataContext* class is very similar to the one exposed by Linq to SQL or the Entity Framework, because it works in a disconnected fashion, letting the user add, update, or remove an entity and then propagate the changes back when the code invokes the *SaveChanges* method.

For example, you can ask for the list of salesmen, inspect some properties using type safe code, make an offline change, and then propagate only these modifications to the service, which, in turn, creates a server Data Context, inserts the deserialized entities into it, and finally, asks Entity Framework to update the data source. This process is completely transparent to you. The client code is shown in Listing 8-21.

LISTING 8-21 Entity update.

```
DataServiceQuery<Salesman> querySingle =
ctx.CreateQuery<Salesman>("Salesmen");

foreach (Salesman s in query)
{
    Console.WriteLine(s.SalesmanDescription);
    s.SalesmanIsAdmin = false;
}

ctx.SaveChanges();

Console.ReadLine();
```

The *DataServiceQuery* class implements the *IEnumerable* interface and the generic version *IEnumerable<T>*, as you may have noticed from the sample presented. This class also implements the *IQueryable<T>* interface, so the client data context exposes a way to query the data context with LINQ queries. These queries are translated into an expression tree that is evaluated and transformed into a WCF Data Service request over the wire when the query is first executed.

You can use the LINQ syntax to express a query, as in Listing 8-22, remembering that every LINQ provider has different support for particular methods. For instance, the first version of ADO.NET Data Services doesn't support the method *Count*, nevertheless, the compiler cannot stop you from running the application as the *IQueryable* interface exposes it.

LISTING 8-22 LINQ to WCF Data Services (client side).

```
var linqQuery = from salesman in ctx.Salesmen
                from estate in salesman.Estates
                where salesman.SalesmanIsAdmin == true
                orderby estate.EstateEuroPrice descending
                select new { Dex = estate.EstateDescription };


foreach (var e in linqQuery)
{
    Console.WriteLine(e.Dex);
}

Console.ReadLine();
```

Security Introduction

In this section, I introduce some important concepts regarding the security mechanism exposed by WCF Data Services.

An important concept to discuss is not a WCF Data Service feature. However, because a service is exposed as an ASP.NET application, every rule that applies to ASP.NET pages and services can be applied to a data service. For example, you can use Windows authentication for services exposed on the intranet, or whenever you have a domain that contains users and groups. In this scenario, you can also use digital certificates in the same way you would any other ASP.NET application.

If you want to expose your service on the Internet and protect it with credentials, you can leverage the .NET Security Principal in the way you prefer. For example, you can use the membership and role manager standard ASP.NET provider if you have a simple service, or you can create a custom provider to use your own storage technique. In case you decide to use the membership and role manager, it is important to disable (or, at least, to not use) the Forms Authentication mechanism because it redirects the request to a login page that is useless in a service request. The client must provide the credential in every request.

If you do not want to use the membership and role manager provider because they are not suitable for your scenario, you can leverage the underlying *GenericPrincipal* or create a custom principal to adhere to the .NET Framework security pillars. You can also integrate your solution with other trusted identity providers by using custom code or frameworks such as Windows Identity Foundation.

These scenarios are possible because a WCF Data Service can be hosted in an on-premises ASP.NET application or can be moved to the cloud. If you resolve to maintain your solution in an on-premises infrastructure, you can use the Internet Information Services (IIS) Windows Activated Service (WAS) to automate the activation of the engine or, even better, you can leverage the Windows Server AppFabric to simplify the management operations.

A WCF Data Service has two other ways to protect access to an entire entity set or to a single entity or a subset. In the examples at the beginning of this chapter, you saw the *InitializeService* static method, and you uncommented the first line to open your entity data model to every request that could reach the service. This internal mechanism can be used to specify access criteria for a single entity set. For example, you can make the *salesmen* entity readable, make the *estates* entity set updatable, and completely hide the other entity sets.

The *enum EntitySetRights* listed in Table 8-1 shows the various permissions of a single entity set.

TABLE 8-1 EntitySetRights Enumeration

Entity Right	Description
All	All operations are permitted.
AllRead	Read operations are permitted.
AllWrite	Read and write operations are permitted.
None	Denies all rights to access data.
ReadMultiple	Permission to read multiple data as in queries for different entities.
ReadSingle	Only access to single entity is permitted. The request for the entity set will be denied.
WriteAppend	Authorization to create a new entity in the entity set.
WriteDelete	Authorization to delete an entity.
WriteMerge	Authorization to update the data. *Merge* is referred to the *Http* method used to update the data.
WriteReplace	Authorization to replace data.

The keyword * indicates that a right is assigned to every entity set.

When the client requests an operation not permitted by an access rule, the code receives a *DataServiceException* exception.

Every service exposes only the operations available on the EDM with some restrictions imposed by the client provider. You can also add some methods to your service to extend its functionality and let the client invoke the methods, because the metadata description instructs the proxy generator (DataSvcUtil.exe) to create a client method in the generated class.

The interesting thing about a new service operation is that it can have two kinds of security implications. The first is the simpler of the two, because it implies the definition of a *ServiceOperationAccessRule* in the same way the *EntitySetRights* does. For every operation, you can instruct the service how to respond to the client request. You can expose an operation, protect it as you want, and let the code verify the request before executing it. An operation is defined by code, so you can define whatever security logic you need. The complete set of rules for a service operation is listed in Table 8-2.

TABLE 8-2 EntitySetRights Enumeration

Entity Right	Description
All	No restriction on service operations.
AllRead	Authorization to read single entity and complete entity sets returned by the service operation.
None	The service operation is not accessible.
ReadSingle	Only access to single entity is permitted by the service operation.
ReadMultiple	The service operation does not restrict access to an entity set.
OverrideEntitySetRights	The service operation rights override the permission defined by the entity set access rule.

You can also define a new service operation by adding a method to the class that represents the WCF Data Service and assigning the classic *WebGet* attribute to it.

Listing 8-23 shows two different security mechanisms applied in a newly defined service operation. You can use this code directly in the WCF Data Service you created at the beginning of the chapter.

LISTING 8-23 Service Operations added to the WCF Data Service.

```
public class EstatesManagement : DataService<Entities>
{
    // This method is called only once to initialize service-wide policies.
    public static void InitializeService(DataServiceConfiguration config)
    {
        // Examples:
        config.SetEntitySetAccessRule("*", EntitySetRights.All);
        config.SetServiceOperationAccessRule("SalesmanAdmin",
            ServiceOperationRights.All);
        config.DataServiceBehavior.MaxProtocolVersion =
            DataServiceProtocolVersion.V2;
    }


    [WebGet]
    public IQueryable<Salesman> SalemanAdmin()
    {
        if (!Thread.CurrentPrincipal.IsInRole("Admin"))
            throw new DataServiceException("You cannot access this method");

        return this.CurrentDataSource.Salesmen;

    }

    [WebGet]
    public IQueryable<Salesman> SalemanForManager()
    {
        if (!Thread.CurrentPrincipal.IsInRole("Manager"))
```

```
            return this.CurrentDataSource.Salesmen.Where(s => s.Estates.Count < 100);

        return this.CreateDataSource().Salesmen;

    }
}
```

In Listing 8-23, the first service operation, named *SalesmanAdmin*, exposes the complete salesmen entity set only to users in the Admin role. The code is straightforward: it checks the role of the user using the standard .NET Framework technique to raise a *DataServiceException* (or a *Security Exception,* if you prefer) when the user doesn't have the correct permission. To access an entity set from a service operation, you have to use the *CurrentDataSource* property exposed by the base class of your service.

The second operation shown in Listing 8-23 illustrates a smart technique to filter data for a particular group of users and can be used for every check you need to perform in a solution. You just check the role and leverage the *IQueryable* interface of the *EntitySet* class to apply a filter on the *salesmen* entity set: for instance, when the user is not a manager, he cannot see any salesman with more than 100 estates assigned.

A similar result can be achieved with another feature of the WCF Data Service base class that is called the *query interceptor.* When a request comes in, it is up to the service to inspect the code to find a method with the *QueryInterceptorAttribute* attribute and execute the method before passing the query to the Entity Framework engine. The query interceptor replies to the request, returning an *Expression<Func<EntitySet, Boolean>>* in which you can express your filter to apply a security algorithm. The returned value is used by the service to enrich the query that will be applied to the EDM.

In Listing 8-24, I applied a different security filter to the *salesmen* entity set, checking whether the user identity contains the string *Roberto.* The code returns a lambda expression that selects the nonadministrative salesmen.

LISTING 8-24 *QueryInterceptor.*

```
    [QueryInterceptor("Salesmen")]
    public Expression<Func<Salesman, Boolean>> OnQuerySalemen()
    {
        if (HttpContext.Current.User.Identity.Name.Contains("Roberto"))
            return s => s.SalesmanIsAdmin == false;
        else
            return s => true;
    }
```

You can also define a query interceptor for CUD operations so that you can selectively choose which users and roles can perform a given operation.

Summary

OData is an emerging protocol for querying and updating data using HTTP, JSON, and Atom Publishing Protocol (AtomPub). Microsoft supports OData with ADO.NET Data Services in .NET Framework 3.5 and WCF Data Services in .NET Framework 4.

Quick Reference

To	Do this
Build a query	Use the OData protocol.
Build an Entity Data Model	Use Linq To SQL or Entity Framework model capabilities, or implement the *IQueryable<T>* interface on your business model.
Create a client service agent	Use the Add Service Reference dialog box to create the proxy and the service-agent entities.
Use WCF Data Services from other platforms	Use the REST/HTTP request using the OData protocol syntax.
Use JSON instead of XML to enable JavaScript client	Set the Accept HTTP header to *application/json*.

Chapter 9

Using SQL Azure

After completing this chapter, you will be able to

- Create a virtual server by using the portal.
- Create administrative and normal users.
- Create databases and configure firewall rules.
- Connect to and use a SQL Azure database from applications.
- Use management tools to administer a database.

The preceding chapters showed how Windows Azure provides a scalable and fault-tolerant environment that lets you create powerful applications without having to purchase and configure hardware and operating systems. This chapter is dedicated to one of the most important features of the platform: Microsoft SQL Azure.

Chapter 4, "Windows Azure Storage," discussed how the Table Service can be a powerful storage solution for cloud and on-premises applications. You can access a storage account via HTTP by using any platform code that is able to understand the REST protocol. Certainly, this way of storing and retrieving data is very interesting—but it is also very far away from a classic solution based on a relational database.

When you have an existing solution and you want to port it to the cloud, the easiest approach is to use the same technology you used in the project and, most importantly, the same data access methodology. SQL Azure lets you do this with little or no modification of your existing code.

Note Because URLs, UI names, and procedures may vary over time, some of them may be out of date by the time you read this. In that case, my best advice is to start looking for the information about the Windows Azure product on the Windows Azure home page (*http://www.azure.com*). Information included in this book was accurate at the time of writing.

SQL Azure Features

Microsoft's goals for the first version of SQL Azure were to provide a basic set of services for both cloud and on-premises applications. Notice in this statement the descriptor "on-premises." It suggests this important concept: that SQL Azure is accessible not only via Windows Azure–hosted applications, but (with varying levels of latency) from anywhere in the world.

The second thing to notice in that statement is that SQL Azure doesn't have all of the same features as Microsoft SQL Server on-premises applications. Some of those features are not useful in a cloud environment, some will be released in future versions, and others will be supplied by third parties.

The set of features in the first version of SQL Azure is called "Core SQL Server database capabilities." This release provides only the database capabilities. It does not contain the Analysis Service engine or the Merge or Transactional Replication engines. You cannot create Online Analytical Processing (OLAP) cubes in the cloud by using this first version—but you can pull data out from the relational database engine and create and process cubes locally.

The second big on-premises SQL Server component lacking in the first version of SQL Azure is Reporting Services. You can currently use a community technical preview (CTP) of SQL Azure Reporting that can consume SQL Azure databases. At the time of this writing, this is how Microsoft describes the service currently available in the CTP (Microsoft Corporation, *Windows Azure* website*, 2011, http://www.microsoft.com/en-us/SQLAzure/reporting.aspx*):

> *Microsoft SQL Azure Reporting lets you use the familiar on-premises tools you're comfortable with to develop and deploy operational reports to the cloud. There's no need to manage or maintain a separate reporting infrastructure, which leads to the added benefit of lower costs (and less complexity). Your customers can easily access the reports from the Windows SQL Azure portal, through a web browser, or directly from your applications.*

Although SQL Azure Reporting is not yet commercially available, you can register to be invited to the community technology preview.

SQL Azure Data Sync will be the replacement for some features of the Replication engines provided by the on-premises version of SQL Server. Again, this technology is actually in CTP1. By the time you read these pages, CTP2 will likely be available. The idea is to extend enterprise data to the cloud, moving the workload to Windows Azure, which will provide a data synchronization engine built on the well-known Microsoft Sync Framework. The replica can be bidirectional, that is, moving both to and from on-premises servers and mobile computers.

Apart from these features, the SQL Azure engine is very similar to the familiar SQL Server database engine. At the time of this writing, here is Microsoft's description of it (Microsoft

Corporation, Windows Azure website, 2011, *http://www.microsoft.com/en-us/sqlazure/database.aspx*):

> *Microsoft® SQL Azure™ Database is a cloud-based relational database service built on SQL Server® technologies. It is a highly available, scalable, multi-tenant database service hosted by Microsoft in the cloud. SQL Azure Database helps to ease provisioning and deployment of multiple databases. Developers do not have to install, setup, patch or manage any software. High availability and fault tolerance is built-in and no physical administration is required.*
>
> *Customers can use existing knowledge in T-SQL development and a familiar relational data model for symmetry with existing on-premises databases. Additionally, customers can get productive on SQL Azure quickly by using the same development and management tools they use for on-premises databases.*

Microsoft is using a modified version of the SQL Server engine to provide a highly available and scalable database service on the Windows Azure Platform. SQL Azure supports T-SQL, so you can use almost any technology that produces queries, such as original equipment manufacturers (ORMs), against a database in the cloud.

The benefits of using a cloud-based relational solution are the same as the benefits offered by the rest of the platform:

- No hardware is required.
- No physical installation is required.
- Patches and updates are applied automatically.
- High availability and fault tolerance are built in.
- Provisioning is simple and you can deploy multiple databases.
- Databases can be scaled up or down based on business needs.
- The infrastructure supports multitenancy.
- There is integration with existing SQL Server tools and technologies.
- Support for T-SQL is based on the familiar relational database model.
- You have the option for the pay-as-you-go pricing.

SQL Azure Database Access

To access a SQL Azure database from the Microsoft .NET Framework code, you can use standard ADO.NET: the *SqlCommand* class to define a command, a *SqlDataReader* to pull data out, or *SqlDataAdapter,* because internally SQL Azure uses a *SqlDataReader* in a traditional manner. You only have to adapt the *SqlConnection* class's connection string. After you change it to the cloud version of the server, you just log on.

The code in Listing 9-1 reads the *customerId* field for every row in the customers table by using the oldest .NET Framework code.

LISTING 9-1 Classic ADO.NET code.

```
using System;
using System.Collections.Generic;
using System.Linq;
using System.Web;
using System.Web.UI;
using System.Web.UI.WebControls;
using System.Data.SqlClient;
using System.Data;

namespace TAServices
{
    public partial class _Default : System.Web.UI.Page
    {
        protected void Page_Load(object sender, EventArgs e)
        {
            try
            {
                using (SqlConnection conn = new SqlConnection())
                {
                    conn.ConnectionString = "some connection string";
                    using (SqlCommand cmd = new SqlCommand())
                    {
                        cmd.Connection = conn;
                        cmd.CommandText = "SELECT CustomerID from customers";
                        conn.Open();

                        using (SqlDataReader dr = cmd.ExecuteReader(
                           CommandBehavior.CloseConnection))
                        {
                            while (dr.Read())
                            {
                                // Do something
                            }
                            dr.Close();
                        }
                    }
                }
            }
            catch (SqlException ex)
            {
                // Something goes wrong
            }
        }
    }
}
```

The classic connection string for a trusted SQL connection is something similar to the following code:

```
Server=myServer;Database=myDb;Trusted_Connection=Yes;
```

If you are using a standard SQL connection instead of a trusted one, you have to modify the connection as shown in the following code:

```
Server=myServer;Database=myDb;Trusted_Connection=Yes; User
     ID=user;Password=password;Trusted_Connection=False;
```

With SQL Azure, the connection cannot be a trusted connection, because the client machine will be always in a different domain than SQL Azure. SQL Azure cannot be in a user domain.

As you learn in the next section, when you create a virtual server to host your database in the cloud, you receive a server name. You can then modify your connection string accordingly:

```
Server=tcp:VirtualServerName.database.windows.net;
     Database=myDb;Trusted_Connection=Yes; User
     ID=user@VirtualServerName;Password=password;Trusted_Connection=False;
```

The two modifications shown in boldface are the server address and the format of the *User ID* setting. As stated in the previous paragraph, the *VirtualServer* name is assigned by the platform when you complete the Create Server wizard. The user format is different because the connection is opened to a front-end node that needs to validate the user to let the connection reach the real server.

You can also use LINQ to SQL or Entity Framework in both .NET Framework 3.5 and 4 from either a Windows Azure hosted service or an on-premises solution. NHibernate and other ORMs also work if they use ADO.NET. When used with Entity Framework, the connection will be similar to the following code:

```
metadata=res://*/ Model.csdl|res://*/ DataModel.ssdl|res://*/DataModel.msl;
provider=System.Data.SqlClient;provider connection string=&quot;Data
Source=VirtualServerName.database.windows.net;Initial Catalog=MyDB;Integrated
Security=False;User ID=user@VirtualServerName;Password=password;
MultipleActiveResultSets=False;Encrypt=True;TrustServerCertificate=False&quot;"
providerName="System.Data.EntityClient"
```

This connection string is essentially identical to the classic version; you just have to modify the server pointer and the user name value. Modifications in the preceding code are in boldface.

Other platforms can also access SQL Azure using native ODBC code and its variants, such as JDBC from the Java environment. Compared to a traditional on-premises solution, you have to adapt the connection string similarly to the ADO.NET managed provider version, but you can use your existing JDBC:SQLServerDriver. You can also use Hibernate on the Java platform because it can use the SQL Server JDBC Driver.

The code that follows is an example of this kind of connection that points to the same database as the previous connection. The highlighted code shows the differences between the code for SQL Server and the code for SQL Azure:

```
hibernate.connection.driver_class=com.microsoft.sqlserver.jdbc.SQLServerDriver
hibernate.connection.url=jdbc:sqlserver://VirtualServerName.database.windows.net:1433;
     databaseName=mydb
hibernate.connection.username=user@VirtualServerName
hibernate.connection.password=password
```

Hypertext Preprocessor (PHP) is another environment that can access SQL Azure, following much the same pattern. You change the connection string and then open the connection:

```
$server = "tcp:VirtualServerName.database.windows.net,1433";
$user = "User@VirtualServerName";
$pass = "password";
$database = "MyDB";
$connectionoptions = array("Database" => $database,
                           "UID" => $user,
                           "PWD" => $pass,
                           "MultipleActiveResultSets" => false);
$conn = sqlsrv_connect($server, $connectionoptions);
```

You've seen now how to connect to a database in the cloud. The next section describes how to create a virtual server, assign an administrative account, and then create a database.

Database Server Creation in the Cloud

The first operation when planning a database in the cloud is creating the server, which you can do using the portal. From the Windows Azure home page, click the Account section, just as you have done in previous chapters. From the Account page, you can access the SQL Azure Developer Portal.

Create a Virtual Server

You can create a virtual server without worrying about payment, because you aren't charged until you create a database on that virtual server.

1. Log on to the portal using your Windows Live ID account. Choose the Database section from the lower-left toolbar. Your subscriptions will appear on the top-left pane. The following figure shows the page containing my subscriptions.

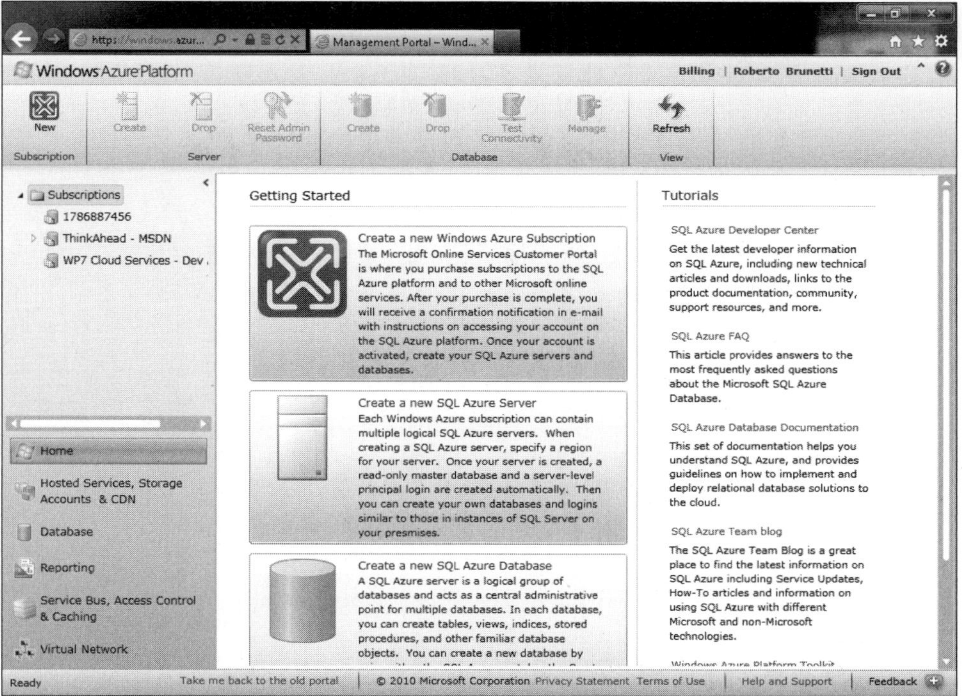

Tip Give meaningful names to the subscription you buy in the Billing Portal, because the Windows Azure Portal, the Windows Azure AppFabric Portal, and the SQL Azure Portal let you choose the project only by name.

2. Choose the project or subscription you want to use to create the database.
3. If this is the first Virtual Server you created in the project, you may have to accept the Terms Of Use by clicking the I Accept button.
4. Click the Create button in the top toolbar to start the Create Server wizard shown in the next figure. The first step in the wizard lets you choose the region where you want your virtual server to be hosted.

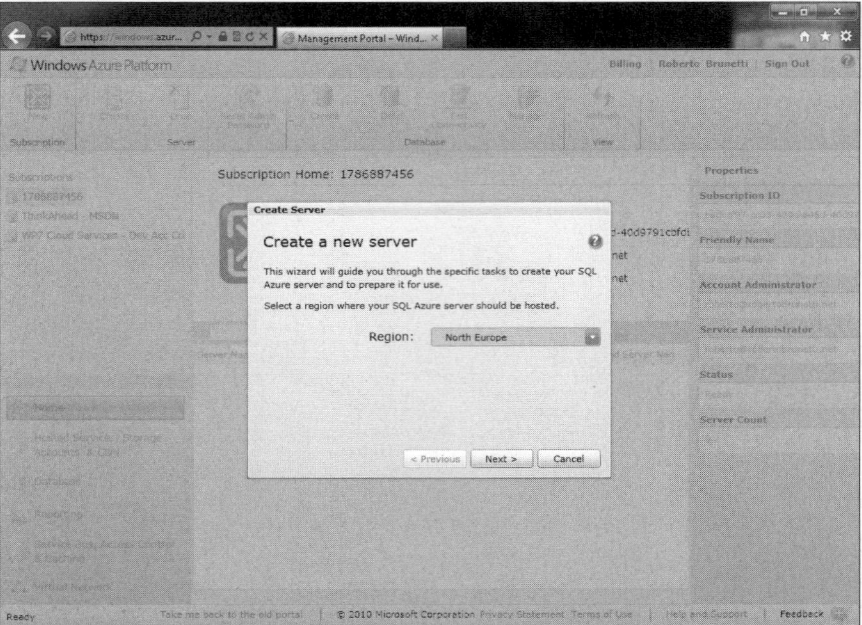

5. Choose the region you prefer, and then click the Next button.
6. Type **myAdmin** as your Administrator Login and **aZureStep_Step** as the password, and then click the Next button. The following figure shows the second step of the wizard.

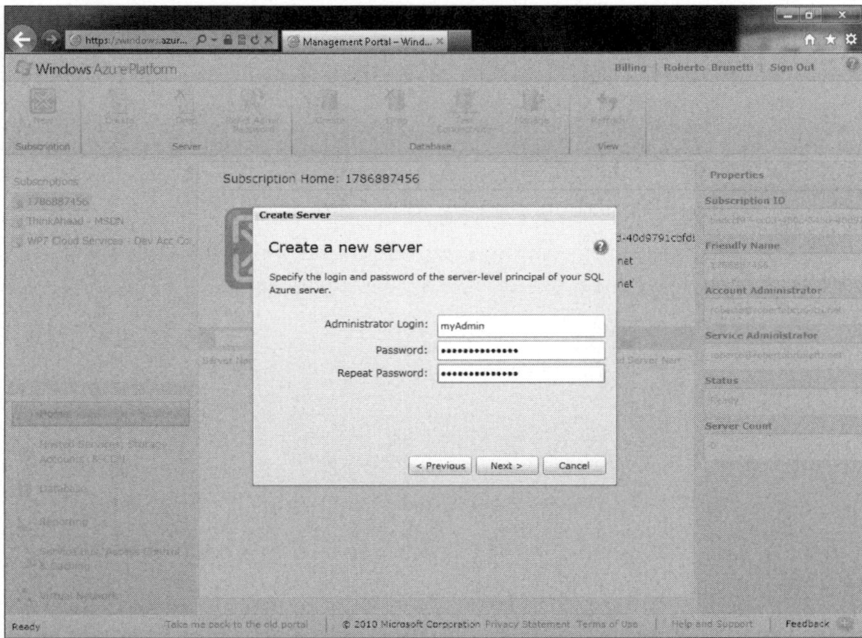

7. In the last page of the wizard, leave all the fields set to their default values, and click the Finish button.

If you followed these steps, you will be redirected to the Subscription Information page that shows you the server name, the administrator name, and the location you selected, as you can see in Figure 9-1.

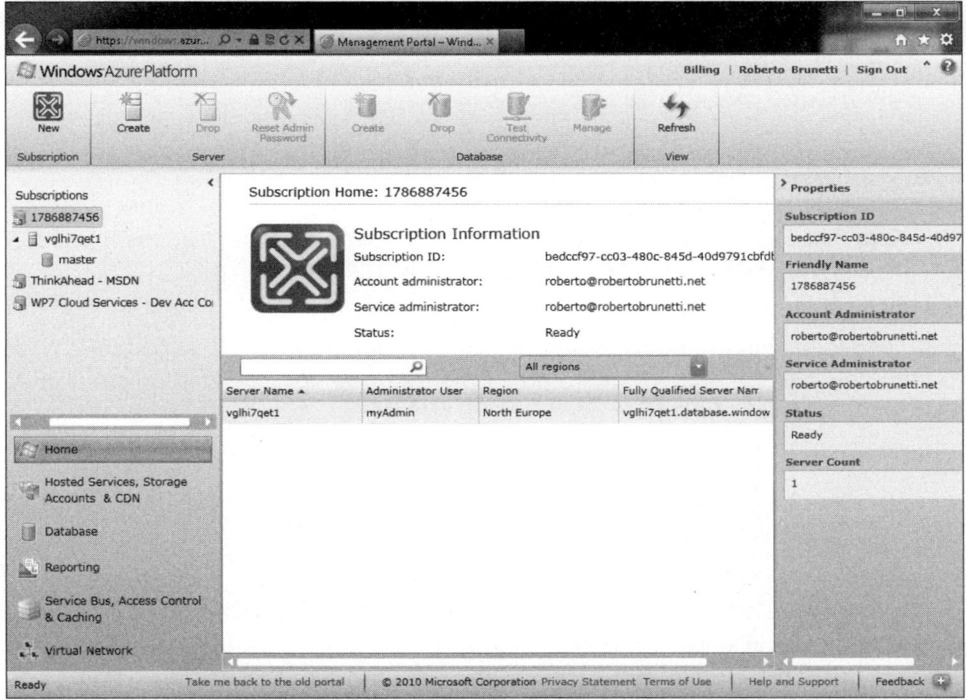

FIGURE 9-1 Subscription Information page.

You have now created a virtual server that can host different databases. The server name is autoassigned, and you must use it in the connection string for both the *Data Source* and the *User ID* parameters, as discussed in the previous section.

From the Subscription Administration page, you can also drop the virtual server if you want to delete it, and you can reset the administrator password whenever you want.

The administrator represents the highest user level. An administrator can be compared to the famous System Administrator (*sa*) in SQL Server. This user can administer the server, create new databases, log on to all databases hosted in this virtual server, and so on.

Figure 9-1 shows the master database, which has the important function (as it does in the on-premises version as well)—of storing system objects and tables.

Create a Database

After requesting the virtual server, you can create a database. Each database is billed based on its size. In other words, there's no difference in cost between creating a single virtual server in a subscription with five databases and creating five virtual servers in five different subscriptions with just one database in each.

You are charged based on database instances per month. Various database editions are available to fulfill different needs. For example, the Windows Azure Platform Development Accelerator Extended edition offers a 10-GB database at a discounted price together with one instance of a hosted service. There is also a SQL Azure Development Accelerator Core that offers a 10-GB database at a discounted price.

Note You are charged only for the data you store in your database. Transaction logs and system objects are not taken into account for billing purposes.

Depending on your Windows Azure subscription, you have particular database creation rights. For example, a user with a Development Accelerator Extended account cannot create a 50 GB database.

Note Pricing and policies can vary over time. I suggest you verify in the billing system which options are available when you create your subscription.

1. Double-click the subscription in the upper-left pane, and then click the virtual server you created in the "Create a Database" procedure.
2. Click the Create button in the upper toolbar. Do not click the Create button you used in the previous procedure. (If you selected the virtual server correctly, the button is unavailable). The following figure shows the Create Database dialog box.

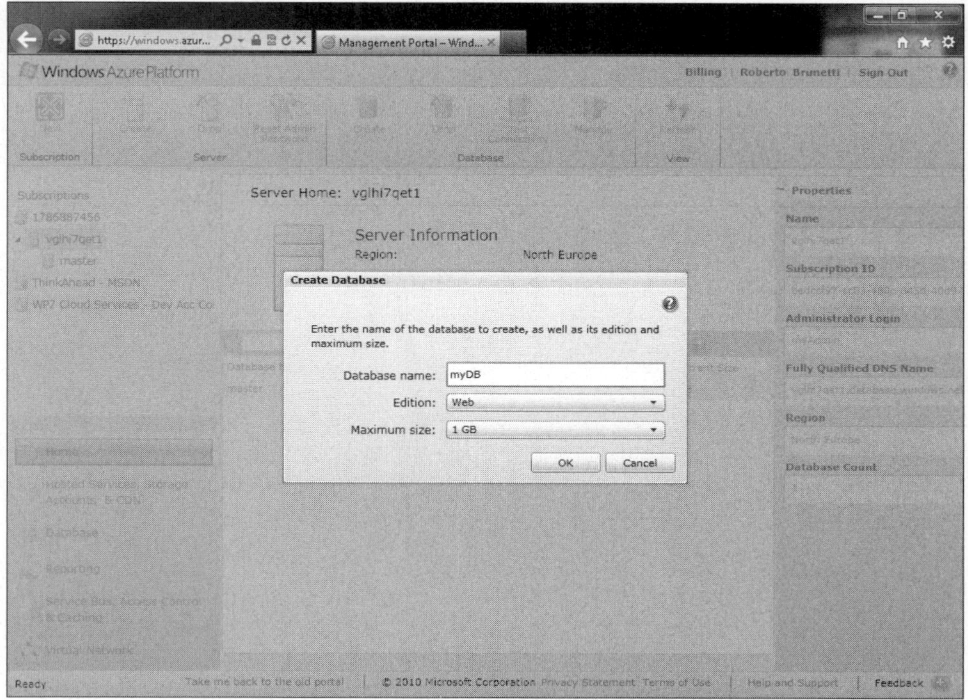

3. Type **myDB** for the database name, and choose the edition and a corresponding size to suit your needs. The Web edition lets you choose from 1 GB and 5 GB database sizes, whereas the Business edition lets you create a database up to 50 GB.

4. Click OK to create the database. The operation takes just a few seconds.

After following these steps, the page presents you with your new database. Figure 9-2 shows a real server with the production database that stores the data for the Save The Planet Windows Phone 7 application. I obscured some sensitive details.

At this point, you have all the information you need to adapt the connection string to your database in the cloud. Follow the connection string guidelines in the section "SQL Azure Database Access" earlier in this chapter.

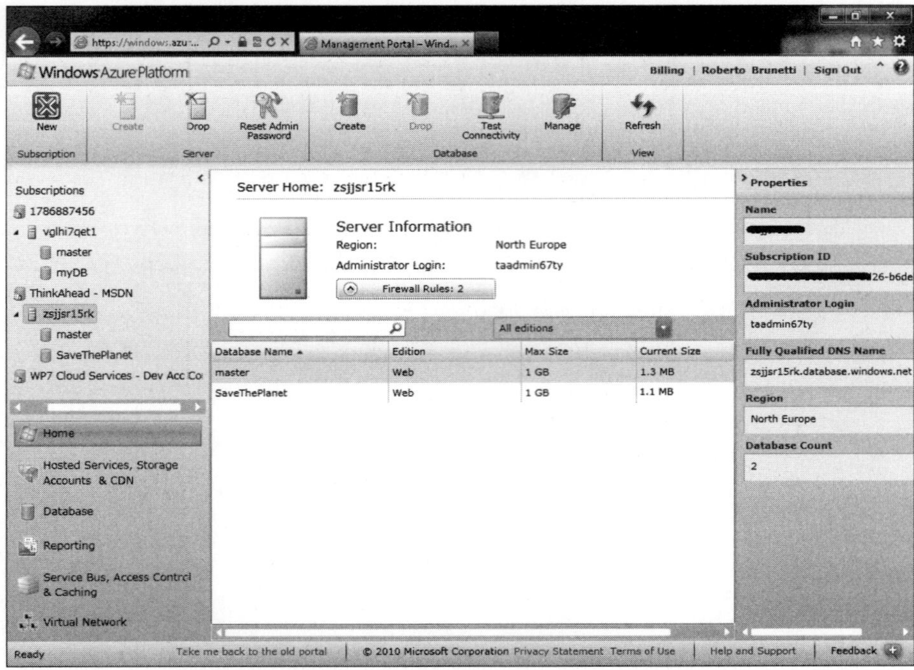

FIGURE 9-2 A real database in production.

All communication between SQL Azure and your application requires encryption: Secure Socket Layer (SSL). If the client application does not validate certificates upon connection, your connection to SQL Azure can be subject to classic "man-in-the-middle" attacks. SSL secures the connection by validating the server certificate and then encrypting all traffic.

If you do not specify *Encrypt=true* in the connection string, the connection and data are still encrypted, but they may not validate the server certificates and would thus be susceptible to the same types of attacks. To validate certificates with ADO.NET, set *Encrypt=True* and *TrustServerCertificate=False* in the database connection string.

Microsoft SQL Server Management Studio R2 also supports certificate validation. You have to set *Encrypt Connection* in the Connection Properties dialog box. SQLCMD.exe supports encrypted connections starting with Microsoft SQL Server 2008 R2. You can use the *-N* command-line option.

Before you can connect a client to the SQL Azure database, you need to perform another small step: opening the firewall to the remote machine.

Configure the Firewall

Firewall configuration is often a pain point when building on-premises solutions, but this procedure shows how you can configure firewall settings in only a minute with SQL Azure.

You need to know that the SQL Azure service is available only through TCP port 1433. It cannot be reached (in this first version) via named pipes or other protocols. To access a SQL Azure database from a client application hosted in your local area network, ensure that your firewall allows outgoing TCP communications on TCP port 1433.

1. In SQL Azure, click the Firewall Rules button from the Server Information Page.
2. To allow connections from a Windows Azure hosted service (a Web or Worker Role), select the Allow Other Windows Azure Services To Access This Server check box.
3. If you need on-premises access or mobile access, you must add a corresponding rule by clicking the Add button.
4. Give the rule a meaningful name and insert the range of IP addresses that can access the virtual server. The modal dialog box shows your current IP address, which must be inserted in the rule when you want to connect to the database with SQL Server Management Studio.
5. Click the OK button.

Figure 9-3 shows the *MicrosoftServices* rule that is automatically created whenever you select the Allow Other Windows Azure Services To Access This Server check box, and a custom rule named All that ranges from the 1.1.1.1 IP address to the 255.255.255.255 IP address.

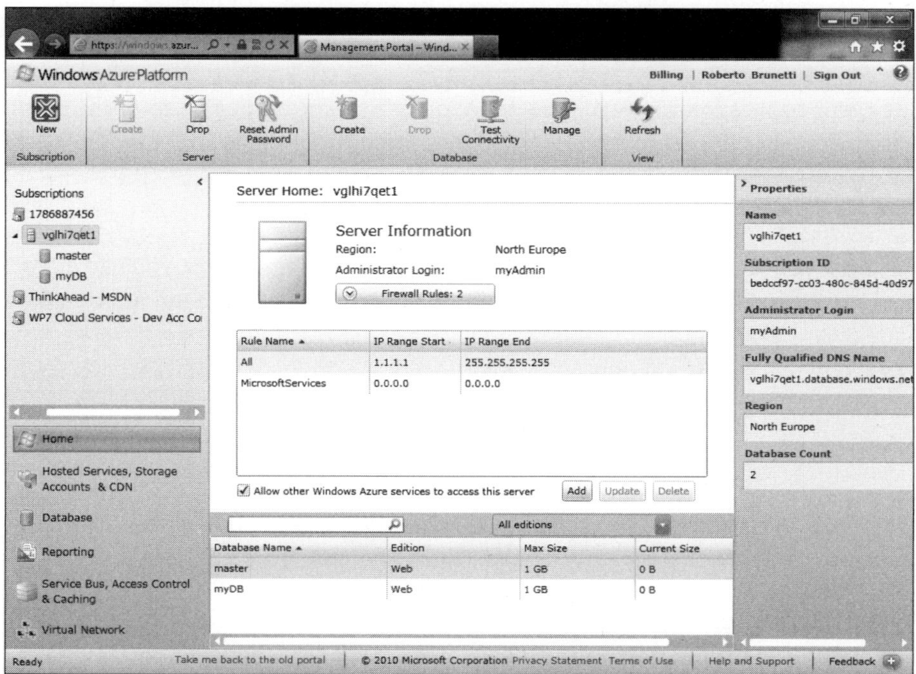

FIGURE 9-3 Firewall rules.

SQL Azure Access

The steps for building and using a SQL Azure database, as you have learned so far, are the following:

1. Create a virtual server from the portal. When you do that, the infrastructure provides you with a server name automatically.
2. Choose an administrative account and a password.
3. Create a database, providing the name and the maximum size.
4. Define applicable firewall rules.

Think for a moment about the steps involved in building a traditional on-premises solution. The process typically starts with hardware selection and includes the licensing considerations for both the operating system and the database engine. Consider as well the installation steps required for a SQL cluster, and the security issues that emerge—even in a simple system. With SQL Azure, you can forget almost all of these concerns. You can pay just $9.00 per month (7.5 euros) for a scalable, redundant database where you can store up to 1 GB of data that you can access securely from anywhere in the world.

Now that your database is ready, you can use your traditional ADO.NET or ODBC code by changing only the connection string. If you are configuring a classic on-premises solution, you probably change the connection string in the *connectionString* section of your App.config or Web.config file, but you can also use a different mechanism if you like.

If the client application is a Web Role or a Worker Role (or both), remember to store the connection string in the service configuration files. Do not use the Web.config or App.config files in this scenario, because you cannot modify them without redeploying the entire solution to Windows Azure.

To add the connection string parameter to the service configuration, you can either use Microsoft Visual Studio or manually add the XML elements to the configuration files. If you decide to use Visual Studio, remember to choose *String* as the type for the parameter setting, as shown in the following figure.

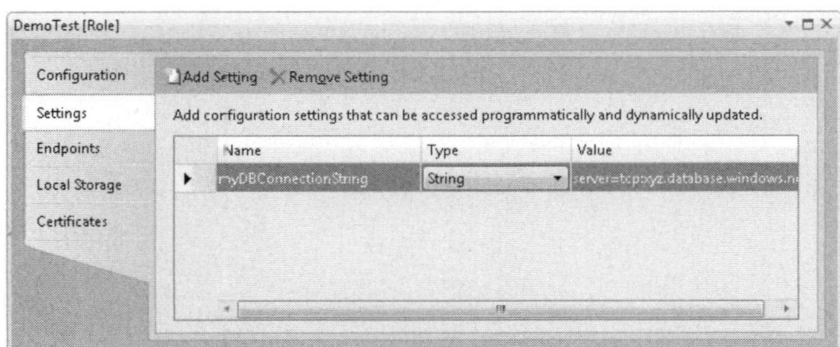

The setting type *Connection String* is dedicated to connections to in storage account projects and is used by the *StorageClient* APIs to build the correct URLs for blobs, tables, and queues.

If you prefer to modify the ServiceConfiguration.cscfg file manually, remember to add the configuration settings to the service definition file before assigning the settings values in the service configuration file.

Listing 9-2 shows the service definition for a Web Role named *WebRole1,* with a setting named *myDBConnectionString*. The service definition contains just the definitions for the various parameters.

LISTING 9-2 ServiceDefinition.csdef.

```
<?xml version="1.0" encoding="utf-8"?>
<ServiceDefinition name="DevLeapCloudService" xmlns="http://schemas.microsoft.com/
ServiceHosting/2008/10/ServiceDefinition">
  <WebRole name="WebRole1">
    <InputEndpoints>
      <InputEndpoint name="HttpIn" protocol="http" port="80" />
    </InputEndpoints>
    <ConfigurationSettings>
      <Setting name="myDBConnectionString" />
    </ConfigurationSettings>
  </WebRole>
</ServiceDefinition>
```

Listing 9-3 presents the value assignments for the ServiceConfiguration.cscfg.

LISTING 9.3 ServiceConfigurtion.cscfg.

```
<?xml version="1.0"?>
<ServiceConfiguration serviceName="DevLeapCloudService" xmlns="http://schemas.
microsoft.com/ServiceHosting/2008/10/ServiceConfiguration">
  <Role name="WebRole1">
    <Instances count="1" />
    <ConfigurationSettings>
      <Setting name="myDBConnectionString"
            value="Server=tcp:VirtualServerName.database.windows.net;
            Database=myDb;Trusted_Connection=Yes; User ID=user@VirtualServerName;
            Password=password;Trusted_Connection=False" />
    </ConfigurationSettings>
  </Role>
</ServiceConfiguration>
```

To change the connection string, you can use the developer portal—without redeploying the entire solution to Windows Azure.

If you created the structure of your tables, views, and stored procedures in the cloud database instance, you can use Visual Studio to connect to them using the same connection string information. In fact, you can use any Visual Studio tool that uses a connection string to connect to a SQL Azure database. For example, you might build your Entity Data Model by connecting the designer to the SQL Azure database.

The following figure shows the classic Visual Studio Add Connection dialog box connecting to the *SaveThePlanet* database in my SQL Azure virtual server.

When the connection is defined, any Visual Studio tool that uses a database can work against SQL Azure database instances. The following figure shows the *SaveThePlanet.Person* table structure and data inside the traditional Visual Studio 2010 IDE.

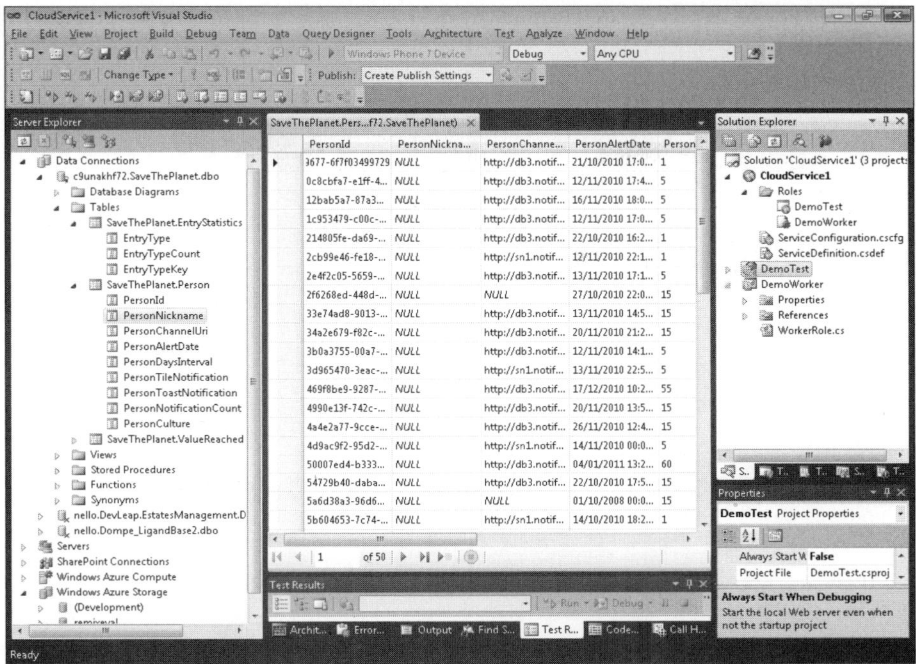

You can also use SQL Management Studio R2 to manage database objects such as tables, views, and stored procedures, as well as logons, users, and groups. Finally, you can use the Query Analyzer to query and manage data.

The following figure shows the Connect To Server dialog box.

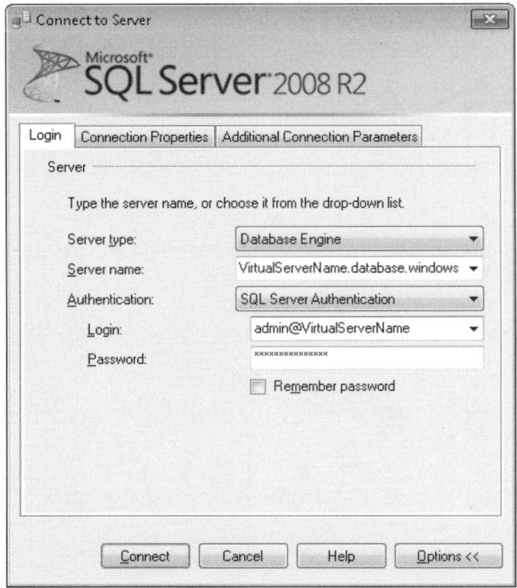

After making a successful connection, SQL Server Management Studio R2 presents the list of databases on the virtual server, shown in the following figure, and you make data requests using the traditional query window.

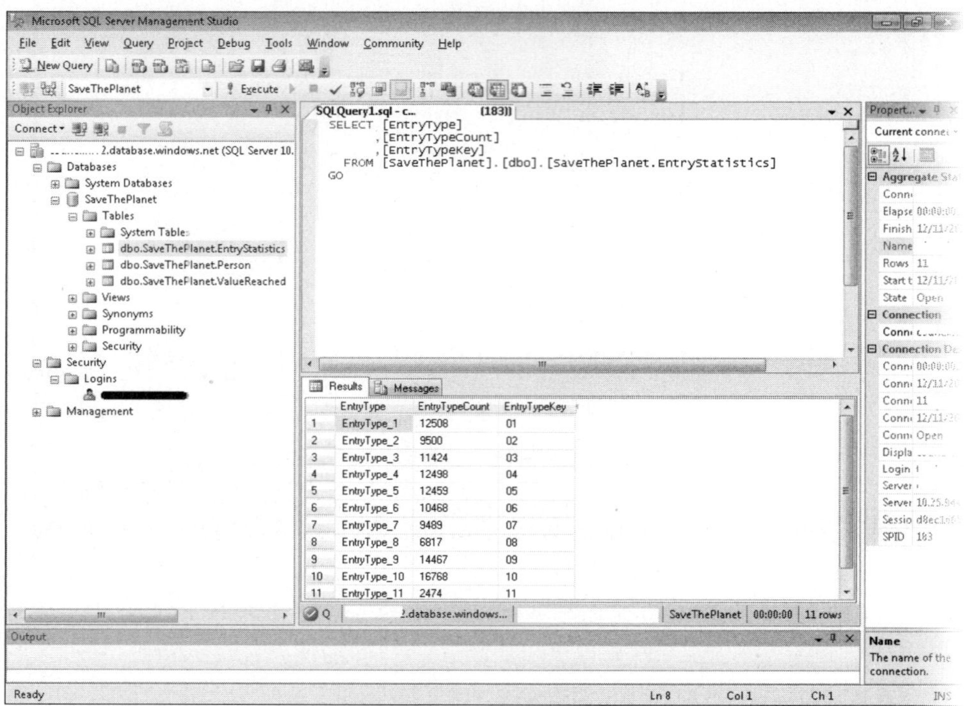

Object Explorer presents a slightly different set of information:

- It lacks the entire Server Object tree because SQL Azure doesn't support Linked Servers or Backup Devices.
- The Management tree contains just the Data-Tier application menu. There are no Database Mail, Distributed Transaction Coordinator, Resource Governor, or Maintenance Plan items.
- Replication engines are not supported in the current version of SQL Azure, so there is nothing related to this feature in the user interface.
- The Security tree presents only the logon menu; logons are equivalent to the on-premises version of SQL Server.
- Some of these features are self-managed by the infrastructure, and some are simply not present at the current time.
- You can still ask for the query execution plan, shown the following figure.

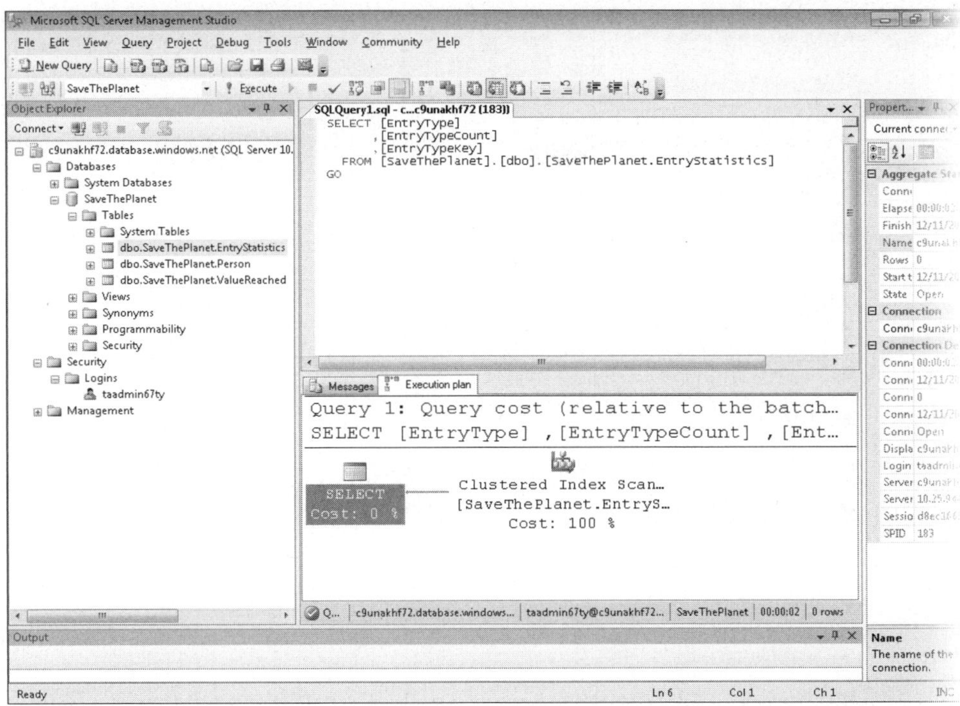

If you normally work with a SQL Server instance on your machine or on your Local Area Network (LAN), you will see a little difference in the performance of the management tool. This is related to the network latency; requests made by the tool have to traverse the Internet until they reach the data center where you decided to host your virtual server.

One of the best ways to work is to use a local database instance to configure the SQL Azure database. You develop by using the local database instance, updating its objects, testing the application against it, and then transfer the completed tested structure to the cloud instance. You can do this using either Visual Studio 2010 or SQL Server 2008 R2. You can also use the tool of your choice to produce the T-SQL script on the local instance and apply it to the cloud.

Not every SQL Server database feature can be used in SQL Azure, so you have to be careful when you create new database objects in your local database instance. For example, you can't use User Defined Types in the current version of SQL Azure, so you must remove those in the generated scripts before applying the scripts to your cloud version.

The next sections analyze the relational engine feature and introduce a tool that simplifies creating a cloud adaptation of a local instance.

SQL Azure Relational Engine Feature

SQL Azure's top features, as listed by Microsoft, are these:

- Tables, views, indexes, roles, stored procedures, triggers, and user defined functions
- Constraints
- Transactions
- Temp tables
- Basic functions (aggregates, math, string, date/time)
- Constants
- Cursors
- Index management and index rebuilding
- Local temporary tables
- Reserved keywords
- Statistics management
- Table variables
- Transact-SQL language elements such as create/drop databases, create/alter/drop tables, create/alter/drop users and logons

As mentioned at the beginning of this chapter, some of the relational database engine functionalities are not supported. For quick reference, the main features not supported are these:

- User-defined types
- Common Language Runtime (CLR)
- Database file placement
- Database mirroring
- Distributed queries
- Distributed transactions
- Filegroup management
- Full Text Search
- Global temporary tables

Note This list may change over time. Read the official guide to verify whether these are supported in the current version of the product.

There are also some differences in the way SQL Azure manages indexes, pages, file groups, and locks with respect to its on-premises counterpart. You need to remove the following keywords from the script generated by the SQL Azure management tool:

- The *USE* statement
- The file group specification for table
- The NOT FOR REPLICATION specification
- PAD_INDEX, ALLOW_ROW_LOCKS, ROWGUIDCOLUMN, ALLOW_PAGE_LOCKS
- Fill Factor
- NEWSEQUENTIALID
- Windows Login

In addition, every table needs a clustered index.

Existing Database Migration

There are different ways to transfer schema and data to SQL Azure.

You can generate a T-SQL script from SQL Server Management Studio 2008 R2, analyze it to remove the unsupported SQL Azure features, and adapt some of the T-SQL statements. Then you can connect the Management Studio tool to the SQL Azure database and run the script against it. You can do the same thing to update an existing database: use your preferred tool to generate an incremental script, adapt it for SQL Azure, and then run it against a SQL Azure database.

After moving the database structure to the cloud, the next step deals with the way you transfer data to and from the SQL Azure instance. An easy (but time consuming) method is to generate *INSERT* statements and run them against the remote database. But a more powerful technique is to use SQL Server Integration Services (SSIS). SQL Azure does not support SQL Server Integration Services. That means only that you cannot run an SSIS package from a SQL Azure instance. However, your local version of SQL Server supports SSIS natively, which means that you can define and launch an SSIS package from SQL Server to pull or push data to SQL Azure. Showing how SSIS works is outside the scope of this book, but you can find plenty of information online.

If you decide to use SSIS, remember that SQL Azure does not support OLE DB, so your connection must be based on ADO.NET.

SQL Azure also supports the *BULK-COPY (BCP)* statement and its cousin, the .NET Framework class *SqlBulkCopy*. This is the fastest technique for inserting large numbers of records into a table.

Currently, SQL Data Sync is in CTP2, but it should be released sometime in 2011. At the time of this writing, its goals are the following (Microsoft Corporation, Windows Azure website, 2011, *http://www.microsoft.com/en-us/sqlazure/datasync.aspx*):

- Extend enterprise data to the cloud rather than replace it.
- Move workloads to the cloud in stages, preserving investment in existing infrastructure.
- Extend data to remote locations such as offices and retail stores.
- Enable new scenarios that span enterprises and the cloud.
- Scale as resources requirements grow.
- Provide no-code sync configuration, which allows you to easily define data to be synchronized with easy-to-use tools.
- Expose a scheduling configuration, allowing you to choose how often data is synchronized.
- Manage conflict handling so that you can handle issues when identical data is changed in multiple locations.
- Provide logging and monitoring: Administration capabilities for tracking data and monitoring potential issues.

SQL Azure Migration Wizard

A simple and effective way to transfer structures and data from a local database instance to a SQL Azure database is to install and use the SQL Azure Migration Wizard. This tool has been available on CodePlex since the CTP version of SQL Azure. At the time of this writing, the current version is 3.5.7. You can download it from *http://sqlazuremw.codeplex.com/*.

You can use the SQL Azure Migration Wizard tool on a local SQL Server 2005 or SQL Server 2008 database to produce a script suitable for SQL Azure. The wizard automatically removes any unsupported feature, adapts the different keywords cited in the previous section, executes the script against a specified SQL Azure database, and moves the data to the cloud.

The tool can also perform the inverse operation: when pointed to a SQL Azure database, it can translate the script into the on-premises SQL Server dialect, and move the remote data to a local copy. It can also move data from one SQL Azure database to another, and analyze local SQL Profiler data for SQL Azure compatibility.

The first screen in the wizard asks what kind of operation you want to perform. The first group of options concerns the analysis feature, which lets you analyze SQL Databases, a TSQL script file, or a SQL Profiler Trace file.

From here you can also analyze and migrate a local database or a TSQL file to SQL Azure. The final option involves migrating a database without analyzing its structure. The following figure shows the first page of the wizard.

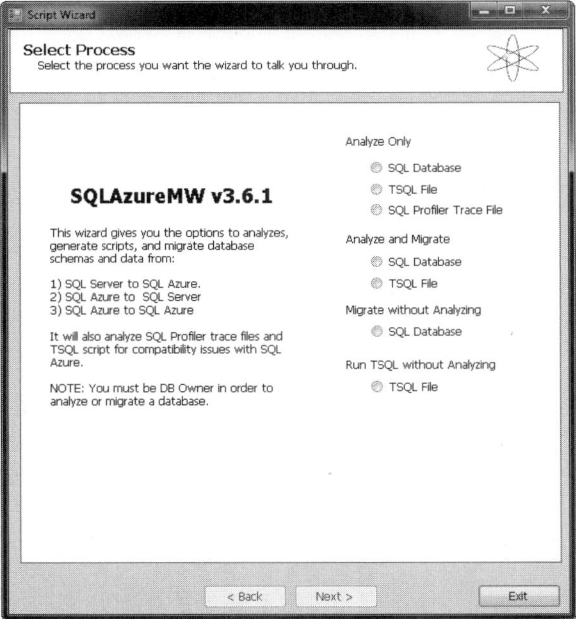

The second step of the wizard asks for the local connection and is shown in the following figure. You can choose whether to connect to the Master DB to ask for the list of every database in the local SQL Server instance.

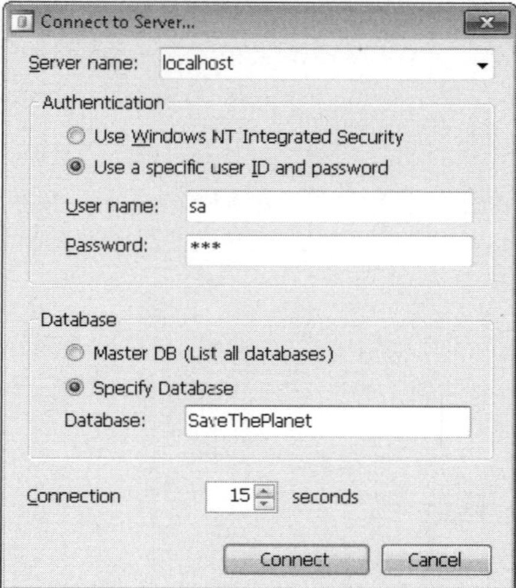

The next step, shown in the following figure, asks which objects you want to analyze and script. The advanced options are very useful for determining the settings to use when the tool generates the script. For example, you might choose to script tables and data but not unique keys and defaults.

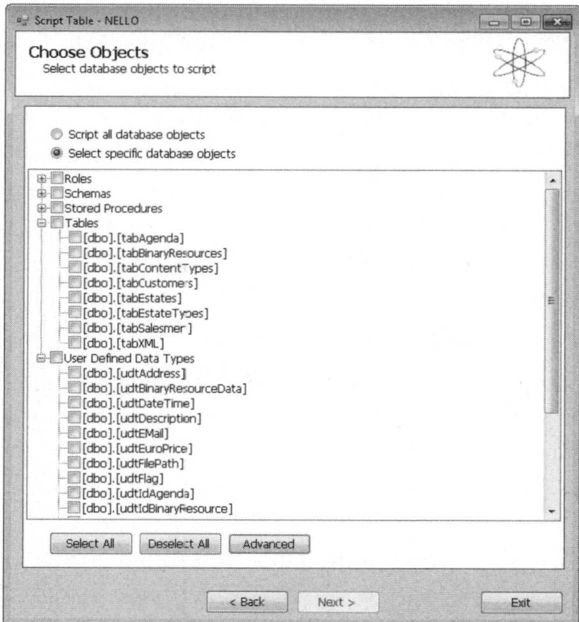

After you chose the objects to script, the tool analyzes the database, produces a script, and displays a summary of the analysis, as shown in the following figure.

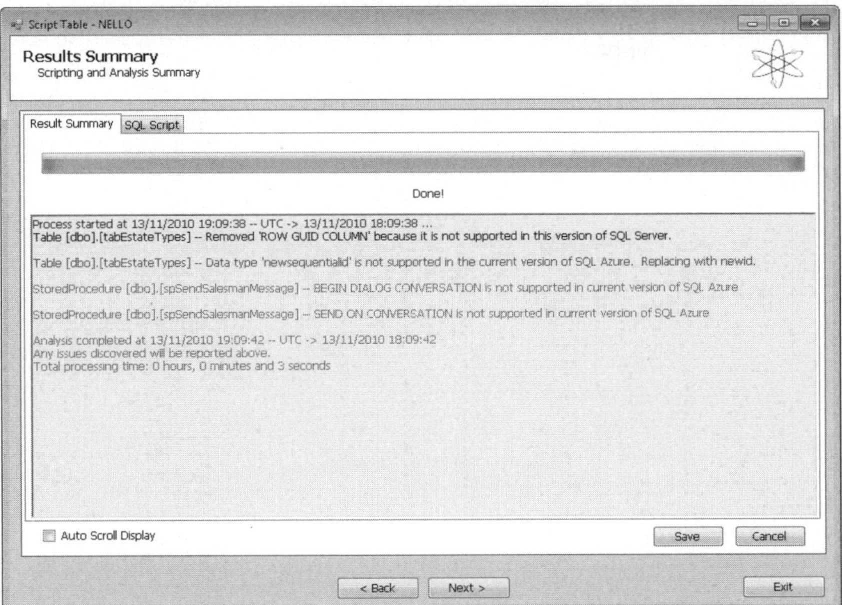

The next step asks you to provide a connection to a SQL Azure database, validates it, and then runs the script against the database in the cloud.

Summary

SQL Azure is an adaptation of SQL Server for the cloud. It provides the same set of fundamental database engine features as its local version. Some local SQL Server features are not available in the current cloud version, and others are simply impractical in the cloud. You can populate SQL Azure databases using SQL Server Integration Services or the SQL Azure Migration Wizard.

Quick Reference

To	Do this
Use the cloud instance of a database	Modify the connection string.
Create a server that can host databases	Use the SQL Azure Portal.
Create a database structure	Use SQL Server Management Studio 2008 R2 or Visual Studio 2010.
Configure port access rules	Use the Firewall Setting rules in the portal and define logins for virtual server.
Migrate an existing database	Consider using the SQL Azure Migration Wizard.

Chapter 10

Accessing Azure Services from Everywhere

After completing this chapter, you will be able to

- Understand how to access a storage account from a client application.
- Write code to use the Storage Client library from a Windows Forms client application.
- Create a basic PHP page to work with the storage account.
- Understand how to make direct calls using REST to access Windows Azure Services.

This chapter is dedicated to some important aspects of a Windows Azure solution. In the preceding chapters, I used Microsoft ASP.NET applications to access cloud-based resources, but any client on any platform can use Windows Azure resources and services. In this chapter, you learn how to configure a client application to access the storage account.

The example you follow in this chapter is a simple Windows Forms application that leverages the storage account features to store and retrieve blobs and entities. I chose Windows Forms to make the point that any client can access Windows Azure services as long as it can consume a standard interface based on HTTP/REST. In the code sample, you use the same library (*StorageClient*) you used in Chapter 4, "Windows Azure Storage," and Chapter 5, "Tables, Queues, and Worker Roles."

Note Because URLs, UI names, and procedures may vary over time, some of them may be out of date by the time you read this. In that case, my best advice is to start looking for the information about the Windows Azure product on the Windows Azure home page (*http://www.azure.com*). Information included in this book was accurate at the time of writing.

Creating the Storage Account Project

In this section, you will create a Storage Account Project using the Windows Azure Management Portal, a client application that uses the *StorageClient* APIs to manage data in the storage account. Then, you use the client application to store and retrieve data.

Create the Storage Account Project

You need to create a Storage Account Project to store and retrieve data. In this procedure, you create a new storage account.

1. Open the browser of your choice and go to the Windows Azure Portal at *http://www.azure.com*.
2. Log on with your Windows Live ID to access the Management Portal.
3. Start the Create A New Storage Account wizard by clicking the New Storage Account button on the top toolbar.
4. Choose a unique name for your storage account. If you choose a name that is already claimed, you receive an error. For example, if you type **azuresbs** in the Enter A URL text box, you receive the error message shown in the following figure.

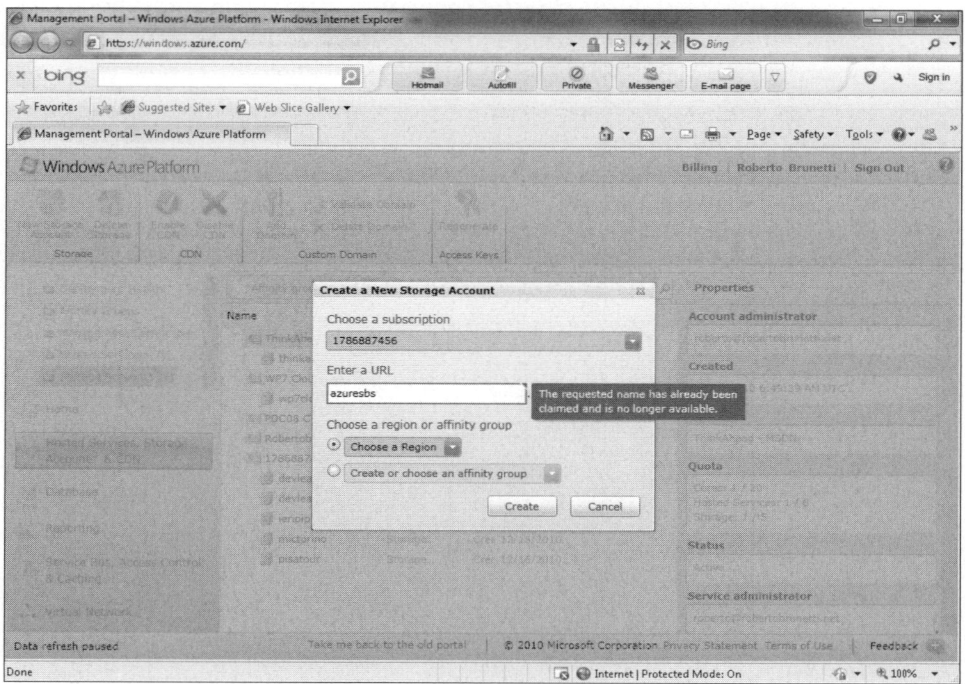

The error occurs because the name *azuresbs* is already claimed. You need to type a unique name that will represent the prefix for the common service URI (*http://servicename.*.core.windows.net*).

5. Choose a unique name for your service and type it in the Enter A URL text box. Continue this process until you choose a name the portal accepts.

6. Choose your preferred region in the first combo box in the Choose A Region Or Affinity Group section. I have chosen **azuresbs3,** as you can see from Figure 10-1.

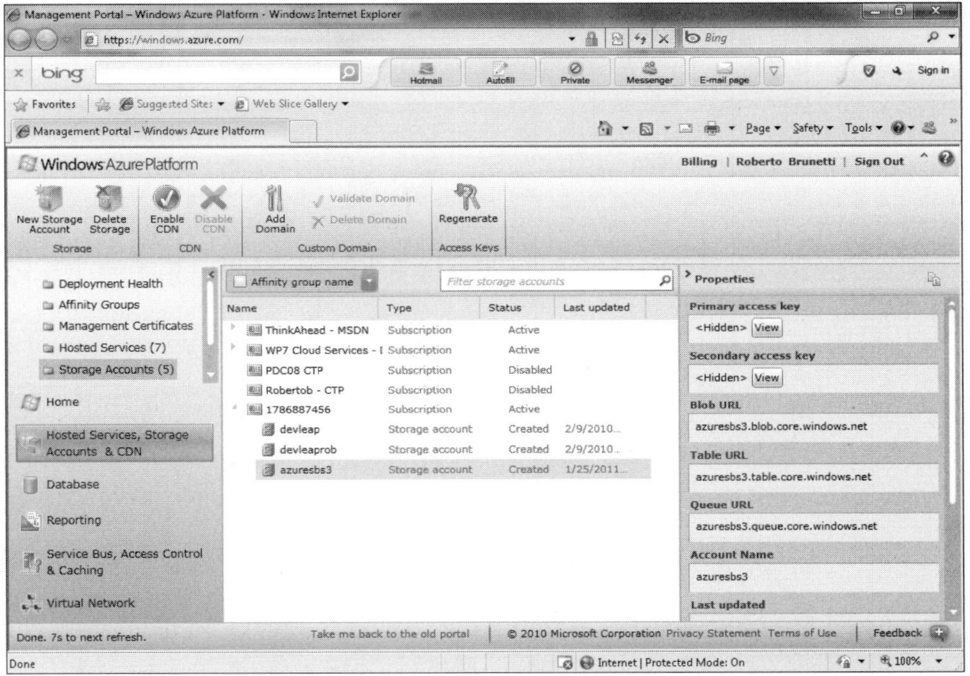

FIGURE 10-1. Storage Accounts management page.

As you learned in Chapter 4, the portal lets you see every detail of the storage account.

Create the Client Application

In this procedure, you store and retrieve data in the storage account from a client application by using a Windows Forms application.

1. Create a new Windows Forms Project using the Microsoft Visual Studio default template, shown in the following figure.

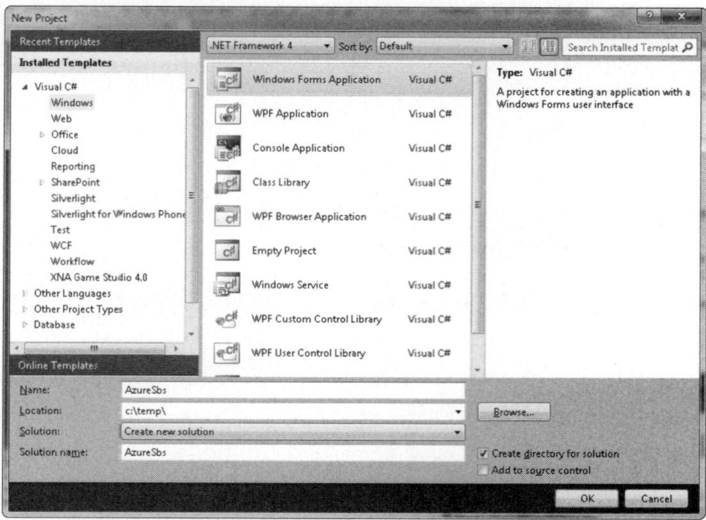

2. Type **AzureSbs** in both the Name and Solution Name text boxes, and click OK to create the project.

3. Add a reference to the *StorageClient* library. Right-click the reference node in the project, and select Add Reference.

4. Click the Browse tab and choose the Ref subdirectory of the Windows Azure SDK. If you installed the SDK in the default directory, your directory is %Program Files%\Windows Azure SDK\<*version*>\ref, which is shown as Ref in the directory in the following figure.

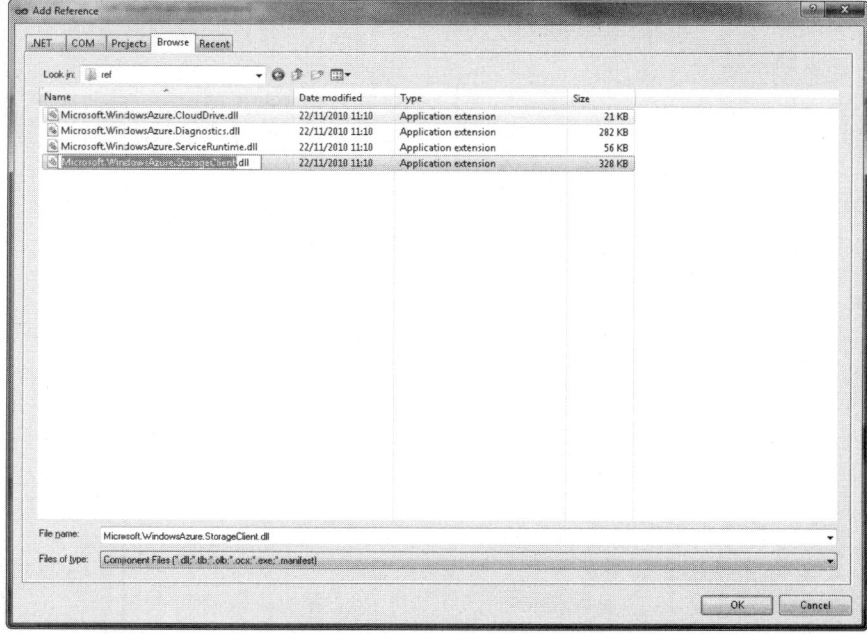

5. Click the OK button to accept the new reference.
6. Make the form a little bit bigger, and drag a *DataGridView* control from the designer toolbox onto the form. Resize the *DataGridView* so that it can show more data like the following figure.

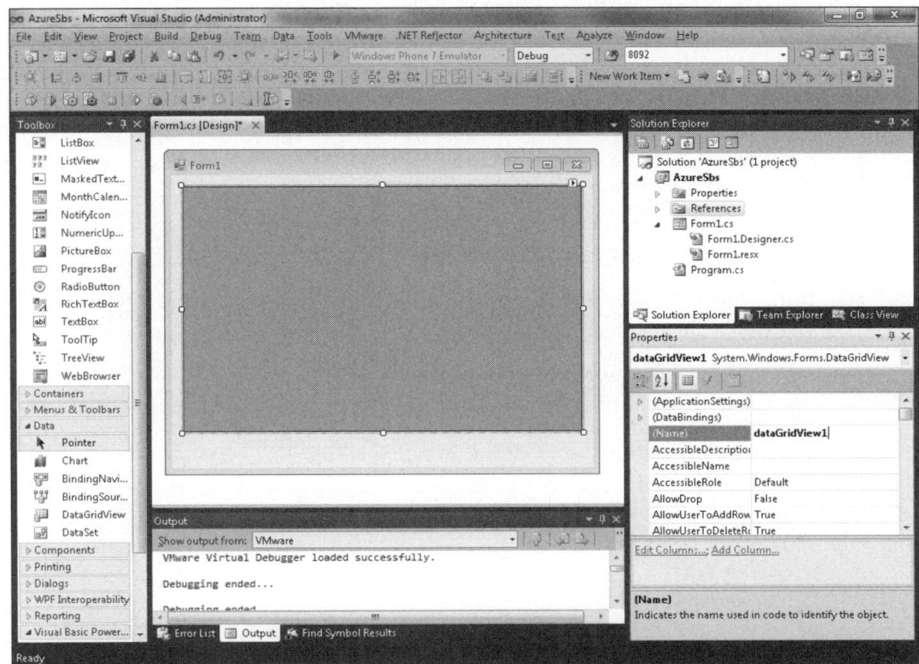

7. Create a new class named **Book** to represent the entity. In the new *Book* class, use the following code to define a book entity that derives from the *StorageClient.TableServiceEntity* base class:

```
using System;
using System.Collections.Generic;
using System.Linq;
using System.Text;
using Microsoft.WindowsAzure.StorageClient;

namespace AzureSbs
{
    public class Book : TableServiceEntity
    {
        public String Title { get; set; }
        public DateTime PublicationDate { get; set; }
    }
}
```

8. Create a new application configuration file to store the connection string to the Storage Account Project.

In a hosted service, it is a good practice to store this kind of data in the service configuration file. In an on-premises solution, you have to store this data in the classic configuration file (Web.config for an ASP.NET application and App.config for a client application).

9. Use the following XML fragment to configure the *DataConnectionString* setting that you will use to retrieve the storage account connection:

```
<?xml version="1.0" encoding="utf-8" ?>
<configuration>
  <appSettings>
    <add key="DataConnectionString" value="UseDevelopmentStorage=true" />
  </appSettings>
</configuration>
```

   In the first test, you use the local storage account simulated service.

10. Add a reference to the *System.Configuration* assembly and to *System.Data.Services.Client*. You need the first one to read the configuration file from the *ConfigurationManager* class, and the second to use the query feature of the Windows Communication Foundation (WCF) Data Services Client library.

11. Double-click a blank area in the form to create the *Form_Load* event handler. Using this method, you request the list of entities stored in the storage account. Replace the default code with the following snippet:

```
using System;
using System.Collections.Generic;
using System.ComponentModel;
using System.Data;
using System.Drawing;
using System.Linq;
using System.Text;
using System.Windows.Forms;
using Microsoft.WindowsAzure.StorageClient;
using Microsoft.WindowsAzure;
using System.Configuration;

namespace AzureSbs
{
    public partial class Form1 : Form
    {
        public Form1()
        {
            InitializeComponent();
        }

        private void Form1_Load(object sender, EventArgs e)
        {
            CloudStorageAccount account =
                CloudStorageAccount.Parse(ConfigurationManager.AppSettings[
               "DataConnectionString"]);
            String baseAddress = account.TableEndpoint.AbsoluteUri;
            StorageCredentials credentials = account.Credentials;
```

```
            CloudTableClient tableClient = account.CreateCloudTableClient();
            tableClient.CreateTableIfNotExist("Books");


            TableServiceContext context = new TableServiceContext(
                baseAddress, credentials);
            dataGridView1.DataSource = context.CreateQuery<Book>("Books").ToList();
        }
    }
}
```

The first line of the preceding code uses the *Parse* method of *CloudStorageAccount* to build the information needed to create the request to the Storage Account Service. The methods take the string stored in the configuration file and expose the information needed to create the URI that points to the service and the access credentials. I built two variables to contain this information to simplify the code.

The next two lines are responsible for creating the table container in the storage account. The sixth line of code creates the client context passing the URI to the Table Storage Account Service and the credentials.

The last line of the code binds the query for the *Books* table, asking for a *book* type. There are some differences from the code used in Chapter 5, which I will explain a little later in the chapter.

12. Before running this project, you have to change the default Target Framework to .NET Framework 4 in the project properties dialog box, which is shown in the next figure. To do this, right-click the Windows Forms Application Project and choose Properties.

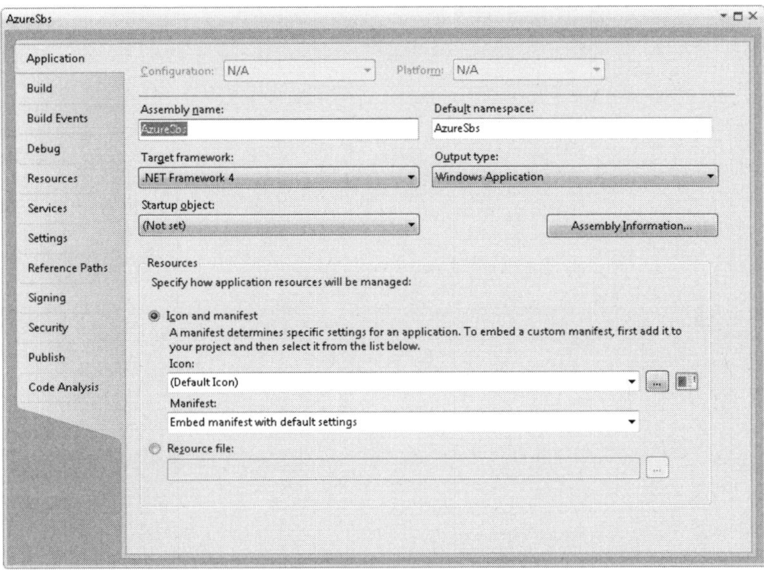

13. Before running the application, check the state of the storage emulator. To do that, from the Start menu, select Windows Azure SDK and then the Storage Emulator User Interface. Verify the running state of the three services. You can click the Start button to start all of them.

14. Run the application to verify that no compilation or running error occurs. The result is an empty grid.

The code for the Windows Form Application Project is slightly different from the code you used in Chapters 4 and 5. Some of the runtime features of the *StorageAccount* class cannot be used outside the Windows Azure hosting environment. For instance, you cannot use the *FromConfigurationSetting* static method to build the URI and credentials; this method uses internal logic to cache the information retrieved from the configuration and leverages the *SetConfigurationSettingPublisher* method to read the account access key from the service configuration file. These methods are useless outside the Windows Azure operating system. If you tried to copy and paste the code presented in Chapter 5 to an out-of-the-cloud application, you would receive an exception like the one presented in the following figure, even if the application were an ASP.NET application.

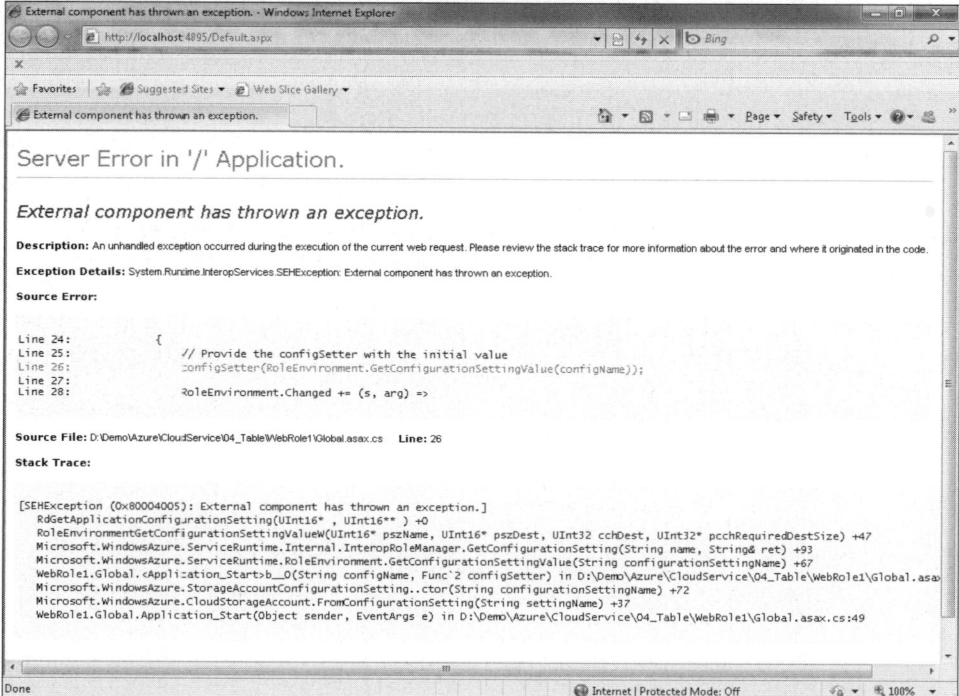

Insert Some Data

Let's try to add some books using very simple code. Refer to Chapter 5 for more complete samples.

1. Add a *TextBox* control and a *Button* control to the form, and leave the default name. Just change the button text to **Add.** The form should look similar to the following figure.

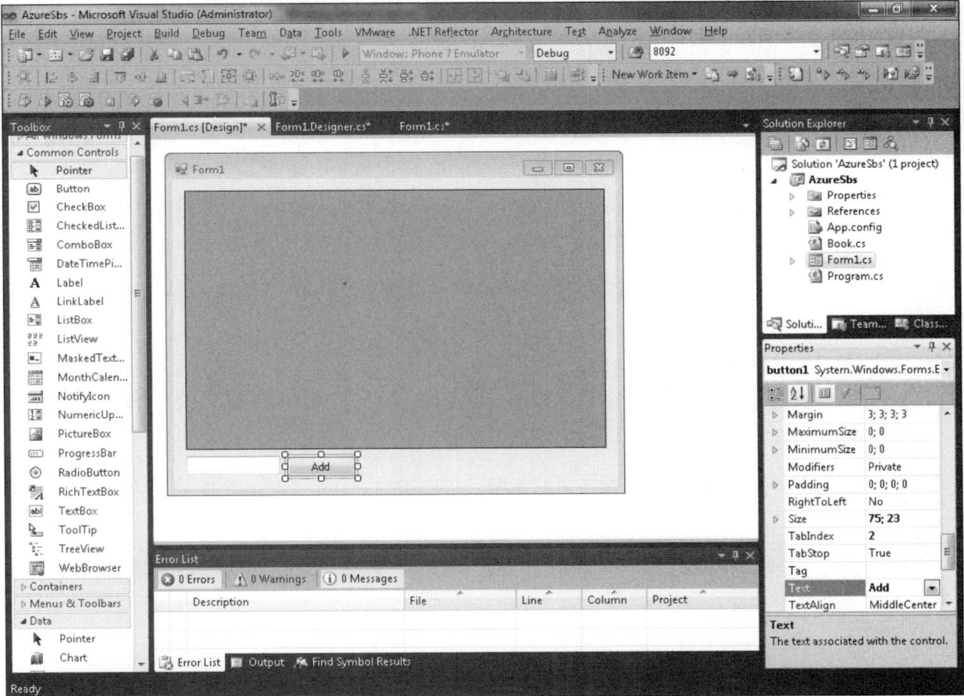

2. Double-click the Add button to create the event handler. Then type the following code in the corresponding method:

```
private void button1_Click(object sender, EventArgs e)
{
    CloudStorageAccount account = CloudStorageAccount.Parse(
       ConfigurationManager.AppSettings["DataConnectionString"]);
    String baseAddress = account.TableEndpoint.AbsoluteUri;
    StorageCredentials credentials = account.Credentials;
    TableServiceContext context = new TableServiceContext(
       baseAddress, credentials);

    Book book = new Book();
    book.PartitionKey = "DEV";
    book.RowKey = Guid.NewGuid().ToString();
```

```
        book.Title = textBox1.Text;
        book.PublicationDate = DateTime.Now;

        context.AddObject("Books", book);
        context.SaveChanges();

        dataGridView1.DataSource = context.CreateQuery<Book>("Books").ToList();
    }
```

The first four lines of code inside the method are identical to the ones presented in the procedure titled "Create the Client Application" earlier in this chapter (see step 11). These lines construct the information needed to build the Table Service context. After that the code creates the context, it creates an entity using the class that derives from the *TableServiceEntity* class, fills it with the Partition and Row keys, and then fills it with the title and publication date. There is no need to recreate the table because the Load event of the form already did it.

The subsequent two lines of code add the entity to the client context and ask the Table Storage Account Service to save the changes.

The last line of code asks the service for the current books list and binds it to the user interface.

3. Start the storage emulator manually if you rebooted your computer since the previous procedure, "Create the Client Application." To find the tool, from the Windows Start menu, select the Windows Azure SDK v1.*x* section.

   This step is necessary because you are running a classic Windows Forms Application Project: there is no automatic interaction with the Windows Azure SDK.

4. Press F5 to start the Windows Forms Application Project, type a book title in the text box, and then click the Add button.

   This is the resulting form.

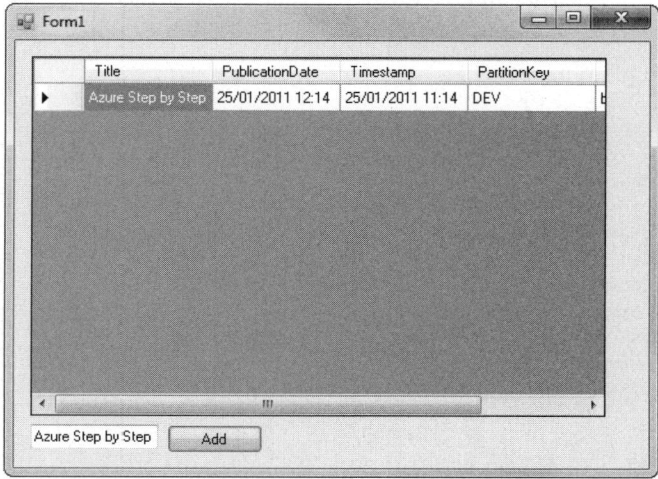

It's time to change the connection string to point to the live storage account and to refactor some code. You can use the following code in the Form1.cs file. (Refer to the "Introduction" for the link to download code samples.)

The code uses generic exception handling to greatly simplify it:

```
using System;
using System.Collections.Generic;
using System.ComponentModel;
using System.Data;
using System.Drawing;
using System.Linq;
using System.Text;
using System.Windows.Forms;
using Microsoft.WindowsAzure.StorageClient;
using Microsoft.WindowsAzure;
using System.Configuration;

namespace AzureSbs
{
    public partial class Form1 : Form
    {
        public Form1()
        {
            InitializeComponent();
        }

        private void Form1_Load(object sender, EventArgs e)
        {
            CloudStorageAccount account = this.CreateAccount();

            try
            {
                CloudTableClient tableClient = account.CreateCloudTableClient();
                tableClient.CreateTableIfNotExist("Books");

                TableServiceContext context = this.CreateContext(account);
                dataGridView1.DataSource =
                   context.CreateQuery<Book>("Books").ToList();
            }
            catch (Exception ex)
            {
                // Exception handling
                // Be specific
            }
        }

        private void button1_Click(object sender, EventArgs e)
        {
            Book book = new Book();
            book.PartitionKey = "DEV";
            book.RowKey = Guid.NewGuid().ToString();

            book.Title = textBox1.Text;
```

```
                book.PublicationDate = DateTime.Now;

                CloudStorageAccount account = this.CreateAccount();
                TableServiceContext context = this.CreateContext(account);

                try
                {
                    context.AddObject("Books", book);
                    context.SaveChanges();

                    dataGridView1.DataSource =
                        context.CreateQuery<Book>("Books").ToList();
                }
                catch (Exception ex)
                {
                    // Exception handling
                    // TODO: Be specific
                }
            }

            private CloudStorageAccount CreateAccount()
            {
                CloudStorageAccount account = CloudStorageAccount.Parse(
                    ConfigurationManager.AppSettings["DataConnectionString"]);
                return account;
            }

            private TableServiceContext CreateContext(CloudStorageAccount account)
            {

                String baseAddress = account.TableEndpoint.AbsoluteUri;
                StorageCredentials credentials = account.Credentials;

                return new TableServiceContext(baseAddress, credentials);
            }
        }
    }
```

To adapt the configuration, you have to remember the account name you chose in the project portal. You can return to the portal at any time to obtain the service name and, even more importantly, the access key. From the storage account detail you saw in Figure 10-1, you can click the View button in the primary or secondary key and then copy the access key to the Clipboard, as shown in the following figure.

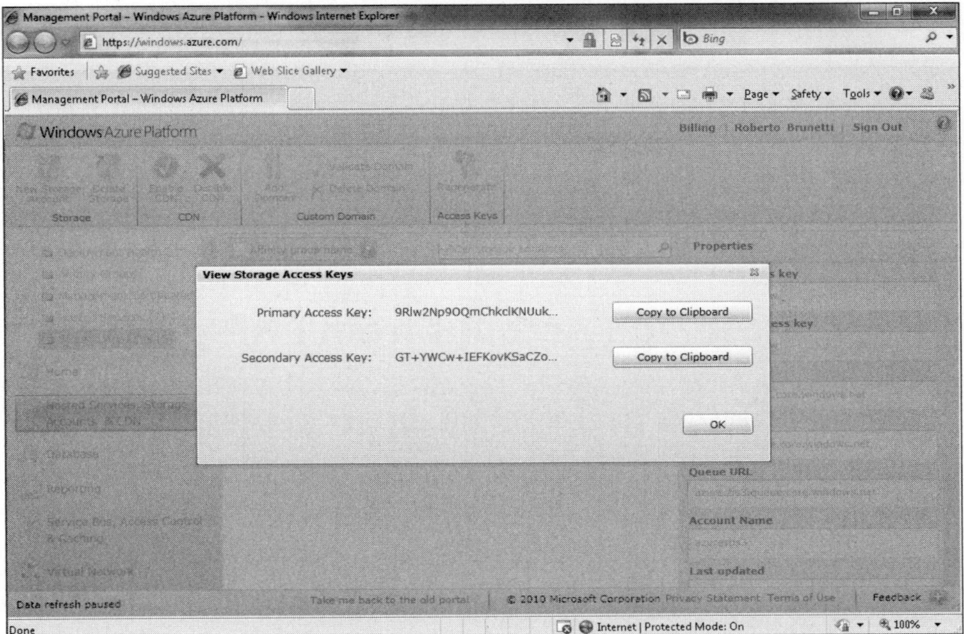

Note Refer to Chapter 5 for a complete discussion of the Table Storage Account Service.

Unfortunately, you cannot use the Visual Studio role configuration designer to insert account and key information, because you are using a Windows Forms application. But you can use the following snippet to configure your service. Remember, your account and key are different from my account and key. The strings you have to change in the App.config file follow:

```
<?xml version="1.0"?>
<configuration>
  <appSettings>
    <add key="DataConnectionString" value="DefaultEndpointsProtocol=https;
         AccountName=azuresbs3;AccountKey=9Rlw2Np9OQm..."/>
  </appSettings>
  <startup>
    <supportedRuntime version="v4.0" sku=".NETFramework,Version=v4.0"/>
  </startup>
</configuration>
```

You can now use the live storage account from an on-premises Windows Forms application.

Run the application now. You end up with an empty grid. Insert some new books, close the application, and then run it again to verify that everything is working properly. You can also try running the sample from another personal computer; you should see the same set of books.

The same concepts apply to a Windows Presentation Foundation application. You can reuse all the code in the code-behind file and in the configuration file.

Accessing the Storage Account from PHP

On the Windows Azure developers home page is a link to the Windows Azure SDK for PHP Developers (currently available as the CodePlex project at *http://phpazure.codeplex.com/*).

The purpose of this project, as stated from the official description at the time of this writing, is the following (Project contributors, CodePlex, 2011, *http://phpazure.codeplex.com*):

> *As part of Microsoft's commitment to Interoperability, this open source project is an effort to bridge PHP developers to Windows Azure. PHPAzure is an open source project to provide a software development kit for Windows Azure and Windows Azure Storage—Blobs, Tables & Queues.*

You have to unzip the package in a folder and then copy the folder into your PHP Project. You can simply create a library directory in the project and add the full path to that directory in the configuration file (Php.ini).

The library offers most of the same facilities as the storage client and can be used, apart from the code syntax, in the same way. For example, the following code uses the same storage account used in previous samples, but in a PHP application. You must define the *Book* class, which will be saved and retrieved from the Books table. The class extends the *TableEntity* base class that is part of the included library:

```
class Contact extends Microsoft_WindowsAzure_Storage_TableEntity
{
    /**
     * @azure Title
     */
    public $Title;
    /**
     * @azure PublicationDate
     */
    public $PublicationDate;
}
```

The schema is defined using "docblock" comments.

The *PartitionKey*, *RowKey*, and *TimeStamp* properties are obtained from the base class so that, as in the preceding Microsoft Visual C# samples, you don't have to expose them directly.

A page can reference the entity (assume it is defined in Entities.php) and the classes to work with tables in the traditional PHP style, as shown in the following code:

```
require 'Microsoft\WindowsAzure\Storage\Table.php';
require 'entities.php';
$storageClient = new
    Microsoft_WindowsAzure_Storage_Table('table.core.windows.net',
    'azuresbs3',
    'eNlSM7B7Bo4dmr1Xr6k5WWJgu4srfd');

if(!$storageClient->tableExists("Books"))
    $storageClient->createTable("Books");
```

The constructor for the *Table* class takes the common part of the URI, the account name, and the primary or secondary access key. The last two lines of code create the table if it does not exist yet.

To insert a new book in the table, the code has to create a new *Book* instance, insert a value in the properties, and call the *insertEntity* method on the *storageClient* class:

```
$book = new Book ('DEV', $_POST['Title']);
$book ->Title = $_POST['Title'];
$book ->PublicationDate = $_POST['Date'];
$result = $storageClient->insertEntity('Books', $book);
```

This code excerpt used the posted title as the *RowKey* value.

Remember that each client library is just a wrapper around REST/HTTP, so you can use any client platform—even the oldest ones—to access the storage account services. This is true for tables as well as for blobs and queues.

Accessing the Storage Account Service directly is a powerful mechanism for data-centric applications, as you've learned in Chapter 4, Chapter 5, and in this chapter. The service, in fact, exposes standard APIs that follow the OData (Open Data Protocol) emerging standard approach.

From an architectural point of view, all the code presented in this chapter is data access layer code—the code uses a storage service. When the application is layered correctly, the business layer invokes this code to store some data. There is no business logic in the code that uses the Storage Client library; it is merely data access code.

If the client application is not data-centric and needs business logic code, it is better to expose a service-oriented architecture (SOA) service to decouple the application logic from the client. The client invokes the SOA service and the service isolates the data access techniques used server-side. At some point in time, you can change the store for your data by changing only the data access layer for the service and not every piece of client access code.

The last chapter of this book is completely dedicated to the architectural aspects introduced here.

Using HTTP and REST

So far, you used the Storage Client APIs from an application that exists outside the cloud. Any Create, Read, Update, Delete (CRUD) operation uses REST and HTTP behind the scenes.

The last code example in this chapter inserts a new book entity into the *Books* table. The storage client wraps this request in a service operation for Microsoft ADO.NET Data Services and transforms the simple method call in a REST request to the service.

Figure 10-2 shows the complete flow of operations performed by the Windows Forms application code when you start the application and insert a new book. You examine the complete flow to learn how to use the underlying REST APIs.

As I've stated throughout this book, many Windows Azure services are exposed via HTTP and REST. If the library you are using does not expose the operation you need in your application, or if the platform you are using has no SDK available, or if you want to have complete control over the operations, you can use REST and HTTP directly. An Apple iPhone is REST/HTTP-capable; an Android device is REST/HTTP-compliant, too. Nearly every platform (including those in the cloud) exposes REST APIs to consume REST services. Figure 10-2 shows an HTTP trace log.

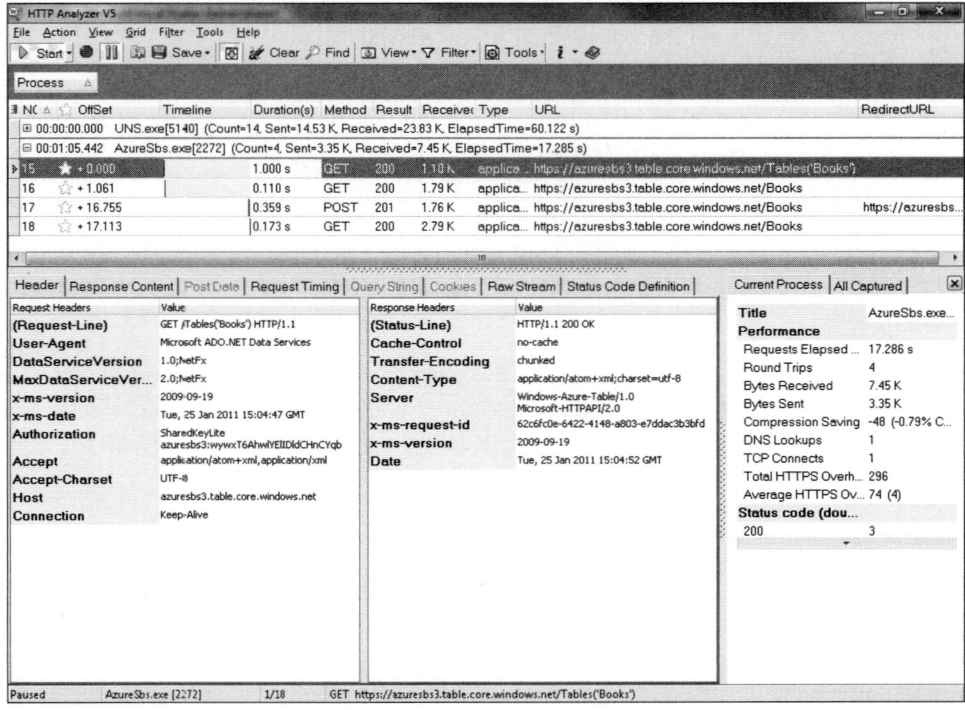

FIGURE 10-2 The HTTP trace log.

The first request you see in Figure 10-2 occurs when the code calls the *CreateIfNotExist* method of the *CloudStorage* class in the *Form1_Load* method:

```
tableClient.CreateTableIfNotExist("Books");
```

The request has a status code of 200, which in the HTTP world means that everything is fine with the request. The URL uses SSL (Secure Socket Layer) over HTTP (usually termed HTTPS), and the URI points directly to the Table Storage Account Service. The beginning of the URI contains the Storage Account Project name to ensure the correctness of the URI with X.509 digital certificates. When you create a new Storage Account Project, the platform releases a digital certificate for the complete URI that lets the client use HTTPS instead of HTTP.

The presented header (the first tab of the lower part of the HTTP Analyzer tool used to analyze HTTP traffic in Figure 10-2) demonstrates the use of the ADO.NET Data Services, which are responsible for converting every method call into a corresponding REST call toward the service. The *TableServiceContext* class derives from the *DataServiceContext* class and adds the Authorization HTTP header using the *ShareKeyLite* algorithm and the provided key.

The response is simply an AtomPub feed, as demonstrated by the Content-Type header of the response, and contains the server identification Windows-Azure-Table/1.0.

The first request has a simple response, because the table already exists in the storage account:

```
<?xml version="1.0" encoding="utf-8" standalone="yes"?>
<entry xml:base="https://azuresbs3.table.core.windows.net/"
    xmlns:d="http://schemas.microsoft.com/ado/2007/08/dataservices"
    xmlns:m="http://schemas.microsoft.com/ado/2007/08/dataservices/metadata"
    xmlns="http://www.w3.org/2005/Atom">
  <id>https://azuresbs3.table.core.windows.net/Tables('Books')</id>
  <title type="text"></title>
  <updated>2011-01-25T15:04:52Z</updated>
  <author>
    <name />
  </author>
  <link rel="edit" title="Tables" href="Tables('Books')" />
  <category term="azuresbs3.Tables"
     scheme="http://schemas.microsoft.com/ado/2007/08/dataservices/scheme" />
  <content type="application/xml">
    <m:properties>
      <d:TableName>Books</d:TableName>
    </m:properties>
  </content>
</entry>
```

The most important part is the *d:TableName* xml element that reports the name of the checked table.

The second line of the trace represents the request made on behalf of the *ToList()* method:

```
dataGridView1.DataSource = context.CreateQuery<Book>("Books").ToList();
```

This request is made to the */Books* resource in *azuresbs3.table.core.windows.net*. Just like the first request in the trace, this request uses HTTPS and contains the Authorization header, because the HTTP protocol is stateless.

This time, as you can see in the following code snippet, the service response is more complex, because it contains the books stored in the Storage Account Table:

```
<?xml version="1.0" encoding="utf-8" standalone="yes"?>
<feed xml:base="https://azuresbs3.table.core.windows.net/"
      xmlns:d="http://schemas.microsoft.com/ado/2007/08/dataservices"
      xmlns:m="http://schemas.microsoft.com/ado/2007/08/dataservices/metadata"
      xmlns="http://www.w3.org/2005/Atom">
  <title type="text">Books</title>
  <id>https://azuresbs3.table.core.windows.net/Books</id>
  <updated>2011-01-25T15:04:53Z</updated>
  <link rel="self" title="Books" href="Books" />
  <entry m:etag="W/&quot;datetime'2011-01-25T15%3A02%3A53.4441536Z'&quot;">
    <id>https://azuresbs3.table.core.windows.net/Books(
      PartitionKey='DEV',
      RowKey='c3c16083-0855-45dc-8b24-16ba2341f25e')</id>
    <title type="text"></title>
    <updated>2011-01-25T15:04:53Z</updated>
    <author>
      <name />
    </author>
    <link rel="edit" title="Books" href="Books(
      PartitionKey='DEV',RowKey='c3c16083-0855-45dc-8b24-16ba2341f25e')" />
    <category term="azuresbs3.Books"
      scheme="http://schemas.microsoft.com/ado/2007/08/dataservices/scheme" />
    <content type="application/xml">
      <m:properties>
        <d:PartitionKey>DEV</d:PartitionKey>
        <d:RowKey>c3c16083-0855-45dc-8b24-16ba2341f25e</d:RowKey>
        <d:Timestamp m:type="Edm.DateTime">
           2011-01-25T15:02:53.4441536Z</d:Timestamp>
        <d:PublicationDate m:type="Edm.DateTime">
           2011-01-25T15:02:52.6407552Z</d:PublicationDate>
        <d:Title>Azure Step by Step</d:Title>
      </m:properties>
    </content>
  </entry>
</feed>
```

The *feed* element contains a reference to the schemas used to format the response, which also uses ADO.NET Data Services.

The *title* element tells the client the operation response, the *id* shows the complete URI of the resource, and the *updated* element informs the client about the exact time of the response.

The *link* reference is relative to *self* for *Books*; the query that the library made is very simple and does not contain other links.

The first entry represents the first book in the table. The *id* tag contains the URI to access the resource directly for querying, updating, or deleting operations. It contains the *PartitionKey* and the *RowKey* assigned during the insert phase.

Some other tags are left blank because they have no meaning. For example, the *author* tag is important when you are reading an *AtomPub* feed of blog posts; but in this case, the *author* tag is completely useless.

Before the actual content of the book, the *link* element contains an *href* reference you can use to perform a delete or an update operation. The category just contains the table name using the data service scheme.

The content of the *content* element is straightforward; every property of the stored entity is represented by a named element that contains the real value.

In the presented Windows Forms application, users can insert a new book. If I test this by typing **SharePoint Developers Reference** in the text box, the application invokes the code to add a new book. The following code is the same code you worked with earlier, before the refactoring phase:

```
CloudStorageAccount account = CloudStorageAccount.Parse(
   ConfigurationManager.AppSettings["DataConnectionString"]);

String baseAddress = account.TableEndpoint.AbsoluteUri;
StorageCredentials credentials = account.Credentials;
TableServiceContext context = new TableServiceContext(baseAddress, credentials);

Book book = new Book();book.PartitionKey = "DEV";
book.RowKey = Guid.NewGuid().ToString();book.Title = textBox1.Text;book.PublicationDate =
DateTime.Now;context.AddObject("Books", book);context.SaveChanges();
```

The Storage Client library accepts the change in the local context, adding a new item with the indicated *Title* and then asks the Table Storage Account Service to perform the insert operation using the following REST call:

```
<?xml version="1.0" encoding="utf-8" standalone="yes"?>
<entry xmlns:d="http://schemas.microsoft.com/ado/2007/08/dataservices"
       xmlns:m="http://schemas.microsoft.com/ado/2007/08/dataservices/metadata"
       xmlns="http://www.w3.org/2005/Atom">
  <title />
  <author>
    <name />
  </author>
  <updated>2011-01-25T15:05:07.3333884Z</updated>
  <id />
  <content type="application/xml">
    <m:properties>
      <d:PartitionKey>DEV</d:PartitionKey>
      <d:PublicationDate m:type="Edm.DateTime">
         2011-01-25T16:05:07.3333884+01:00</d:PublicationDate>
      <d:RowKey>d0c73806-bf1f-49ea-8656-5d6dc64560fc</d:RowKey>
      <d:Timestamp m:type="Edm.DateTime">0001-01-01T00:00:00</d:Timestamp>
      <d:Title>SharePoint Developers Reference</d:Title>
    </m:properties>
  </content>
</entry>
```

The content is an entry that follows the ADO.NET Data Services rules and contains the serialized entity in the *context* element.

It is important to remark that the serialization process is made on the client to call the service via HTTP/REST and is not the way the Table Storage Account Service stores the entity. The service can store the received entity in whatever format it wants and, moreover, this format can change over time. You get to use the service by using the correct schema to pass and receive entities without worrying about the format the service used to store the entities internally.

The last call the code makes before returning the grid to the client is another request to obtain the list of entities:

```
dataGridView1.DataSource = context.CreateQuery<Book>("Books").ToList();
```

This call has the identical format as the second call shown in Figure 1-2, but it contains the newly added book as another entry element. The second book is presented in boldface:

```
<?xml version="1.0" encoding="utf-8" standalone="yes"?>
<feed xml:base="https://azuresbs3.table.core.windows.net/"
  xmlns:d="http://schemas.microsoft.com/ado/2007/08/dataservices"
  xmlns:m="http://schemas.microsoft.com/ado/2007/08/dataservices/metadata"
  xmlns="http://www.w3.org/2005/Atom">
  <title type="text">Books</title>
  <id>https://azuresbs3.table.core.windows.net/Books</id>
  <updated>2011-01-25T15:05:09Z</updated>
  <link rel="self" title="Books" href="Books" />
  <entry m:etag="W/&quot;datetime'2011-01-25T15%3A02%3A53.4441536Z'&quot;">
    <id>https://azuresbs3.table.core.windows.net/Books(PartitionKey='DEV',
      RowKey='c3c16083-0855-45dc-8b24-16ba2341f25e')</id>
```

```
    <title type="text"></title>
    <updated>2011-01-25T15:05:09Z</updated>
    <author>
      <name />
    </author>
    <link rel="edit" title="Books" href="Books(PartitionKey='DEV',
      RowKey='c3c16083-0855-45dc-8b24-16ba2341f25e')" />
    <category term="azuresbs3.Books"
      scheme="http://schemas.microsoft.com/ado/2007/08/dataservices/scheme" />
    <content type="application/xml">
      <m:properties>
        <d:PartitionKey>DEV</d:PartitionKey>
        <d:RowKey>c3c16083-0855-45dc-8b24-16ba2341f25e</d:RowKey>
        <d:Timestamp m:type="Edm.DateTime">
          2011-01-25T15:02:53.4441536Z</d:Timestamp>
        <d:PublicationDate m:type="Edm.DateTime">
          2011-01-25T15:02:52.6407552Z</d:PublicationDate>
        <d:Title>Azure Step by Step</d:Title>
      </m:properties>
    </content>
  </entry>
  <entry m:etag="W/&quot;datetime'2011-01-25T15%3A05%3A09.1698773Z'&quot;">
    <id>https://azuresbs3.table.core.windows.net/Books(PartitionKey='DEV',
      RowKey='d0c73806-bf1f-49ea-8656-5d6dc64560fc')</id>
    <title type="text"></title>
    <updated>2011-01-25T15:05:09Z</updated>
    <author>
      <name />
    </author>
    <link rel="edit" title="Books" href="Books(PartitionKey='DEV',
      RowKey='d0c73806-bf1f-49ea-8656-5d6dc64560fc')" />
    <category term="azuresbs3.Books"
       scheme="http://schemas.microsoft.com/ado/2007/08/dataservices/scheme" />
    <content type="application/xml">
      <m:properties>
        <d:PartitionKey>DEV</d:PartitionKey>
        <d:RowKey>d0c73806-bf1f-49ea-8656-5d6dc64560fc</d:RowKey>
        <d:Timestamp m:type="Edm.DateTime">
          2011-01-25T15:05:09.1698773Z</d:Timestamp>
        <d:PublicationDate m:type="Edm.DateTime">
          2011-01-25T15:05:07.3333884Z</d:PublicationDate>
        <d:Title>SharePoint Developers Reference</d:Title>
      </m:properties>
    </content>
  </entry>
</feed>
```


This exercise is important because it helps you understand how the library makes the call to the service. You can use this technique to learn how to make the query yourself without scanning every REST method interface in the documentation (although having a look at the documentation is always worthwhile).

Summary

In this chapter, you created a simple Windows Forms application that uses the storage account features to store and retrieve blobs and entities. You then saw a simple PHP application that leverages the PHP SDK. The goal was to show you how both platforms (and others as well) can consume the standard HTTP/REST-based interface exposed by the storage account services.

Quick Reference

To	Do this
Work with your storage account in the simplest way	Use the Windows Azure SDK.
Manage storage account data from a .NET application	Use the *StorageClient* library referencing it in the client project.
Store a storage account access key	Use the App.config or Web.config file in an on-premises solution. Use the ServiceConfiguration.cscfg in a Windows Azure solution.
Work with the storage account directly	Use REST/HTTP or REST/HTTPS, following the OData pattern.

Chapter 11

Application Architecture

After completing this chapter, you will be able to

- Understand the characteristics of a multitier application.
- Understand the role of the DAL component.
- Engineer simple data access layer components for different data store technologies.
- Understand the role of the service agent component.

This chapter focuses on application patterns and best practices for a cloud-based solution. The goal is to learn how and when you can best leverage the cloud components in everyday solutions, and to evaluate the impact of using them in modern software architectures. You see some architectural patterns and rules, largely related to the data access layer (DAL) and the business layer of multitier enterprise-level solutions.

Note Because URLs, UI names, and procedures may vary over time, some of them may be out of date by the time you read this. In that case, my best advice is to start looking for the information about the Windows Azure product on the Windows Azure home page (*http://www.azure.com*). Information included in this book was accurate at the time of writing.

Characteristics of a Multitier Solution

A multitier solution is a software project that usually targets many concurrent users. It is divided into *n* layers (usually not fewer than three layers). Applications that use a two-tier scenario are also referred to as *client-server* software. One layer is the back-end server infrastructure, which is generally made up of a database persistence layer. The other layer, the client, includes all the code that accesses the database and renders the user interface.

Generally, in two-tier scenarios, the business logic and domain knowledge required for the solution is implemented within the client software. Sometimes such solutions also include database logic, such as intelligent stored procedures and triggers.

Although client-server architecture is suitable for implementing solutions that will have a relatively small number of users, it presents scalability issues and other limitations compared to other architectural solutions. Software is *scalable* when its performance remains constant and independent regardless of the number of users. Scalable software is not necessarily fast: it simply has a fixed performance score regardless of the number of users served. The very nature of a client-server solution prevents scalability—specifically, an increase in the number of users can have a huge impact on the back-end database layer. For this reason, this book will not cover the client-server architecture in detail.

To achieve better scalability, over the past several years, architectures with at least three tiers have become more and more common. Many modern software solutions are available over a network and/or over the Internet, and they serve a large (and often unpredictable) number of concurrent users. Three-tier solutions present a data access layer, a business layer, and a presentation layer. The *data access layer (DAL)* represents the set of code and data structures used to implement information persistence. The *business layer (BIZ)* defines business logic, workflows, and rules that drive the behavior of the application. The *presentation layer*, or *user interface (UI) layer*, delivers the information to end users and accepts input from them.

The presentation layer, in particular, has become more complex, because it can (and often must) be implemented in many different ways, one for each kind of consumer (web, Windows, smart device, and so on). In general, DAL and BIZ are deployed on specific and dedicated application servers, whereas the UI can be either deployed on consumer devices or delivered to web browsers from specific publishing application servers (web applications on front-end web servers).

Technologies such as Simple Object Access Protocol (SOAP) services, smart clients, smart phones, workflow services, and so on, have influenced many software architects to add other layers. The now-common definition of *n*-tier solution architecture is one in which *n* designates a value greater than or at least equal to three. In general, as you can see from Figure 11-1, these *n* layers are targeted to meet specific application requirements, such as security, workflow definition, and communication.

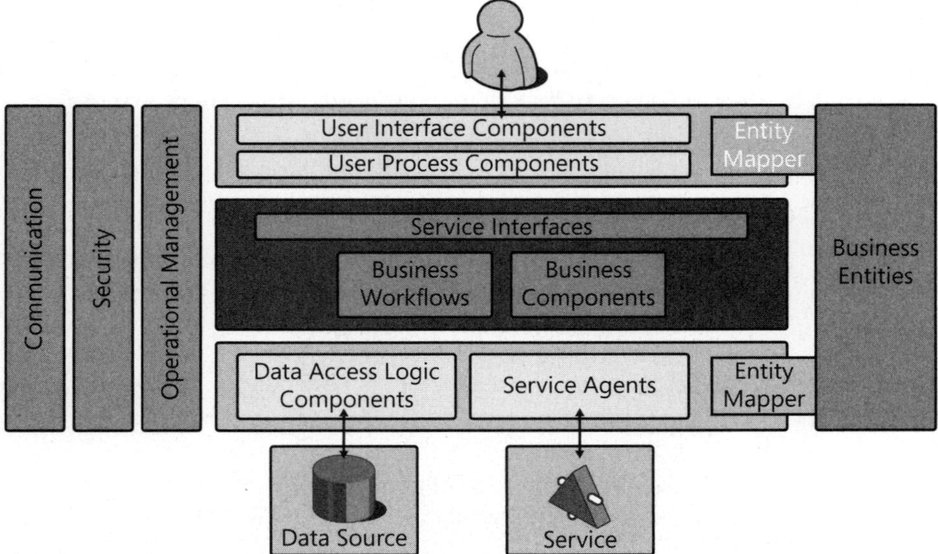

FIGURE 11-1 Schema of a typical *n*-tier architecture.

The main reasons for dividing a software solution's architecture into layers are to improve maintainability, availability, security, and deployment.

Maintainability results from the ability to change and maintain small portions (for example, single layers) of an application without needing to touch the other layers. By working this way, you reduce maintenance time and can also more accurately assess the cost of a fix or a feature change, because you can focus your attention on just the layers involved in the change. For instance, you can adapt the code of the data access layer to work with Microsoft SQL Server instead of Oracle, or you can change a single component to work with the Windows Azure Table Storage Account Service instead of the local SQL Server database. Client-server software is more costly to maintain because any code modifications must be deployed to each client. Well-defined multitier solutions are also available to users more often because critical or highly stressed layers can be deployed in a redundant infrastructure. Think about some native components of the Windows Azure platform: the hosted service can be scaled up in a moment just by increasing the number of instances.

From a security perspective, a layered solution can use different security modules, each one tightly aligned with a particular software layer to make the solution stronger. Last but not least, multitier software is usually deployed more easily, because each layer can be configured and sized somewhat independently from other layers.

In the following pages, I discuss some important points about the various components of a cloud-based architecture.

The Data Access Layer

Every data access layer component has to be stateless. It cannot maintain the state from a request to the subsequent one. This is one of the important points to understand when developing a real scalable solution—if a component maintains the state of a request in memory, the code cannot be spread across servers and thus it does not scale. This is especially applicable to a traditional application. Think about an ASP.NET application that allocates some memory to store session data during request processing. The server memory is not infinite, and at some point in time, when the system has served an extensive number of these types of requests, the memory reaches the maximum available and the garbage collector cannot do anything to clean up session data. If the IT team decides to increase the memory of the server, it moves up the request limit and, as you know, this limit will be reached in a shorter time than expected.

If the components are stateless, they do not need memory when they are not serving requests. In this way, they can theoretically serve an infinite number of subsequent requests from many users. When the number of concurrent requests grows up, the IT team can spread the requests across different servers without any trouble. In Windows Azure, this operation can be done in a matter of seconds, adapting the number of instances by using the Management Portal or the Management APIs.

The role of a data access layer component is to expose data structures that are independent from the underlying data store. Figure 11-1 illustrates the point: the business layer and the user interface layer are isolated from the data store and, as I pointed out, the data access layer can be changed to work with different databases or data services. This level of isolation can be accomplished by developing components that never return a class that is bound with the data access technology. Every public method that can be invoked from the upper layer cannot return a *DataReader* or a specific database structure. If you return a database-specific structure, the code of the upper layers are bound to that data structure, and the application cannot work with different data stores simply by changing the data access layer component.

Listing 11-1 shows the *List* method of a simple DAL component that returns a list of *Salesman* (*SalesmenList* custom collection) by accessing the underlying database (SQL Server in this case). In this code, I use the traditional manual technique to demonstrate the concept.

LISTING 11-1 DAL component using a DataReader.

```
public SalesmenList List()
{
    try
    {
        SalesmenList list = new SalesmenList();

        using (SqlDataReader dr = SqlHelper.ExecSPForReader(
           ConnectionString, "spListSalesmen", null))
        {

            Int32 indexIdSalesman = dr.GetOrdinal("idSalesman");
            Int32 indexSalesmanPassword = dr.GetOrdinal(
               "SalesmanPassword");
            Int32 indexSalesmanDescription = dr.GetOrdinal(
               "SalesmanDescription");
            Int32 indexSalesmanIsAdmin = dr.GetOrdinal("SalesmanIsAdmin");

            while (dr.Read())
            {
                Salesman item = new Salesman();
                item.IdSalesman = dr.GetString(indexIdSalesman);
                item.SalesmanPassword = dr.GetString(indexSalesmanPassword);
                item.SalesmanDescription = dr.GetString(
                   indexSalesmanDescription);
                item.SalesmanIsAdmin = dr.GetBoolean(indexSalesmanIsAdmin);

                list.Add(item);
            }
        }
```

```
            return (list);
        }
        catch (SqlException ex)
        {
            throw new DevLeapDBException("ERR01", ex);
        }
    }
```

The code in Listing 11-1 uses the *SqlHelper* class exposed by the Data Access Application Block of the Enterprise library to execute the stored procedure *spListSalesmen* on a SQL Server database.

The loop reads every *DBDataRecord* and creates a new *Salesman* object with information taken from the database. The new object is added to the collection of salesmen.

This code can be used to access SQL Azure instead of a local database instance without any modification. The *ConnectionString* property used to call the *ExecuteSPForReader* simply reads the connection string from the configuration file:

```
public string ConnectionString
{
    get { return (ConfigurationManager.ConnectionStrings[
       "EstatesManagementConnectionString"].ConnectionString); }
}
```

This property is exposed by the base class (*BaseDal)* from which every DAL component derives. If this code is referenced by a hosted service, you can use it without any modification; remember that the Web.config file (for the Web Role) or App.config file (for the Worker Role) is part of the deployment, and any change to either requires a complete re-deployment. If you want to change the connection string without a redeployment, change the *get* accessor, as shown the following code snippet:

```
public string ConnectionString
{
    get { return (RoleEnvironment.GetConfigurationSettingValue(
       "EstatesManagementConnectionString"); }
}
```

You have to define a setting in the ServiceDefintion.csdef and assign a value to it in the ServiceConfiguration.cscfg. That's it! Your component can work in the cloud, giving you the flexibility to change the connection string without redeployment. This is a good example of code centralization. The *ConnectionString* property is defined in just one place, and the relative code can be changed at any time without causing any problems in other parts of the solution.

You can also perform some tricks in the code to adapt a component to work inside and outside the Windows Azure hosted service. The following code is a simple way to achieve this goal:

```
public string ConnectionString
{
    get
    {
        if(!RoleEnvironment.IsAvailable)
            return (ConfigurationManager.ConnectionStrings[
                "EstatesManagementConnectionString"].ConnectionString);
        else
            return (RoleEnvironment.GetConfigurationSettingValue(
                "EstatesManagementConnectionString");
    }
}
```

A more sophisticated solution would take advantage of some patterns such as factory methods or factory classes.

There is another important point to note: the methods exposed by the data access layer component cannot let the underlying exception bubble up to upper layers. The methods have to catch the data store's specific exception, log it if necessary, and throw an application exception. In the following code, the application exception is represented by a custom *DevLeapDBException* class:

```
catch (SqlException ex)
{
    // Log if necessary

    // Throw Application Exception
    throw new DevLeapDBException("ERR01", ex);
}
```

By using the *DevLeapDBException* class, the data access layer hides the native (SQL) exception to the caller, because the latter has to be independent from the underlying data store.

A DAL component can be considered a mapper between business entities (domain entities) and the database or data service that stores them.

Note A Data Mapper is a software layer that transfers data between database and in-memory objects. You can find a more thorough description of a Data Mapper at *http://www.martinfowler.com/eaaCatalog/dataMapper.html.*

The *Salesman* class is defined in another assembly that is referenced by each layer of the application, as shown in Listing 11-2.

LISTING 11-2 Business entity definition.

```
using System;
using System.Collections.Generic;
using System.Text;

namespace DevLeap.EstatesManagement.Entities
{
    public class Salesman : BaseEntity
    {
        private string _idSalesman;
        private string _salesmanDescription;

        public string SalesmanDescription
        {
            get { return _salesmanDescription; }
            set { _salesmanDescription = value; }
        }
        private string _salesmanPassword;

        public string SalesmanPassword
        {
            get { return _salesmanPassword; }
            set { _salesmanPassword = value; }
        }
        private bool _salesmanIsAdmin;

        public bool SalesmanIsAdmin
        {
            get { return _salesmanIsAdmin; }
            set { _salesmanIsAdmin = value; }
        }

        public string IdSalesman
        {
            get { return _idSalesman; }
            set { _idSalesman = value; }
        }

        public Salesman(): base()
        {
        }
    }

    public class SalesmenList : BaseEntityList<Salesman>
    {
    }
}
```

The *Salesman* class derives from a base class as well as the *SalesmenList* class, which has its own base class. It is always a good idea to have a base class for everything, even when you have nothing to expose in the first version of the solution in the base class. In the near future, the ability to give some entity a common pattern or a new common property is highly likely in agile development practices.

The types presented in Listing 11-2 are simple and look like data transfer objects (DTO) rather than domain model entities. However, remember that this example is just for illustration. In a real solution, these entities would probably include some domain model logic such as validation rules and constraints.

The *BaseEntity* class of the example examined thus far is very simple. The base class for the entity list leverages the generic type feature introduced in Microsoft .NET Framework 2.0 and derives from the *List* base class:

```
using System;
using System.Collections.Generic;
using System.Text;

namespace DevLeap.EstatesManagement.Entities
{
    public class BaseEntity
    {
        public BaseEntity() {}
    }

    public class BaseEntityList<TEntity>: List<TEntity>
        where TEntity: BaseEntity
    {
    }
}
```

You can also leverage generic types in the base class of the DAL components by moving some common methods in the base class without losing type safety. The following code is just an example of this concept. The *SalesmanDal* class instructs the *BaseDal* class regarding the specific type *SalesmanDal* has to use:

```
namespace DevLeap.EstatesManagement.Dal.SQLServer2008
{
    public class SalesmanDal : BaseDal<Salesman, SalesmanList, Int32>
    {
    }
}
```

With this strategy, the *BaseDal* class can expose common methods. For instance, in the following code excerpt, the base class can create a new entity or an entity list by using a common method:

```
namespace DevLeap.EstatesManagement.Dal
{
    public class BaseDal<TEntity, TEntityList, TKey>
        where TEntity: BaseEntity, new()
        where TEntityList: BaseEntityList<TEntity>, new()

    {
       public virtual CreateEntity()
       {
          return new TEntity();
       }
    }
}
```

This code uses *SqlDataReader,* which is the fastest way to read data from an underlying database. If you decide to change databases, you have to adapt only the code inside the DAL components. If you leveraged object-oriented techniques and generic types as well, for every DAL, you probably have to change only some methods in the base class.

A more modern approach to accessing a database is to leverage an Object Relational Mapper (ORM) like LINQ to SQL or ADO.NET Entity Framework. The ORMs do a great job of mapping the relational world of databases with the hierarchical model of the domain entities. Typically, the introduction of an ORM has to be completely transparent to the application. Following the philosophy of "changing just what you need," the introduction of LINQ to SQL in the .NET Framework 3.5 cannot involve more than just a modification of a single layer.

As stated in the book *Programming Microsoft LINQ in .NET Framework 4* by Marco Russo and Paolo Pialorsi (Microsoft Press, 2010), LINQ to SQL can be used to define the mapping from the underlying SQL Server database toward the business entities, without any modification of the application architecture. Let's look more closely at and analyze two ways of using LINQ to SQL.

With LINQ to SQL, you can define a model that shapes .NET classes that are mapped to the underlying database. These classes, known as *LINQ to SQL entities*, can be used by the entire application because they are .NET Framework classes; in fact, you can use the types you define in the LINQ to SQL designer, such as the *Salesman* entity discussed earlier, throughout the application. For example, a presentation layer, implemented by using Windows Presentation Foundation (WPF), could share these defined types with LINQ to SQL and should perform data binding against a sequence of type *IEnumerable<Salesman>* that is obtained by executing a LINQ query directly.

This situation has both advantages and disadvantages. The advantages stem from the agility and ease of use that LINQ to SQL offers. By taking a closer look at the code generated and defined by LINQ to SQL tools (such as SQLMetal or the Object Relational Designer in Microsoft Visual Studio), you can see that these types implement a set of interfaces targeted at the UI data binding: *INotifyPropertyChanging* and *INotifyPropertyChanged.*

On the other hand, the nature of LINQ to SQL means that the data layer is tightly integrated with the SQL Server database. This level of integration might be your goal for a single-database-platform solution, but it can also pose many limitations for your architecture.

In general, a data layer has to be an abstraction of the physical persistence layer, thus allowing changes to the underlying implementation that are transparent to the layers above it. You usually achieve this abstraction by defining a pluggable architecture like the one shown in Figure 11-1, and implementing the code in a way similar to what you have seen in this chapter. *Database independency* means that the communication between the DAL and BIZ layers cannot use anything that is bound to a particular database implementation. However, when you use LINQ to SQL as a pure data layer replacement, you are limited to SQL Server as a database, and your entities will be widely marked in code with attributes that map to SQL Server–specific information. In addition, you might already have a domain model defined simply because you are extending an existing application, or because you do not want to mark your domain model with data-layer-specific (LINQ to SQL) attributes.

To avoid these issues, you can use LINQ to SQL as a replacement for the code presented in the *List* method of the *SalesmanDal* component. The code can be much simpler for every DAL component method, especially for the ones that need to create complex queries. The code in Listing 11-3 can be a LINQ to SQL replacement for the simple *SalesmanDal* code.

LISTING 11-3 A DAL component that uses LINQ to SQL.

```
namespace DevLeap.EstatesManagement.Dal.LINQtoSQL
{
    public class SalesmanDal : BaseDal<Salesman, SalesmanList, Int32>
    {
        public SalesmenList List()
        {
            try
            {
                SalesmenList list = new SalesmenList();

               // Old code
                //using (SqlDataReader dr = SqlHelper.ExecSPForReader(
                //   ConnectionString, "spListSalesmen", null))
                //{

                //    Int32 indexIdSalesman = dr.GetOrdinal("idSalesman");
                //    Int32 indexSalesmanPassword = dr.GetOrdinal(
                //        "SalesmanPassword");
                //    Int32 indexSalesmanDescription = dr.GetOrdinal(
                //        "SalesmanDescription");
                //    Int32 indexSalesmanIsAdmin = dr.GetOrdinal("SalesmanIsAdmin");

                //    while (dr.Read())
                //    {
                //        Salesman item = new Salesman();
                //        item.IdSalesman = dr.GetString(indexIdSalesman);
```

```
                //          item.SalesmanPassword = dr.GetString(
                //              indexSalesmanPassword);
                //          item.SalesmanDescription = dr.GetString(
                //              indexSalesmanDescription);
                //          item.SalesmanIsAdmin = dr.GetBoolean(
                //              indexSalesmanIsAdmin);

                //          list.Add(item);
                //      }
                //}

                // New LINQ to SQL code
                   using (EstatesManagementDataContext context =
                   new EstatesManagementDataContext(this.ConnectionString))
                {
                    context.ObjectTrackingEnabled = false;

                    var query = from s in context.tabSalesmens
                                select new Salesman
                                {
                                    IdSalesman = s.idSalesman,
                                    SalesmanDescription = s.SalesmanDescription,
                                    SalesmanIsAdmin = s.SalesmanIsAdmin,
                                    SalesmanPassword = s.SalesmanPassword
                                }
                    foreach (Salesman s in query)
                    {
                       list.add(s);
                    }
                 }

                 return (list);
            }
            catch (SqlException ex)
            {
                throw new DevLeapDBException("ERR01", ex);
            }
        }
    }
}
```

As you can see, nothing but the query code has changed. The code fills the *SalesmenList* collection using a different data access technique, but the meaning and content has not changed at all. Also, the technique used to catch the exception is exactly the same.

A better solution is to create an entire new DAL component for each different data access logic technology; the new component will receive all the common functionalities from the base class and override the specific behavior. In the preceding example, the inner code for the data querying can be different in every data access scenario, but the rest of the code can be centralized inside the data access layer.

To completely abstract our solution from any specific data layer, including a LINQ to SQL implementation, you must define the real data layer implementation in a dedicated assembly that will be loaded through a data layer factory instead of being referenced directly. The code using LINQ to SQL resides inside this referenced assembly. Only domain model entities can travel across the boundaries between any DAL implementation and the BIZ layer consumer: not data tables, not LINQ to SQL entities—nothing else.

To meet this last requirement, the LINQ to SQL–based data layer translates its own entities back and forth to the domain model entities, as you saw in Listing 11-3.

It is beyond the scope of this book to illustrate techniques or patterns for decoupling the business layer from the data access layer. You can refer to Martin Fowler's *Patterns of Enterprise Application Architecture* (Addison-Wesley, 2002) to obtain a complete understanding of the various patterns.

The same concept can be applied to ADO.NET Entity Framework 3.5: the model can be defined inside the DAL assembly and the data access code can map business entities with the entities defined in the Entity Data Model. One of the main differences of the Entity Data Model from ADO.NET Entity Framework 3.5 and LINQ to SQL is database independency. Unlike LINQ to SQL, Entity Framework natively supports different data providers without any add-in or external component, and many third-party software companies also support this framework. (For more information, see *http://msdn.microsoft.com/en-us/data/dd363565.aspx*).

Because of the native abstraction provided by the Entity Framework, you would probably choose to use it whenever you really needed to abstract from the data layer. However, think carefully about the overall architecture of your solution as well as about the persistence model you are going to use with the Entity Framework. The standard behavior of Entity Framework 3.5 is *not* persistence ignorance. Thus, if you use the standard Entity Data Model as your domain entities, you would miss out on one of the main requirements for true data layer abstraction: the persistence ignorance of the domain model.

In Entity Framework 4.0, the default behavior is identical to the 3.5 version, except that you can choose to define persistence-ignorant Plain Old CLR Objects (POCO) entities to regain true abstraction from the persistence layer. With POCO entities, you can leave your own domain model entities intact, feeding them transparently with Entity Framework. To achieve that goal, you need to set the Code Generation Strategy of the EDMX to None in the Microsoft Visual Studio Designer, and define a custom class that inherits from *ObjectContext*.

The POCO feature doesn't change any code presented in this chapter. DAL components are stateless mappers that translate domain entities, which are completely persistence-ignorant, into something that can be persisted in a data store during CUD (Create, Update, and Delete) operations. They do the inverse when the upper layers request some data.

The code presented in Listing 11-1 was built for a demo application at the end of 2003 and was revised to leverage the generic types that came out in 2005. The data access layer code that uses the *SqlDataReader* hasn't changed, and it is a good choice when you are looking for the fastest performance when reading data from a database. In 2007, thanks to the pluggable mechanism implemented in the architecture, we (the DevLeap company group) introduced a new data access layer component using LINQ to SQL 3.5, and then a new assembly for ADO.NET Entity Framework in .NET 3.5 (in September 2008). Today, we are still using the same entity code we built in 2003 but leveraging new technologies introduced in the .NET Framework since then, and we do not need to rewrite anything but this single component.

Because the development team could use LINQ to SQL or the Entity Framework in the data access layer to map the database world, nothing changed architecturally. Pluggable architecture enabled the development team to replace technologies as needed. If the ORM classes are used directly in the UI or in the business layer code, the solution is not completely persistence-ignorant, because these layers know too much about the storage itself. They do not know field names or table names, but they know they are using an ORM.

The Table Storage Account Service is a new technology for managing data in the cloud, and it exposes a REST service that can store and retrieve application entities that are not mapped to any predefined structure. As you learned in Chapter 5, "Tables, Queues, and Worker Roles," the service accepts an HTTP/HTTPS request with an Atom Publishing Protocol (AtomPub) payload to make CUD operations, and then it provides filtering and searching capabilities when returning AtomPub content.

The service can be consumed directly using REST/HTTP or via the wrapper library named *StorageClient*. In both cases, the role for the data access layer component is to call the service and then map the results to the *SalesmenList* custom collection. The internal code for the method will be different from the code to access a database, but again, architecturally, nothing has changed.

Try to create a REST implementation following the architectural guideline for a data access layer component:

```
namespace DevLeap.EstatesManagement.Dal.LINQtoSQL
{
    public class SalesmanDal : BaseDal<Salesman, SalesmanList, Int32>
    {
        public SalesmenList List()
        {
            try
            {
                SalesmenList list = new SalesmenList();
                HttpRequest request = new HttpRequest();
                // property of the request

                // Send Request
                // Analyze the <entry> in the AtomPub
               foreach(var entry in response)
               {
                   Salesman item = new Salesman();
```

```
                    // Fill item property with xml element value

                    list.Add(item);
                }

                return (list);
            }
            catch (WebException ex)
            {
                throw new DevLeapDBException("ERR01", ex);
            }
        }
    }
}
```

The preceding code is not complete, but its goal is to show only the architectural essentials.

The main difference between this data access layer method and the LINQ to SQL *SqlDataReader* methods is the way I queried the data store. In the traditional data access code (see Listing 11-1), I issued a query to the database and constructed a list of salesmen based on the record returned from the query. I issued an HTTP request (represented by the commented line in the preceding code) to the remote Table Data Service and constructed a list of salesmen based on the *xml* element found in the AtomPub response. Because in this example the XML response is not important, I omitted the related code.

If you prefer to use the *StorageClient* library, the code you use is very similar to the code that uses LINQ to SQL, because the *StorageClient* library exposes an object context, which you learned about in Chapter 5.

First, define the class that must be serialized and passed to the service:

```
using System;
using System.Collections.Generic;
using System.Linq;
using System.Text;
using Microsoft.WindowsAzure.StorageClient;
using System.Data.Services.Common;

namespace DevLeap.EstatesManagement.Dal.AzureStorage
{

    public partial class tseSalesman : TableServiceEntity
    {
        private string _idSalesman;
        private string _salesmanDescription;

        public string SalesmanDescription
        {
            get { return _salesmanDescription; }
            set { _salesmanDescription = value; }
        }
```

```
        private string _salesmanPassword;

        public string SalesmanPassword
        {
            get { return _salesmanPassword; }
            set { _salesmanPassword = value; }
        }
        private bool _salesmanIsAdmin;

        public bool SalesmanIsAdmin
        {
            get { return _salesmanIsAdmin; }
            set { _salesmanIsAdmin = value; }
        }

        public string IdSalesman
        {
            get { return _idSalesman; }
            set { _idSalesman = value; }
        }

        public tseSalesman() : base()
        {
        }
    }
}
```

This class is quite similar to the business entity *Salesman*, but it is really just the class that represents the data access structure. It can be considered the same as the LINQ to SQL entity you saw in the preceding example (Listing 11-3), or the *DBDataRecord* structure you saw in the first example of this chapter (Listing 11-1).

I named the class in the preceding code *tseSalesman* to highlight that it has a different meaning than the business entity *Salesman,* where the prefix *tse* stands for *TableStorageEntity*. The *Salesman* class must be defined in the same project as the data access layer components because it is a DAL structure that cannot be used outside of this layer. If another layer uses this class, the class is bound to the Windows Azure Table Storage Account Service—and, as you know, this would violate the architectural philosophy.

Next, as shown in the following code, define a custom *TableServiceContext* that lets the developer of the data access layer component use a more typed approach to using the base class directly. This class is a data access layer class called *TableServiceEntity*:

```
using System;
using System.Collections.Generic;
using System.Linq;
using System.Text;
using Microsoft.WindowsAzure.StorageClient;
using Microsoft.WindowsAzure;

namespace DevLeap.EstatesManagement.DAL.AzureStorage
{
```

```
    public class EMTableServiceContext : TableServiceContext
    {
        private const String SalesmenTableName = "EMSalesmen";

        #region Ctor & EnsureTablesExist
        public EMTableServiceContext() :
            base(
            CloudStorageAccount.FromConfigurationSetting(
              "AzureStorageConnectionString").TableEndpoint.AbsoluteUri,
            CloudStorageAccount.FromConfigurationSetting(
              "AzureStorageConnectionString").Credentials)
        {
            this.EnsureTablesCreated(CloudStorageAccount.
               FromConfigurationSetting("AzureStorageConnectionString"));
        }
        // Ensure Table Exists
        private static Boolean _tablesCreated = false;
        private static object _tablesCreatedSyncLock = new Object();

        private void EnsureTablesCreated(CloudStorageAccount account)
        {
            if (!_tablesCreated)
            {
                lock (_tablesCreatedSyncLock)
                {
                    if (!_tablesCreated)
                    {
                        CloudTableClient tableClient =
                            account.CreateCloudTableClient();
                        tableClient.CreateTableIfNotExist(SalesmenTableName);

                    }
                }
            }
        }

        #endregion

        public IQueryable<tseSalesman> GetQueryableSalesmen()
        {
            return this.CreateQuery<tseSalesman>(SalesmenTableName);
        }

        public tseSalesman Add(tseSalesman s)
        {
            s.PartitionKey = "A";
            s.RowKey = s.IdSalesman;

            this.AddObject(SalesmenTableName, s);
            this.SaveChanges();
            return s;
        }
    }
}
```

The preceding code is a refined version of some code examples presented in Chapter 5. This class uses the default constructor to call the base *TableServiceContext* constructor, passing the configuration parameter for the URI and credentials.

It also contains a method to check the existence of the table in a centralized place: it is a good idea, architecturally, to place shareable code in a common method. Also, because this code is required only once during the lifetime of the hosting process, you can use the singleton pattern to execute it just one time.

Apart from these two final touches to the code architecture, the class exposes two methods to centralize creation of *DataServiceQuery<tseSalesman>* and adds a new *tseSalesman*.

Here's the *SalesmanDal List* method for the new data access layer. The LINQ to SQL code is commented so that you can focus on the differences between the LINQ to SQL code and the Table Storage Account Service code:

```
namespace DevLeap.EstatesManagement.Dal.AzureStorage
{
    public class SalesmanDal : BaseDal<Salesman, SalesmanList, Int32>
    {
        public SalesmenList List()
        {
            try
            {
                SalesmenList list = new SalesmenList();

                // LINQ to SQL code
                // using (EstatesManagementDataContext context = new
                //    EstatesManagementDataContext(this.ConnectionString))
                // {
                //     context.ObjectTrackingEnabled = false;

                //     var query = from s in context.tabSalesmens
                //                 select new Salesman
                //                 {
                //                     IdSalesman = s.idSalesman,
                //                     SalesmanDescription = s.SalesmanDescription,
                //                     SalesmanIsAdmin = s.SalesmanIsAdmin,
                //                     SalesmanPassword = s.SalesmanPassword
                //                 }
                //     foreach (Salesman s in query)
                //     {
                //        list.add(s);
                //     }
                // }
               using (EMTableServiceContext context = new EMTableServiceContext())
                {

                    var query = from s in context.GetQueryableSalesmen()
                                select new Salesman
                                {
                                    IdSalesman = s.idSalesman,
```

```
                                    SalesmanDescription = s.SalesmanDescription,
                                    SalesmanIsAdmin = s.SalesmanIsAdmin,
                                    SalesmanPassword = s.SalesmanPassword
                                };

                    foreach (Salesman s in query)
                    {
                        list.add(s);
                    }
                }
                return (list);
            }
            // catch (SqlException ex)
            catch (DataServiceQueryException ex)
            {
                throw new DevLeapDBException("ERR01", ex);
            }
        }
    }
}
```

As you can see, there are no architectural differences among the two code approaches. The main difference is the exception type listed in the *catch* block, which the Data Service Client library throws when problems occur. It cannot throw *SqlException* because there is no SQL Server in this example.

The code inside the method is similar to the code used in the LINQ to SQL example; the *TableServiceContext* class is very similar to the *DataContext* class.

All these examples illustrate my main point: good software architecture helps the solution (and you) leverage new technologies because only the pertinent components or layers must be changed.

The Service Agent

Figure 11-1 showed another pillar of modern software architecture: the service agent.

The service agent component is responsible for translating a business layer request in an over-the-wire request to a remote service and translating the received response (or the exception) into something the business layer can use.

The service agent performs the same work as the data access layer component, abstracting the upper layer from the details of communicating with remote services. The services can also be hosted in the same machine in which the service agent resides, but the difference is that the work is handled by the service agent itself (in the code or configuration settings) and it does not influence the business layer.

When Windows Communication Foundation (WCF) was released in 2006, the only necessary task to accomplish to leverage the new technology was change the service agent. The solution didn't need to be rearchitected. If early Web Service code had been spread across layers and methods, it would have been practically impossible to use WCF without checking and testing every line of code.

The Service Agent project also contains the proxy code. The developer has to use the Add Service Reference tool from the service agent component. Every other component of the solution must have no idea what a Service Reference or a proxy to a Web Service is. The business layer invokes methods on the service agent component, passing and receiving business entities.

This was the .NET Framework 1.0 code contained in my Estates Management project at the end of 2003:

```
namespace DevLeap.EstatesManagement.ServiceAgent.WS20
{
    public partial class SalesmanServiceAgent : BaseServiceAgent
    {
        public SalesmenList List()
        {
            try
            {
                SalesmenService ss = new SalesmenService();
                SalesmenList list = SalesmenMapper.FromContract(ss.List());
                return (list);
            }
            catch (Exception ex)
            {
                throw new DevLeapServiceException("ERR01", ex);
            }
        }
```

The Add Web Reference tool that came with Visual Studio 2003 creates a proxy that invokes the various service operations. The tool creates local classes based on the WSDL (Web Service Description Language) to represent the contract entity (Data Transport Object , or DTO). When the service agent calls the operations on the Web Service, it receives a SOAP response that is XML, and the service agent uses it to build a collection of the local defined classes.

These autogenerated classes cannot be considered business entities, because they are defined in the contract between the service and the consumer. They are bound to the contract, not to the client-side application, which is in a completely different boundary from an SOA point of view. Do not think about the consumer as just a Windows Forms or WPF application. The consumer can be an ASP.NET application or another service.

The role of the service agent is to map these autogenerated classes into the client-side business entities. The real map operation was done with the helper class *SalemenMapper*, because in .NET 1.0 there were no extension methods:

```
namespace DevLeap.EstatesManagement.ServiceAgent.WS20
{
    public static class SalesmenEntityMapper
    {
        public static UIBIZ.SalesmenList FromDataContract(SOA.Salesman[] source)
        {
            UIBIZ.SalesmenList result = new UIBIZ.SalesmenList();

            foreach (SOA.Salesman sourceItem in source)
            {
                result.Add(FromDataContract(sourceItem));
            }

            return (result);
        }

        public static UIBIZ.Salesman FromDataContract(SOA.Salesman source)
        {
            UIBIZ.Salesman result = new UIBIZ.Salesman();

            result.IdSalesman = source._idSalesman;
            result.SalesmanDescription = source._salesmanDescription;
            result.SalesmanIsAdmin = source._salesmanIsAdmin;
            result.SalesmanPassword = source._salesmanPassword;
            return (result);
        }

        public static SOA.Salesman ToDataContract(UIBIZ.Salesman source)
        {
            SOA.Salesman result = new SOA.Salesman();

            result._idSalesman = source.IdSalesman;
            result._salesmanDescription = source.SalesmanDescription;
            result._salesmanIsAdmin = source.SalesmanIsAdmin;
            result._salesmanPassword = source.SalesmanPassword;

            return (result);
        }

        public static List<SOA.Salesman> ToDataContract(UIBIZ.SalesmenList source)
        {
            List<SOA.Salesman> result = new List<SOA.Salesman>();

            foreach (UIBIZ.Salesman sourceItem in source)
            {
                result.Add(ToDataContract(sourceItem));
            }

            return (result);
        }

    }
}
```

The *FromDataContract(SOA.Salesman[] source)* method of the *SalesmenMapper* class loops in the array of the *Salesman* passed as a parameter and, for each DTO object, it calls the *FromDataContract(SOA.Salesman source)* method. This method returns a new *Salesman*, the business entity, to the caller that, in turn, returns the business entity typed collection (*SalesmenList*) to the caller.

The mapper also contains the method to transform a business entity back to the DTO correspondent object. The mapper is used in CUD operations.

In 2006, I introduced a new service agent component in the solution to leverage the new WCF features such as in-process communication as well as features based on TCP. The new service agent differs only in the lines of code that call the service and in the configuration file:

```
namespace DevLeap.EstatesManagement.ServiceAgent.WCF30
{
    public partial class SalesmanServiceAgent : BaseServiceAgent
    {
        public SalesmenList List()
        {
            try
            {
                EndpointAddress endpointAddress = new
                   EndpointAddress(ConfigurationManager.AppSettings["ServiceUri"]);

                SalesmanServiceClient service = new SalesmanServiceClient(
                   SalesmanServiceClient.CreateDefaultBinding(), endpointAddress);

                SalesmenList list = SalesmenMapper.FromContract(service.List());
                return (list);
            }
            catch (FaultException<SalesmanFaultException> ex)
            {
                throw new DevLeapServiceException("ERR01", ex);
            }
        }
```

As you can see from the code, a custom *FaultException* was also used, but this new feature is completely hidden from other layers. The business layer continues to talk to the service agent component, receiving and passing business entities.

With the introduction of the Service Bus, some lines of code had to be changed to instruct the infrastructure about the protocols and URLs to use for communicating with the cloud service. These differences are neither in the business processes nor in the user interface presentation, nor are they in the data access layer component. They are related only to the communication infrastructure. The service agent component can be adapted or replaced without even changing the mapper helper class.

The following code is an example of modifying the preceding code to use the Service Bus with the HTTP protocol:

```
namespace DevLeap.EstatesManagement.ServiceAgent.ServiceBus10
{
    public partial class SalesmanServiceAgent : BaseServiceAgent
    {
        public SalesmenList List()
        {
            try
            {
                EndpointAddress endpointAddress = new EndpointAddress(
                   ConfigurationManager.AppSettings["SBNamespace"]);
                ServiceBusEnvironment.SystemConnectivity.Mode =
                   ConnectivityMode.Http;
                ChannelFactory<ISalesmenService> factory = new
                   ChannelFactory<IEstateService>(endpointAddres);
                svc = factory.CreateChannel();
                SalesmenList list = SalesmenMapper.FromContract(svc.List());
                return (list);
            }
            catch (FaultException<SalesmanFaultException> ex)
            {
                throw new DevLeapServiceException("ERR01", ex);
            }

        }
```

You can apply the same concepts on the server side of the services infrastructure. Contracts, services, mappers, and hosts can be defined in the same assembly from a technical point of view, but when you write the code that way, the components are bound together, so it can be very difficult to adapt such monolithic code to new technologies. When you instead separate the service code from the hosting environment, you can reuse the method code with a different host. For example, you can easily change the host to a Windows Azure Worker Role instead of a local Windows Service while still reusing the same contract, Mappers, and services.

In the last few years, the REST protocol has become more popular; it's the perfect protocol in some scenarios. SOAP, on the other hand, is perfect for other scenarios. The use of one over the other is a matter of preference, not a business layer concern or a user interface problem.

Summary

This chapter provided an introduction to some architectural patterns and a few examples of how to create data access layer components and service agent components. The examples show one way you can architect the lower layer of an application. You can modify or replace the components in a layer whenever a new technology appears or requirements change without worrying about the other layers and the overall architecture of the solution.

Index

C

D

E

F

G

H

I

J

K

L

M

N

O

P

T

U

V

W

About the Author

Roberto Brunetti is an experienced consultant, trainer, and author. He's a cofounder of DevLeap, a company focused on providing high-value content and consulting services to professional developers, and the founder of ThinkMobile, the largest Italian community for mobile development. He is a regular speaker at major conferences, and works closely with Microsoft Italy to put on events and build training courses.